Lecture Notes in Computer Science 6570

Commenced Publication in 1973
Founding and Former Series Editors:
Gerhard Goos, Juris Hartmanis, and Jan van Leeuwen

Cristian S. Calude   Grzegorz Rozenberg
Arto Salomaa (Eds.)

Rainbow
of Computer Science

Dedicated to Hermann Maurer
on the Occasion of His 70th Birthday

 Springer

Volume Editors

Cristian S. Calude
The University of Auckland, Department of Computer Science
38 Princes Street, Auckland 1142, New Zealand
E-mail: cristian@cs.auckland.ac.nz

Grzegorz Rozenberg
Leiden University, Leiden Center for Natural Computing
Niels Bohrweg 1, 2333 CA Leiden, The Netherlands
E-mail: rozenber@liacs.nl

Arto Salomaa
University of Turku, Turku Centre for Computer Science (TUCS)
Leminkäisenkatu 14, 20014 Turku, Finland
E-mail: asalomaa@utu.fi

The illustration appearing on the cover of this book is the work
of Daniel Rozenberg (DADARA).

ISSN 0302-9743   e-ISSN 1611-3349
ISBN 978-3-642-19390-3   e-ISBN 978-3-642-19391-0
DOI 10.1007/978-3-642-19391-0
Springer Heidelberg Dordrecht London New York

Library of Congress Control Number: 2011922265

CR Subject Classification (1998): F.1, F.4, F.3, F.2, H.5, I.2.6, K.4

LNCS Sublibrary: SL 1 – Theoretical Computer Science and General Issues

Typesetting: Camera-ready by author, data conversion by Scientific Publishing Services, Chennai, India

Printed on acid-free paper

Springer is part of Springer Science+Business Media (www.springer.com)

Hermann Maurer (picture by Sean Maguire, 2008)

Preface

This book is dedicated to *Hermann Maurer* on the occasion of his 70th birthday in April 2011. The title word *Rainbow* reflects the beauty and variety of the achievements of this outstanding scientist, as well as the diversity and depth of current computer science. Hermann is a true Renaissance man, polymath, *Homo Universalis*, but he still has kept most of his activities on his native Austrian soil. He has been able to combine an exceptionally high level in scientific work with remarkable successes in high administrative and organizational positions. In computer science he has combined profound theory with high-level and unique applications. The high admiration that Hermann enjoys in the scientific community all over the world was witnessed by the enthusiastic response we received to our request to contribute to this book.

Hermann's studies took place in Vienna, where he also had his first positions. After that he was an assistant and associate professor for computer science at the University of Calgary during 1966–1971 and a full professor for applied computer science at the University of Karlsruhe, 1971–1977. Then in 1978 he assumed his main academic position, a full professorship at the Graz University of Technology, where he was also the dean of studies and the dean of the new school of computer science. He has also had long-term visiting positions at SMU (Dallas), University of Brasilia (Brazil), the University of Waterloo and the University of Auckland where he was also an honorary research fellow. Moreover, he has been an adjunct professor at Denver University, advisor to the University of Malaysia at Kuching (UNIMAS) since 1998 and a visiting researcher at Edith Cowan University (Perth, Australia). This list does not do any justice to Hermann's work because usually his stay at a university is not a normal visit but brings forward important innovations.

Hermann's career as a researcher and teacher is outstanding. He is the author of some 20 scientific books and approximately 650 papers in various journals and conference proceedings. He has supervised roughly 400 MSc theses and some 50 PhD theses. He has visited extensively universities and research institutes all over the world, and given invited or keynote lectures at numerous international conferences. Hermann's early pioneering research was in compiler design, formal languages, automata, algorithms and data-structures. His current main research and project areas are networked multimedia/hypermedia systems; electronic publishing and applications to university life, exhibitions and museums; Web-based learning environments; languages and their applications; data structures and their efficient use; telematic services, computer networks, computer-supported new media, dynamic symbolic language, social implications of computers, techniques to fight plagiarism and computers in science fiction. Recently Hermann has been an outspoken critic of some data-mining activities on the Web.

Hermann is or has been the chairman or a member of steering and program committees of numerous international conferences. Apart from his work on the editorial boards of many journals, Hermann founded one of the very first electronic journals, *Journal of Universal Computer Science*. He still continues to be the editor-in-chief of this very successful journal.

To show Hermann's qualities in leadership and administration, we list the following facts.

Hermann was the project manager of a number of pioneering multimillion-dollar undertakings. They include a patent for optical storage device, the development of a color-graphic microcomputer (MUPID), an electronic teaching experiment COSTOC, multi-media projects such as *Images of Austria* (Expo'92 and Expo'93), various electronic publishing projects such as *PC Library, Geothek and Brockhaus Multimedial*. He was responsible for the development of the first second-generation Web-based information system Hyperwave and a modern net-based teaching platform. Hermann organized the multimedia part of a number of museum projects, including Ars Electronica Center (Linz, Austria), the Papa Tongarewa (Wellington, New Zealand), as well as the Odyseeum (Cologne) opened in 2009. He also participated in or headed a number of EU projects.

Hermann was the director of the Research Institute for Applied Information Processing of the Austrian Computer Society for 1983–1998, the chair or vice-chair of the Institute for Information Systems and Computer Media since 1988, the director of the Institute for Hypermedia Systems of Joanneum Research for 1987–2006, the director of the Austrian Web Application Center for 1997–2000, the co-founder and chairman of the board of the Hyperwave AG Munich 1997–2005, the vice-chairman of the same company since then, as well as the founder and scientific advisor of the first research center on knowledge management in Austria. Hermann's enthusiastic leadership often brings forward remarkable results and innovations. Among the editors of this book, the expression *Hermann quality* refers to a high level of excellence.

It is no wonder that Hermann is one of the most decorated computer scientists. He has received a number of awards, among them the Prize for Merits for Information Processing in Austria, the "Enter-Prize" (a play of words with "enterprise") of the Styrian Chamber of Commerce in 1999, the Integrata-Prize (for Human Software) in 2000, and the "AACE Fellowship Award" of the Association for the Advancement of Computing in Education in 2003. Hermann became a foreign member of the Finnish Academy of Sciences in 1996 and a member of the Academia Europaea in 2000, where he was elected chairman of the section "Informatics" in April 2009. His invigorating work in this position is already visible in many ways, for instance, exceptionally good and useful Web pages have been created for the whole academy. He is a life-long honorary member of MCCA, Vienna, and of the Computer Engineering Society, Graz. In 2001 he was awarded the "Austrian Cross of Honours for Arts and Science Class I," as well as the "Large Medal of Honour of the Province of Styria." He received the Honorary Doctorate of the Polytechnical University of St. Petersburg in 1991, of the University Karlsruhe, Germany in 2002, and of the University of Calgary in 2007.

Apart from science, Hermann being *Homo Universalis* is clearly visible in his extra-curricula life and hobbies. Desire to explore the world around us is one of his basic characteristics. Space does not permit us to describe here in any detail Hermann's hobbies or family life. The latter includes trips all over the world, as well as various other activities with his wife Ushi, children and grandchildren. Hermann's friends have the opportunity to learn every year interesting facts about far-away lands and cultures, reading his well-known Christmas letters.

Hermann is a successful writer of science fiction. His novels dwell mostly in the world of computers: future possibilities such as teleportation, but also the dramatic consequences if the administration of the Web falls into wrong hands. Hermann has always been very sportive—mountain climbing, scuba diving and hiking belonging to his hobbies.

Each of the three editors of this book has a warm and close friendship with Hermann, developed over many years. In particular, Cris is grateful to him for being a role model and mentor, Grzegorz for so many years of reliable friendship, and Arto for the happy and productive MSW decade around 1980. We wish Hermann continuing success and satisfaction in science, leadership and life in general, in the years to come.

January 2011

Cristian S. Calude
Grzegorz Rozenberg
Arto Salomaa

Table of Contents

The Practice of Informatics

Algorithmics

Improved Approximations for Hard Optimization Problems via Problem Instance Classification*

Hans-Joachim Böckenhauer, Juraj Hromkovič, and Tobias Mömke

Department of Computer Science, ETH Zurich, Switzerland
{hjb,juraj.hromkovic,tobias.moemke}@inf.ethz.ch

Abstract. Under the usual complexity-theoretic assumptions like $\mathcal{P} \neq \mathcal{NP}$, many practically relevant optimization problems are provably hard to solve or even to approximate. But most of these hardness results are derived for worst-case scenarios, and it is in many cases not clear whether the actual problem instances arising in practical applications exhibit this worst-case behaviour. Thus, a recent branch of algorithmic research aims at a more fine-grained analysis of the hardness of optimization problems. The main idea behind this analysis is to find some parameter according to which one can classify the hardness of problem instances. This approach does not only lead to new hardness results, but can also be used to design improved approximation algorithms for practically relevant subclasses of problem instances.

In this paper, we survey several different approaches for such improved approximation results achieved by a fine-grained classification of problem instances.

1 Introduction

Understanding and classifying the hardness of computational problems is one of the most fundamental goals in computer science. The model of the Turing machine [44] together with the Church-Turing thesis gives us a precise formal model of the class of problems that can be algorithmically solved and thus provides a sharp border between algorithmically solvable and algorithmically unsolvable problems. But every-day experience of the 1960s showed that many problems that are algorithmically solvable in principle are intractable from a practical point of view since all known algorithms are much too time-consuming.

This observation lead to the development of the fundamental concept of computational complexity [31, 43]. But, in contrast to the theory of computability, no formal model yielding a sharp border between "practically" solvable and unsolvable problems has yet been identified.

Instead, the hardness of a problem is often analyzed in a worst-case scenario. But this approach might yield misleading results for some practical applications since, for many problems, only a very few instances of any given length are really

---

* This work was partially supported by SNF grant 200021-132510/1.

C.S. Calude, G. Rozenberg, A. Salomaa (Eds.): Maurer Festschrift, LNCS 6570, pp. 3–19, 2011.

as hard as the worst-case lower bound suggests. To overcome these difficulties, sometimes an average-case analysis is used. But, besides usually being a very challenging task, the results of any average-case analysis heavily depend on the assumed probability distribution of problem instances. Since the distribution of the actual inputs in a practical application usually is not known, this method can often yield misleading results as well. Instead of these traditional approaches, one would like to measure whether a given single problem instance is hard to process. Unfortunately, a sound formal definition of this is unattainable since the solution for a single instance can always be precomputed and integrated into the algorithm, leading to a constant complexity in any case.

One possible way out of this dilemma is to partition the set of problem instances into infinitely many infinitely large classes according to their hardness. Proving membership in one of these classes then gives an *upper* bound on the resources needed to process a specific instance. In a more general scope, the partitioning enables a fine-grained analysis of the hardness of a problem, where classes of tractable inputs can be identified.

One of the first approaches to establish such an infinite partitioning is called parameterized complexity. One identifies a suitable parameter k of the input and tries to bound the running time of the algorithm on an instance of length n by $\mathcal{O}(f(k) \cdot p(n))$ where f is an arbitrary computable function and p is some polynomial function. Intuitively speaking, such a bound on the time complexity means that the running time is exponential only in the parameter, but not in the input length. This parameterization of problem instances has proven to be a very successful technique, see, e.g., the books by Downey and Fellows [23] or Niedermeier [36] for an introduction. In this survey, we summarize some more recent approaches of partitioning the set of problem instances also for determining the hardness of computing *approximate* solutions for optimization problems.

There are several possibilities for directly extending the concept of parameterized complexity to optimization problems, we give a survey of known approaches in Section 3. In Section 4, we discuss the related concept of *stability* of approximation algorithms [7, 11]. Here, the idea is to allow only polynomial running time, but to determine the approximation ratio as a function depending on a parameter of the input. This parameter is typically determined by the distance of the considered problem instance from some set of easily solvable instances.

In Section 5, we survey two recent approaches of instance-classifying algorithm design. *Hybrid algorithms* find a partition of the problem instances such that, for each input, either the best known approximation or the best known running time of an exact algorithm can be significantly improved. For *win/win approximation algorithms*, we are able to prove that, for each input, the approximation ratio of at least one of two related problems can be improved. From another point of view, this means to parameterize the instances of one problem according to their approximability for the other problem.

2   Basic Definitions

In this section, we briefly recall the basic definitions of approximation algorithms. For a more detailed introduction to this topic, we refer to the books by Hromkovič [33], Ausiello et al. [4], or Vazirani [46].

An *optimization problem* U can be described by a quadruple $U = (L, \mathcal{M}, cost, goal)$, where L denotes the set of problem instances, $\mathcal{M}(x)$ is the set of feasible solutions for each problem instance $x \in L$, $cost$ is a function measuring the cost of any feasible solution for a given problem instance, and $goal$ is the optimization goal, i. e., minimization or maximization. An algorithm A is called *consistent* for U if it computes a feasible solution $A(x) \in \mathcal{M}(x)$ for every problem instance $x \in L$.

Let A be a consistent algorithm for an optimization problem $U = (L, \mathcal{M}, cost, goal)$. The *approximation ratio* $R_A(x)$ of A on the input x is defined as $R_A(x) = \max\{cost(A(x))/Opt_U(x), Opt_U(x)/cost(A(x))\}$, where $Opt_U(x)$ denotes the cost of an optimal solution for x. This definition ensures that the approximation ratio yields a value ≥ 1 for both minimization and maximization problems. For $\delta > 1$, we say that A is a δ-*approximation algorithm* for U if, for all $x \in L$, $R_A(x) \leq \delta$.

The definition can be generalized to describe also non-constant approximations by defining $R_A(n) = \max\{R_A(x) \mid x \text{ is input of size } n\}$. For every function $f{:}\mathbb{N} \to \mathbb{R}^+$, we call A an $f(n)$-*approximation algorithm* for U if $R_A(n) \leq f(n)$, for every $n \in \mathbb{N}$.

When dealing with approximations, we usually restrict our attention to optimization problems where (i) the problem instances are recognizable in polynomial time, (ii) the size of any feasible solution is polynomially bounded by the size of the input, (iii) the cost function is polynomial-time computable, and, (iv) for any solution candidate, it can be tested in polynomial time if it is a feasible solution. The class of problems satisfying these conditions is called $\mathcal{NPO}$.

The class $\mathcal{APX}$ is the subclass of problems from $\mathcal{NPO}$ for which there exists a δ-approximation algorithm, where $\delta \geq 1$ is a constant.

A consistent algorithm A for an optimization problem U is called a *polynomial-time approximation scheme (PTAS)* for U if, for every input pair $(x, \varepsilon) \in L \times \mathbb{R}^+$, A computes a feasible solution $A(x)$ with an approximation ratio of at most $1 + \varepsilon$ within a time that is polynomial in the size of x. If the running time can be bounded by a function that is polynomial both in the size of x and in ε^{-1}, we call A a *fully polynomial-time approximation scheme (FPTAS)*. The classes of problems from $\mathcal{NPO}$ admitting a PTAS or an FPTAS are called $\mathcal{PTAS}$ and $\mathcal{FPTAS}$, respectively.

3   Parameterized Approximation Algorithms

The idea behind parameterized algorithmics is the following: Consider some hard (e. g., $\mathcal{NP}$-hard) computing problem. If we want to design an exact algorithm solving the problem, we cannot expect a polynomial running time on all problem instances, unless $\mathcal{P} = \mathcal{NP}$. Nevertheless, the complexity of an algorithm might vary a lot for different instances of the problem. Our goal now is to find a suitable parameterization of the set of inputs describing their hardness. In particular, we are interested in finding a parameter k for any input such that the super-polynomial part of the running time is tied to the value of the parameter only, but does not depend on the size of the input.

This concept was introduced by Downey and Fellows [21, 22, 23]. It can be formalized as follows: Let U be a computing problem and let L be the set of all problem instances of U. We call any polynomial-time computable function $\kappa\colon L \to \mathbb{N}$ a *parameterization* of U if, for infinitely many $k \in \mathbb{N}$, the set $\{x \in L \mid \kappa(x) = k\}$ is infinite. Intuitively speaking, a parameterization κ partitions the set of problem instances into infinitely many infinite subclasses. An algorithm A is called a *κ-parameterized polynomial-time algorithm* for U if A solves U and if there exists a polynomial function p and an arbitrary computable function f such that the running time of A on any problem instance x is bounded by $f(\kappa(x)) \cdot p(|x|)$, where $|x|$ denotes the size of x. If there exists a κ-parameterized algorithm for U, we say that the parameterized problem (U, κ) is *fixed-parameter tractable*. By $\mathcal{FPT}$ we denote the class of all fixed-parameter tractable parameterized problems. If the parameterization is clear from the context, we call a κ-parameterized polynomial-time algorithm simply an *fpt-algorithm.*

There are many different possibilities to choose such parameterizations. One possibility is to use some natural parameter revealing some structure of the input like the maximum vertex degree or the diameter in a graph, the maximum number of occurrences of a variable in a Boolean formula, or the alphabet size in a string. We call these *structural parameterizations* in the following.

Another possibility, which is often used in the existing literature for decision problems, is to consider the size of the solution as a parameter. We call this the *solution-size parameterization,* in the literature it can also be found under the name of *standard parametrization.* A well-known example is the *vertex cover problem*: Given an undirected graph and a natural number k, it asks whether there exists a set C of at most k vertices in the graph such that every edge is incident to at least one vertex from C. This problem, parameterized with the desired size of the vertex cover k as a parameter, is fixed-parameter tractable [21, 23]. Similar results have been proven for many other parameterized decision problems, for an overview and a discussion of several design techniques for parameterized algorithms see, e. g., the books by Downey and Fellows [23] or Niedermeier [36].

On the other hand, many parameterized problems are not fixed-parameter tractable, unless $\mathcal{P} = \mathcal{NP}$. For proving such results, a full complexity theory has been developed, based on the concept of the so-called $W[1]$-*hardness.* See the books by Downey and Fellows [23] or Flum and Grohe [28] for an introduction to parameterized complexity theory.

While parameterized algorithms and parameterized complexity were mainly used for analyzing exact computations, there exist some approaches for extending their applicability to optimization problems and approximation. We will give an overview of these approaches in this section, a further survey can be found in [35].

3.1   Efficient Polynomial-Time Approximation Schemes

Maybe the first attempt to connect parameterized algorithms and approximation was to look at approximation schemes from the point of view of parameterization. Only few optimization problems admit an FPTAS[1], and the running time of many known PTASs often is very high for any reasonable approximation ratio. Here, the concept of parameterization can sometimes help to establish a more fine-grained classification of PTASs. Remember that the input for a PTAS consists of an instance x of the corresponding optimization problem U together with some $\varepsilon > 0$ describing the desired approximation ratio $1 + \varepsilon$. We can view this as a parameterized problem by taking the desired approximation ratio as a parameter, i. e., by setting $\kappa(x, \varepsilon) = 1/\varepsilon$. A PTAS with a running time in $\mathcal{O}(f(1/\varepsilon) \cdot p(|x|))$ for some computable function f and some polynomial function p (or, in other words, an fpt-algorithm according to the parameter $1/\varepsilon$) is called an *efficient polynomial-time approximation scheme (EPTAS)*. This notion was introduced by Cesati and Trevisan [16].

One of the most prominent examples of an EPTAS is the one for the geometric traveling salesman problem given by Arora [3]. Other EPTASs were designed, for example, for scheduling on uniform processors [34], and for many so-called bidimensional problems on planar graphs, including feedback vertex set, vertex cover, minimum maximal matching, and a series of vertex-removal problems [19], see also [20] for an overview of bidimensionality. All of these algorithms are technically too involved to present the details in this survey. Instead, we illustrate the concept of EPTASs with a simple example taken from [9].

The *Steiner tree problem in graphs (STP)* is the following optimization problem: Given a complete edge-weighted graph $G = (V, E, c)$ and a subset $S \subseteq V$ of *terminal vertices*, the goal is to find a minimum-weight subgraph of G spanning all terminals. This problem is $\mathcal{APX}$-hard even in the case when all edge weights are taken from the set $\{1, 2, \ldots, r\}$ for some $r \in \mathbb{N}$, i. e., it does not admit any PTAS, unless $\mathcal{P} = \mathcal{NP}$ [6]. We now consider the following *reoptimization* variant[2] of this problem: Assume that an optimal solution Opt_{old} is given for an STP instance $(G = (V, E, c), S_{old})$, and we now want to compute a solution for a locally modified instance (G, S_{new}), where S_{new} is produced from S_{old} by adding a vertex to it. We call this problem, where the edge costs are again restricted to $\{1, 2, \ldots, r\}$, AddTerm-r-STP. It was shown in [9] that AddTerm-r-STP is $\mathcal{NP}$-hard.

Theorem 1 (Böckenhauer et al. [9]). *There exists an EPTAS for AddTerm-r-STP.*

Proof. Let $G = (V, E, c)$ be an edge-weighted graph, where $c: E \rightarrow \{1, \ldots, r\}$ for some constant $r \in \mathbb{N}$, let $S_{old}, S_{new} \subseteq V$ be two terminal sets such that $S_{new} = S_{old} \cup \{v\}$ for some $v \in V - S_{old}$, and let Opt_{old} be a minimum Steiner tree for

---

[1] Only problems that are not strongly $\mathcal{NP}$-hard, i. e., that become polynomial-time solvable when the input is encoded in unary.

[2] For a motivation and a detailed introduction to the concept of reoptimization, see for instance [10].

(G, S_{old}). Let $1 + \varepsilon$ be the desired approximation ratio, for some $\varepsilon > 0$. Then the following simple algorithm is an EPTAS for AddTerm-r-STP: Let $k := \lceil 1/\varepsilon \rceil$. If S_{new} contains at most $r \cdot k$ vertices, then compute an optimal solution using the Dreyfus-Wagner STP algorithm [26]. Otherwise, take the given old optimal solution and connect the new terminal v to it via an arbitrary edge.

We first analyze the approximation ratio in the second case of this algorithm. Since $|S_{\mathrm{new}}| > k$ and every edge has cost at least 1, the cost of the optimal solution for the new instance is at least $r \cdot k$. Adding one edge to Opt_{old} costs at most r, i.e., the cost of the computed solution T_A can be estimated as $c(T_A) \leq c(Opt_{\mathrm{old}}) + r$. Thus, the approximation ratio is

$$\frac{c(T_A)}{c(Opt_{\mathrm{new}})} \leq \frac{c(Opt_{\mathrm{old}}) + r}{c(Opt_{\mathrm{new}})} \leq \frac{c(Opt_{\mathrm{new}}) + r}{c(Opt_{\mathrm{new}})} = 1 + \frac{r}{c(Opt_{\mathrm{new}})} \leq 1 + \frac{r}{r \cdot k} \leq 1 + \varepsilon.$$

According to [26], the time complexity of calculating an optimal solution in the first case of the algorithm is in $O(n^2 \cdot 3^{r \cdot k})$. The time complexity of the remaining parts is negligible. Since r is a constant and $k = \lceil 1/\varepsilon \rceil$, all requirements for an EPTAS are satisfied.   □

There are close relations between EPTASs and fpt-algorithms. In particular, the existence of an EPTAS is related to the fixed-parameter tractability according to the solution-size parameterization.

Theorem 2 (Cesati and Trevisan [16]). *If an optimization problem U admits an EPTAS, then the solution-size parameterization of U is in $\mathcal{FPT}$.*   □

Corollary 1. *If the solution-size parameterization of an optimization problem U is $W[1]$-hard, then U does not admit an EPTAS, unless $\mathcal{P} = \mathcal{NP}$.*   □

Corollary 1 directly implies that $W[1]$-hardness also rules out the possibility of an FPTAS. Thus, the theory of parameterized complexity can also be used to prove hardness results in classical approximation theory.

3.2   Structural Parameterizations

For using the approach of parameterization, many different structural parameters of the input can be used. For example, for graph problems, one can consider the maximum vertex degree, the diameter, the genus, the treewidth, etc. For satisfiability problems, the maximum length of clauses or the maximum number of occurrences of one variable are possible parameters.

Note that, strictly speaking, some parameters like the treewidth of a graph do not lead to valid parameterizations in the sense of the definition at the beginning of this section, since they are not computable in polynomial time. But there exists an fpt-algorithm (in the strict sense of the definition) for determining the treewidth of a graph. Thus, it is meaningful to use it as a parameter as well; indeed, the treewidth parameterization is one of the most successful ones in parameterized algorithmics.

In this subsection, we give some examples where structural parameters help to yield improved approximations. We start with a problem which has been shown to be inapproximable as well as $W[1]$-hard, but for which we can design a simple constant-factor approximation algorithm with fpt-running time.

The *metric traveling salesman problem (Δ-TSP)* asks for finding a shortest Hamiltonian tour (i.e., a tour visiting each vertex exactly once) in a given edge-weighted complete graph, where the edge-weight function c satisfies the triangle inequality, i.e., for each three vertices u, v, w, we have $c(\{u, v\}) \leq c(\{u, w\}) + c(\{w, v\})$. In the *$\Delta$-TSP with deadlines ($\Delta$-DLTSP)*, we have additionally given a start vertex s and a subset of *deadline vertices* with prescribed deadlines which have to be visited by the tour before the cost of the tour exceeds these deadlines. In other words, the partial tour from s to any deadline vertex x with deadline $d(x)$ has to have a length of at most $d(x)$. It has been shown in [8] that the Δ-DLTSP is not approximable within a ratio of $((1 - \varepsilon)/2)|V|$, for any $0 < \varepsilon < 1$, unless $\mathcal{P} = \mathcal{NP}$, where V denotes the set of vertices in the input graph. The most natural parameterization for this problem is the number of deadline vertices. But, according to this parameterization, the problem is $W[1]$-hard since it was shown in [8] that it is $\mathcal{NP}$-hard even when restricted to instances with only two deadline vertices. Thus, neither approximation nor parameterized algorithms alone can help to solve this problem. But in the following we show that it is fruitful to combine both approaches.

For this, we first extend the notion of fixed-parameter tractability to approximation algorithms. A consistent algorithm A for a parameterized optimization problem (U, κ) is called a *δ-fpt-approximation algorithm* for (U, κ) if A computes an at most δ-approximative solution for every admissible input x for U with a running time bounded by $f(\kappa(x)) \cdot p(|x|)$ for some arbitrary computable function f and some polynomial function p.

Theorem 3 (Böckenhauer et al. [8]). *There exists a 2.5-fpt-approximation algorithm for Δ-DLTSP, parameterized by the number of deadline vertices.*

Proof. Consider a problem instance of Δ-DLTSP, consisting of a complete edge-weighted graph $G = (V, E, c)$ with metric edge-weight function c, a start vertex s, a set D of deadline vertices and a deadline function $d\colon D \to \mathbb{N}$ assigning a deadline to each deadline vertex. Let $k = |D|$ denote the number of deadline vertices.

We consider the following algorithm. It first computes a Hamiltonian tour H_C on all non-deadline vertices (but including the start vertex) using Christofides' algorithm [18]. Then it checks every linear order $\pi = (s, p_1, \ldots, p_k)$ on the vertices from $D \cup \{s\}$ and constructs the corresponding tour $H(\pi)$ visiting these vertices in this order. If this tour does not violate any deadline, the Christofides tour on the remaining vertices is appended at the end. The algorithm outputs the best of all tours constructed this way.

The running time of this algorithm can be estimated by $O(|V|^3 + k!k)$ since there are $k!$ possible orderings to be checked, the checking can be implemented to run in $O(k)$, and Christofides' algorithm has a running time in $O(|V|^3)$ [37]. Thus, this is an fpt-algorithm.

We now estimate the achieved approximation ratio. Consider an optimal solution Opt and the order π_{Opt} of the deadline in it. This order is checked by the algorithm, and the corresponding partial tour $H(\pi_{Opt})$ is no longer than Opt due to the triangle inequality. On the other hand, H_C is a $3/2$-approximation on the subinstance induced by the non-deadline vertices since Christofides' algorithm is $3/2$-approximative. Due to the triangle inequality, including more vertices into this tour cannot decrease the cost, and thus $c(H_C) + c(H(\pi_{Opt})) \leq 3/2 \cdot c(Opt) + c(Opt) = 2.5 \cdot c(Opt)$. □

We can extend the notion of fpt-approximation algorithms also to approximation schemes. An *fpt-AS* for a parameterized optimization problem (U, κ) is a consistent algorithm for U which outputs, for a given instance x of U and a given $\varepsilon > 0$, a $(1 + \varepsilon)$-approximate solution in time $f(\varepsilon, \kappa(x)) \cdot p(|x|)$ for some arbitrary computable function f and some polynomial p. This obviously is a generalization of the notion of an EPTAS because the super-polynomial part of the running time does not only depend on the desired approximation ratio, but also on the parameter $\kappa(x)$.

As an example for an fpt-AS, we mention an algorithm for the *partial vertex cover problem* which was presented in [35]. This is the following optimization problem: Given an undirected graph G and an integer k, the goal is to cover as many edges as possible with some subset of k vertices. This problem was shown to be $W[1]$-hard with respect to the parameter k in [30] and to be $\mathcal{APX}$-hard in [38].

Theorem 4 (Marx [35]). *The partial vertex cover problem admits an fpt-AS with respect to the parameterization $\kappa(G, k) = k$.* □

3.3 Solution-Size Parameterizations

The solution-size parameterization is the most studied type of parameterization for decision problems which seems to be quite natural in many cases and is also related to the existence of EPTASs as already mentioned in Subsection 3.1. But it is not trivial to extend this parameterization to optimization problems. The reason is that, for a hard optimization problem, determining the size of the solution is in most cases as hard as finding the optimal solution itself, but we expect a parameter to be easily computable from the given input.

For overcoming this difficulty, three different, but quite similar approaches were independently proposed in [15,17,24]. The main idea here is to add a parameter to the input describing a range of solution sizes for which the algorithm is expected to compute a good approximative solution. We present the definition from [17] here.

Let U be a minimization problem. A *solution-size δ-fpt-approximation algorithm* for U is a consistent algorithm for U that, given an input x for U and some $k \in \mathbb{N}$ such that the value of the optimal solution $Opt(x)$ satifies $c(Opt(x)) \leq k$, computes a δ-approximate solution in time $O(f(k) \cdot p(|x|))$ for some computable function f and some polynomial function p. For pairs (x, k) such that $c(Opt(x)) > k$, the output of the algorithm can be arbitrary. The definition can be extended to maximization problems in an analogous way.

Not many applications of this concept are known, but some fpt-inapproxima-bility results for the dominating set problem can be found in [25].

4   Stable Approximation Algorithms

In contrast to the parameterized approximation algorithms as described in the preceding section, for *stable* approximation algorithms the parameter is used for measuring the approximation ratio only, maintaining polynomial running time for every problem instance. The main idea is that, for many hard-to-approximate optimization problems, there exists a subset of relatively easily approximable instances, and all other instances can be partitioned into infinitely many classes according to their distance to this easy kernel of the problem, with respect to some appropriate distance measure. Now the goal is to find an algorithm that is consistent for all instances and achieves good approximations for the easy kernel, such that the achieved approximation ratio depends on the distance from the kernel only, but not on the size of the input. This concept of approximation stability was introduced in [7], a detailed survey can be found, e. g., in [11].

More formally, approximation stability can be defined as follows. We start with defining how to measure the distance between problem instances. Let $\overline{U} = (L, \mathcal{M}, cost, goal)$ be an optimization problem and let $U = (L_I, \mathcal{M}, cost, goal)$ be a subproblem of $\overline{U}$, where $L_I \subsetneq L$. Any function $h_L \colon L \to \mathbb{R}^+$ satisfying $h_L(x) = 0$ for all $x \in L_I$ is called a *distance function for U according to L_I*. For any $r \in \mathbb{R}^+$, we define $Ball_{r,h_L}(L_I) = \{w \in L \mid h_L(w) \leq r\}$ to be the set of instances from L which are at distance at most r from L_I.

This definition now enables us to formally define stable approximation algorithms. We consider an ε-approximation algorithm A for U for some $\varepsilon \in \mathbb{R}^+$ which is consistent for $\overline{U}$ and some $p \in \mathbb{R}^+$. We say that A is *p-stable according to h_L* if, for every real number $0 \leq r \leq p$, there exists some $\delta_{r,\varepsilon} \in \mathbb{R}^+$ such that A is a $\delta_{r,\varepsilon}$-approximation algorithm on the subproblem of $\overline{U}$ restricted to the instances in $Ball_{r,h_L}(L_I)$. The algorithm A is called *stable according to h_L* if it is p-stable according to h_L for every $p \in \mathbb{R}^+$. If there exists a $p > 0$ such that A is not p-stable, then A is called *unstable*.

As an example, let us consider the traveling salesman problem (TSP). For general edge weights, the TSP is not approximable within $p(n)$ for any polynomial function p, where n denotes the number of vertices in the input graph. On the other hand, if we restrict the problem to edge-weighted graphs satisfying the triangle inequality, the resulting subproblem Δ-TSP admits a 1.5-approximation due to Christofides' algorithm [18]. The idea now is to take the Δ-TSP as the easy problem kernel and to define some distance to metricity for all other TSP inputs. This can be done by considering a *relaxed triangle inequality*. We say that an edge-weighted graph $G = (V, E, c)$ satisfies the β-triangle inequality for some $\beta \geq 1$ if, for all vertices $u, v, w \in V$, the inequality $c(\{u, v\}) \leq \beta \cdot (c(u, w) + c(w, v))$ holds. Now we can define a distance function h_{TSP} measuring the distance from Δ-TSP for every TSP instance G by $h_{\text{TSP}}(G) = \beta_G - 1$, where $\beta_G \geq 1$ is the minimum value for β such that G satisfies the β-triangle inequality.

It has been shown in [7] that Christofides' algorithm is unstable for h_{TSP}, but a modification of the algorithm can be shown to be stable. Other stable TSP algorithms were developed in [2, 1, 5]; for an overview, see [11].

Theorem 5 (Böckenhauer et al. [7]). *There exists a stable approximation for TSP achieving an approximation ratio of* $1.5 \cdot \beta^2$ *on graphs satisfying the β-triangle inequality.*   □

5   Hybrid Algorithms and Win/Win Approximations

In the previous sections, we have discussed several ways to combine techniques from parameterization and approximation. Another intriguing approach is to use a single parameter for both exact computations and approximations such that, for any value of the parameter, we obtain either an improved exact algorithm or an improved approximation. Algorithms achieving this goal belong to the class of so-called hybrid algorithms which originate from the *algorithm selection problem* [40], the problem to select an appropriate algorithm for an input according to some given selection criteria. A *hybrid algorithm* consists of a collection of algorithms for a problem U and a *selector* S that decides which algorithm from the collection is used for a given input. In the context of this survey, we are interested in those hybrid algorithms that, for a set M of complexity measures, guarantee to compute a good result for any given input with respect to at least one measure $m \in M$.

The set of complexity measures can contain, for example, the worst-case running time and the approximation ratio achievable in polynomial time. An example of a selector S is to identify a parameter of the problem instance and to decide accordingly whether to compute an exact solution or an approximation. The goal is that, according to the value of the parameter, we can either ensure an improved running time or an improved approximation ratio. More precisely, in the case of exact computations, the running time is parameterized with respect to the identified parameter and improves the best known fpt-algorithm for the problem. In the case of approximation, we can ensure that the approximation ratio improves over the best known worst-case approximation ratio, depending on the parameter, similarly as in the case of stable approximation algorithms.

In the following, we give an example of a hybrid algorithm for the maximum cut problem in unweighted graphs (MaxCut). Measured in the number of edges m, the currently best exact algorithm solves MaxCut in time $O(2^{m/5})$ [42]. The worst-case approximation ratio is about 1.1383 using extensive computational power [29]; the best algorithm that is not based on semidefinite programming is 2-approximative and runs in time $O(n+m)$, where n is the number of vertices [41].

The notation O^* denotes an asymptotic upper bound where polynomial factors are omitted.

Theorem 6 (Vassilevska et al. [45]). *For any $\varepsilon > 0$, there is a hybrid algorithm for MaxCut that either computes an exact solution in time $O^*(2^{\varepsilon m})$ or an expected $(4/(2 + \varepsilon))$-approximation in linear time.*

Proof. Given a graph $G = (V, E)$ with $|V| = n$ vertices and $|E| = m$ edges, the hybrid algorithm computes a maximal matching M in linear time, i. e., a matching that contains at least one vertex of every edge from E. Now, the selector decides whether to compute an optimal solution or an approximation depending on the size of M. If $|M| < \varepsilon m/2$, the algorithm computes an exact solution as follows. Let V_M be the set of vertices in M. For each partition of V_M into two sets, the algorithm distributes the vertices from $G \backslash M$ greedily, i. e., the vertices from $G \backslash M$ are distributed one after the other such that each time the cut is maximized. Then it takes the best solution obtained this way. It is clear that this algorithm runs in time $O^*(2^{\varepsilon m})$, since there are $2^{\varepsilon m}$ possible partitions of $\varepsilon m > |V_M|$ vertices. To show that the outcome is an optimal solution, note that at least one of the tested partitions, say (M_1, M_2), coincides with the partition defined by an optimal solution. Since M is a maximal matching, the vertices in $G \backslash M$ form an independent set. Therefore, the optimal distribution of those vertices depends only on M_1 and M_2 and thus greedily distributing the vertices is sufficient.

The remaining case is that $|M| \geq \varepsilon m/2$ and the selector chooses to compute an approximate solution. In this case, the algorithm separately distributes the vertices from M and those from $G \backslash M$ into two sets M_1 and M_2. For each edge $\{u, v\}$ in M, with probability $1/2$ it puts u into M_1 and v into M_2 and with probability $1/2$ it puts u into M_2 and v into M_1. This way, u and v are not in the same set. The algorithm puts each of the remaining vertices with probability $1/2$ to M_1 and otherwise to M_2. Now, the expectation is that half of the edges from E not contained in M are in the cut. Additionally, all $\varepsilon m/2$ edges from M are in the cut. Therefore, the expectation of the total number of edges in the cut is $\varepsilon m/2 + (m - \varepsilon m/2)/2 = m/2 + \varepsilon m/4$.

Since the value of an optimal solution can be trivially bounded from above by m, this results in the approximation ratio $Opt/(m/2 + \varepsilon m/4) \leq m/((2m + \varepsilon m)/4) = 4/(2 + \varepsilon)$.   □

For $\varepsilon < 1/5$, the algorithm from Theorem 6 either improves over the best known exact algorithm or over the best known linear-time approximation algorithm.

We continue with a related concept, the so-called *win/win algorithms*. A win/win algorithm computes — similar to a hybrid algorithm — more than one solution. In contrast to hybrid algorithms, however, win/win algorithms only use a single complexity measure but for a collection of different problems that share the same set of input instances. In other words, given one instance for two problems, a win/win algorithms guarantees to deliver a good solution for at least one of the problems. The win/win approach originates from parameterized computations and is used there as a technique for kernelization. *Kernelization* is a preprocessing that, for a parameterized problem with parameter k, transforms a given problem instance into a new one such that the size of the transformed instance only depends on k. Then it suffices to handle the transformed input instead of the original one. In other words, a kernelization ensures us that we can either directly decide the parameterized problem in polynomial time or we can perform the computations on a smaller instance (possibly with a smaller parameter). An important result in parameterized complexity is that a problem is in $\mathcal{FPT}$ if and only if it has a kernelization. An overview on kernelization techniques can be found, e. g., in [36].

We now sketch an example from Prieto and Sloper [39] that shows how to use win/win algorithms for kernelization. The *k-vertex cover problem* (k-VC) is to decide whether there is a set of k vertices within a graph $G = (V, E)$ such that each edge $e \in E$ is incident to at least one of the vertices. The win/win approach shows that this problem is closely related to the problem of finding a spanning tree in G that has at least k internal vertices (k-IST).

The relation is based on finding a spanning tree in G such that either its leaves form an independent set in G or there are only two leaves. Note that, if there are only two leaves, then the tree is a Hamiltonian path and thus an $(n - 2)$-internal spanning tree in a graph with n vertices.

Lemma 1 (Prieto and Sloper [39]). *Given a graph G, one can find in polynomial time a spanning tree T in G such that either T is a Hamiltonian path or the leaves of T form an independent set.*

Proof. The main ingredient of the proof is to compute a spanning tree T' in G and to transform T' into another spanning tree T that is either a Hamiltonian path or a spanning tree, where the leaves form an independent set. The transformation is done by successively searching for pairs of leaves u, v that are connected in G. By adding the edge $\{u, v\}$ to the spanning tree and removing an edge with at least three incident neighbors from the unique path connecting u and v, we obtain a new spanning tree, where the number of leaves is reduced by at least one. This way, the transformation ends with a tree T such that either no vertex in T has a degree higher than two (i. e., T is a Hamiltonian path) or there is no edge between leaves of T (i. e., the leaves form an independent set). □

If the leaves form an independent set, then the internal vertices form a vertex cover. Therefore, using Lemma 1, we obtain the following win/win result.

Theorem 7 (Prieto and Sloper [39]). *There is a polynomial-time algorithm that, for a given graph G, either computes a vertex cover of at most k vertices or a spanning tree with at least k internal vertices.* □

The stated result is interesting by its own, but additionally one can use it to obtain a kernelization of k-IST.

Theorem 8 (Prieto and Sloper [39]). *For any graph G, one can either find a k-internal spanning tree T in polynomial time or G can be transformed in polynomial time to a graph G' with at most $2k^3 + k^2 + 2k$ vertices such that G has a k-internal spanning tree if and only G' has.* □

The concept of win/win algorithms smoothly translates to approximation. As in win/win algorithms in parameterized computations, we are given one input that is a valid instance of two different problems. But instead of searching for an exact solution, we want to find approximate solutions for these problems. We aim for algorithms that guarantee at least one of the solutions to be improved compared to its known upper bounds on the worst-case approximation ratio. We can see the win/win approximation as a type of parameterization, where the approximation ratio achieved by one of the problems is the parameter for the other one.

An application of Lemma 1, presented in [27], relates the traveling salesman problem with edge costs restricted to 1 and 2, $(1, 2)$-TSP, to the independent set problem (IS). Given a set of edges E, let E_1 be E restricted to the edges of cost 1. The following lemma is a slightly strengthened version of a result from [27].

Lemma 2. *Given a complete weighted graph $G = (V, E, c)$ with edge costs restricted to 1 and 2, one can compute a Hamiltonian path of length L in G and an independent set of size I in the unweighted graph $G' = (V, E_1)$ such that $L - I \leq n - 2$, where $n = |V|$.*

Proof. We apply Lemma 1 to each connected component of G'. Then I is the size of a maximal independent set composed of the leaves of all computed spanning trees within all components. (Note that each such maximal independent set has the same size: It includes all leaves except some of those that are part of a Hamiltonian path within a component.) In particular, each component contributes at least one vertex counted in I.

In order to form a Hamiltonian path of length L, we handle the components of G' separately. For each component C, let T_C be the spanning tree computed for C. We form a path P_C in G by connecting the vertices of C in the order of a depth-first search in T_C starting from a leaf. Note that all edges of P_C that are not in T_C contain at least one leaf of T_C. Thus, we can assign each edge of cost 2 to a leaf of T_C. The leaf from which the depth-first search starts is not assigned to any edge of cost 2. Therefore, for each component C, the number of vertices counted in the independent set I is at least the number of edges of cost 2 in P_C plus one. Finally, we have to connect all paths P_C to one Hamiltonian path in G using edges of cost 2. The claim of the lemma follows immediately, since the number of such edges is the number of components minus one.   □

With this preparation, the actual win/win result is not hard to obtain.

Theorem 9 (Eppstein [27]). *Given a complete weighted graph G with edge weights 1 or 2, there is a win/win approximation algorithm that, for any $\varepsilon > 0$, either computes a $(1 + \varepsilon)$-approximative $(1, 2)$-TSP tour or a $(1/\varepsilon)$-approximative independent set in G', where G' is defined as in Lemma 2.*

Proof. Let L^* be the length of an optimal Hamiltonian tour in G and let I^* be the size of a maximum independent set of G'. If $L \leq (1 + \varepsilon)(n - 1)$, then we are done, because we are sure that $L^* \geq n - 1$. Otherwise, note that $\varepsilon \leq 1$ holds. Using Lemma 2, we get $I \geq L - n + 2 > (1 + \varepsilon)(n - 1) - (n - 1) + 1 \geq \varepsilon n$. Since $I^* \leq n$, the approximation ratio for the maximum independent set is $I^*/I \leq n/(\varepsilon n) = 1/\varepsilon$.   □

The idea of Theorem 9 was used as a technique to find a PTAS for a graph embedding problem in [14].

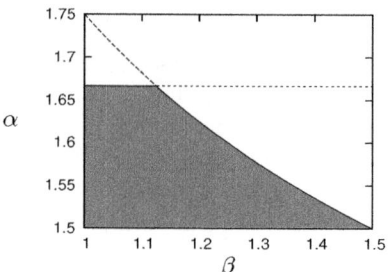

Fig. 1. Upper bound on the approximation ratio from Theorem 11. The horizontal line displays the approximation ratio $\alpha \leq 5/3$ proven in [32].

For some pairs of problems, one can show that, unless $\mathcal{P} = \mathcal{NP}$, there are no win/win algorithms that lead to improved approximation ratios.

Theorem 10 (Eppstein, [27]). *For all $\varepsilon > 0$, unless $\mathcal{P} = \mathcal{NP}$, there is no polynomial-time win/win approximation algorithm for IS and the maximum clique problem that achieves an approximation ratio of $n^{1-\varepsilon}$ for either of the problems, where n is the number of vertices.* □

The pairs of problems considered above for the positive results were related in a way that has similarities with duality in linear programming in the sense that they rely on the interaction of minimization and maximization. To show that this is not a specific property of win/win, we present a win/win approximation from [12] that relates two minimization problems, namely the metric Hamiltonian path problem with prespecified start and end vertex (Δ-HPP$_2$) and the Δ-TSP.

Currently, the algorithm of Christofides [18] has the best proven approximation ratio for the Δ-TSP, which is 1.5. A slight modification of that algorithm was shown by Hoogeveen [32] to be 5/3-approximative for the Δ-HPP$_2$. The two problems are strongly related in the sense that, for any given metric graph, either we are guaranteed to obtain an approximation ratio for Δ-TSP that is significantly better than 1.5-approximative or we can solve the Δ-HPP$_2$ better than 5/3-approximatively for any choice of end-vertices.

To this end, let us consider an algorithm A that works as follows. The input of A is a complete edge-weighted metric graph $G = (V, E, c)$ and two vertices u and v. Then A runs both Christofides' algorithm and Hoogeveen's algorithm on the input using the same minimum-cost spanning tree.

Let Opt_C and Opt_P denote the optimal solutions for the Δ-TSP and the Δ-HPP$_2$ given an input G, u, v and let H_C and H_P be the solutions computed by A. Then we define $\alpha := c(H_P)/c(Opt_P)$ to be the approximation ratio of the computed Hamiltonian path and $\beta := c(H_C)/c(Opt_C)$ to be the approximation ratio of the computed Hamiltonian tour.

Theorem 11 (Böckenhauer et al. [12]). *The approximation ratio α is at most $1 + 1.5/(2\beta)$, independent of the choice of u and v. In particular, only pairs of approximation ratios from or below the shaded area in Figure 1 are possible.* □

6   Conclusion

This paper provides a survey of some currently used ways of classifying instances of hard problems with respect to their computational hardness. On the one hand, this kind of effort shows why some hard problems can be successfully solved in practice. On the other hand, the presented approaches help to understand the nature of the hardness of some algorithmic problems by specifying the properties of the instances that lie in the hardest kernels of the considered problems.

References

1. Andreae, T.: On the traveling salesman problem restricted to inputs satisfying a relaxed triangle inequality. Networks 38(2), 59–67 (2001)
2. Andreae, T., Bandelt, H.J.: Performance guarantees for approximation algorithms depending on parameterized triangle inequalities. SIAM Journal on Discrete Mathematics 8, 1–16 (1995)
3. Arora, S.: Polynomial time approximation schemes for Euclidean traveling salesman and other geometric problems. Journal of the ACM 45(5), 753–782 (1998)
4. Ausiello, G., Crescenzi, P., Gambosi, G., Kann, V., Marchetti-Spaccamela, A., Protasi, M.: Complexity and Approximation. Springer, Berlin (1999)
5. Bender, M., Chekuri, C.: Performance guarantees for TSP with a parametrized triangle inequality. Information Processing Letters 73, 17–21 (2000)
6. Bern, M.W., Plassmann, P.E.: The Steiner problem with edge lengths 1 and 2. Information Processing Letters 32(4), 171–176 (1989)
7. Böckenhauer, H.-J., Hromkovič, J., Klasing, R., Seibert, S., Unger, W.: Towards the notion of stability of approximation for hard optimization tasks and the traveling salesman problem. In: Bongiovanni, G., Petreschi, R., Gambosi, G. (eds.) CIAC 2000. LNCS, vol. 1767, pp. 72–86. Springer, Heidelberg (2000)
8. Böckenhauer, H.-J., Hromkovič, J., Kneis, J., Kupke, J.: The parameterized approximability of TSP with deadlines. Theory of Computing Systems 41(3), 431–444 (2007)
9. Böckenhauer, H.-J., Hromkovič, J., Královič, R., Mömke, T., Rossmanith, P.: Reoptimization of Steiner trees: Changing the terminal set. Theoretical Computer Science 410(36), 3428–3435 (2009)
10. Böckenhauer, H.-J., Hromkovič, J., Mömke, T., Widmayer, P.: On the hardness of reoptimization. In: Geffert, V., Karhumäki, J., Bertoni, A., Preneel, B., Návrat, P., Bielikova, M. (eds.) SOFSEM 2008. LNCS, vol. 4910, pp. 50–65. Springer, Heidelberg (2008)
11. Böckenhauer, H.-J., Hromkovič, J., Seibert, S.: Stability of approximation. In: Gonzalez, T.F. (ed.) Handbook of Approximation Algorithms and Metaheuristics, ch. 31. Chapman & Hall/CRC (2007)
12. Böckenhauer, H.-J., Klasing, R., Mömke, T., Steinová, M.: Improved approximations for TSP with simple precedence constraints. In: Calamoneri, T., Diaz, J. (eds.) CIAC 2010. LNCS, vol. 6078, pp. 61–72. Springer, Heidelberg (2010)
13. Bodlaender, H.L., Langston, M.A. (eds.): IWPEC 2006. LNCS, vol. 4169. Springer, Heidelberg (2006)
14. Cabello, S., Eppstein, D., Klavžar, S.: The Fibonacci dimension of a graph. CoRR abs/0903.2507 (2009)

15. Cai, L., Huang, X.: Fixed-parameter approximation: Conceptual framework and approximability results. Algorithmica 57(2), 398–412 (2010)
16. Cesati, M., Trevisan, L.: On the efficiency of polynomial time approximation schemes. Information Processing Letters 64(4), 165–171 (1997)
17. Chen, Y., Grohe, M., Grüber, M.: On parameterized approximability. In: Bodlaender, H.L., Langston, M.A. (eds.) IWPEC 2006. LNCS, vol. 4169, pp. 109–120. Springer, Heidelberg (2006)
18. Christofides, N.: Worst-case analysis of a new heuristic for the travelling salesman problem. Tech. Rep. 388, Graduate School of Industrial Administration, Carnegie-Mellon University (1976)
19. Demaine, E.D., Hajiaghayi, M.T.: Bidimensionality: New connections between FPT algorithms and PTASs. In: Proc. of the 16th Annual ACM-SIAM Symposium on Discrete Algorithms (SODA 2005), pp. 590–601. SIAM, Philadelphia (2005)
20. Demaine, E.D., Hajiaghayi, M.: The bidimensionality theory and its algorithmic applications. Computer Journal 51(3), 292–302 (2008)
21. Downey, R.G., Fellows, M.R.: Fixed-parameter tractability and completeness i: Basic results. SIAM Journal on Computing 24(4), 873–921 (1995)
22. Downey, R.G., Fellows, M.R.: Fixed-parameter tractability and completeness ii: On completeness for $W[1]$. Theoretical Computer Science 141, 109–131 (1995)
23. Downey, R.G., Fellows, M.R.: Parameterized Complexity. Monographs in Computer Science. Springer, New York (1999)
24. Downey, R.G., Fellows, M.R., McCartin, C.: Parameterized approximation problems. In: Bodlaender, H.L., Langston, M.A. (eds.) IWPEC 2006. LNCS, vol. 4169, pp. 121–129. Springer, Heidelberg (2006)
25. Downey, R.G., Fellows, M.R., McCartin, C., Rosamond, F.A.: Parameterized approximation of dominating set problems. Information Processing Letters 109(1), 68–70 (2008)
26. Dreyfus, S.E., Wagner, R.A.: The Steiner problem in graphs. Networks 1, 195–207 (1971/1972)
27. Eppstein, D.: Paired approximation problems and incompatible inapproximabilities. In: Charikar, M. (ed.) Proc. of the 21st Annual ACM-SIAM Symposium on Discrete Algorithms (SODA 2010), pp. 1076–1086. SIAM, Philadelphia (2010)
28. Flum, J., Grohe, M.: Parameterized Complexity Theory. Springer, Heidelberg (2006)
29. Goemans, M.X., Williamson, D.P.: Improved approximation algorithms for maximum cut and satisfiability problems using semidefinite programming. Journal of the ACM 42(6), 1115–1145 (1995)
30. Guo, J., Niedermeier, R., Wernicke, S.: Parameterized complexity of vertex cover variants. Theory of Computing Systems 41(3), 501–520 (2007)
31. Hartmanis, J., Stearns, R.E.: On the computational complexity of algorithms. Transactions of the American Mathematical Society 117, 285–306 (1965)
32. Hoogeveen, J.A.: Analysis of Christofides' heuristic: some paths are more difficult than cycles. Operations Research Letters 10(5), 291–295 (1991)
33. Hromkovič, J.: Algorithmics for Hard Problems. In: Introduction to Combinatorial Optimization, Randomization, Approximation, and Heuristics. Springer, Berlin (2003)
34. Jansen, K.: An EPTAS for scheduling jobs on uniform processors: Using an MILP relaxation with a constant number of integral variables. SIAM Journal on Discrete Mathematics 24(2), 457–485 (2010)
35. Marx, D.: Parameterized complexity and approximation algorithms. The Computer Journal 51(1), 60–78 (2008)

36. Niedermeier, R.: Invitation to Fixed Parameter Algorithms. Oxford Lecture Series in Mathematics and Its Applications. Oxford University Press, USA (2006)
37. Papadimitriou, C.H., Steiglitz, K.: Combinatorial Optimization: Algorithms and Complexity. Prentice-Hall, Englewood Cliffs (1982)
38. Petrank, E.: The hardness of approximation: gap location. Computational Complexity 4, 133–157 (1994)
39. Prieto, E., Sloper, C.: Either/or: using vertex cover structure in designing FPT-algorithms—the case of k-Internal Spanning Tree. In: Dehne, F.K.H.A., Sack, J.R., Smid, M.H.M. (eds.) WADS 2003. LNCS, vol. 2748, pp. 474–483. Springer, Heidelberg (2003)
40. Rice, J.R.: The algorithm selection problem. Advances in Computers 15, 65–118 (1976)
41. Sahni, S., Gonzalez, T.F.: P-complete approximation problems. Journal of the ACM 23(3), 555–565 (1976)
42. Scott, A.D., Sorkin, G.B.: Faster algorithms for MAX CUT and MAX CSP, with polynomial expected time for sparse instances. In: Arora, S., Jansen, K., Rolim, J.D.P., Sahai, A. (eds.) RANDOM 2003 and APPROX 2003. LNCS, vol. 2764, pp. 382–395. Springer, Heidelberg (2003)
43. Stearns, R.E., Hartmanis, J., Lewis II, P.M.: Hierarchies of memory limited computations. In: Proc. of the 6th Annual Symposium on Switching and Automata Theory, pp. 179–190. IEEE, Los Alamitos (1965)
44. Turing, A.M.: On computable numbers, with an application to the entscheidungsproblem. Proceedings of the London Mathematical Society 2(42), 230–265 (1936)
45. Vassilevska, V., Williams, R., Woo, S.L.M.: Confronting hardness using a hybrid approach. In: Proc. of the 17th Annual ACM-SIAM Symposium on Discrete Algorithms (SODA 2006), pp. 1–10. SIAM, New York (2006)
46. Vazirani, V.V.: Approximation Algorithms. Springer, Heidelberg (2004)

Covering and Packing with Spheres by Diagonal Distortion in $\mathbb{R}^{n\star}$

Herbert Edelsbrunner[1,2] and Michael Kerber[1]

[1] IST Austria (Institute of Science and Technology Austria), Klosterneuburg, Austria
[2] Departments of Computer Science and of Mathematics, Duke University, Durham, North Carolina, and Geomagic, Research Triangle Park, North Carolina, USA

Abstract. We address the problem of covering $\mathbb{R}^n$ with congruent balls, while minimizing the number of balls that contain an average point. Considering the 1-parameter family of lattices defined by stretching or compressing the integer grid in diagonal direction, we give a closed formula for the covering density that depends on the distortion parameter. We observe that our family contains the thinnest lattice coverings in dimensions 2 to 5. We also consider the problem of packing congruent balls in $\mathbb{R}^n$, for which we give a closed formula for the packing density as well. Again we observe that our family contains optimal configurations, this time densest packings in dimensions 2 and 3.

Keywords: Packing, covering, spheres, balls, cubes, lattices, n-dimensional Euclidean space.

1 Introduction

The starting point for the work described in this paper is a perturbation of the integer grid designed to resolve ambiguities in the neighborhood relation of the cubes in an n-dimensional image [7]. Generalizing the perturbation to a 1-parameter family of distortions, we noted its relation with some well-known lattices in the sphere covering and packing literature; see Conway and Sloane [4], Fejes Tóth [8], and Rogers [16]. For example, in $\mathbb{R}^3$, we get the body-centered cubic, or BCC lattice by compressing with a factor $1/2$, and we get the face-centered cubic, of FCC lattice by stretching with a factor 2. We will explain the significance of these lattices for the covering and packing of congruent balls shortly.

Background. In the Euclidean plane, there is a single lattice that gives the thinnest covering of congruent disks as well as the densest packing of congruent disks. This is the hexagonal lattice, which consists of all integer combinations of the vectors

$$v_1 = \frac{1}{2\sqrt{3}} \begin{pmatrix} 1+\sqrt{3} \\ 1-\sqrt{3} \end{pmatrix}, \quad v_2 = \frac{1}{2\sqrt{3}} \begin{pmatrix} 1-\sqrt{3} \\ 1+\sqrt{3} \end{pmatrix}.$$

Placing disks of radius $\sqrt{2}/3$ centered at the lattice points, we get a covering, and reducing the radius to $1/\sqrt{6}$, we get a packing. Both are optimal in the sense that no

---

* This research is partially supported by DARPA under grant HR0011-09-0065 and NSF under grant DBI-0820624.

C.S. Calude, G. Rozenberg, A. Salomaa (Eds.): Maurer Festschrift, LNCS 6570, pp. 20–35, 2011.

other covering achieves a smaller covering density (see Kershner [12]), and no other packing achieves a larger packing density (see Thue [21]). Elegant proofs of both results can be found in Fejes Tóth [8].

The situation gets more complicated already in $\mathbb{R}^3$, where the lattice that gives the thinnest covering is different from the one that gives the densest packing. For covering, the BCC lattice gives the smallest density of a lattice covering (see Bambah [1]), but the existence of an even thinner non-lattice covering has not yet been contradicted. For packing, the FCC lattice gives the highest density (see Gauß[10]), and the claim that no non-lattice packing can be denser has become known as the Kepler Conjecture, one of the foremost mathematical questions of our time [20]. Stated in 1611, the conjecture remained open until Hales gave a computer-assisted proof confirming Kepler's conjecture in 2005 [11].

Even less is known in dimensions beyond 3. The generalization of the BCC lattice gives thin coverings that are known to be optimal among lattice coverings in dimension 4 (see Delone and Ryskov [5]) and in dimension 5 (see Ryskov and Baranovskii [17]). The thinnest known coverings in dimensions 6 to 24 can be found in [18,19] and the related website[1]. In contrast, the generalization of the FCC lattice fails to give the densest packing already in dimension 4. Nevertheless, the densest lattice packings are known in dimensions 4 and 5 (see Korkine and Zolotareff [13]), and in dimensions 6, 7 and 8 (see Blichfeldt [2]). No further optimality results are available until dimension 24 in which the Leech lattice, discovered independently by Witt in 1940 [22] and by Leech in 1965 [15], gives a surprisingly thin covering and dense packing. The optimality among the lattice packings has recently been established by Cohn and Kumar [3].

Results. In this paper, we give a complete analysis of the coverings and packings generated by the lattices obtained by a diagonal distortion of the integer grid. Specifically, we give closed-form expressions of the covering and packing densities as functions of $\delta > 0$, the distortion parameter. The complete analysis is possible because we get only a small number of combinatorially different Delaunay complexes for the 1-parameter family of lattices. For $0 < \delta < 1$, the distortion is a compression, and the Delaunay complex consists of copies of the Freudenthal triangulation of the unit cube. Among these lattices, we find the thinnest coverings for $\delta = 1/\sqrt{n+1}$, giving optimal covering densities among lattices for dimensions 2, 3, 4, and 5. For $\delta = 1$, the distortion is the identity, and the Delaunay complex consists of copies of the unit cube. For $1 < \delta$, the distortion stretches the integer grid, and the Delaunay complex consists of distorted diagonal slices of the unit cube. Among these lattices, we find the densest packings for $\delta = \sqrt{n+1}$, giving optimal packing densities for dimensions 2 and 3.

Outline. Section 2 introduces two decompositions of the n-cube: the Freudenthal triangulation and the slice decomposition. Section 3 explains how a lattice in $\mathbb{R}^n$ defines a covering and a packing, and how we measure their densities. Section 4 gives a complete analysis of the covering density as a function of the distortion. Section 5 does the same for the packing density. Section 6 concludes the paper.

---

[1] http://www.math.uni-magdeburg.de/lattice_geometry/

2   Decomposing the n-Cube

In this section, we introduce the two decompositions of the cube that are instrumental in the analysis of the covering and packing densities of the 1-parameter family of lattices.

Freudenthal triangulation. We write $[n] = \{1, 2, \ldots, n\}$ for the set of coordinate directions in $\mathbb{R}^n$ and e_i for the unit vector in the i-th coordinate direction. The n-dimensional *unit cube*, $\mathbb{U}^n = [0, 1]^n$, has 2^n vertices u_I, each corresponding to a subset $I \subseteq [n]$ such that $u_I = \sum_{i \in I} e_i$. We say u_I *precedes* u_J if $I \subseteq J$ and $I \neq J$. This defines a partial order on the vertices, with a unique smallest vertex $\mathbf{0} = u_\emptyset$, and a unique largest vertex $\mathbf{1} = u_{[n]}$. A *chain* is a sequence of distinct vertices in which each vertex precedes the next one. Its *length* is the number of vertices. Each chain of length $k + 1$ defines a k-simplex, namely the convex hull of its $k + 1$ vertices. The *Freudenthal triangulation* of the n-cube, denoted as $\mathcal{F}^n = \mathcal{F}(\mathbb{U}^n)$, is the set of all simplices defined by chains [9,14]; see Figure 1.

Define the *silhouette* of the n-cube as its projection along the diagonal direction, which is an $(n-1)$-dimensional convex polytope. It is not difficult to see that all vertices other than $\mathbf{0}$ and $\mathbf{1}$ project to vertices of the silhouette. The faces of the silhouette have dimension between 0 and $n - 2$. We can triangulate these faces such that the join of the preimage of every $(k-2)$-simplex with the edge connecting $\mathbf{0}$ with $\mathbf{1}$ gives a k-simplex of the Freudenthal triangulation.

Slice decomposition. Let U_i be the subset of vertices u_J with card $J = i$, and let H_i be the $(n-1)$-dimensional hyperplane orthogonal to the diagonal direction that passes through the vertices of U_i, for $0 \leq i \leq n$. The $n + 1$ hyperplanes cut the n-cube into n *slices*, each of width $1/\sqrt{n}$. We call this the *slice decomposition* of the n-cube, denoted at $\mathcal{S}^n = \mathcal{S}(\mathbb{U}^n)$; see Figure 1. We note that for each edge of the n-cube, there is a unique i such that its endpoints belong to U_{i-1} and to U_i. In other words, the edge does not cross any of the hyperplanes and therefore belongs to a unique slice. It follows that the i-th slice is the convex hull of the points in $U_{i-1} \cup U_i$ and that its number of vertices is $\binom{n}{i-1} + \binom{n}{i}$. Furthermore, the i-th slice is the central reflection of the $(n - i + 1)$-st slice whose vertices are the points in $U_{n-i} \cup U_{n-i+1}$.

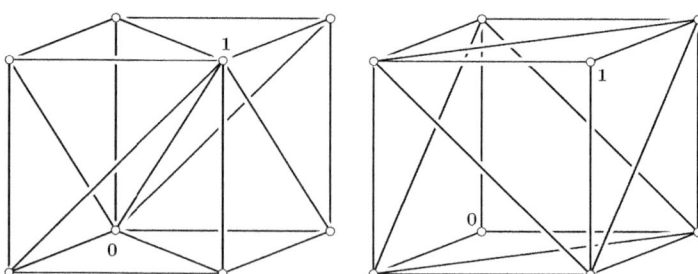

Fig. 1. Left: the Freudenthal triangulation of the 3-cube consisting of six tetrahedra sharing the edge that connects $\mathbf{0}$ with $\mathbf{1}$. Right: the slice decomposition of the 3-cube consisting of two tetrahedra sandwiching an octahedron.

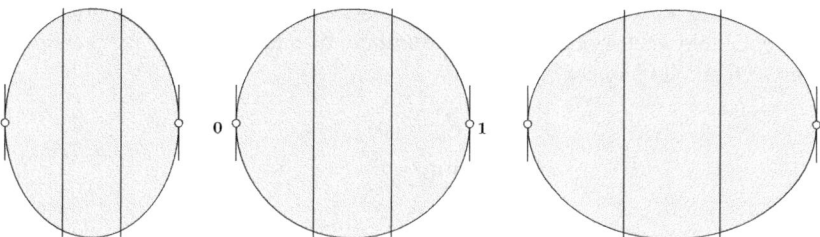

Fig. 2. The sliced circumsphere of the 3-cube in the middle, with its compressed and stretched images on the left and the right

The hyperplanes can also be used to cut the circumscribed $(n-1)$-sphere, S, of the unit n-cube; see Figure 2. For $0 \leq i \leq n$, let $S_i = S \cap H_i$ and note that $S_0 = \mathbf{0}$, $S_n = \mathbf{1}$, and all other S_i are $(n-2)$-dimensional spheres. The radius of S is $\sqrt{n}/2$. We can therefore compute the radius of S_i as

$$r_i = \sqrt{\frac{n}{4} - \left(\frac{\sqrt{n}}{2} - \frac{i}{\sqrt{n}}\right)^2} = \sqrt{i - \frac{i^2}{n}}. \tag{1}$$

As n goes to infinity, the radius of S_1 converges to 1, while the radius of $S_{n/2}$ is $\sqrt{n}/2$ and thus diverges. Remarkably, the points in U_1 are nevertheless vertices of the silhouette of the n-cube. Note that the r_i are also the distances of the vertices of the silhouette from its center.

1 (Silhouette Lemma). *Let s_I and s_J be the projections of u_I and u_J. Assuming $I, J \neq \emptyset, [n]$, both are vertices of the silhouette and $\|s_I\| \leq \|s_J\|$ iff $(\operatorname{card} I - \frac{n}{2})^2 \geq (\operatorname{card} J - \frac{n}{2})^2$.*

This fact will be relevant in Section 5, where we analyze the packing density of a 1-parameter family of lattices. Now consider compressing or stretching the cube and its circumsphere along the diagonal direction. If we compress, we get an ellipsoid of *pancake* type, and the Delaunay complex of the 2^n points is the compressed Freudenthal triangulation; see [7] for a proof. If we stretch, we get an ellipsoid of *cigar* type, and the Delaunay complex of the 2^n vertices is the stretched slice decomposition; see Figure 1.

3   Lattices

In this section, we introduce the 1-parameter family of lattices and explain how they define packings and coverings. Writing V_n for the (n-dimensional) volume of the n-dimensional unit ball, $\mathbb{B}^n = \{x \in \mathbb{R}^n \mid \|x\| \leq 1\}$, we have

$$V_n = \begin{cases} \pi^{\frac{n}{2}} / \left(\frac{n}{2}\right)! & \text{if } n \text{ is even,} \\ \pi^{\frac{n-1}{2}} 2^{\frac{n+1}{2}} / n!! & \text{if } n \text{ is odd,} \end{cases}$$

where $n!! = n \cdot (n-2) \cdot \ldots \cdot 3 \cdot 1$ is the double factorial; see e.g. [4].

Covering and packing. A *lattice* in $\mathbb{R}^n$ consists of all integer combinations of n linearly independent vectors v_i. Important numbers of a lattice $\mathcal{L}$ are its *determinant*, its *covering radius*, and its *packing radius*:

$$\det \mathcal{L} = \det[v_1 v_2 \ldots v_n],$$
$$R(\mathcal{L}) = \max_{x \in \mathbb{R}^n} \min_{a \in \mathcal{L}} \|x - a\|,$$
$$r(\mathcal{L}) = \min_{0 \neq a \in \mathcal{L}} \|a\|/2.$$

Suppose we choose a radius r and replace each point $a \in \mathcal{L}$ by the ball of radius r centered at a. The *density* of the resulting set of balls is the number of balls that contain an average point:

$$\varrho(r) = \frac{V_n r^n}{\det \mathcal{L}}. \tag{2}$$

For $r \geq R(\mathcal{L})$, we get a *covering* in which the balls cover every point at least once. The density is therefore greater than or equal to 1. For $r \leq r(\mathcal{L})$, we get a *packing* in which the balls have disjoint interiors. The density is therefore less than or equal to 1. Two lattices are *isomorphic* if they are related by a similarity. In this case, the two lattices give the same densities. We are interested in finding the lattices that give smallest possible covering density and the largest possible packing density.

The mother of all lattices is the *integer grid*, $\mathcal{L} = \mathbb{Z}^n$. We have $\det \mathcal{L} = 1$, $r(\mathcal{L}) = 1/2$, and $R(\mathcal{L}) = \sqrt{n}/2$. The corresponding packing density is $V_n/2^n$ and the corresponding covering density is $n^{\frac{n}{2}} V_n/2^n$. For small values of n, these are given in Table 1.

Table 1. From left to right: the volume of $\mathbb{B}^n$, the covering density of the integer grid in $\mathbb{R}^n$, and the packing density of the same grid

n	volume of unit ball	covering density	packing density
2	$\pi = 3.141\ldots$	$\pi/2 = 1.570\ldots$	$\pi/4 = 0.785\ldots$
3	$4\pi/3 = 4.188\ldots$	$\sqrt{3}\pi/2 = 2.720\ldots$	$\pi/6 = 0.523\ldots$
4	$\pi^2/2 = 4.934\ldots$	$\pi^2/2 = 4.934\ldots$	$\pi^2/32 = 0.308\ldots$
5	$8\pi^2/15 = 5.263\ldots$	$5\sqrt{5}\pi^2/12 = 9.195\ldots$	$\pi^2/60 = 0.164\ldots$
6	$\pi^3/6 = 5.167\ldots$	$9\pi^3/16 = 17.441\ldots$	$\pi^3/384 = 0.060\ldots$
7	$16\pi^3/105 = 4.724\ldots$	$49\sqrt{7}\pi^3/120 = 33.497\ldots$	$\pi^3/840 = 0.036\ldots$
8	$\pi^4/24 = 4.058\ldots$	$2\pi^4/3 = 64.939\ldots$	$\pi^4/6144 = 0.015\ldots$

Distortion. To describe a 1-parameter family of distortions of the integer grid, we introduce the *diagonal height function*, $\Delta : \mathbb{R}^n \to \mathbb{R}$, which maps every point $x = (x_1, x_2, \ldots, x_n)$ to $\Delta(x) = \langle x, \mathbf{1} \rangle = \sum_{i=1}^{n} x_i$. It is $\sqrt{n}$ times the (signed) Euclidean distance of x from the *diagonal hyperplane*, $\Delta^{-1}(0)$. For each $\delta \in \mathbb{R}$, we construct a lattice $\mathcal{L}_\delta$ by mapping the i-th unit vector to $e_i + D \cdot \mathbf{1}$, where $D = (\delta - 1)/n$. The corresponding linear transformation, $T_\delta : \mathbb{R}^n \to \mathbb{R}^n$, is given by

$$T_\delta(x) = x + D\Delta(x) \cdot \mathbf{1}. \tag{3}$$

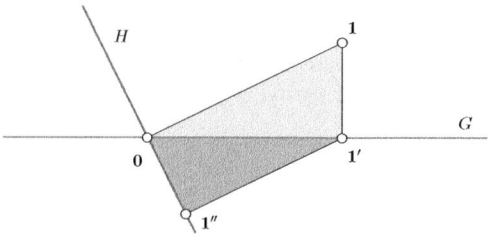

Fig. 3. Two similar right-angled triangles in $\mathbb{R}^n$

Hence, $\mathcal{L}_\delta = T_\delta(\mathbb{Z}^n)$, and we note that $\mathcal{L}_1 = \mathbb{Z}^n$. For vanishing distortion parameter δ, we get a set of points in $\Delta^{-1}(0)$, which has only $n - 1$ dimensions. This set is again a lattice and, more specifically, one in our 1-parameter family, as we now prove.

2 (Lattice Projection Lemma). *The diagonal projection of the n-dimensional integer grid, $T_0(\mathbb{Z}^n)$, is isometric to $T_\delta(\mathbb{Z}^{n-1})$, for $\delta = 1/\sqrt{n}$.*

Proof. Let L be the set of lines in $\mathbb{R}^n$ obtained by drawing a line in diagonal direction through every point in $\mathbb{Z}^n$. Intersecting L with the hyperplane G spanned by the first $n - 1$ coordinate axes, we get $\mathbb{Z}^{n-1}$. Intersecting L with $H = \Delta^{-1}(0)$, wet get $T_0(\mathbb{Z}^n)$. Both are sets in $n - 1$ dimensions, and we can interpolate between them by rotating the hyperplane around $G \cap H$, from G to H. This interpolation is exactly the distortion of $\mathbb{Z}^{n-1}$ defined above. It remains to show that $H \cap L$ is the distorted integer grid for $\delta = 1/\sqrt{n}$. To see this, we consider the two lines in L that pass through $\mathbf{1}$ and through $\mathbf{1}' = (1, \ldots, 1, 0)$ in $\mathbb{R}^n$. They intersect G in $\mathbf{0}$ and $\mathbf{1}'$ and they intersect H in $\mathbf{0}$ and $\mathbf{1}''$, the projection of $\mathbf{1}'$ onto H. The distance between $\mathbf{0}$ and $\mathbf{1}'$ is $\sqrt{n-1}$. To compute the distance between $\mathbf{0}$ and $\mathbf{1}''$, we consider the triangles spanned by $\mathbf{0}$, $\mathbf{1}$, $\mathbf{1}'$ and by $\mathbf{0}$, $\mathbf{1}'$, $\mathbf{1}''$; see Figure 3. The two triangles are similar, which implies that the distance between the two intersection points in H is

$$\| \mathbf{0} - \mathbf{1}'' \| = \| \mathbf{1} - \mathbf{1}' \| \cdot \frac{\| \mathbf{0} - \mathbf{1}' \|}{\| \mathbf{0} - \mathbf{1} \|} \ = \ \sqrt{1 - \frac{1}{n}}.$$

The distortion factor is the ratio of the distance between $\mathbf{0}$ and $\mathbf{1}''$ in H and between $\mathbf{0}$ and $\mathbf{1}'$ in G, which is $\delta = 1/\sqrt{n}$.   ⌑

We will see shortly that the distortion of the $(n - 1)$-dimensional integer grid for $\delta = 1/\sqrt{n}$ provides the thinnest covering in the 1-parameter family we consider in this paper.

Projected Freudenthal simplex. We are interested in the diagonal projection of an n-dimensional Freudenthal simplex and the radius of its circumscribed sphere. Take the n-simplex spanned by the points $y_i = \sum_{j=1}^i e_j$, for $0 \le i \le n$, noting that $y_0 = \mathbf{0}$ and $y_n = \mathbf{1}$. The projection of y_i onto $H = \Delta^{-1}(0)$ is $x_i = T_0(y_i)$, where

$$x_i = \frac{1}{n}(n - i, \ldots, n - i, -i, \ldots, -i)$$

is a point with i equal leading coordinates and $n - i$ equal trailing coordinates. Since $x_0 = x_n$, we get only n different points which span an $(n - 1)$-simplex in H, the projection of the n-simplex. Perhaps surprisingly, it is not difficult to find the center and radius of the circumsphere of the $(n - 1)$-simplex. For that purpose, we consider the point

$$z = \frac{1}{n}(n - 1, n - 2, \ldots, 1, 0)$$

and note that $\Delta(z) = \frac{1}{n} \sum_{i=1}^{n-1} i = \frac{n-1}{2}$. The projection of z onto H is therefore $z' = T_0(z) = z - \frac{n-1}{2n} \cdot \mathbf{1}$, which gives

$$z' = \frac{1}{2n}(n - 1, n - 3, \ldots, -n + 3, -n + 1).$$

To compute the distance between the two projected points, we write the vectors of $2nx_i$, $2nz'$, and $2n(x_i - z')$:

$$(2n - 2i, \ldots, 2n - 2i \; ; \; -2i, \ldots, -2i),$$
$$(n - 1, \ldots, n - 2i + 1 \; ; \; n - 2i - 1, \ldots, -n + 1),$$
$$(n - 2i + 1, \ldots, n - 1 \; ; \; -n + 1, \ldots, n - 2i - 1),$$

showing the 1-st, i-th, $(i + 1)$-st, and n-th coordinates. We can read the difference as a cyclic rotation of the vector $(-n + 1, -n + 3, \ldots, n - 1)$. In other words, all vectors of the form $x_i - z'$ are cyclic rotations of each other, which implies that the $n + 1$ points x_i all have the same distance from z'. This distance is also the radius of the circumscribed sphere of the $(n - 1)$-simplex:

$$R_0 = \sqrt{\frac{(n - 1)(n + 1)}{12n}}. \tag{4}$$

We will use this radius in the analysis of the covering density in Section 4.

4 Covering

To compute the covering radius, we need to understand the Voronoi diagram of $\mathcal{L}_\delta$ or, equivalently, the Delaunay complex. Fortunately, there are only two types.

Radius of a slice. For $\delta > 1$, the Delaunay complex consists of distorted copies of the slice decomposition:

$$\text{Del}(\mathcal{L}_\delta) = T_\delta(\mathcal{S}^n + \mathbb{Z}^n).$$

We may restrict ourselves to the slices in the decomposition of the distorted unit cube. The center of the circumsphere of every slice lies on the diagonal and between the two delimiting hyperplanes. It follows that the circumradii of the slices increase toward the middle, similar to the radii of the $(n - 2)$-spheres in the Silhouette Lemma. For odd n, we have a unique middle slice, and for even n, we have two symmetric slices separated by the middle hyperplane.

Assume first that n is odd. The circumscribed $(n-1)$-sphere of the middle slice passes through two $(n-2)$-spheres of radius

$$r = \sqrt{\frac{n-1}{2} - \frac{(n-1)^2}{4n}} = \frac{1}{2}\sqrt{n - \frac{1}{n}}$$

and distance $2d = \delta/\sqrt{n}$ from each other; see (1). The radius of the $(n-1)$-sphere is therefore

$$R(\delta) = \sqrt{r^2 + d^2} = \frac{1}{2\sqrt{n}}\sqrt{n^2 - 1 + \delta^2}. \tag{5}$$

Now assume that n is even. The radii of the two $(n-2)$-spheres defining a slice next to the middle hyperplane are

$$r = \sqrt{\frac{n-2}{2} - \frac{(n-2)^2}{4n}} = \frac{1}{2}\sqrt{n - \frac{4}{n}}$$

and $\sqrt{n}/2$; see again (1). The distance between the two supporting hyperplanes is $d_1 + d_2 = \delta/\sqrt{n}$. We compute d_1 such that $r^2 + d_1^2 = \frac{n}{4} + d_2^2$. This gives $d_1 = (\delta^2 + 1)/2\delta\sqrt{n}$ and $d_2 = (\delta^2 - 1)/2\delta\sqrt{n}$. The radius of the circumscribed $(n-1)$-sphere is therefore

$$R(\delta) = \sqrt{\frac{n}{4} + d_2^2} = \frac{1}{2\sqrt{n}}\sqrt{\delta^2 + n^2 - 2 + \frac{1}{\delta^2}}. \tag{6}$$

Radius of a simplex. For $0 < \delta < 1$, the Delaunay complex consists of distorted copies of the Freudenthal triangulation:

$$\mathrm{Del}(\mathcal{L}_\delta) = T_\delta(\mathcal{F}^n + \mathbb{Z}^n).$$

All n-simplices are of the same type, and it suffices to compute the circumradius of the one spanned by the images of the points $y_i = \sum_{j=1}^i e_j$, for $0 \le i \le n$. At the beginning of the distortion, when $\delta = 1$, the circumsphere of the Freudenthal n-simplex has radius half the length of the diagonal edge, and at the end, when $\delta = 0$, the circumsphere has a radius specified in (4). We will make use of the fact that the radius of any distorted image of the n-simplex can be expressed in terms of δ and the radii at $\delta = 1$ and at $\delta = 0$. To state the result formally, we let $z(\delta)$ and $R(\delta)$ be the center and the radius of the n-simplex at distortion value $0 \le \delta \le 1$.

3 (Distortion Lemma). *The squared radius of the circumsphere of the distorted image of the Freudenthal n-simplex satisfies $R^2(\delta) = \delta^2 R_1^2 + (1 - 2\delta^2 + \delta^4)R_0^2$.*

A proof is given in Appendix A. Using $R_1^2 = n/4$ and $R_0^2 = (n^2 - 1)/(12n)$ from (4), we get

$$\begin{aligned} R(\delta) &= \sqrt{\frac{\delta^2 n}{4} + \frac{(1 - 2\delta^2 + \delta^4)(n^2 - 1)}{12n}} \\ &= \sqrt{\frac{(n^2 - 1) + (n^2 + 2)\delta^2 + (n^2 - 1)\delta^4}{12n}}. \end{aligned} \tag{7}$$

In summary, we have three different formulas for the covering radius: the one in (5) for $1 \leq \delta$ in odd dimension, the one in (6) for $1 \leq \delta$ in even dimension, and the one in (7) for $0 \leq \delta \leq 1$.

Covering density. Given the radius $R = R(\delta)$, we get the corresponding covering density as $\gamma(\delta) = V_n R^n / \delta$ from (2). We show below that $\gamma(\delta)$ has two local minima: one in the first interval at $\delta = 1/\sqrt{n+1}$, and the other in the second interval at $\delta = \sqrt{n+1}$; see Figure 4. By comparing with the graphs for the packing density in the same figure, we note that the minima for covering coincide with the maxima for packing. We analyze γ, distinguishing between the three cases we encountered for the covering radius.

CASE 1. $0 \leq \delta \leq 1$. Then

$$\gamma(\delta) = \frac{V_n}{(12n)^{\frac{n}{2}}} \cdot \frac{A^{\frac{n}{2}}}{\delta}, \tag{8}$$

where $A = (n^2 - 1) + (n^2 + 2)\delta^2 + (n^2 - 1)\delta^4$. We compute the derivative as

$$\gamma'(\delta) = \frac{V_n}{(12n)^{\frac{n}{2}}} \cdot \frac{\frac{n}{2}\delta A^{\frac{n}{2}-1}A' - A^{\frac{n}{2}}}{\delta^2} = \frac{V_n}{(12n)^{\frac{n}{2}}} \cdot A^{\frac{n}{2}-1} \cdot a,$$

where $a = (2n^2 + n - 1)\delta^2 + (n^2 + 2) - \frac{n+1}{\delta^2}$. The only factor that can vanish is a, so we get $\gamma'(\delta) = 0$ iff $\delta^2 = \frac{1}{n+1}$. This critical point can only be a minimum.

CASE 2.1. $\delta \geq 1$ and n is odd. Then

$$\gamma(\delta) = \frac{V_n}{2^n n^{\frac{n}{2}}} \cdot \frac{B^{\frac{n}{2}}}{\delta}. \tag{9}$$

where $B = \delta^2 + n^2 - 1$. The derivative is

$$\gamma'(\delta) = \frac{V_n}{2^n n^{\frac{n}{2}}} \cdot B^{\frac{n}{2}-1} \cdot b,$$

where $b = (n - 1)(1 - \frac{n+1}{\delta^2})$. The only factor that can vanish is b, so we have $\gamma'(\delta) = 0$ iff $\delta^2 = n + 1$. This can only be a minimum.

CASE 2.2. $\delta \geq 1$ and n is even. Then

$$\gamma(\delta) = \frac{V_n}{2^n n^{\frac{n}{2}}} \cdot \frac{C^{\frac{n}{2}}}{\delta}. \tag{10}$$

where $C = \delta^2 + \frac{1}{\delta^2} + n^2 - 2$. As before, we compute the derivative and get

$$\gamma'(\delta) = \frac{V_n}{2^n n^{\frac{n}{2}}} \cdot C^{\frac{n}{2}-1} \cdot c,$$

where $c = n - \frac{n}{\delta^4} - 1 - \frac{n^2-2}{\delta^2}$. The last factor that can vanish is c, so we have $\gamma'(\delta) = 0$ iff $\delta^2 = n + 1$, as in Case 2.1. Again, this can only be a minimum.

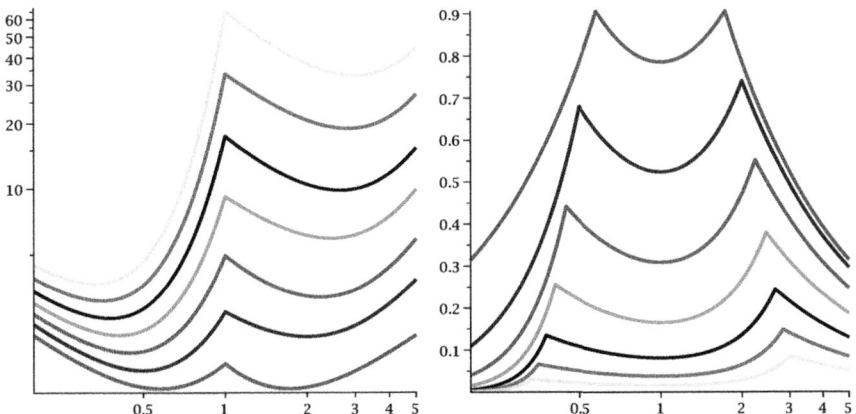

Fig. 4. Left, from bottom to top: the graphs of the covering density in dimensions 2 to 8. All functions have two local minima, the lesser at $\delta = \sqrt{n+1}$ and the global minimum at $\delta = 1/\sqrt{n+1}$. Right, from top to bottom: the graphs of the packing density in dimensions 2 to 8. All functions have two local maxima, the lesser at $\delta = 1/\sqrt{n+1}$ and the global maximum at $\delta = \sqrt{n+1}$. Some of the axes use logarithmic scale for clarity.

Examples. In the plane, the minimum covering density is achieved by the hexagonal lattice, with $\gamma(1/\sqrt{3}) = \gamma(\sqrt{3}) = 1.209\ldots$. More generally, we get

$$\gamma(\delta) = \begin{cases} \frac{\pi}{8}\left(\delta^3 + 2\delta + \frac{1}{\delta}\right) & \text{for } 0 \leq \delta \leq 1, \\ \frac{\pi}{8}\left(\delta + \frac{2}{\delta} + \frac{1}{\delta^3}\right) & \text{for } 1 \leq \delta, \end{cases}$$

using the formulas (8) and (10) for $n = 2$; see the lowest graph in Figure 4 on the left. Note the local maximum for the square lattice, with $\gamma(1) = 1.570\ldots$. We have $\gamma(\delta) = \gamma(1/\delta)$ for all $\delta > 0$. In $\mathbb{R}^3$, we get the thinnest covering for $\mathcal{L}_{1/2}$, with covering density $\gamma(\frac{1}{2}) = 1.463\ldots$. Compare this with $\gamma(2) = 2.094\ldots$ for the FCC lattice and with $\gamma(1) = 2.720\ldots$ for the cubic lattice. More generally, we get

$$\gamma(\delta) = \begin{cases} \frac{\pi(8 + 11\delta^2 + 8\delta^4)^{3/2}}{162\delta} & \text{for } 0 \leq \delta \leq 1, \\ \frac{\pi(8 + \delta^2)^{3/2}}{18\sqrt{3}\delta} & \text{for } 1 \leq \delta; \end{cases}$$

see the second lowest graph in Figure 4 on the left. The lattice $\mathcal{L}_{1/2}$ is isomorphic to the BCC lattice, which is commonly described as the set of integer points plus the integer points shifted by $(\frac{1}{2}, \frac{1}{2}, \frac{1}{2})$.

Recall that for $n = 2$, the two local minima correspond to the same lattice and thus give the same covering density. In contrast, for dimensions $n \geq 3$, we get a smaller density for $\delta = 1/\sqrt{n+1}$ than for $\delta = \sqrt{n+1}$. Using (4) and the Lattice Projection Lemma, we get the corresponding covering radius as the square root of $(n^2 + 2n)/(12n + 12)$. The best covering density within our 1-parameter family is therefore

$$\gamma(1/\sqrt{n+1}) = V_n \sqrt{n+1} \left(\frac{n(n+2)}{12(n+1)}\right)^{\frac{n}{2}};$$

see the left half of Table 2.

Table 2. Left: the covering densities of $\mathcal{L}_\delta$ for $\delta = 1/\sqrt{n+1}$ up to dimension $n = 8$, and the best known covering densities for comparison. Right: the packing densities of $\mathcal{L}_\delta$ for $\delta = \sqrt{n+1}$, and the best known packing densities for comparison. Densities that are known to be optimal for lattices are displayed in bold.

n	covering density		packing density	
	$\gamma(\frac{1}{\sqrt{n+1}})$	best	$\varphi(\sqrt{n+1})$	best
2	**1.209...**		**0.906...**	
3	**1.463...**		**0.740...**	
4	**1.765...**		0.551...	**0.616...**
5	**2.124...**		0.379...	**0.465...**
6	2.551...	2.464...	0.244...	**0.372...**
7	3.059...	2.900...	0.147...	**0.295...**
8	3.665...	3.142...	0.084...	**0.253...**

5 Packing

In this section, we give a formula for the packing density as a function of the distortion parameter.

Packing radius. To get the packing radius of $\mathcal{L}_\delta$, we consider the point $\mathbf{0}$ and find the closest other lattice point. Using the Silhouette Lemma from Section 2, we observe that there are only three possibilities:

$$T_\delta(e_1) = (1 + D, D, \ldots, D),$$
$$T_\delta(e_1 - e_2) = (1, -1, 0, \ldots, 0),$$
$$T_\delta(\mathbf{1}) = (\delta, \delta, \ldots, \delta).$$

The distance to $T_\delta(e_1 - e_2)$ is $\sqrt{2}$, and that to $T_\delta(\mathbf{1})$ is $\delta\sqrt{n}$. The distance to the image of the first unit vector is

$$\|T_\delta(e_1)\| = \sqrt{(1 + D)^2 + (n - 1)D^2} = \sqrt{1 + \frac{\delta^2 - 1}{n}}.$$

Plugging $\delta^2 = n + 1$ into the formula, we get $\|T_\delta(e_1)\| = \sqrt{2}$, and plugging $\delta^2 = 1/(n + 1)$ into it, we get $\|T_\delta(e_1)\| = \delta\sqrt{n}$. We thus have three intervals in which the packing radius has qualitatively different behavior:

$$r(\mathcal{L}_\delta) = \begin{cases} \frac{1}{2}\delta\sqrt{n} & \text{for } 0 \leq \delta \leq \frac{1}{\sqrt{n+1}}, \\ \frac{1}{2}\sqrt{1 + \frac{\delta^2 - 1}{n}} & \text{for } \frac{1}{\sqrt{n+1}} \leq \delta \leq \sqrt{n + 1}, \\ \frac{1}{2}\sqrt{2} & \text{for } \sqrt{n + 1} \leq \delta. \end{cases}$$

Packing density. Given the radius $r = r(\mathcal{L})$, we get the corresponding packing density as $\varphi(\delta) = V_n r^n / \delta$ from (2). In the first interval, the density grows like δ^{n-1}, and in the last interval, it shrinks like $1/\delta$. We now prove that in the middle interval, φ has a single minimum, which it attains at $\delta = 1$. Indeed, we have

$$\varphi(\delta) = \frac{V_n}{2^n n^{\frac{n}{2}}} \cdot \frac{E^{\frac{n}{2}}}{\delta}, \tag{11}$$

where $E = \delta^2 + n - 1$. The derivative with respect to the distortion parameter is

$$\varphi'(\delta) = \frac{V_n}{2^n n^{\frac{n}{2}}} \cdot \frac{\frac{n}{2}\delta E^{\frac{n}{2}-1} E' - E^{\frac{n}{2}}}{\delta^2} = \frac{V_n}{2^n n^{\frac{n}{2}}} \cdot E^{\frac{n}{2}-1} \cdot e,$$

where $e = (n-1)(1 - \frac{1}{\delta^2})$. The only factor that can vanish is e. Restricting ourselves to non-negative values of the distortion parameter, we have $\varphi'(\delta) = 0$ iff $\delta = 1$. This critical point can only be a minimum. In summary, the packing density has local maxima at $\delta = 1/\sqrt{n+1}$ and $\delta = \sqrt{n+1}$, a local minimum at $\delta = 1$, and goes to zero as δ goes to 0 or to ∞; see the graphs in Figure 4.

Examples. In the plane, the maximum packing density is attained for $\delta = 1/\sqrt{3}$ and $\delta = \sqrt{3}$. For both values of the distortion parameter, $\mathcal{L}_\delta$ is isomorphic to the standard hexagonal lattice, with packing density $\varphi(1/\sqrt{3}) = \varphi(\sqrt{3}) = 0.906\ldots$. More generally, we have $\varphi(\delta) = V_2 r^2/\delta$, where $V_2 = \pi$ and $r = r(\mathcal{L}_\delta)$. Using the above formulas for the radius, we thus have

$$\varphi(\delta) = \begin{cases} \frac{\pi\delta}{2} & \text{for } 0 \le \delta \le \frac{1}{\sqrt{3}}, \\ \frac{\pi}{8}(\delta + \frac{1}{\delta}) & \text{for } \frac{1}{\sqrt{3}} \le \delta \le \sqrt{3}, \\ \frac{\pi}{2\delta} & \text{for } \sqrt{3} \le \delta; \end{cases}$$

see the highest graph in Figure 4 on the right. Note that $\varphi(\delta) = \varphi(\frac{1}{\delta})$ for all $\delta > 0$ and that this function has a local minimum for the square lattice at $\varphi(1) = 0.785\ldots$; compare this with the graph of the covering density in the plane. In $\mathbb{R}^3$, we get local maxima at $\delta = 1/2$ and $\delta = 2$. More generally, we have

$$\varphi(\delta) = \begin{cases} \frac{\sqrt{3}\pi\delta^2}{2} & \text{for } 0 \le \delta \le \frac{1}{2}, \\ \frac{\pi(\delta^2+2)^{3/2}}{18\sqrt{3}\delta} & \text{for } \frac{1}{2} \le \delta \le 2, \\ \frac{\sqrt{2}\pi}{3\delta} & \text{for } 2 \le \delta; \end{cases}$$

see the second highest graph in Figure 4 on the right. This function has a local minimum for the cubic lattice at $\varphi(1) = 0.523\ldots$. In contrast to the plane, the values at the two maxima are not the same and we get the higher density at $\varphi(2) = 0.740\ldots$, where $\mathcal{L}_2$ is isomorphic to the FCC lattice. Most commonly, that lattice is described as the set of integer points for which the sum of coordinates is even. This lattice differs from $\mathcal{L}_2$ by a rotation of $60°$ around the line that passes through $\mathbf{0}$ and $\mathbf{1}$.

Recall that for $n = 2$, the two local maxima correspond to the same lattice and thus give the same packing density. In contrast, for dimensions $n \ge 3$, we get a higher density for $\delta = \sqrt{n+1}$ than for $\delta = 1/\sqrt{n+1}$. The best packing density within our 1-parameter family is therefore

$$\varphi(\sqrt{n+1}) = \frac{V_n}{2^{n/2}\sqrt{n+1}};$$

see the right half of Table 2.

6   Discussion

Our simple distortion of the integer grid in diagonal direction leads to a 1-parameter family of lattices that contains optimal lattice coverings in dimensions 2, 3, 4, and 5 and optimal packings in dimensions 2 ad 3. It misses the best lattices in dimensions higher than listed. We therefore pose the question whether our approach can be extended to include the other optimal lattice coverings and packings, in particular the lattices of types D and E and the Leech lattice [4], or even discover lattices with better densities than currently known. Can our 1-parameter analysis be broadened to allow for two or more independent parameters? Alternatively, can we design new 1-parameter families that are easy to analyze and explore the parameter space locally?

References

1. Bambah, R.P.: On lattice coverings by spheres. Proc. Natl. Inst. Sci. India 20, 25–52 (1954)
2. Blichfeldt, H.F.: The minimum values of quadratic forms in six, seven, and eight variables. Math. Zeit. 39, 1–15 (1935)
3. Cohn, H., Kumar, A.: The densest lattice in twenty-four dimensions. Electronic Research Announcements of the Amer. Math. Soc. 10, 58–67
4. Conway, J.H., Sloane, N.J.A.: Sphere Packings, Lattices and Groups. Springer, New York (1988)
5. Delone, B.N., Ryskov, S.S.: Solution of the problem of least dense lattice covering of a four-dimensional space by equal spheres. Izvestiya Akademii Nauk SSSR, Seriya Matem-aticheskaya 4, 1333–1334 (1963)
6. Edelsbrunner, H.: Geometry and Topology for Mesh Generation. Cambridge Univ. Press, Cambridge (2001)
7. Edelsbrunner, H., Kerber, M.: Dual complexes of cubical subdivisions of $\mathbb{R}^n$. IST Austria, Klosterneuburg, Austria (2010) (manuscript)
8. Fejes Tóth, L.: Lagerungen in der Ebene, auf der Kugel und im Raum. Grundlehren der mathematischen Wissenschaften, vol. 65. Springer, Berlin (1953)
9. Freudenthal, H.: Simplizialzerlegung von beschränkter Flachheit. Ann. of Math. 43, 580–582 (1942)
10. Gauss, C.F.: Untersuchungen über die Eigenschaften der positiven ternären quadratischen Formen von Ludwig August Seeber. Göttingische Gelehrte Anzeigen (1831); reprinted in Werke II, Königliche Gesellschaft der Wissenschaften, pp. 188–196 (1863)
11. Hales, T.: A proof of the Kepler conjecture. Ann. Math., Second Series 162, 1065–1185 (2005)
12. Kershner, R.: The number of circles covering a set. Amer. J. Math. 61, 665–671 (1939)
13. Korkine, A., Zolotareff, G.: Sur les formes quadratiques positives. Math. Ann. 11, 242–292 (1877)
14. Kuhn, H.W.: Some combinatorial lemmas in topology. IBM J. Res. Develop. 45, 518–524 (1960)
15. Leech, J.: Notes on sphere packings. Canad. J. Math. 19, 251–267 (1967)
16. Rogers, C.A.: Packing and Covering. Cambridge Tracts in Mathematics and Mathematical Physics, vol. 54. Cambridge Univ. Press, Cambridge (1964)
17. Ryskov, S.S., Baranovskii, E.P.: Solution of the problem of least dense lattice covering of a five-dimensional space by equal spheres. Doklady Akademii Nauk SSSR 222, 39–42 (1975)
18. Schürmann, A., Vallentin, F.: Local covering optimality of lattices: Leech lattice versus root lattice E8. Int. Math. Res. Notices 32, 1937–1955 (2005)

19. Schürmann, A., Vallentin, F.: Computational approaches to lattice packing and covering problems. Discrete Comput. Geom. 35, 73–116 (2006)
20. Szpiro, G.G.: Kepler's Conjecture: How Some of the Greatest Minds in History Helped Solve One of the Oldest Math Problems in the World. Wiley, Hoboken (2003)
21. Thue, A.: Über die dichteste Zusammenstellung von kongruenten Kreisen in einer Ebene. Norske Vid. Selsk. Skr. 1, 1–9 (1910)
22. Witt, E.: Collected Papers. Gesammelte Abhandlungen. Springer, Berlin (1998)

Appendix A

In this appendix, we give a proof of the Distortion Lemma, which is instrumental in the analysis of the covering radius. We begin with a review of weighted points and their polar representation as hyperplanes and points; see e.g. [6].

Weighted points. We construct a convenient framework to express distance relations by generalizing spheres to allow for imaginary radii. A *weighted point* in $n - 1$ dimensions is a point $x_i \in \mathbb{R}^{n-1}$ together with a weight $w_i \in \mathbb{R}$. The *power distance* of a point $z \in \mathbb{R}^{n-1}$ from the weighted point (x_i, w_i) is $\varpi_i(z) = \|z - x_i\|^2 - w_i$. Two weighted points are *orthogonal* if

$$\|x_i - x_j\|^2 = w_i + w_j. \tag{12}$$

If w_i and w_j are both positive then (12) characterizes the situation in which the spheres with centers x_i and x_j and radii $\sqrt{w_i}$ and $\sqrt{w_j}$ intersect each other in a right angle.

Let now H be a hyperplane in $\mathbb{R}^n$, z a point in H, y_i a point in $\mathbb{R}^n$, x_i the orthogonal projection of y_i onto H, and $w_i = -\|x_i - y_i\|^2$ the negative of the squared distance of y_i from H. Then it is easy to see that the square of the distance between z and y_i equals the power distance of z from the point x_i with weight w_i in H: $\|z - y_i\|^2 = \varpi_i(z)$. Letting $w = \|z - y_i\|^2$, we can rewrite this relation as $\|z - x_i\|^2 = w_i + w$. In words, the weighted points (x_i, w_i) and (z, w) in H are orthogonal. We will use this observation to reduce the n-dimensional problem of computing the circumscribed sphere of an n-simplex to the $(n - 1)$-dimensional problem of computing the weighted point that is simultaneously orthogonal to n other weighted points.

Lifting and polarity. It will be convenient to recast the relation between weighted points in $\mathbb{R}^{n-1}$ in terms of hyperplanes (graphs of affine functions) and points in $\mathbb{R}^n$. Given a point $x_i \in \mathbb{R}^{n-1}$ with weight $w_i \in \mathbb{R}$, we introduce the affine function $h_i : \mathbb{R}^{n-1} \to \mathbb{R}$ via $h_i(x) = 2\langle x_i, x \rangle - \|x_i\|^2 + w_i$. Starting with two orthogonal weighted points in $\mathbb{R}^{n-1}$, we thus get

$$\|x_i - x_j\|^2 = w_i + w_j \qquad \text{iff}$$
$$\|x_i\|^2 - 2\langle x_i, x_j \rangle - w_i = -\|x_j\|^2 + w_j \text{ iff}$$
$$h_i(x_j) = \|x_j\|^2 - w_j.$$

This motivates us to introduce the point $p_j = (x_j, \|x_j\|^2 - w_j) \in \mathbb{R}^n$. Traditionally, this point and the hyperplane $\mathrm{graph}(h_j)$ in $\mathbb{R}^n$ are said to be *polar* to each other. We now express what we just proved in terms of these hyperplanes and points.

4 (Ortho-dence Lemma). *The points $x_i, x_j \in \mathbb{R}^{n-1}$ with weights $w_i, w_j \in \mathbb{R}$ are orthogonal iff $p_i \in \mathrm{graph}(h_j)$ iff $p_j \in \mathrm{graph}(h_i)$.*

Proof of Distortion Lemma. We are now ready to formulate the proof of the Distortion Lemma stated in Section 4. Recall that this result concerns the Freudenthal n-simplex with vertices $\sum_{j=1}^{i} e_j$, for $0 \leq i \leq n$, and its distorted images under the linear transformations $T_\delta : \mathbb{R}^n \to \mathbb{R}^n$, for $0 \leq \delta \leq 1$. It will be convenient to translate the n-simplex so it is cut in half by the hyperplane of fixed points, $H = \Delta^{-1}(0)$. We thus define $y_i = v - \frac{1}{2}\mathbf{1} + \sum_{j=1}^{i} e_j$, with $v \cdot \mathbf{1} = 0$, for $0 \leq i \leq n$, and we let Y be the n-simplex spanned by the y_i. This translation does not affect our analysis because $T_\delta(Y)$ is a translate of the distorted original n-simplex, for every δ.

Let $z(\delta)$ be the center and $R(\delta)$ the radius of the circumscribed $(n-1)$-sphere of $T_\delta(Y)$. A benefit of the translation is that $z(\delta) \in H$ for all δ. Indeed, $z(\delta)$ is equally far from the distorted images of y_0 and y_n and therefore lies in the bisector of the two points, which is H. We will see that the set of points $z(\delta)$ is the line segment with endpoints $z_1 = z(1)$ and $z_0 = z(0)$. To show this, we replace each vertex $T_\delta(y_i)$ of the n-simplex by the weighted point $(x_i, w_i(\delta))$, where $x_i = T_0(y_i)$ is the orthogonal projection onto H, and $w_i(\delta) = -\delta^2 \Delta^2(y_i)/n$ is the negative of the squared distance of $T_\delta(y_i)$ from H. By what we said above, the point $z(\delta) \in H$ with weight $R^2(\delta)$ is orthogonal to $(x_i, w_i(\delta))$, for all $0 \leq i \leq n$. Note that in $\mathbb{R}^{n-1}$, we have a common orthogonal weighted point for every generic collection of n weighted points. Here there are $n+1$ weighted points, but two are the same, namely $(x_0, w_0(\delta)) = (x_n, w_n(\delta))$.

In the next step, we replace each $(x_i, w_i(\delta))$ by the affine function $h_i(\delta)$, and we replace each point $z(\delta) \in \mathbb{R}^{n-1}$ with weight $R^2(\delta)$ by the point $p(\delta) = (z(\delta), \|z(\delta)\|^2 - R^2(\delta))$ in $\mathbb{R}^n$. Since $(z(\delta), R^2(\delta))$ is orthogonal to all $(x_i, w_i(\delta))$, the point $p(\delta)$ lies on all hyperplanes of the form $\mathrm{graph}(h_i(\delta))$ in $\mathbb{R}^n$. Now observe what happens when δ changes continuously from 1 to 0. It is convenient to parametrize this motion by $\lambda = \delta^2$, which also goes from 1 to 0. Writing down the formula for the affine map:

$$h_i(\delta)(x) = 2\langle x_i, x \rangle - \|x\|^2 - \frac{\Delta^2(y_i)}{n} \cdot \lambda,$$

we note that changing λ corresponds to an affine vertical translation of each hyperplane. It follows that the common intersection, the point $p(\delta)$, traces out the line segment from $p_1 = p(1)$ to $p_0 = p(0)$ and, more specifically,

$$p(\lambda) = \lambda p_1 + (1 - \lambda)p_0. \tag{13}$$

It follows that the projection to the first $n-1$ coordinates satisfies the same relationship, namely $z(\lambda) = \lambda z_1 + (1 - \lambda)z_0$. Similarly, we have the same relationship for the n-th coordinate. After some rearrangements, we get the squared radius as the linear interpolation of the squared radii at the extremes plus a correction term:

$$R^2(\lambda) = \lambda R_1^2 + (1 - \lambda)R_0^2 + C, \quad \text{with}$$
$$C = \|z(\lambda)\|^2 - \lambda\|z_1\|^2 - (1 - \lambda)\|z_0\|^2.$$

To simplify the remaining computations, we now choose the vector in the initial translation of the n-simplex as $v = -(z_1 + z_0)/2$. With this choice, the midpoint between the two centers is the origin so that $z_1 = -z_0$ and we can write $d^2 = \|z_1\|^2 = \|z_0\|^2$. Furthermore, $\|z(\lambda)\|^2 = 4(\lambda^2 - \frac{1}{2})^2 d^2$ and therefore $C = 4\lambda(\lambda - 1)d^2$. On the other hand, the distance between z_1 and z_0 is $2d = R_0$, so we get $C = \lambda(1 - \lambda)R_0^2$. Adding things up, we get

$$R^2(\lambda) = \lambda R_1^2 + (1 - 2\lambda + \lambda^2)R_0^2.$$

Substituting δ^2 for λ, we get the equation claimed in the Distortion Lemma.

Counting Plane Graphs with Exponential Speed-Up[*]

Andreas Razen and Emo Welzl

Institute of Theoretical Computer Science, ETH Zurich, Switzerland
{razen,emo}@inf.ethz.ch

Abstract. We show that one can count the number of crossing-free geometric graphs on a given planar point set exponentially faster than enumerating them. More precisely, given a set P of n points in general position in the plane, we can compute $\mathrm{pg}(P)$, the number of crossing-free graphs on P, in time at most $\frac{\mathrm{poly}(n)}{\sqrt{8^n}} \cdot \mathrm{pg}(P)$. No similar statements are known for other graph classes like triangulations, spanning trees or perfect matchings.

The exponential speed-up is obtained by enumerating the set of all triangulations and then counting subgraphs in the triangulations without repetition. For a set P of n points with triangular convex hull we further improve the base $\sqrt{8} \approx 2.8284$ of the exponential to 3.347. As a main ingredient for that we show that there is a constant $\alpha > 0$ such that a triangulation on P, drawn uniformly at random from all triangulations on P, contains, in expectation, at least n/α *non-flippable* edges. The best value for α we obtain is 37/18.

Keywords: Counting, crossing-free configurations, plane graphs, triangulations, constrained Delaunay triangulation, edge flips.

1   Introduction

Let P be a finite set of at least three points in the plane. We assume that P is in general position, i.e. no three points are collinear and no four points cocircular. A *geometric graph on P* is a graph defined on the vertex set P whose edges are straight segments connecting the corresponding endpoints. Such a straight-line embedded graph is *crossing-free* if no pair of its edges shares any point except for, possibly, a common endpoint. A crossing-free graph which is maximal, i.e. no edge can be added without incurring a crossing, is called *triangulation*.

We are interested in the number of crossing-free geometric graphs that can be defined on P which we denote by $\mathrm{pg}(P)$. This quantity never exceeds a fixed exponential in $|P|$, a result first established by Ajtai et al. [2] with 10^{13} as base of the exponential. The set of all triangulations of P is denoted by $\mathcal{T}(P)$, and

---

[*] Both authors acknowledge support by SNF project 200021-116741. These results were first presented at the Symposium "Significant Advances in Computer Science" (SACS'07) celebrating 30 years Computer Science at Graz University of Technology, Austria, November 6, 2007.

C.S. Calude, G. Rozenberg, A. Salomaa (Eds.): Maurer Festschrift, LNCS 6570, pp. 36–46, 2011.

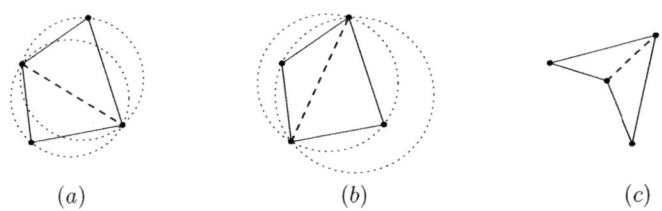

Fig. 1. Flippable edges in (a) and (b); non-flippable edge in (c)

we will write $\mathsf{tr}(P) := |\mathcal{T}(P)|$ for its cardinality. The best-known upper bound for $\mathsf{tr}(P)$ is 30^n [8,11,9], where $n := |P|$. While clearly upper bounds for the total number of crossing-free geometric graphs on a point set P also apply to specific classes of plane graphs (e.g. spanning connected graph, polygonizations, perfect matchings, and spanning trees, to name just a few), better bounds for these classes are known [1,10].

In this paper we will show that there is an absolute constant $c > 1$ such that for any set P of n points in general position $\mathsf{pg}(P) \geq c^n \cdot \mathsf{tr}(P)$, while we are still able to compute $\mathsf{pg}(P)$ in time necessary to enumerate $\mathcal{T}(P)$ times a small polynomial factor in n. The best value for the constant c we obtain is $\sqrt{8}$. Such an enumeration for the set of triangulations is obtained by applying the reverse search technique due to Avis and Fukuda [3]. The fastest algorithm for this enumeration is by Bespamyatnikh [4] and needs time $O(\log \log n)$ per output triangulation.

Recently and independently, Katoh and Tanigawa [6] proposed an idea for *enumerating* crossing-free geometric graph classes relatively similar to our approach by introducing a lexicographic order on the set of triangulations.

In the following assume that the underlying point set P is fixed and write $n := n(P) = |P|$ for its cardinality. Furthermore, let $k := k(P)$ denote the number of points on the boundary of the convex hull of P, thus $n \geq k \geq 3$. By Euler's polyhedral formula any triangulation contains exactly $M := 3n - k - 3$ edges, which we will further distinguish as follows. An edge in a triangulation T is called *flippable* if it is contained in the boundary of two triangles of T whose union is a convex quadrilateral, see Figures $1(a)$ and (b); otherwise the edge is called *non-flippable*, see Figure $1(c)$. We write $\mathsf{fl}(T)$ for the number of flippable edges in T, and similarly $\mathsf{nfl}(T)$ for the number of non-flippable edges. Note that for any triangulation T, clearly, $\mathsf{fl}(T) + \mathsf{nfl}(T) = M$ and $\mathsf{nfl}(T) \geq k$ since edges on the boundary of the convex hull of P are always non-flippable.

Moreover, a flippable edge in T is called *Lawson edge* if the circumcircle of each boundary triangle also contains the respective other boundary triangle in its interior, see the dashed line segment in Figure $1(b)$. Observe that this notion is well-defined since we assumed general position. We denote by $L(T)$ the set of Lawson edges in T, and by $\ell(T)$ its cardinality.

We recall a few definitions and facts about constrained Delaunay triangulations (introduced by Lee and Lin [7]). Given a crossing-free geometric graph G on P, then two points $p, q \in P$ are *visible* from each other if the line segment

pq does not intersect the interior of any edge in G. The *constrained Delaunay triangulation* $T^*(G)$ of G is a triangulation containing the edges of G which has the additional property that the circumcircle of each triangle in $T^*(G)$ does not contain any other point which is visible from all three vertices of the triangle. Lee and Lin showed that for any graph G the constrained Delaunay triangulation $T^*(G)$ exists and is unique if P is in general position. Furthermore, they proved that $T^*(G)$ is obtained from any triangulation containing $E(G)$ by repeatedly flipping a Lawson edge distinct from $E(G)$ as long as possible. Observe that this implies that the procedure terminates with the triangulation $T = T^*(G)$ if and only if $L(T) \subseteq E(G) \subseteq E(T)$.

2   Counting with Exponential Speed-Up

The following theorem is the key to counting and estimating the number of crossing-free graphs in terms of the number of triangulations of a point set P. The basic ingredient is to partition the set of all crossing-free geometric graphs by associating each graph with its constrained Delaunay triangulation. Then the theorem suggests an algorithm for computing $\mathsf{pg}(P)$ in time $O(\mathrm{poly}(n) \cdot \mathsf{tr}(P))$ by enumerating $\mathsf{tr}(P)$ where we apply the reverse search method [3]. We will also show that there is a constant $c > 1$ such that $\mathsf{pg}(P) \geq c^n \cdot \mathsf{tr}(P)$, implying that one may count $\mathsf{pg}(P)$ exponentially faster than enumerating all graphs.

Theorem 1. *For any set P of $n \geq 3$ points in the plane in general position we have*

$$\mathsf{pg}(P) = \sum_{T \in \mathcal{T}(P)} 2^{M - \ell(T)}. \tag{1}$$

(Recall that $\ell(T)$ denotes the number of Lawson edges in T.)

Proof. Consider the following partition of the set of crossing-free geometric graphs on P. For every triangulation T on P there is a partition class consisting of all crossing-free subgraphs G of T that contain the set of Lawson edges of T, i.e., for which

$$L(T) \subseteq E(G) \subseteq E(T). \tag{2}$$

Indeed this defines a partition due to the existence and uniqueness of the constrained Delaunay triangulation. The partition class associated with a triangulation T contains exactly $2^{M - \ell(T)}$ crossing-free geometric graphs. Now, summing over all triangulations yields the statement.   □

Consider the set P_6 of six points in general position as in Figure 2; with four points on the convex hull every triangulation of P_6 has $M = 11$ edges. It can easily be checked that there are exactly six triangulations on P_6 as they are depicted in Figure 2, the Lawson edges are drawn as dashed line segments. Along Theorem 1 we can easily derive that $\mathsf{pg}(P_6) = 6656$.

Actually, from the proof of Theorem 1 we obtain counting algorithms for any graph class (for instance perfect matchings or spanning-trees). We simply iterate over the set of all triangulations of P and for a triangulation T we

$\mathcal{T}(P_6)$:

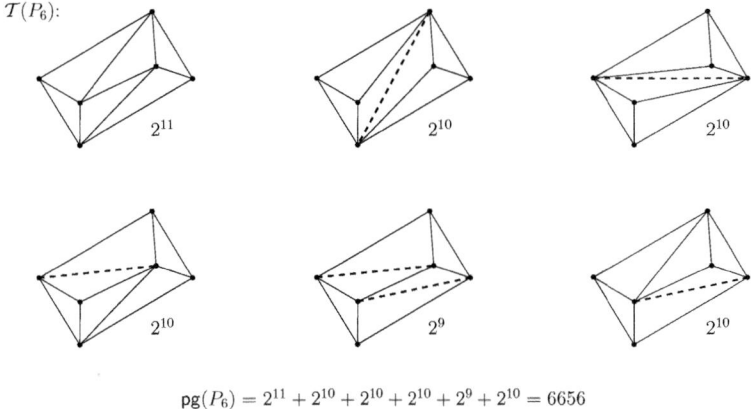

$$\mathsf{pg}(P_6) = 2^{11} + 2^{10} + 2^{10} + 2^{10} + 2^9 + 2^{10} = 6656$$

Fig. 2. Counting crossing-free graphs on a set of 6 points

count the members G of the desired graph class that fulfill the edge containment property (2). In the following we will show that for counting all crossing-free geometric graphs this algorithm yields an exponential speed-up compared to enumerating all graphs (note that computing $\ell(T)$ can be done in polynomial time). As far as perfect matchings are concerned this procedure does not result in a similar speed-up since the number of triangulations can be exponentially larger than the number of perfect matchings (n points in convex position, with n even, have $C_{n-2} \approx 4^n$ triangulations but only $C_{n/2} \approx 2^n$ perfect matchings, where $C_n = \frac{1}{n+1}\binom{2n}{n}$ denotes the n-th Catalan number). For spanning-trees it is open whether every point set allows for more spanning-trees than triangulations, perhaps even exponentially more.

Dividing Identity (1) from Theorem 1 by the total number of triangulations on P, using Jensen's inequality for the (convex) exponential function and linearity of expectation we obtain

$$\frac{\mathsf{pg}(P)}{\mathsf{tr}(P)} = \sum_{T \in \mathcal{T}(P)} 2^{M-\ell(T)} \cdot \frac{1}{\mathsf{tr}(P)} = \mathbb{E}\left[2^{M-\ell(T)}\right] \geq 2^{\mathbb{E}[M-\ell(T)]} = 2^{M-\mathbb{E}[\ell(T)]}, \quad (3)$$

where the expectation of the random variables $2^{M-\ell(T)}$, $M - \ell(T)$ and $\ell(T)$, respectively, is understood with respect to the uniform distribution over all triangulations on P. Hence, by providing an upper bound for $\mathbb{E}\left[\ell(T)\right]$, i.e. the expected number of Lawson edges in a uniformly at random chosen triangulation on P, we obtain a lower bound for the fraction of the number of crossing-free geometric graphs on P versus the number of triangulations of P.

Lemma 1. *For any point set P it holds that*

$$2 \cdot \mathbb{E}\left[\ell(T)\right] = \mathbb{E}\left[\mathsf{fl}(T)\right].$$

Proof. Let S be the set of pairs (e, T) with T a triangulation on P and e a flippable edge in T. Consider an element (e, T) of this set and let e' be the other diagonal of the convex quadrilateral consisting of the boundary triangles of e in T. When flipping e in T, i.e. replacing e by e', we obtain a new triangulation T'. Clearly, $(e', T') \in S$ and flipping e' in T' yields T again. Hence, there is a (canonical) perfect matching between the elements of S. Note that by definition either e or e' is a Lawson edge of its respective triangulation. Therefore,

$$|S| = \sum_{T \in \mathcal{T}(P)} \text{fl}(T) = \mathbb{E}\left[\text{fl}(T)\right] \cdot \text{tr}(P)$$

$$\frac{|S|}{2} = \sum_{T \in \mathcal{T}(P)} \ell(T) = \mathbb{E}\left[\ell(T)\right] \cdot \text{tr}(P),$$

which proves the statement.   □

Recall that $\text{fl}(T) + \text{nfl}(T) = M$. Hence, with Lemma 1, this shows $\mathbb{E}\left[\ell(T)\right] = \frac{1}{2} \cdot (M - \mathbb{E}\left[\text{nfl}(T)\right])$ using linearity of expectation. Plugging this into Inequality (3) we obtain the following estimate.

Theorem 2. *For any set P of $n \geq 3$ points in the plane in general position*

$$\text{pg}(P) \geq 2^{(M + \mathbb{E}[\text{nfl}(T)])/2} \cdot \text{tr}(P). \tag{4}$$

Recall that for any triangulation T we have $\text{nfl}(T) \geq k$ implying that $M + \mathbb{E}\left[\text{nfl}(T)\right] \geq 3n - 3$.

Corollary 1. *For any set P of $n \geq 3$ points in the plane in general position it holds that*

$$\text{pg}(P) \geq \sqrt{8}^{n-1} \cdot \text{tr}(P), \tag{5}$$

which is tight for $n = 3$, and one may count $\text{pg}(P)$ in time at most $\frac{\text{poly}(n)}{\sqrt{8}^n} \cdot \text{pg}(P)$.

At this point let us treat the special case of P being in convex position, that is when $k = n$. Note that in any triangulation of such a point set there are exactly n non-flippable edges, the edges on the boundary of the convex hull of P, and the remaining $n - 3$ edges, the diagonals of the convex n-gon, are flippable. Hence, $\mathbb{E}\left[\text{nfl}(T)\right] = n = k$ and we cannot improve over the statement of Corollary 1 using Theorem 2. However, note that $\sqrt{8} \approx 2.8284$, and for P in convex position it is known that $\frac{\text{pg}(P)}{\text{tr}(P)} = \Theta((\frac{3}{2} + \sqrt{2})^n)$, where $\frac{3}{2} + \sqrt{2} \approx 2.9142$, see [5].

It remains open to show whether the convex n-gon actually minimizes the fraction $\frac{\text{pg}(P)}{\text{tr}(P)}$ over all sets P of n points in general position. In the next section we propose a framework for deriving stronger lower bounds on $\mathbb{E}\left[\text{nfl}(T)\right]$, when the underlying point set is not in convex position.

3   Expected Number of Non-flippable Edges

In the following assume that P has a triangular convex hull (actually, the same arguments also work for point sets where $k \leq 6$). The basic idea for proving a lower bound on the expected number of non-flippable edges is similar to the method in [11] for estimating the number of degree-3 vertices in a random triangulation. There, every vertex receives an initial charge which it then discharges to vertices of degree 3. Here, however, we want to have each vertex in any triangulation ultimately charge non-flippable edges. If every vertex discharges at least 1 on average and each non-flippable edge receives a charge of at most c, then $\mathbb{E}\left[\mathrm{nfl}(T)\right]$ is at least the c-th fraction of the total number of vertices.

To make this more precise denote by P° the set of points in P except for the three extreme points of its convex hull. Then the ground set for our considerations is $P^\circ \times \mathcal{T}(P)$ whose elements are called *vints* (vertex-in-triangulation). The degree of a vint (p, T) is the degree of the vertex p in the triangulation T. For $i \in \mathbb{N}$, a vint of degree i is called i-vint, and given a fixed triangulation T we denote by $v_i = v_i(T)$ the number of i-vints in $P^\circ \times \{T\}$. Observe that in any triangulation $v_1 = v_2 = 0$ and $\sum_{i \geq 3} v_i = |P^\circ| = n - 3$. A proof of the following lemma can be found in [11] (apply the Handshaking Lemma when summing up all degrees in T).

Lemma 2. *Let T be a fixed triangulation and place a charge of $7 - i$ at every i-vint, for $i \geq 3$. Then the weighted sum of charges over all corresponding vints in $P^\circ \times \{T\}$ is at least $|P^\circ|$.*

Note that i-vints with $i \geq 7$ do not receive a positive charge. Hence, it suffices to focus on distributing the charges of 3-, 4-, 5-, and 6-vints. For this we define a relation on the set of vints as in [11]. Let $u = (p_u, T_u)$ and $v = (p_v, T_v)$ be vints, then we say $u \to v$ if $p_u = p_v$ and there is a flippable edge incident to p_u in T_u such that flipping this edge results in the triangulation T_v. Clearly, u is an $(i + 1)$-vint and v an i-vint, for some $i \geq 3$. We denote by $\to^*$ the transitive, reflexive closure of $\to$. If $u \to^* v$ we say that u *may be flipped down to* v.

When discharging we allow every vint to distribute its charge both to lower-degree vints it can be flipped down to and to non-flippable edges. Hereby, a vint (p, T) may only discharge to a non-flippable edge in $E(T)$ that is incident to p or to an edge $qr \in E(T)$ where pqr is a triangle in T. We call such an edge qr a *non-flippable boundary edge of p*. With slight abuse of notation we will also refer to the (non-flippable) incident and boundary edges of the vint (p, T).

The discharging will be done in such a way that finally there is no positive charge left on any vint. Thus, the sum of charges over all vints in $P^\circ \times \mathcal{T}(P)$ which has been distributed among the non-flippable edges is at least $|P^\circ| \cdot \mathrm{tr}(P)$ by Lemma 2. If we can show that during this process a non-flippable edge receives a charge of at most c, then the total number of non-flippable edges in all triangulations of $\mathcal{T}(P)$ is at least $\frac{1}{c}|P^\circ| \cdot \mathrm{tr}(P)$. Hence,

$$\mathbb{E}\left[\mathrm{nfl}(T)\right] \geq \frac{|P^\circ|}{c}. \tag{6}$$

Note that for an edge the property of being non-flippable is by definition equivalent to being incident to a vertex at a (after deleting the edge) reflex angle. In the following we assume the non-flippable edges of the triangulations to be directed towards their endpoint with the reflex angle. Observe that by doing this every non-flippable edge (except for the edges on the boundary of the convex hull) gets directed in a unique way.

3.1   A Simple Charging Scheme

As an instructive example we will now discuss a simple charging scheme by explicitly stating the distribution of the charges from i-vints to non-flippable edges and other vints. This will result in a first non-trivial lower bound for $\mathbb{E}\left[\mathrm{nfl}(T)\right]$.

Consider a 3-vint with an initial charge of 4. Since we assumed general position all three incident edges are non-flippable and directed towards the 3-vint, see Figure 3(a). Hence, this vint may discharge by equally distributing one third of its charge to the incident non-flippable edges. Note, however, that the 3-vint might still receive charge from higher-degree vints, hence at this point we cannot yet explicitly state its maximum possible charge to the incoming edges.

Observe that a 4-vint is always incident to exactly two non-flippable incoming edges since one of the angles between two non-neighboring edges is always reflex, see Figure 3(b). To each of these edges we equally distribute half of the 4-vint's initial charge of 3. In this simple scheme no other vint will discharge to a 4-vint.

When devising the charging scheme for higher-degree vints we further distinguish them according to the number of non-flippable incoming edges. A 5-vint with an initial charge of 2 may occur with two, one or no non-flippable incoming edges, see Figure 4. If the 5-vint is incident to at least one non-flippable edge we equally distribute the vint's charge to all such edges. Note that otherwise all five incident edges are not directed towards the 5-vint but some could still be non-flippable, and we cannot directly discharge as we did in the cases before. However, we may obtain a 3-vint if we can flip two non-neighboring edges when passing the edges in clockwise order around the vint. It is always possible to choose two such flippable edges since the boundary edges of the vint define a 5-gon which has at least three convex angles, hence the corresponding edges are flippable. We give the whole charge of the 5-vint to the resulting 3-vint.

It is crucial to note that a 3-vint may receive such a charge from at most one 5-vint without non-flippable incoming edges. In order to see this recall that we flipped two non-neighboring edges incident to the 5-vint resulting in two of the three boundary edges of the 3-vint. Assume that two 5-vints flip down to the same 3-vint then one boundary edge is obtained in both flips. Reversing the flip of the common boundary edge results in a 4-vint with two non-flippable

(a)   (b)

Fig. 3. Discharging 3-vints in (a) and 4-vints in (b)

Fig. 4. Discharging 5-vints with two, one or no non-flippable incident edges

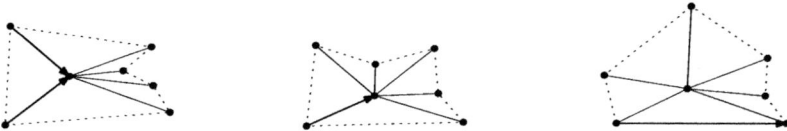

Fig. 5. Discharging 6-vints with at least one non-flippable incident or boundary edge

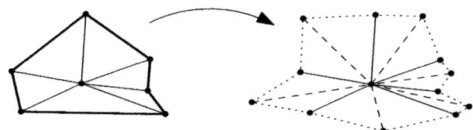

Fig. 6. Discharging 6-vints with neither non-flippable incident nor boundary edges

incoming edges. If this vint is obtained from a 5-vint without non-flippable edges it is necessary (but not sufficient) to flip the edge of the triangle containing both non-flippable edges of the 4-vint. Hence, there was at most one such 5-vint. In this scheme a 3-vint will not be charged by any other higher-degree vint, therefore it may end up with a total charge of at most $4+2=6$. It then discharges uniformly to its three non-flippable incoming edges.

Finally, we have to consider the 6-vints with an initial charge of 1. In case such a vint has at least one non-flippable incoming edge we handle it like we did a 5-vint and equally distribute its charge to all those edges. Otherwise we consider the non-flippable boundary edges of the 6-vint and equally distribute the charge to them, see Figure 5.

If, however, a 6-vint neither has non-flippable incoming edges nor non-flippable boundary edges we let it charge a higher-degree vint for an exception. We flip all boundary edges to obtain a 12-vint of initial charge -5 to which we pass the whole charge of the 6-vint, see Figure 6. Notice that after all 6-vints have discharged any 12-vint still has a negative charge since it may only be charged by at most two 6-vints. To see this note that in order to flip a 12-vint down to a 6-vint from which it received a charge no two neighboring incident edges may be flipped.

Since i-vints with $i \geq 7$ do not have positive charge the average initial charge of 1 per vint has now been discharged onto the non-flippable edges in the triangulations. Let us estimate the maximum charge to such a non-flippable edge. Recall that every non-flippable edge was directed towards a unique vint from which it may be charged, and 6-vints with all incident edges being flippable were the only vints that possibly charge non-flippable boundary edges. Hence, an edge might only receive charge from the one endpoint it is directed to and from at most two 6-vints for which the edge is a non-flippable boundary edge.

In the following we summarize the cases discussed above and list the corresponding maximum charges to an edge depending on the i-vint it is directed towards:

- 3-vint: charge $\leq 1/3 \cdot 6 + 2 = 4$
- 4-vint: charge $\leq 1/2 \cdot 3 + 2 = 3.5$
- 5-vint with two non-flippable edges: charge $\leq 1/2 \cdot 2 + 2 = 3$
- 5-vint with one non-flippable edge: charge $\leq 2 + 2 = 4$
- 6-vint with two non-flippable edges: charge $\leq 1/2 \cdot 1 + 2 = 2.5$
- 6-vint with one non-flippable edge: charge $\leq 1 + 2 = 3$
- i-vint with $i \geq 7$: charge $\leq 2 = 2$.

Therefore, during the discharging of the vints any non-flippable edge received a charge of at most 4 implying that $\mathbb{E}\left[\mathrm{nfl}(T)\right] \geq \frac{n-3}{4}$ because of (6). By Theorem 2 we have

$$\mathsf{pg}(P) \geq 2^{\frac{3n-6+(n-3)/4}{2}} \cdot \mathsf{tr}(P) = \Omega(2^{13n/8}) \cdot \mathsf{tr}(P) = \Omega(3.08^n) \cdot \mathsf{tr}(P),$$

for a set P of n points with triangular convex hull.

3.2   A More Elaborate Charging Scheme

In the following we will improve on the results of the previous section. Note that so far we only allowed 5-vints without non-flippable incoming edges to discharge to a (lower-degree) 3-vint, but we did not yet take into account that we also could have split its charge to 4-vints it can be flipped down to. Also 6-vints may be flipped down to lower-degree vints and charge them.

Furthermore, recall that a 6-vint with no non-flippable incoming edge charged its non-flippable boundary edges crucially. In the worst case an edge might receive an additional charge of 2 from such 6-vints. However, for instance it is clear that such an edge cannot be directed towards a 3-vint, hence we overestimated the corresponding maximum charge. This shows that there is some potential to improve on the bounds we derived in the discussion above.

In order to generalize the approach for obtaining lower bounds on $\mathbb{E}\left[\mathrm{nfl}(T)\right]$ note that we actually solved a linear program in the previous section when determining the way and the amount a vint discharges to non-flippable edges and other vints, and hence also the value of the maximum charge. Indeed we want to find the smallest value α that is larger than every possible charge to a non-flippable edge, such that there is an initial charge of $7-i$ at every i-vint and after the discharging there is no vint with positive charge left. The corresponding linear program looks as follows.

minimize α

s.t. $\alpha \geq \{c_3, c_4, c_{5_2}, c_{5_1}, c_{6_2}, c_{6_1}\} + 2 \cdot b_{6_0}$

$\text{out3} \leq 3 \cdot c_3$	$\text{in3} \geq c_{5_0 \to 3}$	$\text{out3} \geq 4 + \text{in3}$
$\text{out4} \leq 2 \cdot c_4$	$\text{in12} \geq 2 \cdot c_{6_0 \to 12}$	$\text{out4} \geq 3 + \text{in4}$
$\text{out5}_2 \leq 2 \cdot c_{5_2}$		$\text{out5}_2 \geq 2 + \text{in5}_2$
$\text{out5}_1 \leq c_{5_1}$		$\text{out5}_1 \geq 2 + \text{in5}_1$
$\text{out5}_0 \leq c_{5_0 \to 3}$		$\text{out5}_0 \geq 2 + \text{in5}_0$
$\text{out6}_2 \leq 2 \cdot c_{6_2}$		$\text{out6}_2 \geq 1 + \text{in6}_2$
$\text{out6}_1 \leq c_{6_1}$		$\text{out6}_1 \geq 1 + \text{in6}_1$
$\text{out6}_0 \leq \{b_{6_0}, c_{6_0 \to 12}\}$		$\text{out6}_0 \geq 1 + \text{in6}_0$
$\text{out12} \leq 0$		$\text{out12} \geq -5 + \text{in12}$

all variables ≥ 0

The objective is to compute the smallest α larger than every possible charge to an edge. Sets indicated by curly brackets $\{\ldots, \ldots\}$ in the list of constraints are understood as several inequalities of the same form each time replacing one element from the set. The variables c_i (c_{i_j}, resp.) represent the charges to an incoming edge of an i-vint (with j non-flippable incoming edges), b_{6_0} represents the charge of a 6-vint to a non-flippable boundary edge, and $c_{5_0 \to 3}$ ($c_{6_0 \to 12}$) the charge of a 5-vint (6-vint) with no non-flippable incoming edge to a 3-vint (12-vint).

Then we distinguish three types of constraints. First, in the left-most column of constraints for every i-vint (with j non-flippable incoming edges) there is a variable out$i$ (outi_j) that represents the amount of charge that leaves such a vint during the discharging. This amount is upper-bounded by the minimum over all the vint's possibilities to discharge. Then, in the middle column of constraints there is a variable in$i$ (ini_j) for every i-vint (with j non-flippable incoming edges) that represents the charge received from higher- or lower-degree vints. This additional charge to an i-vint is lower-bounded by the maximum over all possible charges from other vints. Note that in the charging scheme from the previous section there are only charges to 3- and 12-vints, therefore the inequalities for 4-, 5-, and 6-vints are not needed since all variables are non-negative. Finally, the right-most column of constraints incorporates the initial charges of $7 - i$ at an i-vint and ensures that after discharging there is no positive charge left.

In a more detailed case distinction which we skip here for brevity we distinguish between i-vints with j non-flippable incoming edges and k non-flippable boundary edges, where $3 \leq i \leq 12$, and $j, k \in \{0, 1, 2\}$. As described before, a vint may discharge to non-flippable incoming or boundary edges or to other vints. The latter case causes more tedious analyses how many lower- and higher-degree vints may actually charge a certain vint. Similarly to above we obtain a linear program that solves to $\frac{37}{18}$ as optimum value.

Corollary 2. *For any set P of $n \geq 3$ points in the plane in general position with triangular convex hull, $\mathbb{E}\left[\text{nfl}(T)\right] \geq \frac{18(n-3)}{37}$. This implies*

$$\text{pg}(P) \geq \Omega(2^{129n/74}) \cdot \text{tr}(P) = \Omega(3.347^n) \cdot \text{tr}(P).$$

The lower bound $\Omega(3.347^n)$ on the fraction $\frac{\mathsf{pg}(P)}{\mathsf{tr}(P)}$ from Corollary 2 compares to $O(4.86^n)$ which is obtained for the so-called double zig-zag chain D_n introduced by Aichholzer et al. [1], with $\mathsf{pg}(D_n) = O(41.19^n)$ and $\mathsf{tr}(D_n) = \Omega(8.48^n)$. Actually, the convex hull of D_n is a quadrilateral but the point set may be slightly altered in order to have triangular convex hull while keeping the asymptotic behavior of the number of crossing-free graphs and triangulations (assume very flat chains and rotate the upper chain clockwise and the lower chain counter-clockwise without changing the point configuration; then add an additional point very far to the right extending both chains in a convex way, i.e. points on the convex hull of a single chain remain on the hull when adding the point).

References

1. Aichholzer, O., Hackl, T., Huemer, C., Hurtado, F., Krasser, H., Vogtenhuber, B.: On the Number of Plane Geometric Graphs. Graphs and Combinatorics 23, 67–84 (2007)
2. Ajtai, M., Chvátal, V., Newborn, M.M., Szemerédi, E.: Crossing-Free Subgraphs. Annals Discrete Math. 12, 9–12 (1982)
3. Avis, D., Fukuda, K.: Reverse Search for Enumeration. Discrete Appl. Math. 65, 21–46 (1996)
4. Bespamyatnikh, S.: An Efficient Algorithm for Enumeration of Triangulations. Comput. Geom. Theory Appl. 23, 271–279 (2002)
5. Flajolet, P., Noy, M.: Analytic Combinatorics of Non-Crossing Configurations. Discrete Math. 204, 203–229 (1999)
6. Katoh, N., Tanigawa, S.: Fast Enumeration Algorithms for Non-Crossing Geometric Graphs. In: Proc. 24th Ann. Symp. on Comput. Geom., pp. 328–337 (2008)
7. Lee, D.T., Lin, A.K.: Generalized Delaunay triangulation for planar graphs. Discrete Comput. Geom. 1, 210–217 (1986)
8. Santos, F., Seidel, R.: A Better Upper Bound on the Number of Triangulations of a Planar Point Set. J. Comb. Theory, Ser. A 102, 186–193 (2003)
9. Sharir, M., Sheffer, A.: Counting Triangulations of Planar Point Sets (2010), http://arxiv.org/abs/0911.3352
10. Sharir, M., Welzl, E.: On the Number of Crossing-Free Matchings, Cycles, and Partitions. SIAM J. Comput. 36, 695–720 (2006)
11. Sharir, M., Welzl, E.: Random Triangulations of Planar Point Sets. In: Proc. 22nd Ann. ACM Symp. on Comput. Geom., pp. 273–281 (2006)

Formal Languages
and Automata

Ancient Typefaces and Parametric Weighted Finite Automata

Jürgen Albert[1] and German Tischler[2]

[1] Dept. of Computer Science, University of Würzburg, Germany
`albert@informatik.uni-wuerzburg.de`
[2] Newton Fellow, Dept. of Informatics, King's College London, WC2R 2LS, UK
`german.tischler@kcl.ac.uk`

Abstract. Generalizations of weighted finite automata where real-valued weights are assigned to all transitions and d-dimensional vectors of real values belong to the states (PWFA) have been studied w.r.t. compact representations of glyphs from ancient fonts, especially from the ubiquitous fraktur-families. It is well-known, that polynomials of arbitrary degree over the unit interval can be generated by simple weighted finite automata in an elegant and compact manner. This result carries over nicely to the representation of typefaces. There it is first applied to the outlines of the glyphs and then to their interiors. Finally, we show that even animated writing, i.e. video-clips of drawing glyphs with a pen as if by a human hand, can be modeled by PWFA.

1 Introduction

There has been a revived interest for computer generated typefaces – beyond D. Knuth's METAFONT or TEX – motivated by recent retrodigitization problems. Those became apparent in celebrated projects like the ,,Million Book Project" initiated at Carnegie Mellon University or ,,Google Books", where reportedly in summer 2010 the number of scanned books passed the mark of 12 million. It was announced that some 130 million unique books will be digitized world-wide by the end of the decade.

Frequently, the accessibility of old books' content suffers from bad physical condition of the original book and/or missing scan-quality or font-families, uncommon nowadays like fraktur which can turn automated optical character recognition into a mission impossible. Fraktur fonts had been popular especially in Scandinavia, Germany and Austria from the 16th century till just after World War II, so there exists an extraordinary wealth of published material without copyright infringements. Figure 1 illustrates typical raw scan data.

We will assume here an extended form of retrodigitization, where not only a searchable plain text results from the OCR processing but instead a mark-up representation together with the necessary fonts to produce a high-quality reprint as a kind of ,,cleaned facsimile". In general, the obtained format will be an XML-document coded in say UTF-8 and TEI-P5 (cf. [18]) accompagnied by suitable style-sheets and vector fonts. Rendering this text again for printing

C.S. Calude, G. Rozenberg, A. Salomaa (Eds.): Maurer Festschrift, LNCS 6570, pp. 49–62, 2011.

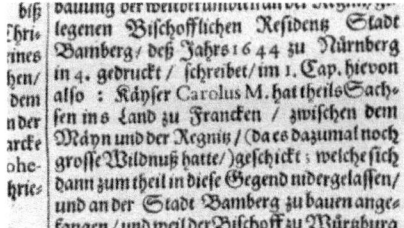

Fig. 1. Fraktur typeface samples from „Matthaeus Merian: Topographia Franco-niae, 1648/1656" and „Johann Kaspar Bundschuh: Geographisch Statistisch-Topographisches Lexikon von Franken, 1799-1804" [21].

on paper or display at a monitor can be regarded as a decoding process after applying a „lossy" image compression method before. In fact, the size of the generated XML-documents and all their style-sheets and font-specifications will usually be much smaller than that for the set of corresponding scans.

Thus, it is not too far-fetched to exploite finite automata with weights; those have shown an amazing efficiency for lossy image compression, and even for video sequences ([7], [8], [12]). The extensions to Parametric Weighted Finite Automata (PWFA) have also been studied w.r.t. representations of polynomially defined curves. A recent overview of weighted automata and variety of applications is found in [9].

Here our topic will mainly be splines, a family of functions that are piece-wise defined by polynomials of low degrees. As the set of PWFA computable sets is effectively closed under set union and invertible affine transformation for each dimension $d \in \mathbb{N}^+$ (cf. [20]), any piece-wise defined polynomial curves can be represented effectively by PWFA. A good overview over splines is given in [10] and a general introduction to classical 2D computer graphics can be found in [15]. Basic constructions of PWFA for single spline curves were first presented in [19].

2 Definitions

In a very general setup weighted finite automata (WFA) are finite automata computing functions over semirings, introduced in [16]. Parametric weighted finite automata (PWFA) are multi-dimensional generalizations of WFA first studied in [4]. Here we will only consider PWFA over the field of real numbers.

Definition 1. *A Parametric Weighte Finite Automaton (PWFA) of dimension $d \in \mathbb{N}^+$ is a quintuple $Z = (Q, \Sigma, W, I, F)$, where*

- *$Q = \{0, \ldots, n-1\}, n \in \mathbb{N}^+$ is a finite non-empty set of states,*
- *$\Sigma = \{0, \ldots, l-1\}, l \in \mathbb{N}^+$ is a finite non-empty alphabet,*
- *$W = (W_0, \ldots, W_{l-1})$ are the weight matrices, where each $W_i \in \mathbb{R}^{n \times n}$ is a matrix of weighted transitions for the input-symbol $i \in \Sigma$,*

- $I = (I_0, \ldots, I_{d-1})$, each $I_j \in \mathbb{R}^{1 \times n}$ is an initial distribution, so the I_j are the rows of the matrix I and
- $F \in \mathbb{R}^{n \times 1}$ is the final distribution.

The function $f : \Sigma^* \mapsto \mathbb{R}^d$ computed by the PWFA Z is defined as

$$f(w) = IW_{a_1} \ldots W_{a_k} F = I \prod_{i=1}^{k} W_{a_i} F$$

for each $w = a_1 \ldots a_k \in \Sigma^*$ and the set $S(Z)$ computed by Z is given by

$$S(Z) = \bigcap_{n=0}^{\infty} T_n(Z)$$

where

$$T_n(Z) = \overline{\bigcup_{i=n}^{\infty} \{f(w) \mid w \in \Sigma^i\}} \ .$$

Here the overline operator denotes the topological closure, i.e. all accumulation points are included in $T_n(Z)$ as well. We will frequently use $T(Z) = T_0(Z)$ as an abbreviation. And Q_Z, Σ_Z, etc. will denote in the following the set of states of the automaton Z, the alphabet of Z, etc. where needed in the constructions.

3 Bézier Curves

Bézier curves are based on the Bernstein polynomials, which in most applications are considered only over the unit interval $[0, 1]$.

A Bernstein polynomial $b_i^n(t)$ (cf. [10]) is given by

$$b_i^n(t) = \binom{n}{i} t^i (1 - t)^{n-i}$$

where $\binom{n}{i} = \frac{n!}{i!(n-i)!}$ if $0 \le i \le n$ and 0 otherwise.

A Bézier curve of degree n is then a real function given by

$$B^n(t) = \sum_{i=0}^{n} b_i^n(t) P_i,$$

where the P_i are real numbers, called the control points of the curve. Each curve $B^n(t)$ is a real-valued polynomial restricted to the unit interval $[0, 1]$. Thus, it is easy to construct a PWFA computing a Bézier curve, as PWFA can represent polynomials compactly and to arbitrary precision (cf. [6]). The control point sequence is often written as a vector, i.e. $S = (P_0, P_1, \ldots, P_n)$.

Example 1. Let $n = 3$ and $S = (0, 0, -\frac{1}{3}, 0)$. Then the polynomial obtained is

$$p(t) = -\frac{1}{3} b_2^3 = -\frac{1}{3}(3t^2 - 3t^3) = t^3 - t^2 \ .$$

In [6] it was shown that any polynomial of degree k requires at most $k+1$ states in a corresponding WFA and this was extended to polynomially defined curves resulting in a PWFA with at most $k + 1$ states, if the maximal degree of the polynomials involved is k [4].

A Bézier curve $B^n(t)$ of degree n can be split into two Bézier curves $C^n(t)$ and $D^n(t)$ of degree n at each point $t_0 \in (0, 1)$ such that

$$B^n(t) = \begin{cases} C^n(\frac{t}{t_0}) & \text{for } t \in [0, t_0) \\ D^n(\frac{t-t_0}{1-t_0}) & \text{for } t \in [t_0, 1] \end{cases}.$$

This property can be used to draw approximations of Bézier curves with arbitrary precision. Any given curve is split into halves recursively until each obtained curve-segment sufficiently resembles a straight line. These straight lines are then rendered.

Parametric curves can be obtained by substituting the real numbers found in a control point vector by vectors taken from a higher dimensional real space. A parametric 2D curve of degree $n = 3$ is e.g. given by some control point vector $S = ((x_0, y_0), (x_1, y_1), (x_2, y_2), (x_3, y_3))$.

In applications we mostly encounter *cubic Bézier curves*, curves of degree $n = 3$, which can be found in the descriptions of font outlines or the modelling of smooth 3D objects. Cubic Bézier curves have an additional very intuitive property describing how the two non-end-points influence the represented curve. If we determine the tangents of a cubic Bézier curve at the points $t = 0$ and $t = 1$, we see that the tangent at P_0 points to P_1 and the tangent at P_3 points to P_2.

Example 2. Consider the control point vector for a cubic Bézier curve $S = ((0, 0), (0, -\frac{1}{3}), (-\frac{1}{3}, -\frac{1}{3}), (0, 0))$, for which we obtain the parametric curve $C(t) = (t^3 - t^2, t^2 - t), t \in [0, 1]$, which starts and ends at the origin. The two tangents intersect the points $(0, -\frac{1}{3})$ and $(-\frac{1}{3}, -\frac{1}{3})$ respectively. It is computed by the PWFA shown in Figure 2.

Our next example is about the best approximation of circles and arcs by cubic Bézier curves, as it is often used in fonts.

Example 3. Assume we want to approximate the top right quarter of the circle of unit radius using a cubic Bézier curve. The choice of the points $P_0 = (1, 0)$

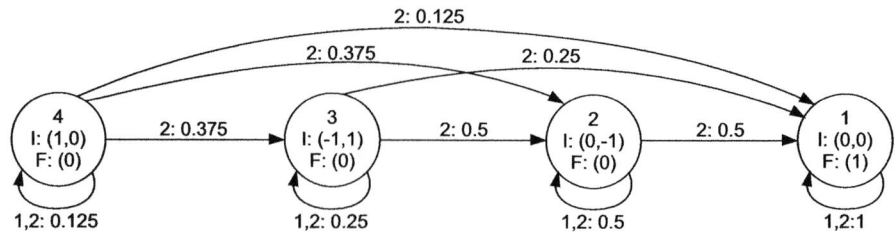

Fig. 2. PWFA computing the set of points $\{(t^3 - t^2, t^2 - t) | t \in [0, 1]\}$

and $P_3 = (0, 1)$ is straightforward and the tangent at P_0 should be vertical whereas the tangent at P_3 should be horizontal. This implies that $P_1 = (1, k_1)$ and $P_2 = (k_2, 1)$ for some real numbers k_1 and k_2. For symmetry reasons it is obvious that $k_1 = k_2 = k$, so $P = ((1, 0), (1, k), (k, 1), (0, 1))$. Thus, we have to find a number k such that the curve is an optimal approximation of the circle sector. The derivation of k can be found in [13,17]. This optimal value is

$$k = 4 \frac{\sqrt{2} - 1}{3} \approx 0.552 \ .$$

In practice, a given curve is first partitioned into segments and then each segment is approximated by a separate Bézier curve that is shifted into the right position (remember that all Bézier curves are defined on $[0, 1]$). This can be simulated easily by PWFA, because there are effective algorithms for set union and invertible affine transformation operations (cf. [20]). As all curve segments are based on polynomials, we can obtain very compact automata. Assume we want to approximate a continuous curve $c(t)$ by some PWFA defined on the interval $[0, 2^q]$ for some natural number q. We partition the curve into a set of segments $c_i(t)$ such that

$$c_i(t) = \begin{cases} c(t + i) & \text{for } 0 \le t < 1 \text{ and } i < 2^q - 1 \\ c(t + i) & \text{for } 0 \le t \le 1 \text{ and } i = 2^q - 1 \\ 0 & \text{otherwise} \end{cases}$$

for $i = 0, \ldots, 2^q - 1$. Then we obtain

$$c(t) = \sum_{i=0}^{2^q - 1} c_i(t - i) \ .$$

Thus, to represent the complete curve, we can use the construction

$$c = \{(t, \textstyle\sum_{i=0}^{2^q - 1} c_i(t - i)) | t \in [0, 2^q - 1]\}$$

$$= \textstyle\bigcup_{i=0}^{2^q - 2} \{(t + i, c_i(t)) | t \in [0, 1)\} \cup \{(t + 2^q - 1, c_{2^q - 1}(t)) | t \in [0, 1]\}$$

$$= \textstyle\bigcup_{i=0}^{2^q - 1} \{(t + i, c_i(t)) | t \in [0, 1]\}$$

where the last step is valid because c is continuous. Now assume, each curve segment $c_i(t)$ is approximated by a Bézier curve of degree n, i.e.

$$c_i(t) \approx p_i(t) = \sum_{j=0}^{n} P_{i,j} b_j^n(t) = \sum_{j=0}^{n} P'_{i,j} x^j$$

for $i = 0, \ldots, 2^q - 1$ such that

$$p(t) = \sum_{i=0}^{2^q - 1} p_i(t - i)$$

is a continuous function. Then we can construct a PWFA X computing $p(t)$ as the set

$$p = \bigcup_{i=0}^{2^q-1} \{(t+i, p_i(t)) | t \in [0,1]\}$$

using

$$|Q_X| = 2\left(\frac{q}{2} + \frac{q}{4} + \ldots + 1\right) + \max\{(n+1), 2\}$$

states. X uses $\max\{n+1, 2\}$ states to represent a PWFA defined polynomial. This maximum will usually be $n + 1$. For sake of completeness, we have also included the case of $n = 0$ (i.e. approximation by piece-wise constant functions). If $n = 0$ we have to introduce an additional state, because we require a linear function for the computation of the first component of the result vectors. The geometric sum stems from a set union construction which yields a tree structured automaton for each of the two components of the result vectors. If the number of sections is not a power of 2, then we can substitute unused intervals by repeating existing intervals. Assume for instance we want to represent the curve $c(t)$ defined on $[0, 3]$ and have decomposed it as

$$c(t) = c_0(t - 0) + c_1(t - 1) + c_2(t - 2)$$

which we compute as

$$c = \{(t+0, c_0(t)) | t \in [0,1]\} \cup \{(t+1, c_1(t)) | t \in [0,1]\} \cup \{(t+2, c_2(t)) | t \in [0,1]\} \ .$$

Then we can repeat the interval $[0, 1]$ for the unused interval $[3, 4]$ by

$$c = \underbrace{\{(t+0, c_0(t)) | t \in [0,1]\}}_{\text{prefix 11}} \cup \underbrace{\{(t+1, c_1(t)) | t \in [0,1]\}}_{\text{prefix 12}} \cup$$
$$\underbrace{\{(t+2, c_2(t)) | t \in [0,1]\}}_{\text{prefix 21}} \cup \underbrace{\{(t+0, c_0(t)) | t \in [0,1]\}}_{\text{prefix 22}} \ .$$

Example 4. Any curve $c(t)$ defined on $[0, 3]$ and built from three Bézier curves can be represented by a PWFA with only ten states. The image computed by the automaton is shown in Figure 3.

For an example let us consider the polynomials

- $(0, 0, \frac{11}{3}, 4) \cong -7x^3 + 11x^2$ for $[0, 1]$,
- $(4, \frac{13}{3}, \frac{13}{6}, 2) \cong 4.5x^3 - 7.5x^2 + x + 4$ for $[1, 2]$ and
- $(2, \frac{11}{6}, 3, 3) \cong -2.5x^3 + 4x^2 - 0.5x + 2$ for $[2, 3]$.

representing a spline in three pieces. As we allow polynomials up to degree 3, we need 4 states representing a polynomial construction. This is identical to the states of the automaton shown in Figure 2. Six more states are required for the set union construction glueing the polynomials together, three for each of the two dimensions, respectively. The number of polynomials is not a power of two, thus we just use the construction described above.

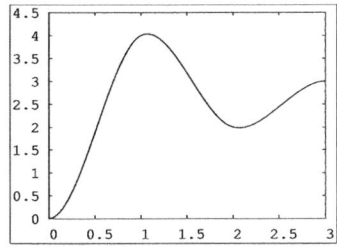

Fig. 3. Function computed on $[0, 3]$ by the PWFA from Example 4

4 Spline Applications

Splines have numerous applications ranging from computer generated fonts over computer aided design (CAD) as used in architecture, engineering, etc. to 3D modelling for animated movies. We will present some examples in this section.

4.1 Scalable Vector Graphics Path Outlines

We will show how an outline of a Scalable Vector Graphics (SVG, cf. [11]) path element can be represented by a real-valued PWFA of dimension 2, where the necessary graphical primitives can either be reproduced exactly or approximated to arbitrary precision.

An SVG path is based on the following primitive instructions (we only provide informal descriptions here, precise definitions can be found in e.g. [11]):

- M: move the pen to a new location and start a new path
- Z: close the current path by drawing a straight line from the current position to the starting point of the path
- L: draw a straight line from the current point to a given point
- H: draw a straight horizontal line from the current point up to a certain horizontal coordinate
- V: draw a straight vertical line from the current point up to a certain vertical coordinate
- C: draw a cubic Bézier curve from the current point to some endpoint, where two control points in between are given
- S: draw a cubic Bézier curve from the current point to some endpoint, where one control point in between is given and the other is computed from the previous curve segment such that the curve is smooth (meaning the curve is continuous and the first derivative exists) at the current point
- Q: draw a quadratic Bézier curve from the current point to some endpoint, where one control point in between are given
- T: draw a quadratic Bézier curve from the current point to some endpoint, where the control point between the end points is computed from the previous curve segment such that the curve is smooth at the current point
- A: draw an elliptical arc from the current point to some point

Actually, each such instruction exists in two variants, namely for absolute and relative coordinates as parameters, resp. We will restrict ourselves to the instruction set for absolute coordinates.

An example of a path according to the SVG 1.1 specifications is:

$$M0,0 \quad C0, -0.333 \quad -0.333, 0.333 \quad 0,0$$

The path describes the cubic Bézier curve represented by the PWFA shown in Figure 2. The pen is first moved to the position $(0,0)$ and then a cubic Bézier curve is drawn to the endpoint $(0,0)$. The control points between the endpoints are (approximately) $(0, -\frac{1}{3})$ and $(-\frac{1}{3}, -\frac{1}{3})$.

We will now reduce the number of instruction types since each drawing instruction can be substituted either by a cubic Bézier curve or an elliptical arc, where only absolute coordinates are used. We use the following steps:

- Trivially, each instruction for relative coordinates can be converted into one that uses absolute coordinates, i.e. we only have to consider paths using instructions M,Z,H,V,L,C,S,Q,T or A.
- The Z, H and V instructions are only convenient notions of the L instruction that have some implicit parameters. Thus, we can assume without loss of generality that each path we are provided with contains only the instructions M,L,C,S,Q,T and A.
- The spline variants S and T can be substituted by the more general variants C and Q respectively by explicitly inserting the implicit control point. This leaves the instructions M,L,C,Q and A.
- Bézier curves have the degree elevation property, i.e. each quadratic Bézier curve can be transformed into an equivalent cubic Bézier curve. More precisely, if a quadratic Bézier curve is given by the control points P_0, P_1 and P_2, then the cubic Bézier curve defined by the control points $P_0, (P_0 + 2P_1)/3$, $(2P_1 + P_2)/3, P_2$ defines the same curve. The remaining instruction types are M,L,C and A.
- A straight line going from P_0 to P_1 can be represented as a cubic Bézier curve using the control points $P_0, (P_0 + P_1)/2, (P_0 + P_1)/2, P_1$. Thus, the instructions M,C and A remain.

The instruction set M,C,A is minimal in the sense that no instruction can be simulated exactly by combinations of the other two. We can however approximate any A instruction as a sequence of C instructions at arbitrary precision. As C instructions can be represented exactly by PWFA, we assume that each encountered A instruction is replaced by a suitable sequence of C instructions and only the instructions M and C remain.

In practice we may skip some of the steps above, e.g. representing a straight line by a cubic Bézier curve is not necessary, as both can be computed by PWFA and the line can be implemented using a smaller amount of resources (states and edges) than the curve. As shown above, a PWFA can represent any finite set of Bézier curves. Thus, each SVG path outline can be computed by some real-valued PWFA of dimension 2.

4.2 Fonts

A typeface, which is also commonly called a font in computer based applications, mainly contains a function of non-empty words over a certain alphabet to a set of shapes. The shapes are called glyphs. Usually, each single alphabet letter is assigned a different glyph. Some fonts also contain glyphs describing words of a length greater than one, e.g. some fonts have a glyph for the word *fi*. Such glyphs for multi-letter words are called ligatures. They are used, if the rendering of a word using two successive single glyphs does not look satisfactory. A font as a whole is in general endowed with some information describing the set of all contained glyphs. This information is called the font metrics. It contains values like baseline, ascent, descent, etc. (cf. [5]).

Each glyph is defined as a relation on the Euclidean plane. When we set a line of text in a certain font, then we have to shift the rendered glyphs to their respective places on the line. This can be understood as a shift along the x axis for each rendered glyph. The shift between two adjacent glyphs *a* and *b* rendered consecutively in one line is given by the horizontal advance parameter of the glyph *a*. In some cases the sole usage of the horizontal advance parameter produces bad looking results, because two adjacent letters appear too close or too far apart. In this case the shift between pairs of glyphs can be changed by adding a so called kerning value.

The glyphs in most computer fonts are either stored as bitmaps or outlines. Bitmap fonts have low rendering complexity and can be optimised for a certain resolution, however they are in general not scalable. Outline fonts (which are sometimes also called vector fonts) store only glyph outlines, which have to be filled by the rendering algorithm. In contrast to bitmap fonts they in general are scalable, but the rendering requires much more complex algorithms. In particular, the rasterization of mathematically defined curves is a non-trivial task.

Clearly, we can use PWFA for typesetting, if the single glyphs of a font can be represented using PWFA. Bitmap fonts can be rendered using ordinary WFA, as they are in fact nothing more than greyscale images. Thus, we will put our emphasis on outline fonts, where we will use PWFA to represent glyph outlines as polynomial relations. We will not discuss the rasterization of such relations, but only the representation of the underlying curves in terms of PWFA.

There is a large variety of font file formats. The two most important formats in applications are the TrueType (cf. [14]) and Adobe PostScript type 1 (cf. [1]) font file formats. The TrueType format is the most common font format in Mac OS and Microsoft Windows. PostScript type 1 fonts, can be found in Adobe's PostScript and Portable Document Format ([2], [3]).

The outlines in a TrueType font are stored as quadratic B-splines. We can either transform them directly to a PWFA or first transform the B-spline representation to a Bézier curve representation and then transform the Bézier curve representation into a PWFA (cf. [19]). The drawing primitives allowed in the PostScript type 1 format are straight lines and cubic Bézier curves. Both can easily be transformed to PWFA form.

Fig. 4. Left: outline of letter S of a fraktur font by cubic Bézier curves in the image. The control points are depicted as little circles, the tangents as lines. Right: resulting glyph for S.

Figure 4 shows a glyph outline consisting of cubic Bézier curves and straight lines on the left. In practice a convenient way to transform a glyph outline of a TrueType or PostScript type 1 font into a PWFA is to use a font editor like FontForge (cf. [22]). First convert the font to an SVG font, which uses SVG paths to describe outlines, and then transform the resulting path into a PWFA.

If we only represent the spline curves defining some glyph by a PWFA, then the description is incomplete, as the interior is missing. The following results show that PWFA can also be used to represent filled outlines defined by glyphs in PostScript type 1 or TrueType fonts.

Lemma 1. *Let X be a PWFA of dimension d such that $S(X) = T(X)$. Then there exists a PWFA Y of dimension d computing the set*

$$S(Y) = \bigcup_{a,\,b \in S(X)} \{xa + (1 - x)b \mid x \in [0, 1]\},$$

which is nothing but the convex hull of $S(X)$.

Proof. Assume that $Q_X = \{1, \ldots, n\}$ for some $n \in \mathbb{N}^+$ and $\Sigma_X = \{1, \ldots, l\}$ for some $l \in \mathbb{N}^+$. Furthermore, assume without loss of generality that $F_X[n] = 1$ and $F_X[i] = 0$ for $1 \le i < n$. Let U_k denote the identity matrix in $\mathbb{R}^{k \times k}$ for each positive natural number k. Let further $\mathcal{O}_{k,m}$ denote the zero matrix in $\mathbb{R}^{k \times m}$ for each pair (k, m) of positive natural numbers. Consider the PWFA Y' of dimension $2d$ such that

- the state set $Q_{Y'} = \{1, \ldots, 2n\}$,
- the input alphabet $\Sigma_{Y'} = \{1, \ldots, 2l\}$,
- the transition matrix $A_{Y_i'}$ is given by

$$A_{Y_i'} = \begin{cases} \begin{pmatrix} A_{X_i} & \mathcal{O}_{n,n} \\ \mathcal{O}_{n,n} & U_n \end{pmatrix} & \text{if } 1 \le i \le l \\ \begin{pmatrix} U_n & \mathcal{O}_{n,n} \\ \mathcal{O}_{n,n} & A_{X_{i-l}} \end{pmatrix} & \text{if } l + 1 \le i \le 2l \end{cases}$$

for $i = 1, \ldots, 2l$,
- the initial matrix $I_{Y'}$ is

$$I_{Y'} = \begin{pmatrix} I_X & \mathcal{O}_{d,n} \\ \mathcal{O}_{d,n} & I_X \end{pmatrix}$$

and
- the final vector $F_{Y'}$ is $F_{Y'} = (F_X^T \; F_X^T)^T$.

Let $p(f_{Y'}(w))$ denote the projection of the vector $f_{Y'}(w)$ to the components $1, \ldots, l$ for each $w \in \Sigma_{Y'}^*$ and let $q(f_{Y'}(w))$ denote the projection of the vector $f_{Y'}(w)$ to the components $l+1, \ldots, 2l$ for each $w \in \Sigma_{Y'}^*$. Then the set P given by

$$P = \overline{\bigcup_{w \in \Sigma_{Y'}^*} \{(p(f_{Y'}(w)), q(f_{Y'}(w)))\}}$$

is the set of all pairs (a, b) such that $a, b \in T(X)$. $S(Y)$ can be expressed as

$$S(Y) = \overline{\bigcup_{w \in \Sigma_{Y'}^*} \{p(f_{Y'}(w)) + x(q(f_{Y'}(w)) - p(f_{Y'}(w))) | x \in [0, 1]\}} \;.$$

Thus, Y can be obtained from Y' using the following steps:

1. Add two states $2n + 1$ and $2n + 2$ representing the real function $f(x) = x$ (cf. [6]). We assume that the state representing the linear function is state $2n + 1$ and the state representing the constant function is $2n + 2$.
2. Set the final vector to 1 for state $2n + 2$ and to zero for each other state.
3. Let $c \in T(X)$ (such a point exists, because $S(X) = T(X)$ implies that $S(X)$ is not empty). Choose $I_Y = (I_X \; I_X \; \mathcal{O}_{d,1} \; c)$ to halve the number of dimensions.
4. Insert a new label $2l + 1$ and assign the transition matrix

$$A_{Y_{2l+2}} = \begin{pmatrix} U_n & \mathcal{O}_{n,n} & -1_n & 1_n \\ \mathcal{O}_{n,n} & U_n & 1_n & \mathcal{O}_{n,1} \\ & \mathcal{O}_{2,\,2n+2} & & \end{pmatrix}$$

to it, where $1_n \in \mathbb{R}^n$ is 1 in component n and 0 otherwise.

Let $h(w) : \Sigma_Y^* \mapsto \Sigma_{Y'}^*$ denote the homomorphism erasing $2l + 1$ and maps any other symbol to itself. When Y reads the symbol $2l + 1$ after it has read some word $w \in \Sigma_{Y'}^*$, then it configures the states computing the linear function to produce a line between the points $p(f_{Y'}(h(w)))$ and $q(f_{Y'}(h(w)))$. Thus, Y is the set of all lines between pairs of (a, b) of points such that $a, b \in T(X)$.

It is easy to see that Lemma 1 can be generalized to the following theorem.

Theorem 1. *Let X and Z be PWFA of dimension d such that $S(X) = T(X)$ and $S(Z) = T(Z)$. Then there is a PWFA Y of dimension d computing the set*

$$S(Y) = \bigcup_{a \in S(X), b \in S(Z)} \{xa + (1 - x)b | x \in [0, 1]\} \;.$$

Proof. We do not construct the automaton Y' as in the proof of Lemma 1 using two copies of X but just one copy of X and one copy of Z. The rest of the construction is analogous.

Applying Theorem 1 to obtain filled glyphs defined by PostScript type 1 or TrueType fonts via PWFA works as follows. TrueType fonts can usually be exactly converted to a PostScript type 1 font. So we assume w.l.o.g. that each used primitive component is a cubic Bézier curve. Furthermore, we can assume as well that there is exactly one connected area to be filled on the glyph. If there are multiple, we will handle them consecutively.

The PostScript type 1 format does not allow outline paths to cross each other. This means each area to be filled is defined by one path describing the outer border and a finite number of paths describing inner borders. We can approximate each glyph outline path from the inside of the glyph at arbitrary precision using polygons. By „from the inside" we mean that each polygon vertex is on the glyph and no polygon edge crosses any glyph outline. We assume that no polygon approximating any outline path crosses itself or a polygon approximating any other outline path. If such a crossing exists, then this can be remedied by using more precise approximations.

An example of such an approximation is shown in Figure 5. The depicted glyph has one outer and one inner border. The area between the polygons approximating the outer border and inner border can be tessellated using filled triangles. A filled triangle is the convex hull of any two edges of the triangle. This leaves the areas between the polygons and the glyph outlines. We have a closer look at how we obtain polygons approximating a glyph outline path from the inside. Observe the outline path shown in the second part of Figure 5. We want to approximate the curve C_1 by a polygon inside the area delimited by C_1, C_2 and C_3. Assume C_1 is given as $C_1(t)$, where $C_1(0)$ denotes the lower end of C_1 and $C_1(1)$ the upper end in the figure. Let $N_1(t)$ denote the unit normal vector of C_1 at t, which points in the direction of the glyph inside. One such vector is depicted in the figure. We define the polygon $P_{1,k}(\delta)$ approximating C_1 as the sequence of vectors

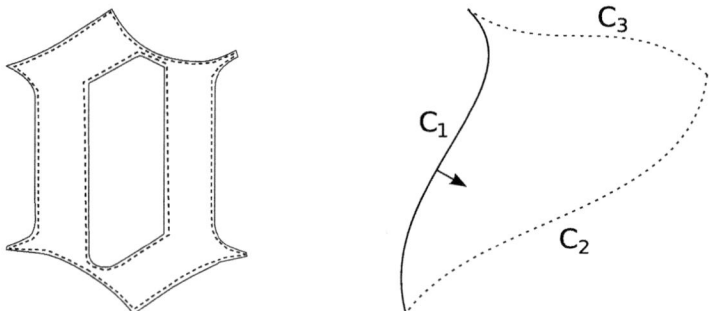

Fig. 5. First a glyph is approximated from the inside using polygons, depicted as dashed lines. Then we take care filling the interior step by step. Herer an outline path consisting of three cubic Bézier curves C_1, C_2 and C_3 is shown. The arrow depicts a normal vector of some point on the curve C_1 pointing to the interior of the glyph.

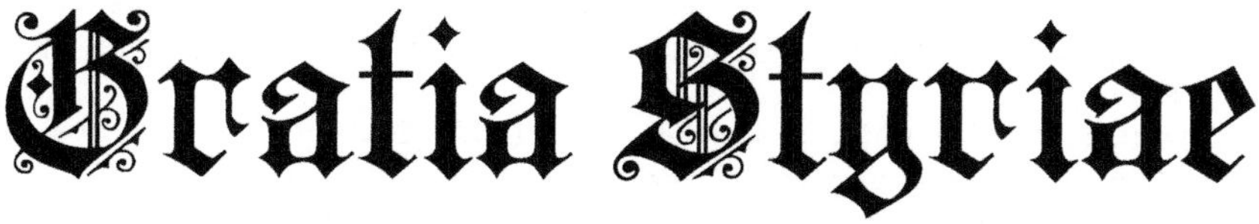

❡rɑtiɑ ⸙tgriɑe

Fig. 6. Text *Gratia Styriae* rendered from a PWFA

$$P_{1,k}(\delta) = C_1(0), C_1\left(\frac{1}{k}\right) + \delta N_1\left(\frac{1}{k}\right), \ldots, C_1\left(\frac{k-1}{k}\right) + \delta N_1\left(\frac{k-1}{k}\right), C_1(1)$$

for $k \geq 2$ and $\delta > 0$. If $P_{1,k}(\delta)$ crosses C_1, then this can be remedied by increasing k, as C_1 is a polynomial and has only finitely many turning points. If we choose k sufficiently large and δ sufficiently small, then there are also no intersections between $P_{1,k}(\delta)$ and C_2 or C_3. We can find a suitable pair of numbers (k, δ) algorithmically by trying each pair $(2^i, 2^{-i})$ for $i = 1, 2, \ldots$ until $P_{1,2^i}(2^{-i})$ no longer crosses C_1, C_2 and C_3. Note that only crossings are forbidden, the approximating polygon is allowed to touch each curve.

Assume we have found a suitable pair (k, δ). Then the sequence $P_{1,k}(\delta)$ has length $k + 1$. We have seen above that each Bézier curve $b(t)$ can be split into two curves $b_1(t)$ and $b_2(t)$ at any point $t \in (0, 1)$. Let $C_{1,1}, \ldots, C_{1,k}$ denote the sequence of cubic Bézier curves obtained by splitting C_1 at the points $\frac{1}{k}, \ldots, \frac{k-1}{k}$. Let further $L_{1,1}, \ldots, L_{1,k}$ denote the sequence of straight lines between the pairs $(P_{1,k}(\delta)_1, P_{1,k}(\delta)_2), \ldots (P_{1,k}(\delta)_k, P_{1,k}(\delta)_{k+1})$. Then we can obtain the area between the curve C_1 and the polygon $P_{1,k}(\delta)$ by filling the areas between each pair $(C_{1,i}, L_{1,i})$ of delimiting curves using the construction of Theorem 1. Using the toolkit we now have at hand, we can render complete texts by PWFA. An example is shown in Figure 6. As all delimiting curves we use are cubic Bézier curves, we can partition each represented text into an arbitrary finite amount of fragments. When we assign these fragments to time steps, we can construct a PWFA which produces the fragments incrementally according to a timeline. Thus, we can render movies showing the drawing of letters as it would be performed by a human hand using PWFA.

Currently, there are experiments underway at our institute, to extend this automata-theoretic kind of representation of glyphs to early medieval manuscripts written in Insular and Carolingian minuscule. One of the goals is to identify individual schools or even single writers by their "typical" glyphs, i.e. by their associated representations of control point vectors and PWFA.

References

1. Adobe Systems Inc: Adobe Type 1 Font Format, 2nd edn. Addison Wesley, Reading (1990)
2. Adobe Systems Inc: PostScript Language Reference, 3rd edn. Addison-Wesley, Reading (1999)
3. Adobe Systems Inc: PDF Reference Version 1.6, 5th edn. Adobe Press (2004)

4. Albert, J., Kari, J.: Parametric weighted finite automata and iterated function systems. In: Proceedings of the Conference Fractals in Engineering, Delft, pp. 248–255 (1999)

5. Anonymous. English Wikipedia article "Typeface" (2010), http://en.wikipedia.org/wiki/Typeface

6. Culik II, K., Karhumäki, J.: Finite automata computing real functions. SIAM Journal on Computing 23(4), 789–814 (1994)

7. Culik II, K., Kari, J.: Image compression using weighted finite automata. Computers & Graphics 17(3), 305–314 (1993)

8. Culik II, K., Kari, J.: Image-data compression using edge-optimizing algorithm for WFA inference. Information Processing and Management 30(6), 829–838 (1994)

9. Droste, M., Kuich, W., Vogler, H.: Handbook of Weighted Automata. Springer, Heidelberg (2009)

10. Farin, G.: Curves and Surfaces for Computer Aided Geometric Design. Academic Press, London (1990)

11. Ferraiolo, J., Fujisawa, J., Jackson, D.: Scalable vector graphics (SVG) 1.1 specification. World Wide Web Consortium, Recommendation REC-SVG11-20030114 (2003)

12. Hafner, U., Albert, J., Frank, S., Unger, M.: Weighted finite automata for video compression. IEEE Journal on selected areas in communication 16, 108–119 (1998)

13. Maisonobe, L.: Drawing an elliptical arc using polylines, quadratic or cubic Bézier curves (2010), http://www.spaceroots.org/documents/ellipse/index.html

14. Microsoft Corporation. Truetype specifications (2003), http://www.microsoft.com/typography/specs/default.htm

15. Pavlidis, T.: Algorithms for Graphics and Image Processing. Computer Science Press (1982)

16. Schützenberger, M.P.: On the definition of a family of automata. Information and Control 4(2-3), 245–270 (1961)

17. Stanislav, G.A.: Drawing a circle with Bézier curves (2010), http://www.whizkidtech.redprince.net/bezier/circle/

18. Text Encoding Initiative (TEI) Consortium. TEI: P5 Guidelines (2010), http://www.tei-c.org/Guidelines/P5/

19. Tischler, G.: Parametric weighted finite automata for figure drawing. In: Domaratzki, M., Okhotin, A., Salomaa, K., Yu, S. (eds.) CIAA 2004. LNCS, vol. 3317, pp. 259–268. Springer, Heidelberg (2005)

20. Tischler, G.: Properties and applications of parametric weighted finite automata. Journal of Automata, Languages and Combinatorics 10(2/3), 347–365 (2005)

21. University Library of Würzburg. Topographia Franconiae (2010), http://franconica.uni-wuerzburg.de/Franconica/ortsregister.html

22. Williams, G.: FontForge (2010), http://fontforge.sourceforge.net/

On Language Decompositions and Primality

Michael Domaratzki[1] and Kai Salomaa[2]

[1] Department of Computer Science, University of Manitoba,
Winnipeg, Manitoba R3T 2N2, Canada
mdomarat@cs.umanitoba.ca
[2] School of Computing, Queen's University, Kingston,
Ontario K7L 3N6, Canada
ksalomaa@cs.queensu.ca

Abstract. Concatenation of strings and languages is a fundamental operation on formal languages. Here we consider the inverse operation of language decomposition, where we want to represent a given language as a non-trivial concatenation of two languages. The associated notions of prime languages and prime decompositions have been originally introduced by Mateescu, A. Salomaa and Yu. We consider also extensions of the decomposability problem with respect to orthogonal concatenation, as well as, more general operations defined by sets of trajectories.

1 Introduction

Concatenation is one of the basic operations on strings and languages. Products or concatenations of languages, viewed as subsets of the free monoid, are used in many applications. However, many apparently simple questions, like the question of determining when two languages commute, turn out to be surprisingly challenging [21,26].

Here we discuss the operation that can be viewed as the inverse of concatenation, that is, we consider the question of decomposing a language L as a concatenation of component languages. We are interested in particular in cases where L is regular. It is known already from Conway [4] (see also [25,29,36]) that it is decidable whether or not a given regular language has a non-trivial decomposition. However, there was no known efficient algorithm for this problem and, recently, the decomposability of regular languages was shown to be PSPACE-complete [27].

Languages that do not have any non-trivial decomposition with respect to concatenation are called prime languages. It turns out that a prime decomposition of a language L, that is, a representation of L as a product of prime languages, need not be unique and some languages, in fact, have no prime decomposition. The notion of prime languages was introduced and prime decompositions were first systematically studied by Mateescu, A. Salomaa and Yu [29,36].

The question whether a language L has a decomposition is represented in a natural way as a two-variable equation $L = X \cdot Y$. We will consider existence of solutions for such equations and their variants where one of the variables

C.S. Calude, G. Rozenberg, A. Salomaa (Eds.): Maurer Festschrift, LNCS 6570, pp. 63–75, 2011.
© Springer-Verlag Berlin Heidelberg 2011

X or Y is a fixed language or where the concatenation is replaced by some other operation. Language equations have been extensively studied and have applications in many areas of computer science. More information on language equations, in general, can be found in [23,25,26,31] and their references.

It should be noted that even the decidability status of the decomposition problem for regular languages with respect to, for example, orthogonal concatenation or shuffle remains open. The shuffle decomposition problem for regular languages has been studied in [2,18].

We consider a general class of operations defined by *shuffle along trajectories* that generalize the operations of concatenation, (unrestricted) shuffle and a large class of other language operations. Trajectory-based operations were originally introduced by Mateescu, Rozenberg and A. Salomaa [28]. We discuss conditions on the sets of trajectories that guarantee that the corresponding decomposition problem for regular languages remains effectively solvable.

We assume that the reader is familiar with the basics of formal languages and, in particular, with the notions of regular languages and finite automata, for more information see e.g. [37,38]. The set of all strings over a finite alphabet Σ is Σ^* and a language is any subset of Σ^*. The empty string is ε. The concatenation of languages L_1 and L_2 is defined as $L_1 \cdot L_2 = \{w_1 w_2 \mid w_i \in L_i, i = 1, 2\}$. We denote a nondeterministic finite automaton, or NFA, as a tuple $A = (Q, \Sigma, \delta, q_0, Q_F)$, where Q is the finite set of states, Σ is the input alphabet, $\delta : (Q \times \Sigma) \to 2^Q$ is the multivalued transition function, $q_0 \in Q$ is the start state and $Q_F \subseteq Q$ is the set of accepting states. The language recognized by A is denoted $L(A)$. The automaton A is deterministic, or a DFA, if for all $q \in Q$ and $\sigma \in \Sigma$, $|\delta(q, \sigma)| \leq 1$.

2   Language Primality and Prime Decompositions

If $L = L_1 \cdot \ldots \cdot L_k$, $k \geq 2$, we say that the languages L_i, $1 \leq i \leq k$, are factors of L and $L_1 \cdot \ldots \cdot L_k$ is a *decomposition of index k* for L. The decomposition is *non-trivial* if $L_i \neq \{\varepsilon\}$, $i = 1, \ldots, k$.

Note that any language L has the trivial decompositions $L \cdot \{\varepsilon\}$ and $\{\varepsilon\} \cdot L$. In the following, unless otherwise mentioned, by a decomposition we always mean a non-trivial decomposition.

A non-empty language $L \neq \{\varepsilon\}$ is said to be *prime* if L has no decompositions of index 2. Clearly a language L has decomposition of index k for some $k \geq 2$ if and only if L has a decomposition of index 2.

In [14] a language L is termed *indecomposable* if the equation $L = L_1 \cdot L_2$ implies that $L = L_1$ or $L = L_2$. Clearly a prime language is always indecomposable, and it can be verified that any indecomposable language distinct from $\emptyset$ and $\{\varepsilon\}$ is also prime [35].

In [29,36] the following method to decide primality of a regular language was given. Let $A = (Q, \Sigma, \delta, q_0, Q_F)$ be a DFA. We say that $P \subseteq Q$ is a *decomposition set* of A if $L(A) = R_1^P R_2^P$, where

$$R_1^P = \{w \in \Sigma^* \mid \delta(q_0, w) \in P\}, \quad R_2^P = \bigcap_{p \in P} \{w \in \Sigma^* \mid \delta(p, w) \in Q_F\}.$$

Proposition 1. [29] *Let L be a regular language recognized by a DFA $A = (Q, \Sigma, \delta, q_0, Q_F)$. For any decomposition $L = L_1 \cdot L_2$ there exists a decomposition set P of A such that $L_i \subseteq R_i^P$, $i = 1, 2$.*

Thus, the factors of an arbitrary decomposition (of index 2) of a regular language L are included in factors of a maximal decomposition that is defined by a decomposition set of the minimal DFA for L.

Corollary 1. *If a regular language L has a decomposition, it has a decomposition where the components are regular.*

With notations as in Proposition 1, for a given DFA A and $P \subseteq Q$ we can construct in polynomial time a DFA for R_2^P and an NFA for the concatenation $R_1^P R_2^P$. Since equivalence of NFA's can be decided in PSPACE [38], Proposition 1 gives a PSPACE algorithm to decide whether or not the language recognized by a DFA is prime. However, the complexity of the primality problem was left open in [29], see also [15].

Recently, DFA primality was shown to be PSPACE-hard by Martens, Niewerth and Schwentick [27]. Interestingly, the primality problem for regular languages is closely connected with typing problems for XML schemas, and the authors of [27] were motivated by applications in distributed XML documents.

Below, using a construction appearing already in [29] we give an alternative proof for PSPACE-hardness of deciding whether an NFA recognizes a prime language (which is a weaker result).

Proposition 2. *Given an NFA A it is PSPACE-hard to decide whether or not $L(A)$ is prime.*

Proof. We use a reduction from the PSPACE-hard problem of deciding NFA universality [30]. Our reduction is similar to the one used originally in [29] for showing that primality of a context-free language in undecidable.

Let Σ be the input alphabet for A and denote $\Omega = \Sigma \cup \{a, b\}$ where a and b are new symbols not occurring in Σ. We define

$$L_0 = aL(A)ba + a\Sigma^*bb + b\Sigma^*aa + b\Sigma^*ab.$$

Given A as input, it is easy to construct (in polynomial time) an NFA B for the language L_0.

We claim that L_0 is prime if and only if $L(A) \neq \Sigma^*$. For the "only if" direction we note that if $L(A) = \Sigma^*$, then $L_0 = (a\Sigma^*b + b\Sigma^*a)(a + b)$.

For the "if" direction, suppose that $L(A) \neq \Sigma^*$ and consider an arbitrary decomposition $L_0 = M_1 \cdot M_2$ of L_0, where $M_1 \neq \{\varepsilon\} \neq M_2$.

We observe that since L_0 is prefix-free and suffix-free,

$$M_i \text{ cannot contain a complete word of } L_0, \ i = 1, 2. \tag{1}$$

Now suppose that M_2 contains a word of length at least two, $w = w'xy$, $w' \in \Omega^*$, $x, y \in \{a, b\}$. (Since $L_0 \subseteq \{a, b\}\Sigma^*\{a, b\}^2$, the last two symbols of w must be in $\{a, b\}$.)

Since, by (1), M_2 cannot contain a complete word of L_0, the language M_1 must have a word w_z beginning with z, both for $z = a$ and $z = b$. This leads to a contradiction for all choices of $x, y \in \{a, b\}$, because, for any $v \in \Sigma^*$, $w_a vaa, w_a vab \notin L_0$ and $w_b vba, w_b vbb \notin L_0$.

Hence we can conclude that any word of M_2 has length at most one. Now (1) implies that $\varepsilon \notin M_2$. Since L_0 contains strings ending with a and strings ending with b the only possibility is that $M_2 = \{a, b\}$.

Since $L(A) \neq \Sigma^*$, we can choose $u \in \Sigma^* - L(A)$. Now $aubb \in L_0$ which implies $aub \in M_1$. Since $a \in M_2$, we get $auba \in M_1 \cdot M_2 = L_0$, which is a contradiction.   ∎

Thus, already based on the work by Mateescu, A. Salomaa and Yu [29] it could be shown that NFA primality is PSPACE-hard, although this was not explicitly mentioned in [29]. In order to establish the stronger result for DFA's, [27] uses a different construction and a reduction from *DFA concatenation universality* [20], that is, the problem of deciding whether the concatenation of languages recognized by two given DFA's equals Σ^*.

Theorem 1. [27] *The problem of deciding primality of $L(A)$ for a given DFA A is PSPACE-complete.*

Next we consider the question of representing a (regular) language as a product of prime languages. A *prime decomposition* of a language L is a decomposition of L, where each of the factors is a prime language.

Clearly, every finite language has a prime decomposition, however, a prime decomposition for a finite language need not be unique even if we disregard the order of factors in the product [29]. For example,

$$(\varepsilon + a^2)(\varepsilon + a^2 + a^3 + a^4) = (\varepsilon + a^2 + a^3)^2,$$

where both factors on both sides of the equation are prime.

There exist infinite languages without any prime decomposition. An example given in [15] is the language

$$H = \varepsilon + \{ a^{i_1} b^{i_1} a^{i_2} b^{i_2} \cdots a^{i_r} b^{i_r} \mid r \geq 1, \ 1 \leq i_1 < i_2 < \cdots < i_r \}.$$

This means that in any decomposition of H as a product $M_1 \cdot \ldots \cdot M_k$, one of the languages M_i, $1 \leq i \leq k$, can be further decomposed in a non-trivial way, and the process can be continued to yield a decomposition of an arbitrary index. However, all known examples of languages that provably have the above property are non-regular, and even non-context-free [15].

Open problem 2.1. *Do all regular languages have a prime decomposition?*

The situation is essentially different if we restrict consideration to prefix-free languages since it is known that the monoid of prefix codes is a free monoid [32]. Any prefix-free regular language has a unique prime decomposition if it is additionally required that the components are regular and prefix-free [5]. Interestingly, the analogous property does not hold for infix-free regular languages [16].

Note that, because languages can be decomposed in various ways, simply the existence of a prime decomposition for L does not imply any upper bound for the index of possible decompositions of L. A language L is said to be *strongly prime decomposable*[15] if the maximum index of any decomposition of L is bounded by a constant. If L is strongly prime decomposable, any refinement of an arbitrary decomposition of L has to result in a prime decomposition in a finite number of steps. The condition guarantees the existence of a prime decomposition but not its uniqueness.

Using techniques based on Proposition 1, [15] gives an effective characterization of strongly prime decomposable regular languages and using the characterization establishes that all unary regular languages have a prime decomposition.

Theorem 2. [15] *Every regular language over a unary alphabet has a prime decomposition.*

There exist non-regular unary languages that provably have no prime decomposition [15,34]. Recently, more general types of (prime) decompositions of languages, including infinitary decompositions, have been studied in [35].

2.1 Orthogonal Concatenation

The question of decomposability of languages becomes more involved if we consider the operation of non-ambiguous, or orthogonal, concatenation [6]. We say that L is the *orthogonal concatenation* of languages L_1 and L_2, denoted, $L = L_1 \odot_\perp L_2$, if for every string $w \in L$ there exist *unique* strings $w_1 \in L_1$ and $w_2 \in L_2$ such that $w = w_1 \cdot w_2$. We say that L is $\perp$-*prime* if L has only trivial decompositions (where one of the components is $\{\varepsilon\}$) as the orthogonal concatenation of two languages.

Note that the orthogonal product of given languages L_1 and L_2 need not be defined. If we define the product of L_1 and L_2 to consist of those words that have a unique representation as the concatenation of strings in L_1 and L_2 we get the related, but different, operation of *unique concatenation* considered in [33].

Techniques such as the one used for Proposition 1 fall apart when trying to determine, for a given regular language L, whether or not L has a non-trivial orthogonal factorization. Thus, we do not know whether for regular languages the existence of an orthogonal decomposition is even decidable. Note that given regular languages L_1 and L_2 we can effectively decide whether or not $L_1 \odot_\perp L_2$ is defined and, in the positive case, construct a DFA for $L_1 \odot_\perp L_2$. However, a simple brute-force search seems not sufficient to decide $\perp$-primality for regular languages (even in the case where the components are required to be regular) because there is no known state complexity upper bound for regular solutions for X and Y in an equation $L = X \odot_\perp Y$ [6].

Open problem 2.2. *Is $\perp$-primality decidable for regular languages?*

It has been shown by Anselmo and Restivo [1] that existence of solutions for one-variable equations involving orthogonal concatenation and regular constant languages is decidable. Their proof relies on power series techniques.

Theorem 3. [1] *For given regular languages L_1 and L_2, it is decidable whether or not the equation $L_1 = L_2 \odot_\perp X$ has a solution for X. A possible solution is unique and has an effective construction.*

It seems conceivable that the analogy of Corollary 1 would not hold for orthogonal concatenation [6], that is, there could be regular languages L such that $L = M_1 \odot_\perp M_2$ where M_1 and M_2 are non-regular while L has only trivial representations as the orthogonal product of regular languages.

3   Trajectory-Based Operations

Shuffle on trajectories is a system for defining a class of language operations in a uniform way. In particular, a binary language is given which specifies the shuffling operations which are allowed. The operations defined by shuffle on trajectories can then only interleave the characters in the input words, preserving their order, but can not delete them. In particular, each trajectory $t \in \{0,1\}^*$ with $|t|_0 = n$ and $|t|_1 = m$ specifies the manner in which we can form the shuffle on trajectories of two words of length n (as the left input word) and m (as the right input word). The word resulting from the shuffle along t will have a letter from the left input word in position i if the i-th symbol of t is 0, and a letter from the right input word in position i if the i-th symbol of t is 1.

By using shuffle on trajectories, we can examine the sets of trajectories and their effect on different language equations. Here, we focus on decompositions, but other language equations can be examined (see the first author [10] for a survey of shuffle on trajectories which includes results on language equations).

3.1   Shuffle on Trajectories

The original definition of shuffle on trajectories is due to Mateescu *et al.* [28]. We first define the shuffle of two words x and y over an alphabet Σ on a trajectory t, a word over $\{0,1\}$. We denote the shuffle of x and y on trajectory t by $x \, \shuffle_t \, y$.

If $x = ax'$, $y = by'$ (with $a, b \in \Sigma$) and $t = et'$ (with $e \in \{0,1\}$), then

$$x \shuffle_{et'} y = \begin{cases} a(x' \shuffle_{t'} by') & \text{if } e = 0; \\ b(ax' \shuffle_{t'} y') & \text{if } e = 1. \end{cases}$$

If $x = ax'$ ($a \in \Sigma$), $y = \epsilon$ and $t = et'$ ($e \in \{0,1\}$), then

$$x \shuffle_{et'} \epsilon = \begin{cases} a(x' \shuffle_{t'} \epsilon) & \text{if } e = 0; \\ \emptyset & \text{otherwise.} \end{cases}$$

If $x = \epsilon$, $y = by'$ ($b \in \Sigma$) and $t = et'$ ($e \in \{0,1\}$), then

$$\epsilon \shuffle_{et'} y = \begin{cases} b(\epsilon \shuffle_{t'} y') & \text{if } e = 1; \\ \emptyset & \text{otherwise.} \end{cases}$$

We let $x \shuffle_\epsilon y = \emptyset$ if $\{x, y\} \neq \{\epsilon\}$. Finally, if $x = y = \epsilon$, then $\epsilon \shuffle_t \epsilon = \epsilon$ if $t = \epsilon$ and $\emptyset$ otherwise.

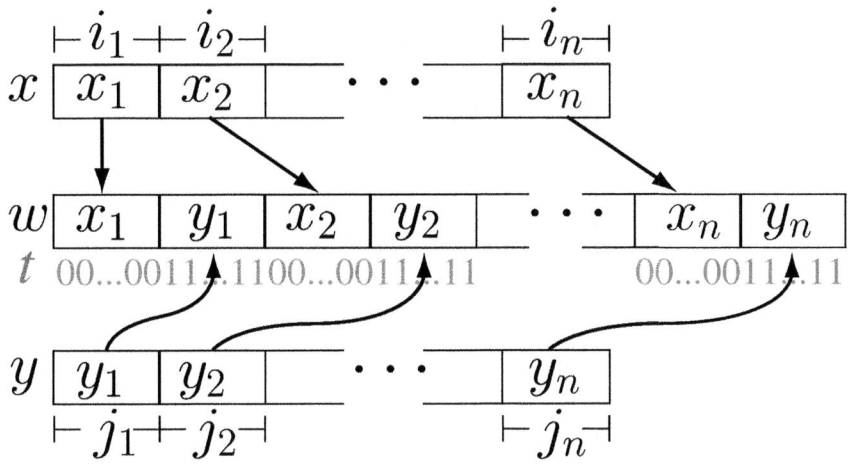

Fig. 1. Illustration of shuffle on trajectories

Alternatively, we can see that if $t = \prod_{k=1}^{n} 0^{i_k} 1^{j_k}$ for some $n \geq 0$ and $i_k, j_k \geq 0$ for all $1 \leq k \leq n$, then

$$x \sqcup_t y = \{\prod_{k=1}^{n} x_k y_k \ : \ x = \prod_{k=1}^{n} x_k, y = \prod_{k=1}^{n} y_k,$$
$$\text{with } |x_k| = i_k, |y_k| = j_k \text{ for all } 1 \leq k \leq n\}$$

if $|x| = |t|_0$ and $|y| = |t|_1$. On the other hand, $x \sqcup_t y = \emptyset$ if $|x| \neq |t|_0$ or $|y| \neq |t|_1$. This alternative definition of shuffle on trajectories is illustrated graphically in Figure 1: for each block of 0s in the trajectory the next block from the left operand (x) is added to the result (w), while if the block contains 1s, the right operand (y) is used.

To illustrate the concept more concretely, we note that if $x = abaac$, $y = ccab$, $t_1 = 011001100$ and $t_2 = 010000111$ then

$$x \sqcup_{t_1} y = accbaabac,$$
$$x \sqcup_{t_2} y = acbaaccab.$$

We extend shuffle on trajectories to sets $T \subseteq \{0, 1\}^*$ of trajectories as follows:

$$x \sqcup_T y = \bigcup_{t \in T} x \sqcup_t y.$$

Further, for $L_1, L_2 \subseteq \Sigma^*$, we define

$$L_1 \sqcup_T L_2 = \bigcup_{\substack{x \in L_1 \\ y \in L_2}} x \sqcup_T y.$$

We can see that if $T = 0^*1^*$, we have that $L_1 \sqcup_T L_2 = L_1 L_2$, i.e., $T = 0^*1^*$ gives the concatenation operation. If $T = (0 + 1)^*$, then $L_1 \sqcup_T L_2 = L_1 \sqcup L_2$, i.e., $T = \{0,1\}^*$ gives the shuffle operation. See Mateescu *et al.* [28] for the fundamental study of shuffle on trajectories.

3.2 Deletion along Trajectories

We now consider deletion on trajectories, which serves as an inverse for shuffle on trajectories. This inverse is important for solving language equations involving shuffle on trajectories. The concept of deletion along trajectories was independently introduced by Domaratzki [8,9] and Kari and Sosík [24]. Deletion on trajectories uses trajectories in a similar manner as in shuffle on trajectories. The trajectories model language operations which delete an occurrence of the right argument from the left argument in a controlled, scattered way.

Let $x, y \in \Sigma^*$ be words with $x = ax'$, $y = by'$ $(a, b \in \Sigma)$. Let t be a word over $\{0,1\}$ such that $t = et'$ with $e \in \{0,1\}$. Then we define $x \rightsquigarrow_t y$, the deletion of y from x along trajectory t, as follows:

$$x \rightsquigarrow_t y = \begin{cases} a(x' \rightsquigarrow_{t'} by') & \text{if } e = 0; \\ x' \rightsquigarrow_{t'} y' & \text{if } e = 1 \text{ and } a = b; \\ \emptyset & \text{otherwise.} \end{cases}$$

Also, if $x = ax'$ $(a \in \Sigma)$ and $t = et'$ $(e \in \{0,1\})$, then

$$x \rightsquigarrow_t \epsilon = \begin{cases} a(x' \rightsquigarrow_{t'} \epsilon) & \text{if } e = 0; \\ \emptyset & \text{otherwise.} \end{cases}$$

If $x \neq \epsilon$, then $x \rightsquigarrow_\epsilon y = \emptyset$. Further, $\epsilon \rightsquigarrow_t y = \epsilon$ if $t = y = \epsilon$. Otherwise, $\epsilon \rightsquigarrow_t y = \emptyset$.

Let $T \subseteq \{0,1\}^*$. Then

$$x \rightsquigarrow_T y = \bigcup_{t \in T} x \rightsquigarrow_t y.$$

We extend this to languages as expected: Let $L_1, L_2 \subseteq \Sigma^*$ and $T \subseteq \{0,1\}^*$. Then

$$L_1 \rightsquigarrow_T L_2 = \bigcup_{\substack{x \in L_1 \\ y \in L_2}} x \rightsquigarrow_T y.$$

For example, if $T = 0^*1^*$, then $\rightsquigarrow_T$ is the right-quotient operation. If $T = 1^*0^*$, then $\rightsquigarrow_T$ is the left-quotient operation, while if $T = (0+1)^*$, then $\rightsquigarrow_T$ is the scattered deletion operation (see, e.g., Ito *et al.* [19]).

The main motivation for the introduction of $\rightsquigarrow_T$ is that it serves as an inverse to $\sqcup\!\sqcup_T$ in the sense of Kari [22]. Thus, we note that by using these inverses, language equations such as, for example,

$$X \sqcup\!\sqcup_T R_1 = R_2$$

or

$$R_1 \rightsquigarrow_T X = R_2$$

are solvable if R_1, R_2 and T are regular languages. We refer the reader to the survey [10] for pointers to results on one-variable language equations involving shuffle and deletion along trajectories.

3.3   Language Decomposition Involving Trajectories

We now consider language equations with two variables involving shuffle on trajectories. In particular, we are interested in the equation

$$L = X_1 \sqcup\!\sqcup_T X_2.$$

where L is a constant language and X_1, X_2 are unknowns. We are interested in the effect of the complexity of L and T on the decidability of the existence of solutions to this equation.

For example, if $T = 0^*1^*$, then we get the equation

$$L = X_1 X_2 \tag{2}$$

where L is a fixed language and X_1, X_2 are unknown. This is the language equation corresponding to the decomposition problem studied in Section 2.

It is known that if L is a regular language, we can determine if a solution to (2) exists. Furthermore, as seen in Section 2, we know that if a solution X_1, X_2 exists, there exists a maximal regular solution; i.e., there exists R_1, R_2 such that $X_i \subseteq R_i$ for $i = 1, 2$ and $L = R_1 R_2$.

To contrast equation (2), we note that if $T = \{0, 1\}^*$, then the equation obtained is

$$L = X_1 \sqcup\!\sqcup X_2. \tag{3}$$

The problem of, given L, do non-trivial X_1 and X_2 exist satisfying equation (3) is an open problem, despite a significant amount of attention. The problem appears to first have been considered by Mateescu, and was studied by Câmpeanu *et al.* [2] and Ito [18].

With the problem (3) in mind, it is clear that no general result, applicable to all T, is known about the equation $L = X_1 \sqcup\!\sqcup_T X_2$. It is an open problem to determine necessary and sufficient conditions on a set of trajectories T such that it is decidable whether a nontrivial decomposition of an input language L exists. Here, we recall results which are applicable to a class of trajectories which ensures decidability [12,9].

Recall that a language $L \subseteq \Sigma^*$ is *bounded* if there exist $w_1, w_2, \ldots, w_n \in \Sigma^*$ such that $L \subseteq w_1^* w_2^* \cdots w_n^*$. We further say that L is *letter-bounded* if we can choose $w_i \in \Sigma$ for all $1 \leq i \leq n$; that is, if $L \subseteq a_1^* a_2^* \cdots a_n^*$ for $a_i \in \Sigma$ for $1 \leq i \leq n$. Thus, for example, the set $T = 0^*1^*0^*$ is letter-bounded, while $T = (01)^*$ is bounded (but not letter-bounded) while it is known that $T = (0+1)^*$ is not bounded. The following result is due to the authors [12,9].

Theorem 4. *Let $T \subseteq \{0, 1\}^*$ be a letter-bounded regular set of trajectories. Then given a regular language R, it is decidable whether there exist X_1, X_2 such that $X_1 \sqcup\!\sqcup_T X_2 = R$.*

The main tool for proving Theorem 4 is the following lemma [12]:

Lemma 1. *Let $T \subseteq \{0, 1\}^*$ be a letter-bounded regular set of trajectories. Then for all regular languages R, there are only finitely many regular languages L'*

such that $L' = R \leadsto_T L$ for some language L. Furthermore, given effective constructions for T and R, we can effectively construct a finite set $\mathcal{S}$ of regular languages such that if $L' = R \leadsto_T L$ for some language L, then $L' \in \mathcal{S}$.

Thus, if we are provided a regular language R and a set of trajectories T, and wish to determine if there exist X_1 and X_2 such that $R = X_1 \sqcup\!\sqcup_T X_2$, Lemma 1 shows that there are only finitely many choices for each X_1 and X_2. As we have mentioned, Theorem 4 was known for catenation, $T = 0^*1^*$. However, it also holds for, e.g., the following operations: insertion $(0^*1^*0^*)$, k-insertion $(0^*1^*0^{\leq k}$ for fixed $k \geq 0)$, and bi-catenation $(1^*0^* + 0^*1^*)$, which were previously unknown.

We also note that if the equation $X_1 \sqcup\!\sqcup_T X_2 = R$ has a solution, where R is a regular language and T is a letter-bounded regular set of trajectories, then the equation also has solution $Y_1 \sqcup\!\sqcup_T Y_2 = R$ where Y_1, Y_2 are regular languages. This result is well-known for $T = 0^*1^*$ (see, e.g., Choffrut and Karhumäki [3]).

We recall that, as mentioned, for $T = (0+1)^*$, the two-variable decomposition problem is open [2]:

Open problem 3.1. *Given a regular language R, is it decidable whether there exist X_1, X_2 (with $X_1, X_2 \neq \{\epsilon\}$) such that $R = X_1 \sqcup\!\sqcup X_2$?*

We now turn to another class of trajectories for which we can give positive decidability results about the shuffle decomposition problem. Recall that a language L is k-thin if $|L \cap \Sigma^n| \leq k$ for all $n \geq 0$. The authors [13] have shown that if $T \subseteq \{0,1\}^*$ is a 1-thin set of trajectories, given a regular language R, it is decidable whether there exist X_1 and X_2 such that $R = X_1 \sqcup\!\sqcup_T X_2$. However, even for 2-thin sets of trajectories, the problem remains open [13]:

Open problem 3.2. *Given a k-thin ($k \geq 2$) set of trajectories $T \subseteq \{0,1\}^*$, is it decidable, given a regular language R, whether R has a shuffle decomposition with respect to T?*

3.4   Unary Languages

For unary languages, the class of sets of trajectories for which the decomposition problem is decidable is much enlarged compared to binary alphabets, due to the fact that sets of trajectories are equivalent with respect to unary languages if and only if their commutative images are equal [13]. Let Ψ be the Parikh mapping. We say that two sets of trajectories T_1 and T_2 are *letter-equivalent* if and only if $\Psi(T_1) = \Psi(T_2)$. The following result [13] shows that letter-equivalence is sufficient to decide the shuffle decomposition problem for unary regular languages:

Theorem 5. *Let T_1 and T_2 be letter-equivalent sets of trajectories. If T_1 is letter-bounded, then given a unary regular language R, it is decidable whether there exist X_1, X_2 such that $R = X_1 \sqcup\!\sqcup_{T_2} X_2$.*

Note that T_2 is not required to be regular in this theorem. However, this result is not enough to characterize the sets of trajectories for which the unary version of the shuffle decomposition problem is decidable:

Open problem 3.3. *Given a regular set of trajectories $T \subseteq \{0,1\}^*$:*

(a) can we decide whether T is letter equivalent to a letter-bounded regular set of trajectories?
(b) if so, can we effectively find such a letter-bounded regular set of trajectories?

3.5   Undecidability of Decomposition Problems

We now turn to undecidability. It has been shown [2] that it is undecidable whether a context-free language has a nontrivial shuffle decomposition with respect to the set of trajectories $\{0,1\}^*$. This result can be extended for arbitrary complete regular sets trajectories [12]. (Note that if T is a complete set of trajectories, then any language L has decompositions $L \sqcup_T \{\epsilon\}$ and $\{\epsilon\} \sqcup_T L$. Below we exclude these trivial decompositions; all other decompositions of L are said to be nontrivial.)

Theorem 6. *Let T be any fixed complete regular set of trajectories. For a given context-free language L it is undecidable whether or not there exist languages $X_1, X_2 \neq \{\epsilon\}$ such that $L = X_1 \sqcup_T X_2$.*

3.6   Open Problems

Without trying to be exhaustive, we note some open problems related to shuffle decomposition. These problems are in addition to those noted above (in particular, the shuffle decomposition problem for arbitrary shuffle and for 2-thin sets of trajectories).

The first open problem arises from a result of the authors [13]:

Theorem 7. *There exists a fixed linear context-free set of trajectories T_0 such that it is undecidable whether $L = R_1 \sqcup_{T_0} X$ has a solution X for given regular languages L, R_1 over a given alphabet Σ.*

This result is interesting as it provides a rare example of a problem whose inputs are regular languages, but which is undecidable (another example is given by Hinz and Dassow [17]). However, the related shuffle decomposition problem is open:

Open problem 3.4. *Is it possible to construct a fixed context-free set of trajectories T such that for a given regular language L it is undecidable whether there exist languages $X_1, X_2 \neq \{\epsilon\}$ such that $L = X_1 \sqcup_T X_2$?*

Also open are other forms of language equations more general than we have considered above. We mention only two here:

Open problem 3.5. *Find necessary and sufficient conditions on sets of trajectories T_1, T_2 so that, given a regular language R, it is decidable whether there exist nontrivial languages X_1, X_2, X_3 satisfying $(X_1 \sqcup_{T_1} X_2) \sqcup_{T_2} X_3 = R$.*

Open problem 3.6. *Given regular languages R_1, R_2, is it decidable whether there exists nontrivial languages X_1, T (with $T \subseteq \{0,1\}^*$) such that $X_1 \sqcup_T R_1 = R_2$ or $R_1 \sqcup_T X_1 = R_2$?*

References

1. Anselmo, M., Restivo, A.: On languages factorizing the free monoid. Internat. J. Algebra and Computation 6, 413–427 (1996)
2. Câmpeanu, C., Salomaa, K., Vágvölgyi, S.: Shuffle decompositions of regular languages. Internat. J. Foundations of Computer Science 13, 799–816 (2002)
3. Choffrut, C., Karhumäki, J.: Fatou properties of rational languages. In: Martin-Vide, C., Mitrana, V. (eds.) Where Mathematics, Computer Science, Linguistics and Biology Meet, pp. 227–235 (2000)
4. Conway, J.H.: Regular Algebra and Finite Machines. Chapman and Hall, Boca Raton (1971)
5. Czyzowicz, J., Fraczak, W., Pelc, A., Rytter, W.: Linear-time prime decomposition of regular prefix codes. Internat. J. Foundations of Computer Science 14, 1019–1031 (2003)
6. Daley, M., Domaratzki, M., Salomaa, K.: Orthogonal concatenation: Language equations and state complexity. J. Universal Comput. Sci. 16, 653–675 (2010)
7. Domaratzki, M.: Semantic shuffle on and deletion along trajectories. In: Calude, C.S., Calude, E., Dinneen, M.J. (eds.) DLT 2004. LNCS, vol. 3340, pp. 163–174. Springer, Heidelberg (2004)
8. Domaratzki, M.: Deletion along trajectories. Theoret. Comput. Sci. 320, 293–313 (2004)
9. Domaratzki, M.: Trajectory-Based Operations. PhD thesis, Queen's University (2004)
10. Domaratzki, M.: More Words on Trajectories. Formal Language Theory Column, Bull. Eur. Assoc. Theor. Comp. Sci. 86, 107–145 (2005)
11. Domaratzki, M., Rozenberg, G., Salomaa, K.: Interpreted trajectories. Fundamenta Informaticae 73, 182–193 (2006)
12. Domaratzki, M., Salomaa, K.: Decidability of trajectory-based equations. Theoret. Comput. Sci. 345, 304–330 (2005)
13. Domaratzki, M., Salomaa, K.: Restricted sets of trajectories and decidability of shuffle decompositions. Internat. J. Foundations of Computer Science 16, 897–912 (2005)
14. Frid, A.: Commutation of binary factorial languages. In: Harju, T., Karhumäki, J., Lepistö, A. (eds.) DLT 2007. LNCS, vol. 4588, pp. 193–204. Springer, Heidelberg (2007)
15. Han, Y.-S., Salomaa, A., Salomaa, K., Wood, D., Yu, S.: On the existence of prime decompositions. Theoret. Comput. Sci. 376, 60–69 (2007)
16. Han, Y.-S., Wang, Y., Wood, D.: Infix-free regular expressions and languages. Internat. J. Found. Comput. Sci. 17, 379–393 (2006)
17. Hinz, F., Dassow, J.: An undecidability result for regular languages and its application to regulated rewriting. Bulletin of the EATCS 38, 168–174 (1989)
18. Ito, M.: Shuffle decomposition of regular languages. J. Universal Comput. Sci. 8, 257–259 (2002)
19. Ito, M., Kari, L., Thierrin, G.: Shuffle and scattered deletion closure of languages. Theor. Comp. Sci. 245, 115–133 (2000)
20. Jiang, T., Ravikumar, B.: Minimal NFA problems are hard. SIAM J. Comput. 22, 1117–1141 (1993)
21. Karhumäki, J., Petre, I.: Two problems on commutation of languages. In: Current Trends in Theoretical Computer Science– The Challenge of the New Century, vol. 2, pp. 477–494. World Scientific, Singapore (2004)

22. Kari, L.: On language equations with invertible operations. Theor. Comp. Sci. 132, 129–150 (1994)
23. Kari, L., Konstantinidis, S.: Language equations, maximality and error-detection. J. Comput. System Sci. 70, 157–178 (2005)
24. Kari, L., Sosík, P.: Aspects of shuffle and deletion on trajectories. Theoret. Comput. Sci. 332, 47–61 (2005)
25. Kari, L., Thierrin, G.: Maximal and minimal solutions to language equations. J. Comput. System Sci. 53, 487–496 (1996)
26. Kunc, M.: What do we know about language equations? In: Harju, T., Karhumäki, J., Lepistö, A. (eds.) DLT 2007. LNCS, vol. 4588, pp. 23–27. Springer, Heidelberg (2007)
27. Martens, W., Niewerth, M., Schwentick, T.: Schema design for XML repositories: Complexity and tractability. In: Proceedings of ACM Symposium on Principles of Database Systems, PODS 2010, June 6–11 (2010)
28. Mateescu, A., Rozenberg, G., Salomaa, A.: Shuffle on trajectories: Syntactic constraints. Theoret. Comput. Sci. 197, 1–56 (1998)
29. Mateescu, A., Salomaa, A., Yu, S.: Factorizations of languages and commutativity conditions. Acta Cybernetica 15, 339–351 (2002)
30. Meyer, A.R., Stockmeyer, L.J.: The equivalence problem for regular expressions with squaring requires exponential time. In: Symposium on Switching and Automata Theory, SWAT 1972, pp. 125–129. IEEE Society Press, Los Alamitos (1972)
31. Okhotin, A.: Decision problems for language equations. J. Comput. System Sci. 76, 251–266 (2010)
32. Perrin, D.: Codes conjugués. Inform. and Control 20, 221–231 (1972)
33. Rampersad, N., Ravikumar, B., Santean, N., Shallit, J.: State complexity of unique rational operations. Theoret. Comput. Sci. 410, 2431–2441 (2009)
34. Rampersad, N., Shallit, J.: Private communication (2006)
35. Salomaa, A., Salomaa, K., Yu, S.: Variants of codes and indecomposable languages. Information and Computation 207, 1340–1349 (2009)
36. Salomaa, A., Yu, S.: On the decomposition of finite languages. In: Proc. Developments in Language Theory, DLT 1999, pp. 22–31. World Scientific Publ. Co., Singapore (2000)
37. Shallit, J.: A Second Course in Formal Languages and Automata Theory. Cambridge University Press, Cambridge (2009)
38. Yu, S.: Regular languages. In: Rozenberg, G., Salomaa, A. (eds.) Handbook of Formal Languages, vol. I, pp. 41–110. Springer, Heidelberg (1997)

A Unifying Kleene Theorem for Weighted Finite Automata

Zoltán Ésik[1,*] and Werner Kuich[2,**]

[1] Dept. of Computer Science, University of Szeged, Hungary
[2] Institut für Diskrete Mathematik und Geometrie,
Technische Universität Wien, Austria

Abstract. We state two variants of the Theorem of Kleene-Schützenberger: one for arbitrary semirings and proper finite automata; the other for Conway semirings and arbitrary finite automata. Considering finite automata over partial Conway semirings over an ideal, we show that these two variants are special cases of a unifying theorem.

1 Introduction

In this paper we develop the theory of weighted finite automata by an algebraic treatment using semirings, formal power series and matrices. By the use of these mathematical constructs, definitions, constructions, and proofs are obtained that are very satisfactory from a mathematical point of view. The use of these mathematical constructs yields the following advantages:

(i) The constructions needed in the proofs are mainly the usual ones.
(ii) The proofs are separated from the constructions and do not need the intuitive contents of the constructions. Often they are shorter than the usual proofs.
(iii) The results are more general than the usual ones. Depending on the semiring used, the results are valid for classical finite automata, finite automata with ambiguity considerations, probabilistic finite automata, etc.

The reader is assumed to have some basic knowledge of finite automata (see Maurer [15], Hopcroft, Ullman [10], Salomaa [16]).

The paper consists of this and three more sections.

In Section 2 we introduce the algebraic structures needed: partial Conway semirings over an ideal, and power series and matrices over these semirings.

Finite automata are introduced in Section 3. Starting with the classical nondeterministic finite automaton and Kleene's Theorem we generalize to (weighted)

---

[*] Partially supported by the TÁMOP-4.2.1/B-09/1/KONV-2010-0005 program of National Development Agency of Hungary, the Austrian-Hungarian Action Foundation, grant 77öu9, and the National Foundation of Hungary for Scientific Research, grant no. K 75249.
[**] Partially supported by the Austrian-Hungarian Action Foundation, grant 77öu9.

C.S. Calude, G. Rozenberg, A. Salomaa (Eds.): Maurer Festschrift, LNCS 6570, pp. 76–89, 2011.

finite automata over a semiring with two variants of the Theorem of Kleene-Schützenberger.

In the last section, we generalize again and prove a Kleene type theorem unifying these two variants of the Theorem of Kleene-Schützenberger.

2   Preliminaries

By a *semiring* we mean a set S together with two binary operations $+$ and $\cdot$ and two constant elements 0 and 1 such that

- (i) $\langle S, +, 0 \rangle$ is a commutative monoid,
- (ii) $\langle S, \cdot, 1 \rangle$ is a monoid,
- (iii) the distributivity laws $s_1 \cdot (s_2 + s_3) = s_1 \cdot s_2 + s_1 \cdot s_3$ and $(s_1 + s_2) \cdot s_3 = s_1 \cdot s_3 + s_2 \cdot s_3$ hold for every $s_1, s_2, s_3 \in S$,
- (iv) $0 \cdot s = s \cdot 0 = 0$ for every $s \in S$.

If the operations and the constant elements of S are understood then we denote the semiring simply by S. Otherwise, we use the notation $\langle S, +, \cdot, 0, 1 \rangle$. In the sequel, S will denote a semiring.

Intuitively, a semiring is a ring (with unity) without subtraction. A typical example is the semiring of nonnegative integers $\mathbb{N}$. A very important semiring in connection with language theory is the *Boolean* semiring $\mathbb{B} = \{0, 1\}$ where $1 + 1 = 1 \cdot 1 = 1$. Clearly, all rings (with unity), as well as all fields, are semirings, e. g., integers $\mathbb{Z}$, rationals $\mathbb{Q}$, reals $\mathbb{R}$, complex numbers $\mathbb{C}$ etc.

Let $\mathbb{N}^{\infty} = \mathbb{N} \cup \{\infty\}$. Then $\langle \mathbb{N}^{\infty}, +, \cdot, 0, 1 \rangle$ and $\langle \mathbb{N}^{\infty}, \min, +, \infty, 0 \rangle$, where $+, \cdot$ and min are defined in the obvious fashion (observe that $0 \cdot \infty = \infty \cdot 0 = 0$), are semirings.

Let $\mathbb{R}_+ = \{a \in \mathbb{R} \mid a \geq 0\}$ and $\mathbb{R}_+^{\infty} = \mathbb{R}_+ \cup \{\infty\}$. Then $\langle \mathbb{R}_+, +, \cdot, 0, 1 \rangle$, $\langle \mathbb{R}_+^{\infty}, +, \cdot, 0, 1 \rangle$ and $\langle \mathbb{R}_+^{\infty}, \min, +, \infty, 0 \rangle$ are all semirings. Moreover, the semirings $\langle \mathbb{N}_+^{\infty}, \min, +, \infty, 0 \rangle$, $\langle \mathbb{R}_+^{\infty}, \min, +, \infty, 0 \rangle$ are called *tropical semirings*. A further example is provided by the semiring $\langle [0, 1], \max, \cdot, 0, 1 \rangle$, where max has its usual meaning.

Let Σ be a finite alphabet and denote by Σ^* the free monoid of all words over Σ including the empty word ε. Then each subset of Σ^* is called *formal language over* Σ. We define, for formal languages $L_1, L_2 \subseteq \Sigma^*$, the *product* of L_1 and L_2 by

$$L_1 \cdot L_2 = \{w_1 w_2 \mid w_1 \in L_1, w_2 \in L_2\}.$$

Then $\langle 2^{\Sigma^*}, \cup, \cdot, \emptyset, \{\varepsilon\} \rangle$ is a semiring, called the *semiring of formal languages over* Σ. Here 2^U denotes the power set of the set U and $\emptyset$ denotes the empty set.

If U is a set, $2^{U \times U}$ is the set of binary relations over U. Define, for two relations R_1 and R_2, the product $R_1 \cdot R_2 \subseteq U \times U$ by

$$R_1 \cdot R_2 = \{(u_1, u_2) \mid \text{there exists an } u \in U \text{ such that}$$
$$(u_1, u) \in R_1 \text{ and } (u, u_2) \in R_2\}$$

and, furthermore, define

$$\Delta = \{(u, u) \mid u \in U\}.$$

Then $\langle 2^{U \times U}, \cup, \cdot, \emptyset, \Delta \rangle$ is a semiring, called the *semiring of binary relations over* U.

We will call a *star semiring* any semiring equipped with an additional unary operation $*$.

A semiring $(S, +, \cdot, 0, 1)$ is called *complete* if it has sums for all families $(s_i \mid i \in I)$ of elements of S, where I is an arbitrary index set, such that the following conditions are satisfied:

(i) $\sum_{i \in \emptyset} s_i = 0$, $\sum_{i \in \{j\}} s_i = s_j$, $\sum_{i \in \{j,k\}} s_i = s_j + s_k$, for $j \neq k$,

(ii) $\sum_{j \in J}(\sum_{i \in I_j} s_i) = \sum_{i \in I} s_i$, if $\bigcup_{j \in J} I_j = I$ and $I_j \cap I_{j'} = \emptyset$ for $j \neq j'$,

(iii) $\sum_{i \in I}(s \cdot s_i) = s \cdot \left(\sum_{i \in I} s_i\right)$, $\sum_{i \in I}(s_i \cdot s) = \left(\sum_{i \in I} s_i\right) \cdot s$.

This means that a semiring S is complete if it is possible to define "infinite sums" (i) that are an extension of the finite sums, (ii) that are associative and commutative and (iii) that satisfy the distributivity laws (see Bloom, Ésik [2], Conway [4], Eilenberg [6], Kuich [13]).

Recall that in formal language theory, the Kleene-iteration L^* of a language $L \subseteq \Sigma^*$ is defined by $L^* = \bigcup_{n \geq 0} L^n$. Analogously, in complete semirings for each element s we can define the *star* s^* of s by

$$s^* = \sum_{j \geq 0} s^j,$$

where $s^0 = 1$ and $s^{j+1} = s \cdot s^j = s^j \cdot s$ for $j \geq 0$. Hence, with this star operation, each complete semiring is a star semiring called a *complete star semiring*.

The following semirings are complete star semirings:

(i) The Boolean semiring $\langle \mathbb{B}, +, \cdot, *, 0, 1 \rangle$ with $0^* = 1^* = 1$.

(ii) The semiring $\langle \mathbb{N}^\infty, +, \cdot, *, 0, 1 \rangle$ with $0^* = 1$ and $a^* = \infty$ for $a \neq 0$.

(iii) The semiring $\langle \mathbb{R}_+^\infty, +, \cdot, *, 0, 1 \rangle$ with $a^* = 1/(1-a)$ for $0 \leq a < 1$ and $a^* = \infty$ for $a \geq 1$.

(iv) The tropical semirings $\langle \mathbb{R}_+^\infty, \min, +, *, \infty, 0 \rangle$ and $\langle \mathbb{N}^\infty, \min, +, *, \infty, 0 \rangle$ with $a^* = 0$ for all $a \in \mathbb{R}_+^\infty$ resp. all $a \in \mathbb{N}^\infty$.

(v) The semiring $\langle 2^{\Sigma^*}, \cup, \cdot, *, \emptyset, \{\varepsilon\} \rangle$ of formal languages over a finite alphabet Σ with $L^* = \bigcup_{n \geq 0} L^n$ for all $L \subseteq \Sigma^*$.

(vi) The semiring $\langle 2^{U \times U}, \cup, \cdot, *, \emptyset, \Delta \rangle$ of binary relations over U with star operation defined by $R^* = \bigcup_{n \geq 0} R^n$ for all $R \subseteq U \times U$. The relation R^* is called the *reflexive and transitive closure* of R, i.e., the smallest reflexive and transitive binary relation over U containing R.

We now define formal power series (see Kuich, Salomaa [14]). Let Σ be a (finite) alphabet. Mappings r from Σ^* into S are called *(formal) power series*. The values of r are denoted by (r, w), where $w \in \Sigma^*$, and r itself is written as a formal sum

$$r = \sum_{w \in \Sigma^*} (r, w)w.$$

The values (r, w) are also referred to as the *coefficients* of the series. The collection of all power series r as defined above is denoted by $S\langle\!\langle \Sigma^* \rangle\!\rangle$.

Given $r \in S\langle\!\langle \Sigma^* \rangle\!\rangle$, the subset of Σ^* defined by

$$\{w \mid (r, w) \neq 0\}$$

is termed the *support* of r and denoted by $\mathrm{supp}(r)$. The subset of $S\langle\!\langle \Sigma^* \rangle\!\rangle$ consisting of all series with a finite support is denoted by $S\langle \Sigma^* \rangle$. Series of $S\langle \Sigma^* \rangle$ are referred to as *polynomials*.

Examples of polynomials belonging to $S\langle \Sigma^* \rangle$ for every S are 0, w, sw, $s \in S$, $w \in \Sigma^*$, defined by:

$$(0, w) = 0 \text{ for all } w,$$
$$(w, w) = 1 \text{ and } (w, w') = 0 \text{ for } w \neq w',$$
$$(sw, w) = s \text{ and } (sw, w') = 0 \text{ for } w \neq w'.$$

Note that w equals $1w$.

We introduce two operations inducing a semiring structure to power series. For $r_1, r_2 \in S\langle\!\langle \Sigma^* \rangle\!\rangle$, we define the *sum* $r_1 + r_2 \in S\langle\!\langle \Sigma^* \rangle\!\rangle$ by $(r_1 + r_2, w) = (r_1, w) + (r_2, w)$ for all $w \in \Sigma^*$. For $r_1, r_2 \in S\langle\!\langle \Sigma^* \rangle\!\rangle$, we define the *(Cauchy) product* $r_1 r_2 \in S\langle\!\langle \Sigma^* \rangle\!\rangle$ by $(r_1 r_2, w) = \sum_{w_1 w_2 = w} (r_1, w_1)(r_2, w_2)$ for all $w \in \Sigma^*$. Clearly, $\langle S\langle\!\langle \Sigma^* \rangle\!\rangle, +, \cdot, 0, \varepsilon \rangle$ and $\langle S\langle \Sigma^* \rangle, +, \cdot, 0, \varepsilon \rangle$ are semirings.

For $s \in S$, $r \in S\langle\!\langle \Sigma^* \rangle\!\rangle$, we define the *scalar products* $sr, rs \in S\langle\!\langle \Sigma^* \rangle\!\rangle$ by $(sr, w) = s(r, w)$ and $(rs, w) = (r, w)s$ for all $w \in \Sigma^*$. Observe that $sr = (s\varepsilon)r$ and $rs = r(s\varepsilon)$.

A series $r \in S\langle\!\langle \Sigma^* \rangle\!\rangle$, where every coefficient equals 0 or 1, is termed the *characteristic series* of its support L, in symbols, $r = \mathrm{char}(L)$.

It will be convenient to use the notations $S\langle \Sigma \cup \{\varepsilon\} \rangle$, $S\langle \Sigma \rangle$ and $S\langle \{\varepsilon\} \rangle$ for the collection of polynomials having their supports in $\Sigma \cup \{\varepsilon\}$, Σ and $\{\varepsilon\}$, respectively.

Let $r_i \in S\langle\!\langle \Sigma^* \rangle\!\rangle$, $i \in I$, where I is an arbitrary index set. Then, for $w \in \Sigma^*$ let $I_w = \{i \mid (r_i, w) \neq 0\}$. Assume now that for all $w \in \Sigma^*$, I_w is finite. Then we call the family of power series $\{r_i \mid i \in I\}$ *locally finite*. In this case we can define the sum $\sum_{i \in I} r_i$ by

$$\left(\sum_{i \in I} r_i, w\right) = \sum_{i \in I_w} (r_i, w)$$

for all $w \in \Sigma^*$.

A power series $r \in S\langle\!\langle \Sigma^* \rangle\!\rangle$ is called *proper* if $(r, \varepsilon) = 0$. The *star* r^* of a proper power series $r \in S\langle\!\langle \Sigma^* \rangle\!\rangle$ is defined by

$$r^* = \sum_{n \geq 0} r^n .$$

Since r is proper we infer $(r^n, w) = 0$ for each $n > |w|$. Hence, $\{r^n \mid n \geq 0\}$ is locally finite, $(r^*, w) = \sum_{0 \leq n \leq |w|} (r^n, w)$, and the star of a proper power series is well-defined.

We now introduce matrices. Let $m, n \geq 1$. Mappings A from $\{1, \ldots, m\} \times \{1, \ldots, n\}$ into a semiring S are called *matrices* over S. The values of A are denoted by A_{ij}, where $1 \leq i \leq m$, $1 \leq j \leq n$. The values A_{ij} are also referred to as the *entries* of the matrix A. In particular, A_{ij} is called the (i, j)-*entry* of A. The collection of all matrices as defined above is denoted by $S^{m \times n}$. If $m = 1$ or $n = 1$ then A is called *row* or *column vector*, respecively.

We introduce some operations and special matrices inducing a monoid or semiring structure to matrices. For $A_1, A_2 \in S^{m \times n}$ we define the *sum* $A_1 + A_2 \in S^{m \times n}$ by $(A_1 + A_2)_{ij} = (A_1)_{ij} + (A_2)_{ij}$ for all $1 \leq i \leq m$, $1 \leq j \leq n$. Furthermore, we introduce the *zero matrix* $0 \in S^{m \times n}$. All entries of the zero matrix 0 are 0. By these definitions, $\langle S^{m \times n}, +, 0 \rangle$ is a commutative monoid.

For $A_1 \in S^{m \times n}$ and $A_2 \in S^{n \times p}$ we define the *product* $A_1 A_2 \in S^{m \times p}$ by

$$(A_1 A_2)_{i_1 i_3} = \sum_{1 \leq i_2 \leq n} (A_1)_{i_1 i_2} (A_2)_{i_2 i_3} \qquad \text{for all } 1 \leq i_1 \leq m, \, 1 \leq i_3 \leq p.$$

Furthermore, we introduce the *matrix of unity* $E \in S^{n \times n}$. The diagonal entries E_{ii} of E are equal to 1, the off-diagonal entries $E_{i_1 i_2}$, $i_1 \neq i_2$, of E are equal to 0, $1 \leq i, i_1, i_2 \leq n$.

It is easily shown that matrix multiplication is associative, the distributivity laws are valid for matrix addition and multiplication, E is a multiplicative unit and 0 is a multiplicative zero. So we infer that $\langle S^{n \times n}, +, \cdot, 0, E \rangle$ is a semiring for each $n \geq 1$.

Suppose that S is a semiring and I is an ideal of S, so that $0 \in I$, $I + I \subseteq I$ and $IS \cup SI \subseteq I$. Observe that $I = S$ iff $1 \in I$. A *partial star semiring S over the ideal I* is a semiring S equipped with a star operation $^* : I \to S$.

If S is a partial star semiring over the ideal I, we define, for $r \in S\langle\langle \Sigma^* \rangle\rangle$ with $(r, \varepsilon) \in I$, the star $r^* \in S\langle\langle \Sigma^* \rangle\rangle$ of r inductively as follows:

$$(r^*, \varepsilon) = (r, \varepsilon)^*, \quad (r^*, w) = (r, \varepsilon)^* \sum_{uv = w, \, u \neq \varepsilon} (r, u)(r^*, v), \; w \in \Sigma^*, \; w \neq \varepsilon.$$

(See Theorem 3.5 of Kuich, Salomaa [14] and Bloom, Ésik [2].) If $\langle S, +, \cdot, {}^*, 0, 1 \rangle$ is a star semiring then the *star operation* in the star semiring $\langle S\langle\langle \Sigma^* \rangle\rangle, +, \cdot, {}^*, 0, \varepsilon \rangle$ will be always defined as above.

Let S be a partial star semiring over the ideal I. Then for $A \in I^{n \times n}$ we define $A^* \in S^{n \times n}$ inductively as follows:

(i) For $n = 1$ and $A = (a)$, $a \in I$, we define $A^* = (a^*)$.

(ii) For $n > 1$ we partition A into blocks $A = \begin{pmatrix} a & b \\ c & d \end{pmatrix}$ with $a \in I^{1 \times 1}$, $b \in I^{1 \times (n-1)}$, $c \in I^{(n-1) \times 1}$, $d \in I^{(n-1) \times (n-1)}$, and define $A^* = \begin{pmatrix} \alpha & \beta \\ \gamma & \delta \end{pmatrix}$ with $\alpha \in S^{1 \times 1}$, $\beta \in S^{1 \times (n-1)}$, $\gamma \in S^{(n-1) \times 1}$, $\delta \in S^{(n-1) \times (n-1)}$, by

$$\alpha = (a + bd^*c)^*, \quad \beta = \alpha bd^*, \quad \gamma = \delta ca^*, \quad \delta = (d + ca^*b)^*.$$

(See Theorem 3.3 of Conway [4], Theorem 4.21 of Kuich, Salomaa [14], Bloom, Ésik [2] and Theorem 2.5 of Kuich [13].) If $\langle S, +, \cdot, *, 0, 1 \rangle$ is a star semiring then the *star operation* in the star semiring $\langle S^{n \times n}, +, \cdot, *, 0, E \rangle$ will always be defined as above.

In Bloom, Ésik, Kuich [3], a *partial Conway semiring* S *over the ideal* I is defined as a partial star semiring S over I satisfying the following two axioms:

1. *Sum star identity*:
$$(a + b)^* = a^*(ba^*)^*$$
   for all $a, b \in I$.

2. *Product star identity*:
$$(ab)^* = 1 + a(ba)^*b$$
   for all $a, b \in S$ such that $a \in I$ or $b \in I$.

A *Conway semiring* is a partial Conway semiring S which is a star semiring (i.e., $I = S$).

When $a \in I$ we will denote $aa^* = a^*a$ by a^+ and call $^+$ the *plus* operation.

Example. Let S be a semiring and Σ be an alphabet. Clearly, the collection of proper power series of $S\langle\langle \Sigma^* \rangle\rangle$ forms an ideal $I = \{ r \in S\langle\langle \Sigma^* \rangle\rangle \mid (r, \varepsilon) = 0 \}$. Moreover, $S\langle\langle \Sigma^* \rangle\rangle$ is a partial star semiring over I that is also a partial Conway semiring over I (see Droste, Kuich [5]).

It is known (Conway [4], Bloom, Ésik [2], Ésik, Kuich [8]) that when S is a Conway semiring then $S\langle\langle \Sigma^* \rangle\rangle$, Σ an alphabet, and $S^{n \times n}$, $n \geq 1$, are again Conway semirings. More generally, but with the same proofs, we have:

Theorem 1. *Suppose that S is a partial Conway semiring over the ideal I. Then*

(i) $S\langle\langle \Sigma^* \rangle\rangle$, Σ *an alphabet, is a partial Conway semiring over the ideal* $\{ r \in S\langle\langle \Sigma^* \rangle\rangle \mid (r, \varepsilon) \in I \}$;

(ii) $S^{n \times n}$, $n \geq 1$, *is a partial Conway semiring over the ideal* $I^{n \times n}$. *Moreover, the* matrix star identity *holds in* $S^{n \times n}$:
$$\begin{pmatrix} a & b \\ c & d \end{pmatrix}^* = \begin{pmatrix} \alpha & \beta \\ \gamma & \delta \end{pmatrix}$$

for all possible decompositions of a sqare matrix in $I^{n \times n}$ into a, b, c, d. Here $\alpha, \beta, \gamma, \delta$ are as in the definition of the star of a matrix.

For later use, we state the following theorem.

Theorem 2. *Suppose that S is a partial Conway semiring over the ideal I. If*
$$A = \begin{pmatrix} a & b \\ c & d \end{pmatrix} \in I^{n \times n}$$

then
$$A^+ = \begin{pmatrix} (a + bd^*c)^+ & (a + bd^*c)^*bd^* \\ (d + ca^*b)^*ca^* & (d + ca^*b)^+ \end{pmatrix} \in I^{n \times n}.$$

If $\langle S, +, \cdot, 0, 1 \rangle$ is a complete semiring, then so are $\langle S\langle\!\langle \Sigma^* \rangle\!\rangle, +, \cdot, 0, \varepsilon \rangle$ and $\langle S^{n \times n}, +, \cdot, 0, E \rangle$ by the following definitions:

If $r_i \in S\langle\!\langle \Sigma^* \rangle\!\rangle$ for $i \in J$, then $\sum_{i \in J} r_i = \sum_{w \in \Sigma^*} \left(\sum_{i \in J} (r_i, w) \right) w$;

if $A_i \in S^{n \times n}$ for $i \in J$, then $\left(\sum_{i \in J} A_i \right)_{kj} = \sum_{i \in J} (A_i)_{kj}$ for $1 \leq k, j \leq n$.

Here J is an arbitrary index set. Moreover, each complete star semiring is a Conway semiring (see Conway [4], Bloom, Ésik [2], Kuich [12], Hebisch [9]) and the star operation in the complete semirings $S\langle\!\langle \Sigma^* \rangle\!\rangle$ and $S^{n \times n}$ is the same as the star operation in the Conway semirings $S\langle\!\langle \Sigma^* \rangle\!\rangle$ and $S^{n \times n}$, respectively. Hence, the semirings (i)–(vi) are all Conway semirings.

3   Finite Automata

Usually, a nondeterministic finite automaton without ε-moves is defined as follows (see Maurer [15], Hopcroft, Ullman [10]). A *nondeterministic finite automaton* (in the classical sense)

$$\mathcal{A} = (Q, \Sigma, \delta, q_1, F)$$

is given by

  (i)   a finite nonempty *set of states Q*,
 (ii)   an *input alphabet Σ*,
(iii)   a *transition function $\delta : Q \times \Sigma \to 2^Q$*,
 (iv)   an *initial state $q_1 \in Q$*,
  (v)   a *set of final states $F \subseteq Q$*.

The transition function δ is extended to a mapping $\hat{\delta} : Q \times \Sigma^* \to 2^Q$ by

$$\hat{\delta}(q, \varepsilon) = \{q\}, \quad \hat{\delta}(q, wx) = \{p \mid p \in \delta(r, x) \text{ for some } r \in \hat{\delta}(q, w)\},$$

for $q \in Q$, $w \in \Sigma^*$ and $x \in \Sigma$.

A word $w \in \Sigma^*$ is *accepted* by $\mathcal{A}$ if $\hat{\delta}(q_1, w) \cap F \neq \emptyset$. The *language $|\mathcal{A}|$ accepted by $\mathcal{A}$*, is defined by

$$|\mathcal{A}| = \{w \in \Sigma^* \mid \hat{\delta}(q_1, w) \cap F \neq \emptyset\}.$$

Kleene [11] introduced regular expressions to characterize the languages accepted by finite automata (see also Salomaa [16]). Assume that Σ and $U = \{\cup, {}^*, \emptyset, [,]\}$ are disjoint alphabets. A word E over $\Sigma \cup U$ is a *regular expression over Σ* if

  (i) E is the symbol $\emptyset$,
 (ii) E is a symbol of Σ, or else
(iii) E is of one of the forms $[E_1 \cup E_2]$, $[E_1 E_2]$, or E_1^*, where E_1 and E_2 are regular expressions over Σ.

Each regular expression E over Σ *denotes a language $|E|$ over Σ* according to the following conventions:

(i) The language denoted by $\emptyset$ is the empty language.

(ii) The language denoted by $a \in \Sigma$ consists of the word a.

(iii) For regular expressions E_1 and E_2 over Σ, $||[E_1 \cup E_2]|| = |E_1| \cup |E_2|$, $||[E_1 E_2]|| = |E_1||E_2|$, $|E_1^*| = |E_1|^*$.

Theorem 3. (Kleene's Theorem [11]) *Let Σ be an alphabet and let L be a formal language over Σ. Then the following statements are equivalent:*

(i) L is accepted by a nondeterministic finite automaton with input alphabet Σ;
(ii) L is denoted by a regular expression over Σ.

Observe that a language over Σ is denoted by a regular expression over Σ iff it is an element of the sub-star semiring of 2^{Σ^*} generated by the sets $\{a\}$, $a \in \Sigma$. Hence, we can reformulate Theorem 3 to

Corollary 1. *Let Σ be an alphabet and let L be a formal language over Σ. Then the following statements are equivalent:*

(i) L is accepted by a nondeterministic finite automaton with input alphabet Σ;
(ii) L is an element of the sub-star semiring of 2^{Σ^*} generated by the singleton sets corresponding to the elements of Σ.

It is this formulation of Kleene's Theorem which we will generalize. In a first step we define finite automata over a semiring S and an alphabet Σ.

A *finite automaton (of dimension $n \geq 0$ over the semiring S and the alphabet Σ)*

$$\mathbf{A} = (\alpha, A, \beta)$$

is given by

(i) an *initial vector* $\alpha \in (S\langle\{\varepsilon\}\rangle)^{1 \times n}$,

(ii) a *transition matrix* $A \in (S\langle\Sigma \cup \{\varepsilon\}\rangle)^{n \times n}$,

(iii) a *final vector* $\beta \in (S\langle\{\varepsilon\}\rangle)^{n \times 1}$.

It is called *proper* if $A \in (S\langle\Sigma\rangle)^{n \times n}$. If S is a star semiring or $\mathbf{A}$ is proper then A^* is defined and the behavior of $\mathbf{A}$ is

$$|\mathbf{A}| = \sum_{1 \leq i,j \leq n} \alpha_i (A^*)_{ij} \beta_j = \alpha A^* \beta \,.$$

The *(directed) graph* of a proper finite automaton $\mathbf{A} = (\alpha, A, \beta)$ of dimension n is constructed in the usual manner. It has nodes $1, \ldots, n$ and an edge from node i to node j if $A_{ij} \neq 0$. The *weight* of this edge is $A_{ij} \in S\langle\Sigma\rangle$. The *initial* (resp. *final*) *weight* of a node i is given by α_i (resp. β_i). A node is called *initial* (resp. *final*) if its initial (resp. final) weight is unequal to 0. The *weight* of a path is the product of the weigths of its edges. It is easily shown that $(A^k)_{ij}$ is the sum of the weights of paths of length k from node i to node j. When S is complete, since $(A^*)_{ij} = \sum_{k \geq 0}(A^k)_{ij}$, $(A^*)_{ij}$ is the sum of the weights of the paths from node i to node j. Hence, $\alpha_i(A^*)_{ij}\beta_j$ is this sum for nodes i and j, multiplied on the left and right by the initial weight of node i and the final weight of node

j, respectively. Eventually, the behavior of $\mathbf{A}$ is the sum of all these terms with summation over all initial states i and all final states j.

Assume that $\mathbf{A} = (\alpha, A, \beta)$ is a proper finite automaton of dimension n over the semiring 2^{Σ^*} and the alphabet Σ and $\mathcal{A} = (Q, \Sigma, \delta, q_1, F)$ is a nondeterministic finite automaton. Then $\mathbf{A}$ and $\mathcal{A}$ *correspond to each other* if the following conditions are satisfied:

(i) $|Q| = n$; so we may assume $Q = \{q_1, \ldots, q_n\}$, where i corresponds to q_i, $1 \le i \le n$.
(ii) $a \in A_{ij} \Leftrightarrow q_j \in \delta(q_i, a)$, $1 \le i, j \le n$, $a \in \Sigma$.
(iii) $\alpha_1 = \{\varepsilon\}$, $\alpha_i = \emptyset$, $2 \le i \le n$.
(iv) $\beta_i = \{\varepsilon\} \Leftrightarrow q_i \in F$, $\beta_i = \emptyset \Leftrightarrow q_i \notin F$.

It is easily seen that $|\mathbf{A}| = |\mathcal{A}|$ if $\mathbf{A}$ and $\mathcal{A}$ correspond to each other. This is due to the fact that

$$w \in (A^k)_{ij} \Leftrightarrow q_j \in \hat{\delta}(q_i, w), \quad 1 \le i, j \le n, \ k \ge 0, \ w \in \Sigma^*, \ |w| = k\,,$$

and

$$w \in (A^*)_{ij} \Leftrightarrow q_j \in \hat{\delta}(q_i, w), \quad 1 \le i, j \le n, \ w \in \Sigma^*\,.$$

(In the complete star semiring $(2^{\Sigma^*})^{n \times n}$ we have $A^* = \bigcup_{k \ge 0} A^k$.) Hence,

$$|\mathbf{A}| = \alpha A^* \beta = \bigcup_{1 \le i, j \le n} \alpha_i (A^*)_{ij} \beta_j = \bigcup_{q_j \in F} (A^*)_{1j} =$$
$$\bigcup_{q_j \in F} \{w \mid q_j \in \hat{\delta}(q_1, w)\} = \{w \mid \hat{\delta}(q_1, w) \cap F \ne \emptyset\} = |\mathcal{A}|\,.$$

This shows that finite automata over a semiring S and an alphabet Σ are really generalizing nondeterministic finite automata with input alphabet Σ.

Kleene's Theorem, Theorem 3, can be generalized in two variants to the Theorem of Kleene-Schützenberger (See Schützenberger [18], and Conway [4], Eilenberg [6], Salomaa, Soittola [17], Kuich, Salomaa [14], Bloom, Ésik [2], Kuich [13], Berstel, Reutenauer [1], Ésik, Kuich [7]). The first variant considers proper finite automata over arbitrary semirings, the second variant arbitrary finite automata over Conway semirings.

Theorem 4. *Let S be a semiring, Σ be an alphabet and r be a power series in $S\langle\langle \Sigma^* \rangle\rangle$. Then the following two statements are equivalent.*

(i) r is the behavior of a proper finite automaton over S and Σ;
(ii) r can be obtained from $S\langle\{\varepsilon\}\rangle \cup \Sigma$ by finitely many applications of the operations sum, product and star, where the star is applied only to proper power series.

Theorem 5. *Let S be a Conway semiring, Σ be an alphabet and r be a power series in $S\langle\langle \Sigma^* \rangle\rangle$. Then the following two statements are equivalent.*

(i) r is the behavior of a finite automaton over S and Σ;
(ii) r can be obtained from $S\langle\{\varepsilon\}\rangle \cup \Sigma$ by finitely many applications of the operations sum, product and star.

As before, Theorem 5 can be reformulated to

Corollary 2. *Let S be a* Conway *semiring, Σ be an alphabet and r be a power series in $S\langle\!\langle\Sigma^*\rangle\!\rangle$. Then the following two statements are equivalent.*

(i) r is the behavior of a finite automaton over S and Σ;
(ii) r is an element of the sub-star semiring of $S\langle\!\langle\Sigma^*\rangle\!\rangle$ generated by $S\langle\{\varepsilon\}\rangle \cup \Sigma$.

The next theorem shows that, in case S is a Conway semiring, the sets of power series characterized by Theorems 4 and 5 coincide.

Theorem 6. *Let S be a Conway semiring and Σ be an alphabet. Then for each finite automaton $\mathbf{A}$ over S and Σ a proper finite automaton $\mathbf{A}'$ over S and Σ can be constructed such that $|\mathbf{A}| = |\mathbf{A}'|$.*

Proof. Let $\mathbf{A} = (\alpha, A, \beta)$ be of dimension n with $A_0 = (A, \varepsilon)\varepsilon$ and $A_1 = \sum_{a\in\Sigma}(A, a)a$. Then we construct $\mathbf{A}' = (\alpha', A', \beta')$ of dimension n by $\alpha' = \alpha$, $A' = A_0^* A_1$, $\beta' = A_0^*\beta$ and obtain

$$|\mathbf{A}'| = \alpha(A_0^* A_1)^* A_0^*\beta = \alpha(A_0 + A_1)^*\beta = \alpha A^*\beta = |\mathbf{A}|. \qquad \square$$

The power series characterized by Theorem 4 are called *rational* power series. This set of rational power series is usually denoted by $S^{\mathrm{rat}}\langle\!\langle\Sigma^*\rangle\!\rangle$.

4   A Unifying Kleene Theorem

In this section we establish a Kleene theorem for partial Conway semirings. To this end, we define a general notion of (finite) automaton in partial Conway semirings (see Bloom, Ésik, Kuich [3]).

Throughout this section, S denotes a partial Conway semiring over an ideal I of S, S_0 a subsemiring of S and Σ a subset of I.

Suppose that S is a partial Conway semiring over I, S_0 is a subsemiring of S and Σ is a subset of I. An *automaton* over (S_0, Σ) is a triplet $\mathbf{A} = (\alpha, A, \beta)$ consisting of an *initial vector* $\alpha \in S_0^{1\times n}$, a *transition matrix* $A \in (S_0\langle\Sigma\rangle)^{n\times n}$, where $S_0\langle\Sigma\rangle$ is the set of all finite sums of terms sa, $s \in S_0$, $a \in \Sigma$, and a *final vector* $\beta \in S_0^{n\times 1}$. The integer n is called the *dimension* of $\mathbf{A}$. The *behavior* of $\mathbf{A}$ is $|\mathbf{A}| = \alpha A^*\beta$. (Since $A \in I^{n\times n}$, A^* exists.)

We say that $s \in S$ is *recognizable* over (S_0, Σ) if s is the behavior of some automaton over (S_0, Σ). We let $\mathbf{Rec}_{S,I}(S_0, \Sigma)$ denote the set of all elements of S which are recognizable over (S_0, Σ).

Next we define rational elements. Suppose that S is a partial Conway semiring over I, S_0 is a subsemiring of S and Σ is a subset of I. The set of *rational* elements over (S_0, I), $\mathbf{Rat}_{S,I}(S_0, \Sigma)$, is the least set containing $S_0 \cup \Sigma$ and closed under the rational operations $+, \cdot, ^*$, where * is only applied to elements of I.

In the proof of our Kleene theorem, we will make use of the following fact.

Lemma 1. *Suppose that each entry of the $n\times n$ matrix A is in $\mathbf{Rat}_{S,I}(S_0, \Sigma)\cap I$. Then the same holds for the matrix A^+.*

Proof. We prove this fact by induction on n. When $n = 1$, our claim is clear. Assuming that $n > 1$ write $A = \begin{pmatrix} a & b \\ c & d \end{pmatrix}$, where a is 1×1, d is $(n-1) \times (n-1)$. Then A^+ is given by Theorem 2. We only show that each entry of the submatrix $(a+bd^*c)^+$ is in $\mathbf{Rat}_{S,I}(S_0, \Sigma) \cap I$. But $a+bd^*c = a+bc+bd^+c$. By the induction hypothesis, each entry of d^+ is in $\mathbf{Rat}_{S,I}(S_0, \Sigma) \cap I$. Since $\mathbf{Rat}_{S,I}(S_0, \Sigma)$ is closed under sum and product, and since each entry of a, b or c is also in this set, it follows that each entry of $a + bd^*c$ is in $\mathbf{Rat}_{S,I}(S_0, \Sigma) \cap I$. Thus, using the induction hypothesis again, it follows that each entry of $(a + bd^*c)^+$ is in $\mathbf{Rat}_{S,I}(S_0, \Sigma) \cap I$. $\qquad\square$

Theorem 7. *Suppose that S is a partial Conway semiring over I, S_0 is a sub-semiring of S and Σ is a subset of I. Then $\mathbf{Rec}_{S,I}(S_0, \Sigma) \subseteq \mathbf{Rat}_{S,I}(S_0, \Sigma)$.*

Proof. Let $\mathbf{A} = (\alpha, A, \beta)$ be an automaton over (S_0, Σ). Then $|\mathbf{A}| = \alpha A^* \beta = \alpha\beta + \alpha A^+ \beta$. Clearly, $\alpha\beta \in S_0$. By the previous lemma, $A^+ \in \mathbf{Rat}_{S,I}(S_0, \Sigma)$. Since $S_0 \subseteq \mathbf{Rat}_{S,I}(S_0, \Sigma)$ and since $\mathbf{Rat}_{S,I}(S_0, \Sigma)$ is closed under sum and product, it follows that $\alpha A^* \beta$ is in $\mathbf{Rat}_{S,I}(S_0, \Sigma)$. $\qquad\square$

We now prove a certain converse of the previous proposition.

Theorem 8. *Suppose that S is a partial Conway semiring over I, S_0 is a sub-semiring of S and Σ is a subset of I. Moreover, assume that*

(i) $1 \in I$, *or*
(ii) if $s + a \in I$, for $s \in S_0$, $a \in I$, then $s = 0$.

Then $\mathbf{Rat}_{S,I}(S_0, \Sigma) \subseteq \mathbf{Rec}_{S,I}(S_0, \Sigma)$.

Proof. Suppose that $s \in \mathbf{Rat}_{S,I}(S_0, \Sigma)$. We have to show that there is an automaton $\mathbf{A}$ over (S_0, Σ) whose behavior is s. In case of assumption (i) we show additionally: This automaton $\mathbf{A}$ over (S_0, Σ) has the property that *the product of the initial and final vector of $\mathbf{A}$ is 0.*

Assume that $s = a$ for some $a \in \Sigma$. Then define the following automaton $\mathbf{A}_a$ of dimension 2:

$$\mathbf{A}_a = \left((1\ 0), \begin{pmatrix} 0 & a \\ 0 & 0 \end{pmatrix}, \begin{pmatrix} 0 \\ 1 \end{pmatrix} \right).$$

We have

$$|\mathbf{A}_a| = (1\ 0) \begin{pmatrix} 1 & a \\ 0 & 1 \end{pmatrix} \begin{pmatrix} 0 \\ 1 \end{pmatrix} = a.$$

Next, let $s \in S_0$. Then in case of assumption (i) define the following automaton $\mathbf{A}_s$ of dimension 2:

$$\mathbf{A}_s = \left((s\ 0), \begin{pmatrix} 0 & 1 \\ 0 & 0 \end{pmatrix}, \begin{pmatrix} 0 \\ 1 \end{pmatrix} \right)$$

We have

$$|\mathbf{A}_s| = (s\ 0) \begin{pmatrix} 1 & 1 \\ 0 & 1 \end{pmatrix} \begin{pmatrix} 0 \\ 1 \end{pmatrix} = s.$$

In case of assumption (ii) define the following automaton $\mathbf{A}_s$ of dimension 1:

$$\mathbf{A}_s = (s, 0, 1)$$

We have

$$|\mathbf{A}_s| = s \cdot 0^* \cdot 1 = s.$$

In the induction step there are three cases to consider. Suppose that $s = s_1 + s_2$ or $s = s_1 s_2$ such that there exist automata $\mathbf{A}_i = (\alpha_i, A_i, \beta_i)$ over (S_0, Σ) with $|\mathbf{A}_i| = s_i$, satisfying in case of assumption (i) $\alpha_i \beta_i = 0$, $i = 1, 2$. We construct automata $\mathbf{A}_1 + \mathbf{A}_2$, $\mathbf{A}_1 \cdot \mathbf{A}_2$ defining $s_1 + s_2$ and $s_1 s_2$, respectively. Let

$$\mathbf{A}_1 + \mathbf{A}_2 = \left(\left(\alpha_1 \; \alpha_2 \right), \begin{pmatrix} A_1 & 0 \\ 0 & A_2 \end{pmatrix}, \begin{pmatrix} \beta_1 \\ \beta_2 \end{pmatrix} \right)$$

and

$$\mathbf{A}_1 \cdot \mathbf{A}_2 = \left(\left(\alpha_1 \; 0 \right), \begin{pmatrix} A_1 & \beta_1 \alpha_2 A_2 \\ 0 & A_2 \end{pmatrix}, \begin{pmatrix} \beta_1 \alpha_2 \beta_2 \\ \beta_2 \end{pmatrix} \right).$$

Then

$$|\mathbf{A}_1 + \mathbf{A}_2| = \left(\alpha_1 \; \alpha_2 \right) \begin{pmatrix} A_1^* & 0 \\ 0 & A_2^* \end{pmatrix} \begin{pmatrix} \beta_1 \\ \beta_2 \end{pmatrix}$$
$$= \alpha_1 A_1^* \beta_1 + \alpha_2 A_2^* \beta_2$$
$$= |\mathbf{A}_1| + |\mathbf{A}_2|,$$

and

$$|\mathbf{A}_1 \cdot \mathbf{A}_2| = \left(\alpha_1 \; 0 \right) \begin{pmatrix} A_1^* & A_1^* \beta_1 \alpha_2 A_2^+ \\ 0 & A_2^* \end{pmatrix} \begin{pmatrix} \beta_1 \alpha_2 \beta_2 \\ \beta_2 \end{pmatrix}$$
$$= \alpha_1 A_1^* \beta_1 \alpha_2 \beta_2 + \alpha_1 A_1^* \beta_1 \alpha_2 A_2^+ \beta_2$$
$$= \alpha_1 A_1^* \beta_1 \alpha_2 A_2^* \beta_2$$
$$= |\mathbf{A}_1| \cdot |\mathbf{A}_2|.$$

Also, in case of assumption (i)

$$\left(\alpha_1 \; \alpha_2 \right) \left(\beta_1 \; \beta_2 \right)^T = \alpha_1 \beta_1 + \alpha_2 \beta_2 = 0$$

and

$$\left(\alpha_1 \; 0 \right) \left(\beta_1 \alpha_2 \beta_2 \; \beta_2 \right)^T = \alpha_1 \beta_1 \alpha_2 \beta_2 = 0.$$

Next, we show that when $s = r^+$ for some $r \in I$ which is the behavior of an automaton $\mathbf{A} = (\alpha, A, \beta)$ over (S_0, Σ), satisfying in case of assumption (i) $\alpha \beta = 0$, then s is the behavior of an automaton $\mathbf{A}^+$. Since

$$r = |\mathbf{A}| = \alpha A^* \beta = \alpha \beta + \alpha A^+ \beta \in I,$$

we infer for both assumptions $|\mathbf{A}| = \alpha A^+ \beta$. Now let

$$\mathbf{A}^+ = (\alpha, A + \beta \alpha A, \beta).$$

By $(A + \beta\alpha A)^* = A^*(\beta\alpha A^+)^*$, we have

$$|\mathbf{A}^+| = \alpha A^*(\beta\alpha A^+)^*\beta = \alpha A^+\beta(\alpha A^+\beta)^* = (\alpha A^+\beta)^+ = |\mathbf{A}|^+ = s.$$

Moreover, we have that $\alpha\beta = 0$ in case of assumption (i).

Finally, when $s = r^*$ and $|\mathbf{A}| = r$, then $|\mathbf{A}^+ + \mathbf{A}_1| = r^* = s$.   □

Remark. Note that the assumption (ii) in the above theorem holds whenever each $t \in S$ has at most one representation $t = s + a$ with $s \in S_0$ and $a \in I$. This happens when S is the *direct sum* of S_0 and I.

We have proved:

Theorem 9. *Suppose that S is a partial Conway semiring over I, S_0 is a subsemiring of S and Σ is a subset of I. Moreover, assume that*

(i) $1 \in I$, *or*
(ii) $s + a \in I$, $s \in S_0$, $a \in I$, *implies* $s = 0$.

Then $\mathbf{Rat}_{S,I}(S_0, \Sigma) = \mathbf{Rec}_{S,I}(S_0, \Sigma)$.

If the basic semiring is $S\langle\langle\Sigma^*\rangle\rangle$ and $S_0 = S\langle\{\varepsilon\}\rangle$, our Theorem 9 unifies Theorems 4 and 5.

If S is a Conway semiring, choose assumption (i): $S\langle\langle\Sigma^*\rangle\rangle$ is again a Conway semiring, $I = S\langle\langle\Sigma^*\rangle\rangle$ and $\varepsilon \in I$.

If S is an arbitrary semiring and the finite automata are proper, choose assumption (ii): I is now the set of proper power series; and $s\varepsilon + r \in I$, $s \in S$, $r \in I$ implies $s = 0$.

References

1. Berstel, J., Reutenauer, C.: Les séries rationelles et leurs langages. Masson (1984); English translation: Rational Series and Their Languages. EATCS Monographs on Theoretical Computer Science, vol. 12. Springer, Heidelberg (1988)
2. Bloom, S.L., Ésik, Z.: Iteration Theories. EATCS Monographs on Theoretical Computer Science. Springer, Heidelberg (1993)
3. Bloom, S.L., Ésik, Z., Kuich, W.: Partial Conway and iteration semirings. Fund. Inform. 86, 19–40 (2008)
4. Conway, J.H.: Regular Algebra and Finite Machines. Chapman & Hall, Boca Raton (1971)
5. Droste, M., Kuich, W.: Semirings and formal power series. In: Droste, M., Kuich, W., Vogler, H. (eds.) Handbook of Weighted Automata. EATCS Monographs on Theoretical Computer Science, pp. 3–28. Springer, Heidelberg (2009)
6. Eilenberg, S.: Automata, Languages and Machines, vol. A. Academic Press, London (1974)
7. Ésik, Z., Kuich, W.: Inductive *-semirings. Theoretical Computer Science 324, 3–33 (2004)
8. Ésik, Z., Kuich, W.: Modern Automata Theory, http://www.dmg.tuwien.ac.at/kuich
9. Hebisch, U.: The Kleene theorem in countably complete semirings. Bayreuther Mathematische Schriften 31, 55–66 (1990)

10. Hopcroft, J.E., Ullman, J.D.: Introduction to Automata Theory, Languages, and Computation. Addison-Wesley, Reading (1979)
11. Kleene, S.C.: Representation of events in nerve nets and finite automata. In: Shannon, C.E., McCarthy, J. (eds.) Automata Studies, pp. 3–41. Princeton University Press, Princeton (1956)
12. Kuich, W.: The Kleene and the Parikh theorem in complete semirings. In: Ottmann, T. (ed.) ICALP 1987. LNCS, vol. 267, pp. 212–225. Springer, Heidelberg (1987)
13. Kuich, W.: Semirings and formal power series: Their relevance to formal languages and automata theory. In: Rozenberg, G., Salomaa, A. (eds.) Handbook of Formal Languages, ch. 9, vol. 1, pp. 609–677. Springer, Heidelberg (1997)
14. Kuich, W., Salomaa, A.: Semirings, Automata, Languages. EATCS Monographs on Theoretical Computer Science, vol. 5. Springer, Heidelberg (1986)
15. Maurer, H.: Theoretische Grundlagen der Programmiersprachen. B.I. Wissenschaftsverlag (1969)
16. Salomaa, A.: Formal Languages. Academic Press, London (1973)
17. Salomaa, A., Soittola, M.: Automata-Theoretic Aspects of Formal Power Series. Springer, Heidelberg (1978)
18. Schützenberger, M.P.: On the definition of a family of automata. Inf. Control 4, 245–270 (1961)

Local Squares, Periodicity and Finite Automata[*]

Mari Huova, Juhani Karhumäki, Aleksi Saarela, and Kalle Saari

Department of Mathematics and Turku Centre for Computer Science TUCS
University of Turku, FI-20014 Turku, Finland
{mahuov,karhumak,amsaar,kasaar}@utu.fi

Abstract. We consider the general problem when local regularity implies the global one in the setting where local regularity means the existence of a square of certain length in every position of an infinite word. The square can occur as centered or to the left or to the right from each position. In each case there are three variants of the problem depending on whether the square is that of words, that of abelian words or, as an in between case, that of so called k-abelian words. The above nine variants of the problem are completely solved, and some open problems are addressed in the k-abelian case. Finally, an amazing unavoidability result for 2-abelian squares is obtained.

1 Introduction

Questions when local properties imply global ones are of fundamental importance in many area of mathematics. Among the most well known problems of this type is Burnside Problem [3]. It asks whether a finitely generated group, where each of its subgroups generated by a single element is finite, is necessarily finite as well. A remarkable paper of Adian and Novikov [1] shows that the answer to this question is "no" – that is we do not have the above desired implication. In the case of free semigroups the situation is the same, only the proof is much simpler application of avoidability properties of words, see [14] or [11].

Positive results of the above nature are recently discovered and studied in connection with infinite words. Here the local regularity is described, e.g., as a property that the word contains a certain repetition everywhere, and the global one as the requirement that the word is (ultimately) periodic. A remarkable result here is the characterization of [13] stating that a one-way infinite word is ultimately periodic if and only if each of its long enough prefixes ends up with a repetition of a word of order at least $\varphi + 1$, where φ is the golden ratio. Consequently, the local regularity "having always a square" does not imply the global one while "having always a cube" does so. The analysis of [13] was refined in [8], see also [10], by restricting the length of the repetition in the local regularity condition. A general treatment of these questions can be found in Chapter 8 of [12].

---

[*] Supported by the Academy of Finland under grants 121419 and 134190 and by the Väisälä Foundation.

C.S. Calude, G. Rozenberg, A. Salomaa (Eds.): Maurer Festschrift, LNCS 6570, pp. 90–101, 2011.

In this note we define the local regularity as the existence of a square at each position of the word. We obtain three variants of the problem depending on whether the square is centered, to the left or to the right of each position, respectively. In addition, in each case we obtain three subproblems corresponding to the cases where squares are those of ordinary words, those of abelian words or, as an in between case, those of so-called k-abelian words described in a moment. We parameterize all of these nine problems by adding a restriction on the length of the square. With this setting we completely characterize when the local regularity, i.e. having a square of certain length everywhere, implies the global periodicity, i.e. being ultimately periodic.

The method used here is that from [8]. Namely, for a fixed length n we can construct a finite automaton accepting, as infinite runs, exactly those words which obey a given local regularity constrain. Then the existence of intersecting loops characterizes whether a nonperiodic word of the required form can exist. It follows from the method that whenever a non-ultimately periodic word is found, actually nondenumerably many of those are constructed. Despite of the simplicity of the approach, computer verifications are crucial for our results. The above is easily modified for two-way infinite words.

Our results have another interesting interpretation. Let us consider a one-way infinite word as a dynamical process where it is defined step by step. Assume further that in this process we preserve a given local regularity property. Then our results have identified the exact borderlines, with respect to the length of squares, of *predictable* vs *chaotic behavior* in all of our nine problems. In the predictable case we obtain only periodic words while in the chaotic case we obtain nondenumerably many (nonperiodic) words in our process.

We conclude this introduction by defining informally the notion of k-*abelian equivalence*. For a natural number k two words are k-abelian equivalent if they possess common prefixes and suffixes of length $k - 1$, respectively, and each factor of length k occurs equally many times in these words. The value $k = 1$ corresponds to the *abelian equivalence*. The condition for prefixes and suffixes is introduced in order to locate the k-abelian equivalence properly in between the ordinary equivalence (equality) and the abelian equivalence. Finally, a k-abelian square is a word of the form uv where u and v are k-abelian equivalent.

Our last section analyzes some basic properties of the k-abelian equivalence, as well as points out some intriguing open questions. More precisely, we characterize in the binary alphabet the 2-abelian and 3-abelian equivalence classes, as well as analyze the numbers of these equivalence classes of words of length n. In the case $k = 2$ we obtain an exact quadratic formula, while in the case $k = 3$ we obtain an estimate $\Omega(n^4)$. In general, we obtain a polynomial upper bound, although the degree of the polynomial is exponential in k. We conclude by considering avoidability questions for k-abelian powers. More precisely, we ask what is the smallest alphabet size when 2-abelian cubes (resp. 2-abelian squares) can be avoided in infinite words. Obviously, these values are in between the corresponding values for word- and abelian repetitions, that is either 2 or 3, and 3 or 4, respectively, see [11] and [5]. For cubes we check by a computer that there exist binary words of length 100000, avoiding 2-abelian cubes. This makes us to conjecture that 2-abelian cubes can be avoided in the binary alphabet, exactly as ordinary cubes. On the other hand 2-abelian squares – quite surprisingly – can not be avoided in a ternary alphabet. The longest word avoiding such squares is of length 537. Hence the smallest alphabet they can be avoided in is quartic.

2   Preliminaries

In this section we fix our terminology, and in particular define our crucial notions. For words we refer to [12] and for automata to [7].

We denote by Σ a finite alphabet and Σ^+ and Σ^ω the sets of nonempty finite words and one-way infinite words over Σ, respectively. An element $w \in \Sigma^\omega$ is *ultimately periodic* if it can be written in the form $w = uvv \cdots = uv^\omega$ for some finite words u and v. This notion extends in a natural way to two-way infinite words: two-way infinite word w is *ultimately periodic to the right* if it can be written in the form $w = uv$ where u is one-way infinite word to the left and v is ultimately periodic word in Σ^ω. Similarly, we define *two-way ultimately periodic words to both directions*. In our considerations, words of these forms are viewed as *globally regular* words. *Local regularity* is defined in our considerations as a repetition such as a square, a cube etc.

We consider three types of equivalence relations on Σ^+: the ordinary equality of words, the abelian (or commutative) equivalence of words, and, as an in between case, so-called k-abelian equivalence of words. The last one is defined as follows. Let k be a natural number. Two finite words u and v are *k-abelian equivalent* if and only if

- $\mathrm{pref}_{k-1}(u) = \mathrm{pref}_{k-1}(v)$ and $\mathrm{suf}_{k-1}(u) = \mathrm{suf}_{k-1}(v)$
- for all $x \in \Sigma^k$, $\#(x, u) = \#(x, v)$,

where pref_{k-1} (resp. suf_{k-1}) refers to the maximal prefix (resp. suffix) of length at most $k - 1$ and $\#$ counts the number of (possibly overlapping) occurrences of x in the word. Let us denote this equivalence relation by $\equiv_{a,k}$. Then, clearly, $\equiv_{a,1}$ coincides with $\equiv_a$, the usual abelian equivalence relation on words.

The first condition is introduced in order to have the following relations, which are straightforward to conclude:

$$u = v \Rightarrow u \equiv_{a,k} v \Rightarrow u \equiv_a v, \quad \text{for all k.}$$

Indeed, for words $u = 1101$ and $v = 0110$ we have $u \neq_a v$ while u and v satisfy the second condition above for $k = 2$. The notion of abelian and k-abelian repetitions are now defined in a natural way. For example, word w is *k-abelian square* if it can be written as $w = uv$ where $u \equiv_{a,k} v$. It follows that we can talk about words *avoiding*, e.g., 2-abelian squares.

3   Local Squares vs. Periodicity

We examine the following problem: for a given number n, if a binary right-infinite word contains at every position a square of a word of length at most n, is the word necessarily ultimately periodic?

To make this question precise, we must define what having a square at every position means. We give three different definitions, which lead to three variations of the problem.

A word w contains everywhere a

- *left square* of length at most n, if every factor of w of length $2n$ has a nonempty square as a suffix,
- *right square* of length at most n, if every factor of w of length $2n$ has a nonempty square as a prefix,
- *centered square* of length at most n, if every factor of w of length $2n$ has a nonempty square exactly in the middle, i.e. is of the form $uxxv$, where $|u| = |v|$ and $x \neq 1$.

In addition to ordinary squares, we can give similar definitions for k-abelian squares. We will study the cases $k = 1$ and $k = 2$, i.e. abelian and 2-abelian equivalences. This gives a total of nine variations of the problem.

We begin by giving a method to solve the following problem: for a number n, if a binary right-infinite word contains everywhere a left square of length at most n, is the word necessarily ultimately periodic? This method can then be modified for the other eight variations of the problem.

We define an automaton as follows: the set of states is Σ^{2n-1}, where $\Sigma = \{a, b\}$. If $c, d \in \Sigma$, $u \in \Sigma^{2n-2}$ and cud has a nonempty square as a suffix, then the value of the transition function at (cu, d) is defined as $\delta(cu, d) = ud$; otherwise δ is undefined. All states are initial and final. The automaton is deterministic, except that there are many initial states.

The following theorems give a way to solve our problem.

Theorem 1. *Let $w = uv$, where $u \in \Sigma^{2n-1}$ and $v \in \Sigma^\omega$. The word w contains a left square of length at most n everywhere if and only if the above automaton accepts every prefix of v starting from the state u.*

Proof. Follows from the definition of the automaton. □

Theorem 2. *There exists a binary aperiodic right-infinite word that contains a left square of length at most n everywhere if and only if the above automaton has two intersecting cycles.*

Proof. If the automaton has two intersecting cycles, then there is a state u and words s, t such that $\delta(u, as) = u = \delta(u, bt)$. Now every word in $\{as, bt\}^\omega$ contains a left square of length at most n everywhere, and there are aperiodic words in this set.

If there are no intersecting cycles and $uv \in \Sigma^\omega$ is such that $\delta(u, t)$ is defined for every prefix t of v, then there must be a cycle such that $\delta(u, t)$ is in that cycle for every long enough prefix t. Then v must be ultimately periodic. □

If the automaton does not have intersecting cycles, then there are only ultimately periodic words that contain a left square of length at most n everywhere. The number of these words can be countably infinite. For example, for every m the word $(ab)^m a^\omega$ has a left square of length at most two everywhere. However, there are only finitely many possible periodic parts, because the automaton has only finitely many cycles. Thus the situation is very structured.

On the other hand, if the automaton has two intersecting cycles, then there are aperiodic words that contain a left square of length at most n everywhere. Moreover, the number of such words is uncountable, and the situation can be viewed as chaotic.

The existence of intersecting cycles is fairly easy to check algorithmically: we determine the strongly connected components (for example with Tarjan's algorithm) and check whether in some component there is a state from which there are two transitions into the same component.

Using this method we can see that the smallest value of n for which there is an aperiodic word containing a left square of length at most n everywhere is $n = 5$. This was already proved in [8]. The automaton has two strongly connected components that contain intersecting cycles. A representation of one of them is in Fig. 1; the other component can be obtained by exchanging the letters. Here we have omitted those states, which have only one transition coming to them and only one transition leaving from them. In addition to these two components, there are also components consisting of a single cycle, and components consisting of a single state. Every cycle generates ultimately periodic words and single states may generate prefixes of infinite words, but only intersecting cycles can generate aperiodic infinite words.

We can use the same method for k-abelian squares: in the definition of the transition function we simply require cud to have a suffix that is a k-abelian square instead of an ordinary square. For 2-abelian left squares the smallest possible value is also $n = 5$; the automaton still has two strongly connected components that contain intersecting cycles, but they are slightly more complicated, see Fig. 2. For abelian left squares the smallest possible value is $n = 3$. The automaton has two strongly connected components that contain intersecting cycles, which have sizes 18 and 12, and two one-state cycles. There are so many transitions that it would be difficult to draw a clear picture. In fact, the automaton is almost the whole De Bruijn graph; there are only eight states from which there is only one transition.

The method can also be modified for right squares: in the definition of the transition function we require cud to have a prefix that is a square. If δ_L, δ_R are the transition functions for left and right squares, then $\delta_L(cu, d) = ud$ if and only if $\delta_R(du^R, c) = u^R c$, where u^R is the reverse of u. Thus the automaton

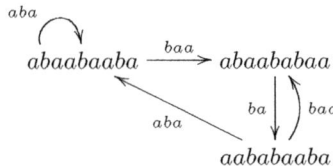

Fig. 1. A component of the automaton for left squares of length $n = 5$

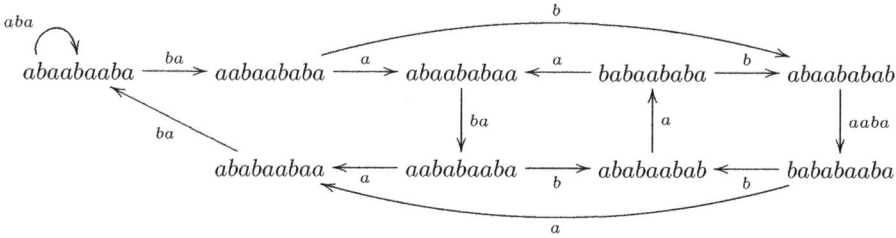

Fig. 2. A component of the automaton for left 2-abelian squares of length $n = 5$

for right squares is obtained from the automaton for left squares by reversing transitions and relabeling states and transitions. It follows that the automaton for left squares has two intersecting cycles if and only if the automaton for right squares has.

Finally, we can define a similar automaton for centered squares. It turns out that in this case the ultimate periodicity is harder to avoid: in the abelian case the smallest value of n for which there is an aperiodic word containing a centered abelian square of length at most n everywhere is $n = 8$. The automaton has one strongly connected component that contains intersecting cycles. This component has 148 states. In the 2-abelian case the smallest possible value is $n = 12$. The automaton has two strongly connected components that contain intersecting cycles. Both components have 222 states. Small parts of these two automata are represented in Fig. 3. These parts are sufficient to generate some examples of aperiodic words that satisfy the conditions. The automata contain also many other intersecting cycles, which are not represented here. Abelian squares (left, right and centered) were studied in [2]. In particular there it was proved that there are some connections with the Thue-Morse morphism and its generalizations.

For ordinary centered squares the situation changes completely: no finite value of n is large enough. This can be proved using the Critical Factorization Theorem (see [4]). The first part of the next theorem is Theorem 8.3.5 in [12].

Theorem 3. *If there is an n such that $w \in \Sigma^\omega$ has a centered square of length at most n everywhere, then w is ultimately periodic. On the other hand, there are aperiodic two-way infinite words that have centered squares everywhere.*

Proof. From the existence of such a number n it follows that the local period of w is at most n at every position. By the Critical Factorization Theorem, also the

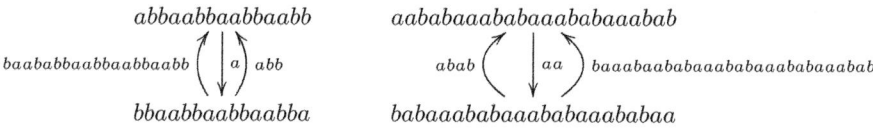

Fig. 3. Small parts of the automata for centered abelian and 2-abelian squares of lengths $n = 8$ and $n = 12$

global period of every prefix of w is bounded by n. Now w must be ultimately periodic by the theorem of Fine and Wilf.

Suppose that a finite word w does not have a centered square at some position, say $w = uv$, where no suffix of u is a prefix of v. Now w can be extended to both directions so that it has a centered square at this position: $vtuvtu$ is a proper extension for every word t. We can repeat this for other positions, and as a limit we get a two-way infinite word that has a centered square everywhere. The t-words can be chosen easily so that the infinite word is aperiodic.   □

Above we have studied one-way infinite words. The same questions can be asked also for two-way infinite words. In this case the answers are the same as for one-way infinite words.

Theorem 4. *There is a binary aperiodic right-infinite word containing an ordinary (2-abelian, abelian) left (right, centered) square of length at most n everywhere if and only if there is such a two-way infinite word.*

Proof. If there is an aperiodic right-infinite word, then the automaton has two intersecting cycles, say $\delta(u, as) = u = \delta(u, bt)$ for some state u and words s, t. Now every two-way infinite word formed of as and bt satisfies the conditions, and there are aperiodic such words.

On the other hand, if there is an aperiodic two-way infinite word, then it is aperiodic to the left or to the right. If it is aperiodic to the right, then the automaton has two intersecting cycles. If it is aperiodic to the left, then the automaton, where all transitions are reversed, has two intersecting cycles. But then also the original automaton has two intersecting cycles.   □

We summarize the results obtained in this section by presenting in Table 1 the minimal values of n for which there are aperiodic right-infinite words containing an ordinary (or 2-abelian or abelian) left (or right or centered) square of length at most n everywhere.

We conclude this section with two remarks on general k-abelian case. First, for left and right squares the values of Table 1 would remain as 5; the k-abelian case is in between of those of words and 2-abelian cases. For the centered variant of the problem the exact borderline for k-abelian repetitions when $k \geq 3$ is unknown. It looks that our straightforward computations might easily be infeasible.

Table 1. Optimal values for local regularity which does not imply global regularity in our problems

	words	2-abelian	abelian
left	5	5	3
right	5	5	3
centered	∞	12	8

4   k-Abelian Equivalence: Observations and Open Problems

In this section we give characterizations of the equivalence classes of 2-abelian and 3-abelian words over a binary alphabet. We count the number of the equivalence classes of 2-abelian words over a binary alphabet and the size of each such an equivalence class. We examine the number of the equivalence classes also in general and give an open problem of the subject. In addition, we formulate an open problem concerning avoidability of 2-abelian repetitions. We then end this section by a discussion that indicates that 2-abelian words sometimes behave like ordinary words and sometimes like abelian words.

First we give characterizations for the equivalence classes for 2- and 3-abelian words over binary alphabet by which we mean that we define a representative for each equivalence class.

Example 1. In a binary alphabet $\Sigma = \{a, b\}$ the characterization of the equivalence classes of 2-abelian words can be given in the form:

$$aa^k b^l (ab)^m a^n \quad \text{or} \quad bb^k a^l (ba)^m b^n,$$

where $k, l, m \geq 0$ and $n \in \{0, 1\}$. So, we have in the beginning of the word all the factors of form aa and bb.

We remark that the above characterization is not unambiguous in a few cases, for example if there does not exist the factor bb but aa exists. Then we may express the same class in two different ways, $aa^k b^1 (ab)^m a^n$ or $aa^{k-1} b^0 (ab)^{m+1} a^n$. The following characterization of the equivalence classes of 3-abelian words is not unambiguous either in some cases. The equivalence class of a word depends in fact on the number of factors of the form aaa, bbb and 3-letter factors containing aa or bb. Clearly, the length of the word and the first and the last two letters are significant, too.

Example 2. In the alphabet $\Sigma = \{a, b\}$ the characterization of the equivalence classes of 3-abelian words can be given in the following form containing eight possible combinations:

$$\left.\begin{array}{l} aaa^k b^l (aabb)^m \\ bbb^k a^l (aabb)^m \\ abb^k a^l (aabb)^m \\ baa^k b^l (aabb)^m \end{array}\right\} \text{or} \left.\right\} * \text{ connected with } * \left\{\begin{array}{l} (aab)^g (ab)^h b^i a^j \text{ or} \\ (abb)^g (ab)^h b^i a^j, \end{array}\right.$$

where $k, l, m, g, h \geq 0$, $i \in \{0, 1\}$ and $j \in \{0, \ldots, 2 - i\}$. If we restrict to classes with $k > 1$ and $l > 2$, the given representation is unambiguous.

Now we can count the number of the equivalence classes of 2-abelian words in the binary alphabet $\Sigma = \{a, b\}$.

Example 3. If the length of the word is one there exist two equivalence classes, namely a and b. If the length is two there exist four equivalence classes aa, ab, ba and bb.

We consider next the words of length $n > 2$ and containing k a-letters and hence $n - k$ b-letters. We have a correspondence between the number of different letters and the number of the equivalence classes:

number of a-letters   number of classes
$k = 0 \lor k = n$ $\Rightarrow 1$
$k = 1 \lor k = n - 1$ $\Rightarrow 3$
$1 < k < n - 1$ $\Rightarrow 2\min(k, n - k) + \min(k - 1, n - k) + \min(k, n - k - 1)$

From these we obtain the number of the equivalence classes of words with length $n > 2$:

$$\begin{cases} 8 + \sum_{k=2}^{n-2}(4\min(k, n - k) - 1), & \text{if } 2 \nmid n \\ 6 + 2n + \sum_{k=2}^{\frac{n}{2}-1}(4\min(k, n - k) - 1) + \sum_{k=\frac{n}{2}+1}^{n-2}(4\min(k, n - k) - 1), & \text{if } 2 \mid n \end{cases}$$

If we count the given sums we get as a conclusion the following theorem.

Theorem 5. *The number of 2-abelian equivalence classes consisting of words of length n over a binary alphabet is $n^2 - n + 2$ and thus the number is $\Theta(n^2)$, where $n > 0$ is the length of words and alphabet is binary.*

We can also examine the sizes of the equivalence classes in the case of binary alphabet and 2-abelian equivalence. Consider the words beginning with a, ending with b and containing factors of the form aa, ab, ba and bb k-, $(k-1)$-, l- and m-times, respectively. Then the equivalence class contains $\binom{l+k-1}{k-1}\binom{m+k-1}{k-1}$ such words. Similarly, there exist $\binom{l+k}{k}\binom{m+k-1}{k-1}$ words in the equivalence class containing words beginning and ending with a and having factors of the form aa, ab, ba and bb k-, k-, l- and m-times, respectively. Results for words beginning with b are similar and these four cases cover all the possible 2-abelian words over binary alphabet.

From the characterization of the equivalence classes of 3-abelian words in example 2 we see that the number of the equivalence classes in this case is $\Omega(n^4)$. We have five independent variables, k, l, m, g and h, and if we restrict $k > 1$ and $l > 2$, each combination of these five values gives a different equivalence class. If we now fix the length of the words to be n we obtain a relation

$$k + l + 4m + 3g + 2h + \alpha = n,$$

where $\alpha \in \{2, 3, 4\}$ depending on i and j. We may restrict to analyze words long enough and to subsets of the equivalence classes and hence the equation can be modified to the form:

$$12k' + 12l' + 4(3m') + 3(4g') + 2(6h') = 12n'.$$

Now we may count the number of solutions of equation $\sum_{i=1}^{5} x_i = N$, where $x_i > 0$ for all $i \in \{1, \ldots, 5\}$ and N is fixed. The number of solutions is $\Theta(N^4)$ which implies that the number of 3-abelian equivalence classes of words of length n is $\Omega(n^4)$.

Contrary to the 2-abelian case the exact formula for the number of the 3-abelian equivalence classes is not a polynomial. This can be concluded from the list of the equivalence classes for small values of n, see [6].

Theorem 6. *The number of k-abelian equivalence classes over Σ^n is $O(n^{|\Sigma|^k-1})$.*

Proof. An equivalence class over Σ^n with a representative $u \in \Sigma^n$ is uniquely determined by the $|\Sigma|^k$ nonnegative integers $|u|_z$, where $z \in \Sigma^k$, and the prefix and suffix of u of length $k - 1$. Since the number of length-k factors in a word of length n is $n - k + 1$, counting multiplicities, the number of distinct equivalence classes is at most

$$|\Sigma|^{2(k-1)} \cdot \left| \left\{ (i_1, i_2, \dots, i_{|\Sigma|^k}) \mid i_j \geq 0 \text{ and } i_1 + \cdots + i_{|\Sigma|^k} = n - k + 1 \right\} \right|$$

$$= |\Sigma|^{2(k-1)} \cdot \binom{n - k + |\Sigma|^k}{|\Sigma|^k - 1}$$

$$= O(n^{|\Sigma|^k-1}).$$

□

It is likely that the real upper bound is smaller than the given one and hence we can state an open problem:

Open problem 1: Give a better estimate to the number of the equivalence classes of k-abelian words.

Finally, we give an open problem concerning k-abelian repetitions. It is known that cubes are avoidable over the binary alphabet, for example the infinite word of Thue-Morse accomplishes this property, see [11]. On the other hand, it is easy to see that abelian cubes are not avoidable. Though, for abelian words over binary alphabet the repetitions of fourth order are avoidable (see [5]) and so in k-abelian case the order of repetition that can be avoided in a binary alphabet is either three or four. We formulate this in the case of 2-abelian words as an open problem:

Open problem 2: Does there exist an infinite binary word that avoids 2-abelian cubes?

The analysis we made with computers reveals that there exist cube-free 2-abelian words longer than 100 000 letters. This does not prove the existence of such an infinite word but supports the assumption that cubes would be avoidable for 2-abelian words over binary alphabet, exactly as in the case of words.

The problem could also be expressed in terms of the size of an alphabet in which cubes can be avoided. The size of the alphabet is now two or three because abelian cubes are avoidable over ternary alphabet, see [5].

A similar question can be asked for 2-abelian squares. Already squares are avoidable for words over 3-letter alphabet (see [11]) but for abelian words over ternary alphabet the maximal length of a word avoiding squares is seven, as can be easily checked. It is known, although this is not easy to prove, that there exists an infinite abelian word avoiding squares over 4-letter alphabet, see [9]. This indicates that for k-abelian words avoiding squares the size of a smallest alphabet is at least three and at most four. In the case $k = 2$ we discovered the following result:

Theorem 7. *The smallest alphabet in which the 2-abelian squares can be avoided is a 4-letter alphabet.*

We executed with a computer a similar construction of square-free 2-abelian words over ternary alphabet than in the case of cube-free 2-abelian words over binary alphabet. The maximal length of square-free 2-abelian words that could be constructed is 537 letters and every longer word over ternary alphabet contains a 2-abelian square. The constructed word of this maximal length 537 is given in example 4. This word is unique up to the permutations of the alphabet. With earlier results mentioned above this shows that the alphabet to avoid squares have to contain at least four letters, and this is, indeed, enough. The behavior of 2-abelian words is in this situation similar with abelian words.

Example 4. The word of length 537 over ternary alphabet $\Sigma = \{a, b, c\}$ that avoids 2-abelian squares:

abcbabcacbacabacbabcbacabcbabcabacabcacbacabacbabcbacbcacbabcacbcabcba
bcabacbabcbacbcacbacabacbabcbacabcbabcabacabcacbacabacbabcbacbcacbacab
acbcabacabcacbcabcbacbcacbacabacbabcbacbcacbabcacbcabcbabcabacbabcbacb
cacbacabacbabcbacabcbabcabacabcacbacabacbabcbacbcacbacabacbcabacabcacb
cabcbabcabacabcacbacabacbabcbacabcbabcabacabcacbcabcbabcabacbabcbacbca
cbabcacbcabcbabcabacabcacbcabcbacbcacbacabacbcabacabcacbcabcbabcabacab
cacbacabacbabcbacabcbabcabacabcacbcabcbabcabacbabcbacbcacbabcacbcabcba
bcabacabcacbacabacbabcbacabcbabcabacabcacbabcba.

References

1. Adian, S.I., Novikov, P.S.: Infinite periodic groups I, II, III. Izv. Akad. Nauk SSSR. Ser. Mat. 32(1,2,3), 212–244, 251–524, 709–731 (1968)
2. Avgustinovich, S., Karhumäki, J., Puzynina, S.: On abelian versions of Critical Factorization Theorem. In: Proceedings of the 13th Mons. Theoretical Computer Science Days (2010)
3. Burnside, W.: On an unsettled question in the theory of discontinuous groups. Quart. J. Pure and Appl. Math. 33, 230–238 (1902)
4. Choffrut, C., Karhumäki, J.: Combinatorics of words. In: Rozenberg, G., Salomaa, A. (eds.) Handbook of Formal Languages, vol. 1, pp. 329–438. Springer, Heidelberg (1997)
5. Dekking, F.M.: Strongly nonrepetitive sequences and progression-free sets. J. Combin. Theory Ser. A 27(2), 181–185 (1979)
6. Harmaala, E.: Private communication
7. Hopcroft, J.E., Ullman, J.D.: Introduction to Automata Theory, Languages, and Computation. Addison-Wesley, Reading (1979)

8. Karhumäki, J., Lepistö, A., Plandowski, W.: Locally periodic versus globally periodic infinite words. J. Combin. Theory Ser. A 100(2), 250–264 (2002)
9. Keränen, V.: Abelian squares are avoidable on 4 letters. In: Kuich, W. (ed.) ICALP 1992. LNCS, vol. 623, pp. 41–52. Springer, Heidelberg (1992)
10. Lepistö, A.: On Relations between Local and Global Periodicity. PhD thesis, University of Turku (2002)
11. Lothaire, M.: Combinatorics on Words. Addison-Wesley, Reading (1983)
12. Lothaire, M.: Algebraic Combinatorics on Words. Cambridge University Press, Cambridge (2002)
13. Mignosi, F., Restivo, A., Salemi, S.: Periodicity and the golden ratio. Theoret. Comput. Sci. 204(1-2), 153–167 (1998)
14. Morse, M., Hedlund, G.A.: Unending chess, symbolic dynamics and a problem in semigroups. Duke Math. J. 11, 1–7 (1944)

P and dP Automata: A Survey

Gheorghe Păun[1,2] and Mario J. Pérez-Jiménez[2]

[1] Institute of Mathematics of the Romanian Academy
PO Box 1-764, 014700 Bucureşti, Romania
[2] Department of Computer Science and Artificial Intelligence
University of Sevilla
Avda. Reina Mercedes s/n, 41012 Sevilla, Spain
gpaun@us.es, marper@us.es

Abstract. This is a quick survey of basic notions and results related to P automata (P systems with symport/antiport rules working in the accepting mode), with some emphasis on the recently introduced dP automata (a distributed version of the standard P automata), ending with some open problems and research topics which we find of interest in this area.

1 Introduction

Membrane computing is a branch of natural computing aiming to abstract computing models from the structure and the functioning of the biological cell; the basic model of this research area (usually called a *P system*) consists of a hierarchical arrangement of membranes which delimit compartments where multisets of objects evolve according to given rules inspired by biology. Some rules are mimicking the biochemical reactions, other rules correspond to processes specific to cells, such as the selective passage of chemicals across membranes, in the form of symport and antiport operations (couples of molecules pass together, in the same direction in the case of symport and in opposite directions in the case of antiport, through specific protein channels). This is the framework where the present paper is placed: cell-like models, with the multisets of objects processed by communication only (moving them across membranes), using symport and antiport rules. Such systems were initially used in the generative manner (one starts from an initial configuration and one proceeds by a maximally parallel use of rules until reaching a halting configuration, one where no rule can be applied; the contents of a designated membrane in the halting configuration is considered as the result of the computation).

Many variations of this basic model can be found in the membrane computing literature. We mention only the much investigated classes of tissue-like P systems and of spiking neural P systems. The reader is refereed to [15], [17], and to the domain website [21] for details.

The idea of using a P system in the accepting mode has appeared already "from the old times": start a computation by introducing a multiset in a specified membrane and, if (and only if) the computation halts, then this multiset is

C.S. Calude, G. Rozenberg, A. Salomaa (Eds.): Maurer Festschrift, LNCS 6570, pp. 102–115, 2011.
© Springer-Verlag Berlin Heidelberg 2011

accepted. In the systems using only communication rules, such as those based on symport/antiport rules, a string can also be accepted in a natural way: just arrange in a sequence the objects (described by symbols) taken from the environment by the system during a halting computation. This idea was followed first in [6] (the paper was presented during the Workshop on Membrane Computing, Curtea de Argeş, 2002) and, almost concomitantly, in [10].

The devices introduced in the first paper are called *P automata*. They are usual P systems with symport/antiport rules supplemented with certain features: a set of accepting configurations (called "states" in [6]) is given and a mapping which associates a string with a multiset. The computation proceeds as usual in a P system with symport/antiport rules and it is considered successful only if it halts in an accepting state. In each step, the system takes some objects from the environment, hence a sequence of multisets can be associated with a successful computation. This sequence is "translated" into a string by the mapping mentioned above. Several papers were devoted to these devices (in particular, characterizations of regular, context-free, and recursively enumerable languages were obtained, and complexity investigations were carried out); we refer to [5] for details, including references.

A simplified version of P automata was considered in [10]: successful computations are defined by halting only, and the mapping which passes from multisets (of objects introduced in the system) to strings is very simple – either all symbols are introduced in the accepted string (if several symbols are taken in the same step, then any permutation of them is introduced in the string, hence a set of strings can be associated with one computation), or only the objects from a given set, which is like in Chomsky grammars and Lindenmayer systems, where terminal and non-terminal symbols are considered and the strings in a language consists of only terminals.

From now on we will work only with P automata in the sense of [10]. We call *extended* the automata which consider terminal symbols (hence they discard the non-terminal ones). We will give precise definitions in the next section.

Note that any P system is a distributed parallel device, with several compartments/membranes working simultaneously, but the input (in the case of P automata) is taken from the environment only by the skin region. Looking for a computing model which can take parts of a global input and introduce them as "local" inputs in different components and then process these inputs separately in order to answer a "global question", so-called *dP systems* were recently introduced in [16]. In the general case, such systems consist of a given number of components in the form of a usual P system, of any type, which can have their separate inputs and communicate from skin to skin membranes by means of antiport rules like in tissue-like P systems. In this framework, communication complexity issues can be investigated, as in [12]. (Some previous proposals towards a communication complexity of P systems were made in [1], but mainly related to the communication effort in terms of symport/antiport rules in a usual P system, not an explicitly distributed one.) The case of P automata was considered in some details – and this leads to the notion of *dP automata*. The possibility of accepting languages of various types in Chomsky hierarchy in a distributed way, using a bounded number of communication rules and also with some (linear) speed-up was proven.

The study of dP automata was continued in [9], by comparing their power with that of usual P automata and with families of languages in the Chomsky hierarchy. As expected, due to the distribution (and synchronization), dP automata are strictly more powerful than P automata. Also expected is the fact that each regular languages can be recognized by a P automaton.

In the present note, we recall the results from [16] and [9]. A theorem from [9] gives a representation of recursively enumerable (RE) languages starting from languages recognized by dP automata, similar to the representation of RE languages in terms of context-sensitive languages; it is not shown in [9] whether this new representation is non-trivial, in the sense that the relation between the family of languages recognized by dP automata and the family of context-sensitive languages is not settled (the inclusion is obvious, but it is not shown to be proper). We clarify here this point, by finding a context-sensitive language which cannot be accepted by a dP automaton. Along the paper as well as in the end of it, we formulate a series of open problems and research topics (especially about dP automata) which we find of interest.

2   dP Automata

We directly introduce the dP automata, by whose particularization we get the notion of a P automaton.

The reader is assumed to be familiar with basics of membrane computing, e.g., from [15], [17], and of formal language theory, e.g., from [19], [20].

In what follows, V^* is the free monoid generated by the alphabet V, λ is the empty word, $V^+ = V^* - \{\lambda\}$, and $|x|$ denotes the length of the string $x \in V^*$. REG, LIN, CF, CS, RE denote the families of regular, linear, context-free, context-sensitive, and recursively enumerable languages, respectively. As usual in membrane computing, the multisets over an alphabet V are represented by strings in V^*; a string and all its permutations correspond to the same multiset, with the number of occurrences of a symbol in a string representing the multiplicity of that object in the multiset. (We work here only with multisets of finite multiplicity.) The terms "symbol" and "object" are used interchangeably, all objects are here represented by symbols.

A *dP automaton* (of degree $n \geq 1$) is a construct

$$\Delta = (O, E, \Pi_1, \ldots, \Pi_n, R),$$

where:

(1) O is an alphabet (of objects);
(2) $E \subseteq O$ (the objects available in arbitrarily many copies in the environment);

(3) $\Pi_i = (O, \mu_i, w_{i,1}, \ldots, w_{i,k_i}, E, R_{i,1}, \ldots, R_{i,k_i})$ is a symport/antiport P system of degree k_i (O is the alphabet of objects, μ_i is a membrane structure of degree k_i, $w_{i,1}, \ldots, w_{i,k_i}$ are the multisets of objects present in the membranes of μ_i in the beginning of the computation, E is the alphabet of objects present – in arbitrarily many copies – in the environment, and $R_{i,1}, \ldots, R_{i,k_i}$ are finite sets of symport/antiport rules associated with the membranes of μ_i; the symport rules are of the form $(u, in), (u, out)$, where $u \in O^*$, and the antiport rules are of the form $(u, out; v, in)$, where $u, v \in O^*$; note that we do not have an output membrane), with the skin membrane labeled with $(i, 1) = s_i$, for all $i = 1, 2, \ldots, n$;

(4) R is a finite set of rules of the form $(s_i, u/v, s_j)$, where $1 \le i, j \le n, i \ne j$, and $u, v \in O^*, uv \ne \lambda$.

The systems $\Pi_1, \ldots, \Pi_n$ are called *components* of Δ and the rules in R are called *communication rules*. For a rule $(s_i, u/v, s_j)$, $|uv|$ is the *weight* of this rule.

Each component can take an input, work on it, and communicate with other components. The communication is done by means of rules in R, but, because the environment is common, the components can also communicate, in two steps, through the environment. In the constructions involved in the proofs of the results recalled below this latter possibility is systematically avoided, but from a formal point of view this raises already a research topic: Is any difference between the power and/or the efficiency of dP systems whose components are allowed and those whose components are not allowed to communicate through the environment? How this communication can be avoided? (Some suggestions are given in [16], e.g., to consider a "local environment" for each component, not accessible to other components.)

A halting computation with respect to Δ accepts the string $x = x_1 x_2 \ldots x_n$ over O if the components $\Pi_1, \ldots, \Pi_n$, starting from their initial configurations, using the symport/antiport rules as well as the inter-components communication rules, in the non-deterministic maximally parallel way, bring from the environment the substrings $x_1, \ldots, x_n$, respectively, and eventually halts.

The dP automata are synchronized devices, a universal clock exists for all components, marking the time in the same way for the whole dP automaton.

Three communication complexity measures were defined in [16], following [1], counting the number of communication steps (parameter $ComN$), of communication rules ($ComR$), or the total weight of communication rules ($ComW$) used during a computation. Based on these measures, the notions of *weak parallelizability* and of *efficient parallelizability* are introduced. For instance, a language $L \subseteq V^*$ is said to be (n, m)-*weakly ComX parallelizable*, for some $n \ge 2, m \ge 1$, and $X \in \{N, R, W\}$, if there is a dP automaton Δ with n components and there is a finite subset F_Δ of L such that each string $x \in L - F_\Delta$ can be written as $x = x_1 x_2 \ldots x_n$, with $||x_i| - |x_j|| \le 1$ for all $1 \le i, j \le n$, each component Π_i of Δ takes as input the string $x_i, 1 \le i \le n$, and the string x is accepted by Δ by a halting computation δ such that $ComX(\delta) \le m$. A language L is said to be *weakly ComX parallelizable* if it is (n, m)-weakly $ComX$ parallelizable for some $n \ge 2, m \ge 1$.

Note that (i) the string is distributed in equal parts, modulo one symbol, to the components of the dP automaton (like in communication complexity area, [12]; one says that the string is distributed *in a balanced way*) and (ii) the communication complexity, in the sense of measure $ComX$, is bounded by the constant m. It is said nothing about the length of the computation, that is why a stronger version of parallelizability is introduced, the efficient one. In what follows, we allow the dP system to perform communications of an arbitrary complexity, while the length of the computation is not taken into consideration, hence we ignore these aspects.

Specifically, for a dP automaton Δ of degree n we define the language $L(\Delta)$, of all strings $x \in O^*$ such that we can write $x = x_1 x_2 \ldots x_n$, with $||x_i| - |x_j|| \leq 1$ for all $1 \leq i, j \leq n$, each component Π_i of Δ takes as input the string $x_i, 1 \leq i \leq n$, and the computation halts.

Note again that, like in the communication complexity area, the string is distributed in equal parts, modulo one symbol, to the components of the dP automaton. This acts like a strong restriction for our devices. If this condition is not imposed, hence any decomposition of the string x can be considered, then a superlanguage of $L(\Delta)$ is obtained. Like in [16], [9], in what follows we only consider the balanced distribution case; the study of the unbalanced case remains a topic for future research (we will mention this question again in the last section).

We denote by LdP_n the family of languages $L(\Delta)$, for Δ of degree at most n. A dP automaton of degree 1 is a usual P automaton – of a non-extended type: all symbols are introduced in the accepted string. If a terminal set of objects is considered, then we obtain an extended P automaton (formally, we have a device $\Pi = (O, T, \mu, w_1, \ldots, w_m, E, R_1, \ldots, R_m)$, with $T \subseteq O$, working as a usual P automaton and considering only the symbols from T in the accepted strings and ignoring those from $O - T$). We denote by LP the family of languages recognized by non-extended P automata (hence $LP = LdP_1$) and by ELP the family of languages recognized by extended P automata. (Note that we ignore the weight of symport and antiport rules, but these parameters, usual when investigating symport/antiport P systems, can be considered also here.) If the subscript n in LdP_n is arbitrary, then we replace it by $*$.

A terminal alphabet can be considered also for dP automata, but this is not of much interest: $ELdP_1 = ELP$, which is known to equals RE.

3 On the Power of P Automata

Extended P automata were proved already in [10] to be computationally universal:

Theorem 1. $ELP = RE$.

Actually, rather simple P automata (e.g., with only one membrane), also working in the deterministic way, are shown to be able to simulate language accepting register machines. In turn, because in the non-extended case the number of objects present in the system is comparable with the number of objects taken from the environment (the initial multisets are fixed), hence with the length of the accepted string, we immediately have:

Theorem 2. $LP \subseteq CS$.

However, we know no other result about non-extended P automata reported before the introduction of dP automata, which is somehow strange, because the power of non-extended P automata raise interesting (and intuitively non-trivial) problems.

Some of these problems were addressed in [9]; we will recall the respective results, after recalling an example, which can illustrate the way a P automaton works. The automaton (with six membranes) is given first formally and then in Figure 1, represented as usual in membrane computing (with the rules near the membranes with which they are associated).

$$\Pi = (O, \mu, w_1, w_2, w_3, w_4, w_5, w_6, E, R_1, R_2, R_3, R_4, R_5, R_6),$$
$$O = \{a, b, c, d, e, f, g, \#\},$$
$$\mu = [\,[\,[\ ]_3[\ ]_4\,]_2[\ ]_5[\ ]_6\,]_1,$$
$$w_1 = c,$$
$$w_2 = de,$$
$$w_3 = \lambda,$$
$$w_4 = \#,$$
$$w_5 = fgg,$$
$$w_6 = \#,$$
$$E = \{a, b, c, d\},$$
$$R_1 = \{(c, out; aa, in),\ (a, out; c, in),\ (d, out; bb, in),\ (b, out; d, in)\},$$
$$R_2 = \{(e, out),\ (ae, in),\ (d, out; fe, in),\ (be, in),\ (g, in),\ (\#, in),\ (\#, out)\},$$
$$R_3 = \{(gab, in),\ (g, out)\},$$
$$R_4 = \{(\#, out; ga, in),\ (\#, out; gb, in)\},$$
$$R_5 = \{(f, out; c, in),\ (gg, out; d, in)\},$$
$$R_6 = \{(\#, out; e, in),\ (eg, in)\}.$$

This automaton recognizes the non-regular language $L(\Pi) = \{(a^2 c)^s (b^2 d)^s \mid s \geq 1\}$ – we denote it by L_1, for a later reference.

We start by bringing the object e out of membrane 2, at the same time with introducing two copies of a from the environment. If e will enter membrane 6, then the computation never halts, hence the object e should be "kept busy" by means of a copy of object a, which brings e back to membrane 2 (while the other copy of a exits, in exchange with one copy of object c). This process is repeated for a number of times and then, instead of going out, the object c enters membrane 5, releasing from here the object f. Together with e, object f enters membrane 2, releasing d. From now on, d plays the same role as c before and b

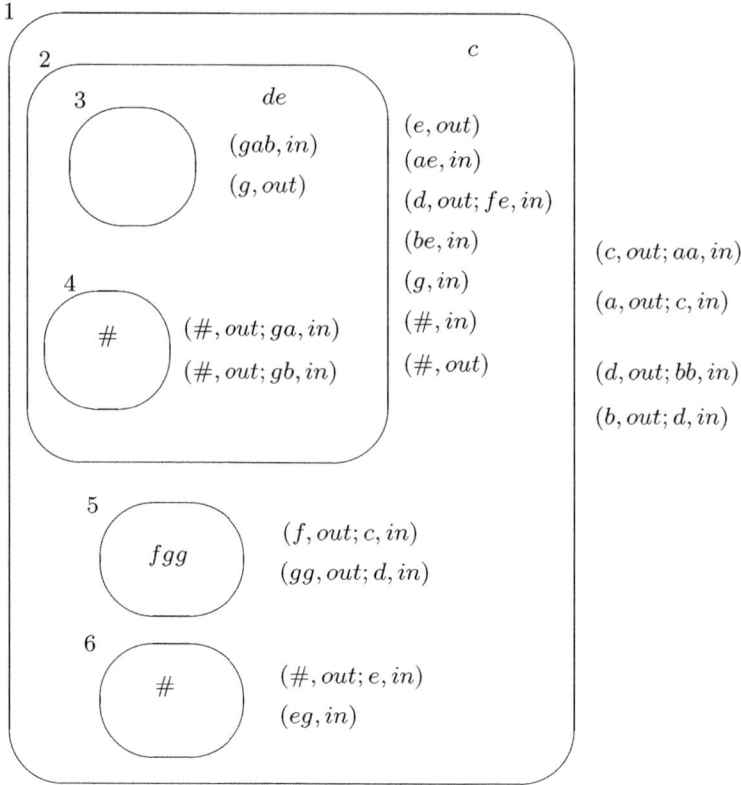

Fig. 1. A P automaton recognizing the language L_1

plays the role of a, hence we bring inside a string of the form $(bbd)^s$, $s \geq 1$. After a while, also d enters membrane 5, releasing the two copies of g. One is used for moving the object e inside membrane 6 without releasing the trap object #, while the other copy of g enters membrane 2, and start here checking whether the number of copies of a and b stored here are equal. If this is not the case, then g together with exceeding a or with an exceeding b enters membrane 4, and the trap object # is brought to region 2, hence the computation never stops.

Therefore, we have $L_1 \in LP$. The idea of the system in Figure 1 can be extended so that we can check the equality of three blocks of repeated symbols, hence also non-context-free languages can be obtained. We summarize these remarks as:

Theorem 3. *LP contains linear non-regular, as well as non-context-free languages.*

Thus, the non-extended P automata can recognize "complex" languages – but they fail to recognize other "simple" languages. Here are two necessary conditions for a language to be in LP proved in [9].

We start with an easy result, refuting however many languages.

Lemma 1. *For every language $L \subseteq V^*, L \in LP$, which is not regular there is a string $w \in L$ which can be written in the form $w = w_1 a b w_2$, for some $w_1, w_2 \in V^*$ and $a, b \in V$ (not necessarily distinct) such that $w_1 b a w_2 \in L$.*

This lemma implies, for instance, that the linear language

$$L_2 = \{(ab)^n (ac)^n \mid n \geq 1\}$$

is not in LP. Actually, a more general consequence of Lemma 1 is drawn in [9]:

Theorem 4. *All families of languages which include strictly the family of regular languages and are closed under λ-free morphisms contain languages which are not in LP.*

We pass now to the second necessary condition for a language to be in LP.

Lemma 2. *Let V be an alphabet with at least two elements and $f : V^* \longrightarrow V^*$ an injective mapping. The language $L_f = \{w f(w) \mid w \in V^*\}$ is not in the family LP.*

The proof is based on the observation that the number of configurations of a P automaton which has brought inside m symbols is bounded by a polynomial in m, but there are more than 2^m different strings of length m over an alphabet with more than two symbols (hence exponentially many), which makes impossible the matching between the two halves of the strings. We will extend this proof idea to dP automata in the next section.

As a consequence of the previous lemma, for instance, the context-sensitive language, $L_3 = \{w f(w) \mid w \in \{a, b\}^*\}$ for $f(a) = a', f(b) = b'$, is not in LP.

Pleasantly enough (and somewhat expected), P automata can recognize all regular languages:

Theorem 5. $REG \subset LP$.

4   On the Power of dP Automata

Let us first note that the language L_2 is in LdP_2 and the same is true for L_3; this language is recognized by the dP automaton (of degree 2, with arbitrarily many communications) indicated in Figure 2, hence we have

Theorem 6. $LdP_n - LP \neq \emptyset$ for all $n \geq 2$.

The following theorem is classic in formal language theory – see, e.g., [20]:

Theorem 7. *For every language $L \in RE, L \subseteq V^*$, there is a language $L' \in CS$ and two symbols $a, c \notin V$ such that: (i) $L' \subseteq L\{c\}a^*$, (ii) for each $w \in L$ there is $i \geq 0$ such that $w c a^i \in L'$.*

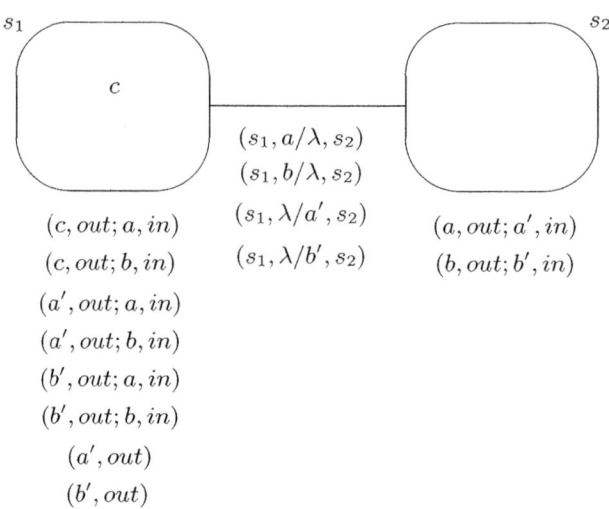

$$(c, out; a, in)$$
$$(c, out; b, in)$$
$$(a', out; a, in)$$
$$(a', out; b, in)$$
$$(b', out; a, in)$$
$$(b', out; b, in)$$
$$(a', out)$$
$$(b', out)$$

Fig. 2. A dP automaton accepting the language L_3

Otherwise stated, the two languages are "the same" up to a tail of arbitrary length added to strings in L.

Because the initial configuration of a dP automaton is given and the objects brought into the system from the environment are part of the recognized string, the workspace of the automaton is linearly bounded with respect to the string, hence Theorem 2 can be extended to:

Theorem 8. $LdP_* \subseteq CS$.

In [9] it is conjectured that the above inclusion is proper. We confirm here this hypothesis:

Lemma 3. *The language* $L_4 = \{(ww')^s \mid w \in \{a, b\}^+, s \geq 2\}$, *where* w' *is obtained from* w *by priming the symbols* a *and* b, *is not in the family* LdP_*.

Proof. Assume that $L_4 = L(\Delta)$ for some dP automaton Δ with n components, $\Pi_1, \ldots, \Pi_n, n \geq 2$. Consider the sublanguage H_n of L_4 consisting of strings with n blocks ww', i.e.,

$$H_n = \{(ww')^n \mid w \in \{a, b\}^+\} \subset L_4.$$

Because of the balanced distribution of inputs to the n components of Δ, each Π_i has to take from the environment a string ww'. Consider the strings w of length m, for some arbitrarily large m, and examine the state of the dP automaton in the moment when component Π_1 has "read" from the environment the symbols of w. (There is a step when exactly the symbols of w were introduced in Π_1: the next symbol is primed and, if it enters the system at the same time with a symbol from w, which is not primed, then a substring $c'd$ can appear, $c, d \in \{a, b\}$, which is contradictory.)

At this moment, the whole dP automaton contains a number of symbols bounded from above by $t_0 + m + 2m(n-1)$, where t_0 is the number of objects present in the initial configuration, m objects are introduced by Π_1 and each of the other $n-1$ components have introduced at most $2m$ objects each. If these objects were identical, then they are distributed in the regions of the system – assume that their number is k – in a number of ways which is bounded from above by $(t_0 + m + 2m(n-1))^k$. Here we have four objects a, b, a', b', as well as some possibly different objects present in the initial configuration. In total, a fixed number, let us say r. Thus, all these objects can be distributed in the k regions of Δ in a number of ways which is at most $(t_0 + m + 2m(n-1))^{kr}$. Consequently, there are polynomially many configurations of Δ reached after having the string w read by Π_1.

However, there are 2^m strings of length m over $\{a, b\}$, hence, for a large enough m, there are strings $w_1, w_2 \in \{a, b\}^+$ of length m such that $w_1 \neq w_2$, but the dP automaton reaches the same configuration after reading w_1 or w_2. This means that after reading w_1, Π_1 can continue by reading w_2' and the computation stops like when Π_1 started by reading w_2, hence a string $w_1 w_2' z$ is accepted (we do not care about the form of z), which is not in L_4, a contradiction.   □

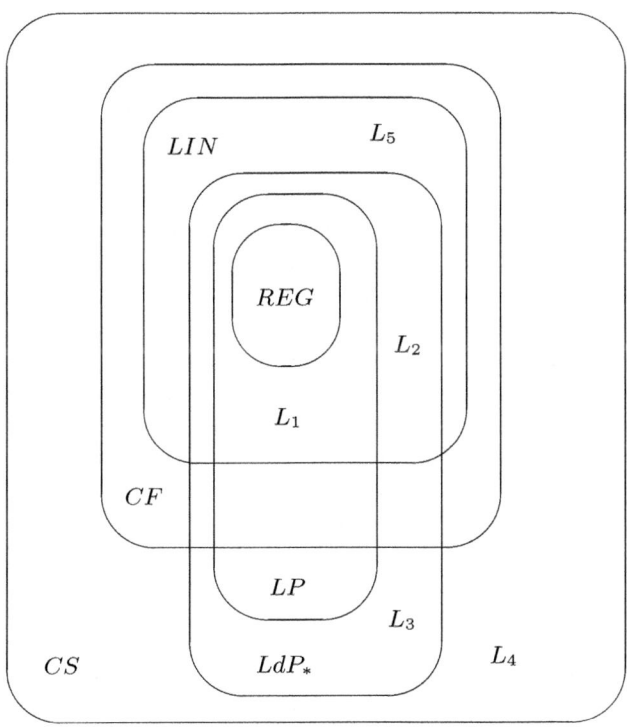

Fig. 3. The place of the families LP and LdP in Chomsky hierarchy

Therefore, the following counterpart of Theorem 7, proved in [9], is of interest:

Theorem 9. *For every language $L \in RE, L \subseteq V^*$, there is a language $L' \in LdP_2, X \in \{N, R, W\}$, and an alphabet U disjoint of V such that: (i) $L' \subseteq LU^*$, (ii) for each $w \in L$ there is $y \in U^*$ such that $wy \in L'$.*

We believe that a similar result is valid also for languages recognized by P automata, but this time with the "tail" placed in the left hand of the string. Specifically, a result of the following form is *conjectured* in [9]:

For every language $L \in RE, L \subseteq V^*$, there is a language $L' \in LP$, and an alphabet U disjoint of V as well as $c, e \notin V \cup U$ such that: (i) $L' \subseteq U^*\{c\}L\{e\}$, (ii) for each $w \in L$ there is $y \in U^*$ such that $ycwe \in L'$.

Moreover, it is conjectured that

$$L_5 = \{w \ mi(w) \mid w \in \{a, b\}^*\} \notin LdP_*,$$

hence, actually, there are linear languages which cannot be accepted by dP automata ($mi(x)$ denotes the mirror image of the string x).

The results from the previous two sections are synthesized in the diagram from Figure 3, based on a similar diagram from [9]; the languages L_1, L_2, L_3, L_4 are specified above and L_5 is only conjectured.

5   Further Research Topics

Of course, many problems and research topics remain to be considered. Several were mentioned in [16] and [9], many others can be imagined.

We recall first some questions from [16]. For instance, we mentioned the notions of parallelizability (recognizing the strings of a language by using a finite number of communication steps) and of efficient parallelizability (to also speed-up the computation, in comparison with a non-distributed automaton). These problems make sense both for the case of the balanced distribution of the string (which is taken as an hypothesis in communication complexity area) and for the arbitrary distribution (which makes sense from the computational complexity point of view). Is it a difference between the two cases? (Anyway, the speed-up obtained by distribution on a given number of "processors" cannot be more than linear, but this is still of interest in some practical cases.) In general, it is of interest to transfer to dP systems, in particular, to dP automata, notions and techniques currently used in communication complexity area, [12].

Then, focusing on P and dP automata as language accepting devices, there are many problems of a classic language theory type which are natural to be raised. For instance, the properties of the language families LP, LdP_*, and $LdP_n, n \geq 2$ (e.g., closure, decidability, descriptional complexity) are of interest (especially because they are not equal to families in Chomsky hierarchy). A related issue is to compare these families with other language families, such as Lindenmayer languages [18], Marcus contextual languages [14], families from the regulated rewriting area [7], etc. Does the number of components induce an infinite hierarchy of the recognized languages? (We only know that $LP = LdP_1 \subset LdP_2 \subseteq LdP_3 \subseteq \ldots \subseteq LdP_*$.) Are there languages which can be recognized by a dP automaton of degree n but not by an automaton of a greater degree? (The problem makes sense only for the balanced case.)

A large research area appears if we want to accept multisets instead of strings, and the problems appear already from the definition. We recall from [9] some hints in this respect.

One way to accept multisets is to reduce this case to accepting strings, taking into account that a multiset can be represented as a string. However, several questions appear in this framework. Consider an alphabet of objects, $A = \{a_1, a_2, \ldots, a_n\}$ and a multiset $M : A \longrightarrow \mathbf{N}$ over A. Any string $w \in A^*$ such that $\Psi_A(w) = (M(a_1), \ldots, M(a_n))$ represents the multiset M (Ψ_A is the Parikh mapping associated with A). Otherwise stated, all permutations of such a string w represent the same multiset. Is the permutation we choose significant from the point of view of accepting it by means of a dP automaton? A way to decrease this wildness of equivalent representations is to look for specified permutations of a string. In particular, we can take the *canonical representation* of M, that is $w_A(M) = a_1^{M(a_1)} \ldots a_n^{M(a_n)}$, hence based on the given ordering of the elements of A. However, we can take any other ordering of A as initially given, and the multiset is the same, but then the canonical representation will be different. Is this important from the point of view of accepting a multiset, by means of a string representation of it, by a dP automaton? A different way of using a P automaton, hence also a dP automaton, in order to recognize a multiset is to start by introducing the multiset in a specified region – to be closer to the case of string recognition, let us assume that this is the skin region – and to accept it if the computation halts. The question now is how to distribute the multiset among the components of the dP automaton, and again we have the two possibilities mentioned above: distributing the objects in the ordering imposed by a given ordering of the alphabet A, and distributing the objects of the multiset in an arbitrary manner – again with two cases for each possibility: a balanced distribution or an arbitrary distribution. (Balanced here is defined in terms of the cardinality of multisets, which is consistent with the definition of a balanced distribution for strings.)

A similarly large panoply of research issues can be based on using different ingredients and features in the considered automata. For instance, what about working in the asynchronous manner or with other types of parallelism, different from the maximal one considered above? What about taking some suggestions from [2], and consider dP automata with identical (or similar, e.g., of the same degree) components, maybe surrounded by separate environments? Then, we can add further tools for controlling the computations, such as promoters, inhibitors, channel states (for the inter-components communication rules), and so on. The use of promoters/inhibitors is particularly attractive, because they can help in easily halting the computations.

For instance, the "difficult" language $L_6 = \{a^n b^{2^n} \mid n \geq 1\}$ (it is non-semilinear) can be recognized by a dP automaton of degree 2 as that in

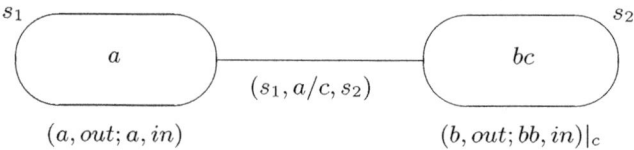

$$(s_1, a/c, s_2)$$

$(a, out; a, in)$ $(b, out; bb, in)|_c$

Fig. 4. A simple dP automaton with promoters

Figure 4, where $(b, out; bb, in)|_c$ means that c is a promoter of the antiport rule $(b, out; bb, in)$, the rule can be applied only if (at least one occurrence of) c is present in the membrane; the promoter is not involved in the rule (is not "consumed", it can promote at the same time any number of different rules). The automaton takes the input in a non-balanced way: a^n is read by the first component and b^{2^n} by the second one. The computation stops when the promoter c goes to the first component, in exchange of the unique object a present here.

The power of the promoter is visible. We do not know whether this feature can be removed, or whether the input can be read in a balanced way (probably not, hence this can be an example of a language which can be recognized only in the non-balanced way); note also that we perform only one communication.

Instead of using c as a promoter, we can use a as an inhibitor of the rule $(b, out; bb, in)$ and the work of the system is similar.

There also are several research issues related to the computational complexity of P and dP automata (for P automata, such investigations were already done, e.g., in [4]), or dealing with infinite strings or infinite alphabets (some references for P automata are [11], [8]). And, of course, we can also take into consideration the descriptional complexity, especially the weight of symport and antiport rules.

Like in [9], we conclude with the belief that P and dP automata deserve further research efforts.

Acknowledgements

Work supported by Proyecto de Excelencia con Investigador de Reconocida Valía, de la Junta de Andalucía, grant P08 – TIC 04200.

References

1. Adorna, H., Păun, G., Pérez-Jiménez, M.J.: On communication complexity in evolution-communication P systems. In: Proc. 8th Brainstorming Week on Membrane Computing, Sevilla, and Romanian J. Information Theory and Applications (February 2010) (to appear)
2. Colomer, M.A., Lavín, S., Marco, I., Margalida, A., Pérez-Hurtado, I., Pérez-Jiménez, M.J., Sanuy, D., Serrano, E., Valencia-Cabrera, L.: Studying the evolution of Pyrenean Chamois by using P systems. In: Pre-proc. Conf. on Membrane Computing, CMC11, Jena, Germany (August 2010)
3. Csuhaj-Varjú, E.: P automata. In: Mauri, G., et al. (eds.) WMC 2004. LNCS, vol. 3365, pp. 19–35. Springer, Heidelberg (2005)

4. Csuhaj-Varjú, E., Ibarra, O.H., Vaszil, G.: On the computational complexity of P automata. Natural Computing 5, 109–126 (2006)
5. Csuhaj-Varjú, E., Oswald, M., Vaszil, G.: P automata. In: [17], ch. 6, pp. 144–167
6. Csuhaj-Varjú, E., Vaszil, G.: P automata or purely communicating accepting P systems. In: Păun, G., Rozenberg, G., Salomaa, A., Zandron, C. (eds.) WMC 2002. LNCS, vol. 2597, pp. 219–233. Springer, Heidelberg (2003)
7. Dassow, J., Păun, G.: Regulated Rewriting in Formal Language Theory. Springer, Berlin (1989)
8. Dassow, J., Vaszil, G.: P finite automata and regular languages over countably infinite alphabets. In: Hoogeboom, H.J., Păun, G., Rozenberg, G., Salomaa, A. (eds.) WMC 2006. LNCS, vol. 4361, pp. 367–381. Springer, Heidelberg (2006)
9. Freund, R., Kogler, M., Păun, G., Pérez-Jiménez, M.J.: On the power of P and dP automata. In: Annals of Bucharest University. Mathematics-Informatics Series (2010) (in press)
10. Freund, R., Oswald, M.: A short note on analysing P systems. Bulletin of the EATCS 79, 231–236 (2002)
11. Freund, R., Oswald, M., Staiger, L.: ω-P automata with communication rules. In: Martin-Vide, C., et al. (eds.) WMC 2003. LNCS, vol. 2933, pp. 203–217. Springer, Heidelberg (2004)
12. Hromkovic, J.: Communication Complexity and Parallel Computing: The Application of Communication Complexity in Parallel Computing. Springer, Berlin (1997)
13. Oswald, M.: P Automata. PhD Thesis, TU Vienna (2003)
14. Păun, G.: Marcus Contextual Grammars. Kluwer, Dordrecht (1997)
15. Păun, G.: Membrane Computing. An Introduction. Springer, Berlin (2002)
16. Păun, G., Pérez-Jiménez, M.J.: Solving problems in a distributed way in membrane computing: dP systems. Int. J. of Computers, Communication and Control 5(2), 238–252 (2010)
17. Păun, G., Rozenberg, G., Salomaa, A. (eds.): Handbook of Membrane Computing. Oxford University Press, Oxford (2010)
18. Rozenberg, G., Salomaa, A.: The Mathematical Theory of L Systems. Academic Press, New York (1980)
19. Rozenberg, G., Salomaa, A. (eds.): Handbook of Formal Languages, 3 volumes. Springer, Berlin (1998)
20. Salomaa, A.: Formal Languages. Academic Press, New York (1973)
21. The P Systems Website, http://ppage.psystems.eu

On the General Coloring Problem⋆

N.W. Sauer⋆⋆

University of Calgary and Technische Universität Wien
nsauer@ucalgary.ca

Abstract. Generalizing relational structures and formal languages to structures whose relations are evaluated by elements of a lattice, we show that such structure classes form a Heyting algebra if and only if the evaluation lattice is a Heyting algebra. Hence various new and some older results obtained for Heyting algebras can be applied to such structure classes.

Keywords: Generalized homomorphisms, Heyting algebras.

1 Introduction

In between 1980 and 1986 H. Maurer published together with various collaborators, A. Salomaa, I.H. Sudborough, E. Welzl, D. Wood, a substantial volume of work concerning interpretations, colorings, complexity of graphs and grammatical language families. For some of this work see [1], [2], [3], [4]. Many of the questions addressed fall into the area now called constrained satisfaction problems and or deal with gaps and dualities within, as is now recognized, the general setting of Heyting algebras. In this paper we will provide a very general frame within which questions asked in the early Maurer papers can be addressed and show that in this context, elements from Heyting algebras are sufficient and necessary for the labelling values. Then we will point to the beautiful theory on gaps and dualities completed in recent years. Nevertheless some of the direct constructions for special cases given in the Maurer papers are still of interest. No attempt has been made to relate those new results to grammatical families. See [10] for grammatical families which form a Heyting algebra and for which then the general theory of gaps and duals applies as well.

2 Heyting Categories and Heyting Algebras

A *Heyting algebra* H is a bounded lattice such that for all $a, b \in H$ there is a largest element $x \in H$, called the *relative complement of a with respect to b*, so that $a \wedge x \leq b$. We will denote this largest element by b^a. In particular then $a \wedge b^a \leq b$ and and $b \leq b^a$ and hence $a \wedge b^a = a \wedge b$. Hence a relative complement of

---

⋆ 2000 Mathematics Subject Classification. Primary: 03E02. Secondary: 22F05, 05C55, 05D10, 22A05, 51F99.

⋆⋆ Supported by NSERC of Canada Grant # 691325.

C.S. Calude, G. Rozenberg, A. Salomaa (Eds.): Maurer Festschrift, LNCS 6570, pp. 116–126, 2011.

a with respect to b is unique. In discussions of applications of Heyting algebras to intuitionistic logic this largest element is denoted by $a \rightarrow b$. As we wish to reserve the $\rightarrow$ arrow for indicating functions and in particular homomorphisms and b^a satisfies many standard laws of arithmetic we prefer to use b^a. ($b^{a+c} = b^a \times b^c$, $(b^a)^c = b^{a \times b}$ etc., see [5] for a complete discussion of that arithmetic). With $+$ for $\vee$ and $\times$ for $\wedge$.) If a bounded lattice L is given we will denote by $\mathbf{1}$ the largest and by $\mathbf{0}$ the smallest element of L. It is known that every Heyting algebra is distributive and hence that a finite lattice is a Heyting algebra if and only if it is distributive. Every Boolean algebra is a Heyting algebra. See [6], [7], [8], [9].

3   Examples

For two graphs G and H a function $f : V(\mathrm{G}) \rightarrow V(\mathrm{H})$ is a homomorphism if $(f(x), f(y)) \in E(\mathrm{H})$ whenever $(x, y) \in E(\mathrm{G})$. Changing notation slightly we may consider a graph to consist of a set G together with a labelling σ of the pairs in G^2 with $\mathbf{0}$ and $\mathbf{1}$. Then $f : G \rightarrow H$ is a homomorphism if: $\sigma_{\mathrm{G}}(x, y) = \mathbf{1}$ implies $\sigma_{\mathrm{H}}(f(x), f(y)) = \mathbf{1}$. That is we have a labelling in the two element Boolean lattice $\{\mathbf{1}, \mathbf{0}\}$ and homomorphisms map pairs labelled $\mathbf{1}$ to pairs labelled $\mathbf{1}$. (Pairs labelled $\mathbf{0}$ maybe mapped to pairs labelled $\mathbf{0}$ or $\mathbf{1}$.)

Let $GTOP$ be the set of oriented graphs whose edges are labeled by open subsets of the Euclidean plane. That is we wish to express the fact that two points are related by being in some common open subset of $\mathfrak{R}^2$. (Or fix a topology T and use the open sets of T as labels.) A function $f : V(\mathrm{G}) \rightarrow V(\mathrm{H})$ is a *homomorphism* of G $\in GTOP$ to H $\in GTOP$ if for every edge $(a, b) \in E(\mathrm{G})$ the label of (a, b) is a subset of the label of $(f(a)), f(b))$, that is the open sets containing the points become smaller. It is not difficult to check that the open subsets of a topology T form a Heyting algebra under $\subseteq$ with $B^A = \mathrm{interior}(\bar{A} \cup B)$ for $\bar{A}$ the complement of A in T.

Let $\mathbb{N}$ be the set of natural numbers and $\omega = \{0\} \cup \mathbb{N}$. Let G be a graph with $V(\mathrm{G}) = G$ which has two types of edges, say red and blue edges. We stipulate that homomorphisms have to map red to red and blue to blue edges. More formally we may say that there are two binary relations R and B on G which have to be preserved under homomorphisms. Or, there are two labelings σ and μ, of the pairs in G^2 with $\mathbf{0}$ and $\mathbf{1}$ and homomorphisms are functions which do not increase the labels in either of the two labelings. A condition which can easily be extending to labels out of a lattice. Of course we might have infinitely many labelings. In order to include even more general cases we could express that situation as follows. Given is a set $\mathcal{I}$ of pairwise disjoint two element sets. The structures under consideration consist of a finite set A and a function σ which assigns to every $w \in \bigcup_{I \in \mathcal{I}} A^I$ a value in $\{\mathbf{0}, \mathbf{1}\}$. This provides a cryptomorphic version for the class of all finite directed graphs with $|\mathcal{I}|$ many different edge types.

Similar to above we can of course represent more general relational structures and sets of words, languages. We will define the operations of $+$ and $\times$ and an exponentiation of such structures. Of course when interested in a special category of structures one has then to check that those operations preserve the category, or class of structures of interest. This is quite easily seen for relational structures but represents difficulties for grammatical languages. Some information on that has been obtained in [10] and has also been discussed in the papers [1], [2],[3] and [4].

4   Labelling with Elements of a Heyting Algebra

Let $A \neq \emptyset$ be a set, thought of as an alphabet, and $\mathcal{I}$ a set of pairwise disjoint non empty index sets and L a bounded lattice and σ a function which assigns to every element $w \in \bigcup_{I \in \mathcal{I}} A^I$ a lattice element $\sigma(w) \in L$. Such a quadruple $(A; \mathcal{I}, L, \sigma)$ will be called a *function structure* with base set A. We will denote by $\mathbf{0}$ the zero element of L and by $\mathbf{1}$ the one element of L. The meet in L will be denoted by $\wedge$ and the join by $\vee$. For $w \in \bigcup_{I \in \mathcal{I}} A^I$ we will often write w_i for $w(i)$. For $I \in \mathcal{I}$ and $w \in A^I$ we can then represent the function w by the "word" $(w_i; i \in I)$, which is even more suggestive if I is ordered. Let $\mathfrak{F}(\mathcal{I}, L)$ be the class of function structures of the form $(A; \mathcal{I}, L, \sigma)$. The elements of $\mathfrak{F}(\mathcal{I}, L)$ will be called $(\mathcal{I}, L)$-structures.

Let $\mathrm{A} = (A; \mathcal{I}, L, \sigma_\mathrm{A}) \in \mathfrak{F}(\mathcal{I}, L)$ and $\mathrm{B} = (B; \mathcal{I}, L, \sigma_\mathrm{B}) \in \mathfrak{F}(\mathcal{I}, L)$. We extend functions $f : A \to B$ to functions from $\bigcup_{I \in \mathcal{I}} A^I$ to $\bigcup_{I \in \mathcal{I}} B^I$ via, for every $I \in \mathcal{I}$:

$$f(w)(i) = f(w(i)) \text{ for all } i \in I, \quad \text{that is } f(w) = f \circ w.$$

The function $f : A \to B$ is a *homomorphism of* A *to* B if:

$$\sigma_\mathrm{A}(w) \leq \sigma_\mathrm{B}(f(w)) \text{ for all } w \in \bigcup_{I \in \mathcal{I}} A^I. \tag{1}$$

Note that this notion of homomorphism specializes to the standard one for graphs and relational structures in case L is the two element Boolean lattice.

We write $\mathrm{A} \to \mathrm{B}$ if there is a homomorphism of A to B and $\mathrm{A} \sim \mathrm{B}$ if $\mathrm{A} \to \mathrm{B}$ and $\mathrm{B} \to \mathrm{A}$. Note that the relation $\to$ is transitive and that the relation $\sim$ is an equivalence relation on $\mathfrak{F}(\mathcal{I}, L)$. A homomorphism is an isomorphism if it is bijective and the inverse is a homomorphism. It follows that if f is an isomorphism then equality holds in Inequality 1. For $\mathrm{A} \in \mathfrak{F}(\mathcal{I}, L)$ let $\tilde{\mathrm{A}}$ denote the $\sim$ equivalence class of $\mathfrak{F}(\mathcal{I}, L)$ containing the structure A. Let $\mathfrak{L}(\mathcal{I}, L)$ be the set, and as we will see the lattice, of $\sim$ equivalence classes of $\mathfrak{F}(\mathcal{I}, L)$.

Note that for $I \in \mathcal{I}$:

$$(A \times B)^I = \{((w_i, v_i); i \in I) \mid \text{ with } w_i \in A \text{ and } v_i \in B \text{ for all } i \in I\}.$$

Then $\mathrm{A} \times \mathrm{B}$ is the $(\mathcal{I}, L)$-structure $(A \times B; \mathcal{I}, L, \sigma_{\mathrm{A} \times \mathrm{B}})$ so that for $I \in \mathcal{I}$:

$$\sigma_{\mathrm{A} \times \mathrm{B}}((w_i, v_i); i \in I) = \sigma_A(w_i; i \in I) \wedge \sigma_B(v_i; i \in I).$$

Note that $\mathrm{A} \times \mathrm{B} \to \mathrm{A}$ via $\pi_\mathrm{A} : \mathrm{A} \times \mathrm{B} \to \mathrm{A}$ with $\pi_\mathrm{A}((w_i, v_i); i \in I) = \{w_i \mid i \in I\}$ for all $I \in \mathcal{I}$ and similar for $\pi_\mathrm{B} : \mathrm{A} \times \mathrm{B} \to \mathrm{B}$. If $\mathrm{A}' \to \mathrm{A}$ and $\mathrm{B}' \to \mathrm{B}$ then

$A' \times B' \to A \times B$. Hence if $A' \sim A$ and $B' \sim B$ then $A' \times B' \sim A \times B$. If $C \to A$ via a homomorphism φ_A and $C \to B$ via a homomorphism φ_B then $C \to A \times B$ via $\varphi : C \to A \times B$ with $\varphi(u_i; i \in I) = ((\varphi_A(u_i), \varphi_B(u_i); i \in I)$ for all $I \in \mathcal{I}$, implying that $\times$ is the categorical product of the homomorphism category on $\mathfrak{F}(\mathcal{I}, L)$.

More generally, if L is complete, let $(A_j; j \in J)$ be structures in $\mathfrak{F}(\mathcal{I}, L)$. Then $\prod_{j \in J} A_j$ is the $(\mathcal{I}, L)$-structure $(\prod_{j \in J} A_j; \mathcal{I}, L, \sigma_{\prod_{j \in J} A_j})$ so that

$$\sigma_{\prod_{j \in J} A_j}((w_{j,i}; j \in J); i \in I) = \bigwedge_{j \in J} \sigma_{A_j}(w_{j,i}; i \in I).$$

Then $\prod_{j \in J} A_j \to A_j$ for every $j \in J$ and if $A'_j \to A_j$ for every $j \in J$ then $\prod_{j \in J} A'_j \to \prod_{j \in J} A_j$ and hence if $A'_j \sim A_j$ for every $j \in J$ then $\prod_{j \in J} A'_j \sim \prod_{j \in J} A_j$. If $C \to A_j$ for every $j \in J$ then $C \to \prod_{j \in J} A_j$.

Let 2 be the Boolean 2-element lattice and $\mathcal{I} = \{\{x, y\}\}$. Then an $(\mathcal{I}, 2)$-structure $G = (G; \mathcal{I}, 2, \sigma_G)$ has an obvious interpretation as an ordinary graph without loops if for all $v, w \in G^{\{x,y\}}$ we have $\sigma_G(v) = \sigma_G(w)$ if $w(x) = v(y)$ and $w(y) = v(x)$ and if $\sigma_G(v) = \mathbf{0}$ if $v(x) = v(y)$. Let $H = (H; \mathcal{I}, 2, \sigma_H)$ be another graph. The product of G with H contains two element subsets of the form $\{(a, c), (b, c)\}$ with $a, b \in G$ and $c \in H$. Let $v(x) = a$ and $v(y) = b$ and $w(x) = w(y) = c$. Then $\sigma_{G \times H}((v_x, w_x), (v_y, w_y)) = \sigma_G(v) \wedge \sigma_H(w) = \mathbf{0}$. Hence the usual product of graphs and more generally relational structures agrees with the definition given above.

For $A \cap B = \emptyset$ let $A + B = (A \cup B; \mathcal{I}, L, \sigma_{A+B})$ be the function structure with:

$$\sigma_{A+B}(w) = \begin{cases} \sigma_A(w) & \text{if } \{w(i) \mid i \in I\} \subseteq A, \\ \sigma_B(w) & \text{if } \{w(i) \mid i \in I\} \subseteq B, \\ \mathbf{0} & \text{otherwise.} \end{cases}$$

If $A \cap B \neq \emptyset$ let $B' = (B'; \mathcal{I}, L, \sigma_{B'})$ be isomorphic to B and then let $A + B$ be equal to $A + B'$, effectively defining $A + B$ for isomorphism classes. Note that $A' \to A$ and $B' \to B$ implies $A' + B' \to A + B$ and if $A' \sim A$ and $B' \sim B$ then $A' + B' \sim A + B$. Note that $A \to A + B$ and $B \to A + B$ and if $A \to C$ and $B \to C$ then $A + B \to C$ implying that $+$ is the categorical sum of the homomorphism category on $\mathfrak{F}(\mathcal{I}, L)$. Of course, if L is complete, the notion of $+$ for two $(\mathcal{I}, L)$-structures can be extended in an obvious way to $\sum_{j \in J} A_j$.

The fact that $A' \sim A$ and $B' \sim B$ implies $A' \times B' \sim A \times B$ and $A' + B' \sim A + B$ and if $A' \to B'$ then $A \to B$ makes it possible to extend the notions of $\times$ and $+$ and $\to$ for $\mathfrak{F}(\mathcal{I}, L)$ structures to the $\sim$ equivalence classes of $\mathfrak{F}(\mathcal{I}, L)$.

The reader only interested in finite structures can restrict the class of structures $A = (A; \mathcal{I}, L, \sigma)$ in $\mathfrak{F}(\mathcal{I}, L)$ to those for which A is finite and every $I \in \mathcal{I}$ is finite and disregard any mention of infinite cardinals. The class of such structures is denoted by $\mathfrak{F}_{\text{fin}}(\mathcal{I}, L)$.

Given an infinite cardinal κ let $\mathfrak{F}_\kappa(\mathcal{I}, L)$ be the class of $(\mathcal{I}, L)$ structures whose base set has cardinality less than κ. Obviously $\mathfrak{F}_\kappa(\mathcal{I}, L)$ is closed under the operations of $+$ and $\times$. Let $\mathfrak{L}_\kappa(\mathcal{I}, L)$ denote the lattice of $\sim$ equivalence classes in $(\mathfrak{F}_\kappa(\mathcal{I}, L)$. We will usually tacitly assume that κ is understood, that is given in the preamble like, we are considering finite graphs only, and often just write $\mathfrak{L}(\mathcal{I}, L)$ and $\mathfrak{F}(\mathcal{I}, L)$. If L is complete then $\times$ and $+$ can be extended to infinite products and sums, but with the possibility of increasing the cardinality of the set of $(\mathcal{I}, L)$ structures under consideration. In many instances we also wish to restrict the arity of the functions in $\bigcup_{I \in \mathcal{I}} A^I$, say finite graphs with $\aleph_\omega$ many different edge types. So, for a cardinal λ let $\mathfrak{F}_{\langle \kappa, \lambda \rangle}(\mathcal{I}, L)$ be the class of structures $A = (A; \mathcal{I}, L, \sigma_A)$ in $\mathfrak{F}_\kappa(\mathcal{I}, L)$ for which the cardinality of the index sets $I \in \mathcal{I}$ is less than λ. Again, the class $\mathfrak{F}_{\langle \kappa, \lambda \rangle}(\mathcal{I}, L)$ is closed under $+$ and $\times$ and hence we obtain the corresponding lattice $\mathfrak{L}_{\langle \kappa, \lambda \rangle}(\mathcal{I}, L)$. There may be other understood restrictions leading to a sublattice of $\mathfrak{L}(\mathcal{I}, L)$. For example the evaluation functions σ should not change under certain permutations of some of the index sets I.

Lemma 1. *The structure consisting of $\mathfrak{L}(\mathcal{I}, L)$ as base set and $+$ as join and $\times$ as meet and $\rightarrow$ for the order relation $\leq$ is a bounded lattice. (For the infinite case replace $\mathfrak{L}(\mathcal{I}, L)$ by $\mathfrak{L}_{\langle \kappa, \lambda \rangle}(\mathcal{I}, L)$.)*

Proof. The relation $\rightarrow$ is transitive and hence it follows easily that $(\mathfrak{L}(\mathcal{I}, L); \leq)$ is a partial order. The facts that if $C \rightarrow A$ and $C \rightarrow B$ then $C \rightarrow A \times B$ and if $A \rightarrow D$ and $B \rightarrow D$ then $A + B \rightarrow D$ imply that $(\mathfrak{L}(\mathcal{I}, L); \leq, +, \times)$ is a lattice.

The one element of $\mathfrak{L}(\mathcal{I}, L)$ is the $\sim$ equivalence class containing a structure whose base is a singleton set, say $\{x\}$, with $\sigma(v) = \mathbf{1}$ for all $I \in \mathcal{I}$ and $v \in \{x\}^I$. (That is, v is the constant map to x.) The zero element of $\mathfrak{L}(\mathcal{I}, L)$ is the $\sim$ equivalence class containing a structure whose base is a singleton set, say $\{y\}$, with $\sigma(v) = \mathbf{0}$ for all $I \in \mathcal{I}$ and $v \in \{y\}^I$. $\qquad\square$

If the lattice $\mathfrak{L}(\mathcal{I}, L)$ is a Heyting algebra then it is distributive. In general, even if L is not a Heyting algebra:

Lemma 2. *The lattice $\mathfrak{L}(\mathcal{I}, L)$ is distributive.*

Proof. Let $(\mathcal{I}, L)$-structures A, B, C be given with the base sets A of A and B of B and C of C with A and B disjoint. Then the base set of $D_l := C \times (A + B)$, say D_l, is the set of pairs $\{(c, x) \mid c \in C \text{ and } x \in A \cup B\}$. The base set of $D_r := (C \times A) + C \times B$, say D_r, is the set of all pairs of the form $\{(c, x) \mid c \in C \text{ and } x \in A\} \cup \{(c, x) \mid c \in C \text{ and } x \in B\}$. Then $D_l = D_r := D$. For a given string $s := \{(c_i, x_i) \mid i \in I\}$ let $\mathbf{c} = \sigma_C(c_i; i \in I)$. If $x_i \in A$ for all $i \in I$ then:

$$\sigma_{D_l}(s) = \mathbf{c} \wedge \sigma_A(x_i; i \in I) = \sigma_{D_r}(s)$$

and similar if $x_i \in B$ for all $i \in I$. Note that $C \times A$ and $C \times B$ are disjoint. If there is an $i \in I$ with $x_i \in A$ and a $j \in I$ with $x_j \in B$ then $(c_i, x_i) \in C \times A$ and $(c_j, x_j) \in C \times B$ and hence

$$\sigma_{D_l}(s) = \mathbf{c} \wedge \sigma_A(x_i; i \in I) = \mathbf{c} \wedge \mathbf{0} = \mathbf{0} = \sigma_{D_r}(s).$$

It follows that the identity map is an isomorphism of $C \times (A + B)$ to $(C \times A) + (C \times B)$. $\qquad\square$

Definition 1. *Let* A, B *be structures in* $\mathfrak{F}(\mathcal{I}, L)$ *and* L *a Heyting algebra. Let* $f = (f_i; i \in I \in \mathcal{I})$ *be functions of* A *into* B *and* $a = (a_i; i \in I) \in A^I$ *then*

$$f(a) = (f_i(a_i); i \in I) \in B^I.$$

Let B^A *be the function structure* $(B^A; \mathcal{I}, L, \sigma_{B^A})$ *so that for* $I \in \mathcal{I}$ *and* $f = (f_i \mid i \in I)$ *with* f_i *a function from* A *to* B *for all* $i \in I$:

$$\sigma_{B^A}(f) = \bigwedge_{a \in A^I} \left(\sigma_B(f(a))\right)^{\sigma_A(a)}. \tag{2}$$

The power on the right hand side of (2) is exponentiation in the Heyting algebra L.

There are of course conditions on the lattice L and the class of structures under consideration to ensure that Definition 1 is viable. One is that the meet in Equality (2) exists in L and the other that the cardinality of B^A is not larger than or equal to κ when considering structures in $\mathfrak{F}_\kappa(\mathcal{I}, L)$. Both conditions will be satisfied if $\kappa = \aleph_0$ and I is finite for every $I \in \mathcal{I}$. That is, if considering finite structures with finite signature, or considering finite structures and a complete lattice L. Or the case where κ is a strong limit cardinal and L is κ-meet complete. (That is if L is closed under the infimum of fewer than κ elements.) More precisely, if κ is a strong limit cardinal and $\lambda \leq \kappa$ and L is λ-meet complete then the class $\mathfrak{F}_{\langle \kappa, \lambda \rangle}(\mathcal{I}, L)$ is closed under exponentiation.

Lemma 3. *Let* A, B *be structures in* $\mathfrak{F}(\mathcal{I}, L)$. *Then* $X \to B^A$ *for every* $X \in \mathfrak{F}(\mathcal{I}, L)$ *with* $A \times X \to B$.

Proof. Let $X = (X; \mathcal{I}, L, \sigma_X)$ be an $(\mathcal{I}, L)$ structure and h a homomorphism of $A \times X$ into B. For $x \in X$ let $f_x : A \to B$ be the function with $f_x(a) = h(a, x)$. For $I \in \mathcal{I}$ let $a = (a_i; i \in I) \in A^I$ and $x = (x_i; i \in I) \in X^I$ and $f = (f_{x_i} \mid i \in I)$ then:

$$\sigma_A(a) \wedge \sigma_X(x) = \sigma_{A \times B}((a_i, x_i); i \in I) \leq$$
$$\sigma_B(h(a_i, x_i); i \in I) = \sigma_B(f_{x_i}(a_i); i \in I) = \sigma_B(f(a)),$$

implying that $\sigma_X(x) \leq \left(\sigma_B(f(a))\right)^{\sigma_A(a)}$ for every word $(a_i \mid i \in I)$. Hence:

$$\sigma_X(x) \leq \bigwedge_{a \in A^I} \left(\sigma_B(f(a))\right)^{\sigma_A(a)} = \sigma_{B^A}(f).$$

It follows that the function $\varphi : X \to B^A$ with $\varphi(x) = f_x$ for $x \in X$ is a homomorphism of X into B^A. $\square$

Then $B \to B^A$ because $A \times B \to B$.

Lemma 4. *Let* A, B *be structures in* $\mathfrak{F}(\mathcal{I}, L)$. *Then* $A \times B^A \to B$.

Proof. Let $e : A \times B^A \to B$ be the function with $e(a, f) = f(a)$, the evaluation function. We will show that e is a homomorphism of $A \times B^A$ into B.

$$\sigma_{A \times B^A}((a_i, f_i); i \in I) = \sigma_A(a_i; i \in I) \wedge \sigma_{B^A}(f_i; i \in I) \leq$$
$$\sigma_A(a_i; i \in I) \wedge \sigma_B(f_i(a_i); i \in I)^{\sigma_A(a_i; i \in I)} \leq$$
$$\sigma_B(f_i(a_i); i \in I) = \sigma_B(e(a_i, f_i); i \in I). \qquad \square$$

Lemma 5. *Let* A_0, B_0, A_1, B_1, *be structures in* $\mathfrak{F}(\mathcal{I}, L)$. *If* $B_0 \to B_1$ *and* $A_1 \to A_0$ *then* $B_0^{A_0} \to B_1^{A_1}$. *If* $B_0 \sim B_1$ *and* $A_1 \sim A_0$ *then* $B_0^{A_0} \sim B_1^{A_1}$.

Proof. As the second assertion follows from the first we will prove the first. Let A_0, B_0, A_1, B_1, be structures in $\mathfrak{F}(\mathcal{I}, L)$. Let $B_0 \to B_1$ and $A_1 \to A_0$.

Using Lemma 3 we get for $i \in 2$: $A_0 \times B_i^{A_0} \to B_i$ implying $A_1 \times B_i^{A_0} \to B_i$ implying $B_i^{A_0} \to B_i^{A_1}$. $A_i \times B_0^{A_i} \to B_0 \to B_1$ implying $B_0^{A_i} \to B_1^{A_i}$. Hence: $B_0^{A_0} \to B_0^{A_1} \to B_1^{A_1}$. $\qquad \square$

It follows from Lemma 5 that the exponentiation of structures can be carried to exponentiation of the elements of $\mathfrak{L}(\mathcal{I}, L)$ via: For two elements $\tilde{A}$ and $\tilde{B}$ in $\mathfrak{L}(\mathcal{I}, L)$ let $\tilde{B}^{\tilde{A}}$ be the element in $\mathfrak{L}(\mathcal{I}, L)$ containing the structure A^B.

The exponentiation given in Definition 1 has the property that the cardinality of the base set of B^A is equal to the cardinality of the base set of B power the cardinality of the base set of A. The lattice $\mathfrak{L}(\mathcal{I}, L)$ has *natural exponentiation* if it does have exponentiation and for all $\tilde{A}$ and $\tilde{B}$ in $\mathfrak{L}(\mathcal{I}, L)$ there exists an element $C \in \tilde{B}^{\tilde{A}}$ for which the cardinality of its base set is less than or equal to the cardinality of the base set of B power the base set of A. Remember that if an exponentiation, that is relative complements, exist then they are unique.

Theorem 1. *Let* κ *be a strong limit cardinal and* $\lambda \leq \kappa$ *and* L *be* λ-*meet complete. Then* $\mathfrak{L}_{\langle \kappa, \lambda \rangle}(\mathcal{I}, L)$ *is a Heyting algebra with natural exponentiation if* L *is a Heyting algebra and if* $\mathfrak{L}_{\langle \kappa, \lambda \rangle}(\mathcal{I}, L)$ *is a Heyting algebra with natural exponentiation hen* L *is a Heyting algebra.*

Proof. Let L be a Heyting algebra. Then $\mathfrak{L}_{\langle \kappa, \lambda \rangle}(\mathcal{I}, L)$ is a bounded lattice according to Lemma 1. It follows from Lemma 3 and Lemma 4 that for two elements $\mathbf{a}$ and $\mathbf{b}$ in $\mathfrak{L}(\mathcal{I}, L)$ the element $\mathbf{b^a}$ is the maximum of all elements $\mathbf{x} \in \mathfrak{L}(\mathcal{I}, L)$ with $\mathbf{a} \times \mathbf{x} \to \mathbf{b}$. Hence $\mathfrak{L}_{\langle \kappa, \lambda \rangle}(\mathcal{I}, L)$ is a Heyting algebra.

Let $\mathfrak{L}_{\langle \kappa, \lambda \rangle}(\mathcal{I}, L)$ be a Heyting algebra with natural exponentiation. Denote the constant function from $I \in \mathcal{I}$ to 0 by c_I. For $\mathbf{a} \in L$ let $\underline{\mathbf{a}}$ be the structure in $\mathfrak{F}_{\langle \kappa, \lambda \rangle}(\mathcal{I}, L)$ with base set $\{0\}$ and $\sigma_{\underline{\mathbf{a}}}(c_I) = \mathbf{a}$ for every $I \in \mathcal{I}$. Then $\mathbf{a} \leq \mathbf{b}$ in L if and only if $\underline{\mathbf{a}} \to \underline{\mathbf{b}}$ in $\mathfrak{F}_{\langle \kappa, \lambda \rangle}(\mathcal{I}, L)$. Let $\mathbf{a}, \mathbf{b} \in L$. The exponentiation in $\mathfrak{L}_{\langle \kappa, \lambda \rangle}(\mathcal{I}, L)$ is natural and hence there exists a singleton structure E in $\underline{\mathbf{b}}^{\underline{\mathbf{a}}}$. We may assume without loss that this singleton is the number 0, say $E = (\{0\}, \mathcal{I}, L, \sigma_E)$. For $I \in \mathcal{I}$ let $\mathbf{c}(I) = \sigma_E(c_I)$.

Let $\mathbf{x} \in L$ with $\mathbf{a} \wedge \mathbf{x} \leq \mathbf{b}$. Then $\underline{\mathbf{a}} \times \underline{\mathbf{x}} \to \underline{\mathbf{b}}$ which in turn implies $\mathbf{x} \leq \sigma_E(c_I)$ for all $I \in \mathcal{I}$. Hence, because relative complements are unique, $\sigma_E(c_I) = \sigma_E(c_J)$ for all $I, J \in \mathcal{I}$ and $\sigma_E(c_I)$ is the relative complement of $\mathbf{a}$ with respect to $\mathbf{b}$. $\qquad \square$

As $\aleph_0$ is a strong limit cardinal we obtain for $\mathfrak{F}_{\langle\aleph_0,\aleph_0\rangle}(\mathcal{I},L) = \mathfrak{F}_{\mathrm{fin}}(\mathcal{I},L)$:

Corollary 1. $\mathfrak{L}_{\mathrm{fin}}(\mathcal{I},L)$ *is a Heyting algebra with natural exponentiation if and only if L is a Heyting algebra with natural exponentiation.*

5   Meet Irreducible Elements

An element c in a lattice L is *meet irreducible* if $a \wedge b = c$ implies $a = c$ or $b = c$. The question of whether the complete graphs are meet irreducible in the homomorphism lattice of graphs is equivalent to the seemingly intractable Hedetniemi conjecture. See [11], [12], [13]. A structure $A = (A;\mathcal{I},L,\sigma) \in \mathfrak{F}(\mathcal{I},L)$ is *finite* if its base set A is finite. As most of the interest in Hedetniemi's conjecture concerns finite structures we will restrict to finite structures in this section.

Let $A = (A;\mathcal{I},L,\sigma_A) \in \mathfrak{F}(\mathcal{I},L)$ be finite. Then there exists a smallest number n so that A has a homomorphism f into A with $|f(A)| = n$. It is easy to see that any two homomorphic images of A to A with this minimal number n of elements in the base set are isomorphic. Such minimal images are called *core* of A. Let $B = (B;\mathcal{I},L,\sigma_B)$ be a core of A then every homomorphism of B into B is an isomorphism and there exists a homomorphism of A into B which is the identity on B, hence B is a retract of A. A structure $A \in \mathfrak{F}(\mathcal{I},L)$ is a *core* if every homomorphism of A to A is an isomorphism. Every $\sim$ equivalence class with at least one finite structure in it, contains up to isomorphism a unique core which is the core of every element in that $\sim$ equivalence class.

For the lattice $\mathfrak{L}(\mathcal{I},L)$ the following necessary condition exists for meet irreducibility.

Theorem 2. *Let $C = (C;\mathcal{I},L,\sigma_C) \in \mathfrak{F}(\mathcal{I},L)$ be a finite core and $\mathbf{a} \neq \mathbf{c} \neq \mathbf{b}$ three elements in L with $\mathbf{a}\wedge\mathbf{b} = \mathbf{c}$ and $J \in I$ and a word $w \in A^J$ with $\sigma_C(w) = \mathbf{c}$.*

Then there exist finite structures A_0 and B_0 in $\mathfrak{F}(\mathcal{I},L)$ with $A_0 \not\sim C \not\sim B_0$ so that $A_0 \times B_0 \sim C$.

Proof. Let $A = (C;\mathcal{I},\sigma_A)$ with $\sigma_A(v) = \sigma_C(v)$ for all $v \in \bigcup_{I \in \mathcal{I}} A^I$ with $v \neq w$ and let $\sigma_A(w) = \mathbf{a}$. Let $B = (C;\mathcal{I},\sigma_B)$ with $\sigma_B(v) = \sigma_C(v)$ for all $v \in \bigcup_{J \neq I \in \mathcal{I}} B^I$ and let $\sigma_B(v) = \mathbf{c}$ for all $v \in A^J$ with $v \neq w$ and let $\sigma_B(w) = \mathbf{b}$. The first coordinate projection π_1 is a homomorphism of $A \times B$ to C, because:

For $v,u \in C^I$ and $v \neq w$ we have $\pi_1((v_i,u_i);i \in I) = (v_i;i \in I)$ and $\sigma_{A \times B}((v_i,u_i);i \in I) = \sigma_A(v_i;i \in I) \wedge \sigma_B(u_i;i \in I) = \sigma_C(v_i;i \in I) \wedge \sigma_B(u_i;i \in I) \leq \sigma_C(v_i;i \in I)$. For $v = w$ and $u \neq w$ we have $u,v \in A^J$ and $\pi_1((w_i,u_i);i \in I) = (w_i;i \in I)$ and $\sigma_{A \times B}((v_i,u_i);i \in I) = \sigma_A(w_i;i \in I) \wedge \sigma_B(u_i;i \in I) = \sigma_A(w_i;i \in I) \wedge \mathbf{c} \leq \mathbf{c} = \sigma_C(w_i;i \in I)$. For $v = w$ and $u = w$ we have $w \in A^J$ and $\pi_1((w_i,w_i);i \in I) = (w_i;i \in I)$ and $\sigma_{A \times B}((v_i,u_i);i \in I) = \sigma_A(w_i;i \in I) \wedge \sigma_B(u_i;i \in I) = \mathbf{a} \wedge \mathbf{b} = \mathbf{c} = \sigma_C(w_i;i \in I)$.

Assume for a contradiction that $A \to C$ via a homomorphism, say f. The function f is an endomorphism of C into C because $\sigma_A(w) = \mathbf{a} > \mathbf{c} = \sigma_C(w)$. Because C is a core, f is one-to-one and an automorphism of C and hence has an inverse f^{-1}. But $\sigma_C(f \circ w) \geq \mathbf{a}$ and $\sigma_C(w) = \mathbf{c} < \mathbf{a}$ and $f^{-1} \circ (f \circ w) = w$, a contradiction. Hence $A \nrightarrow C$ and similarly $B \nrightarrow C$.

Let $A_0 = A + C$ and $B_0 = B + C$.   □

Hedetniemi's conjecture says that the complete graphs are meet irreducible within the homomorphism lattice of graphs, or equivalently if the chromatic number of two graphs having chromatic number n is equal to n. Given a lattice L and a single two element index set I the obvious choice for complete graphs is to assign a value $\mathbf{a} \in L$ to all of the vertices and another value $\mathbf{b}$ to all of the two element subsets to obtain the analogue of complete ordinary graphs without loops. Of course in order to avoid trivial cases we have to choose $\mathbf{b} \not\leq \mathbf{a}$ and because of Theorem 2 both $\mathbf{a}$ and $\mathbf{b}$ irreducible in L. Which in many cases excludes the choice of $\mathbf{a} = \mathbf{0}$. Let $\mathfrak{G}(L)$ be the class of graphs whose vertices and edges are labeled by elements of the lattice L, and by misuse of notation also the resulting $\sim$ equivalence classes. For $\mathbf{a}, \mathbf{b}$ meet irreducible elements of L with $\mathbf{b} \not\leq \mathbf{a}$ denote by $K_{n,L,\mathbf{a},\mathbf{b}} \in \mathfrak{G}(L)$ the structure on n vertices labeled by $\mathbf{a}$ and the two element subsets labelled by $\mathbf{b}$, called *complete structures of* $\mathfrak{G}(L)$.

Then considering for example the lattice $L = \{\mathbf{1}, \mathbf{0}, \mathbf{a}, \mathbf{b}\}$ on four elements with $\mathbf{a} \not\leq \mathbf{b} \not\leq \mathbf{a}$ there are three types of complete structures. Labelling the points with $\mathbf{a}$ or $\mathbf{b}$ and the edges then with $\mathbf{b}$ or $\mathbf{a}$ respectively, or with $\mathbf{1}$. It is not difficult, but requires a few case distinctions, to show that any one of those complete structures will be meet irreducible if and only if the corresponding complete graph on the same number of vertices is meet irreducible.

Problem 1. Is it the case that for all Heyting algebras L the generalized complete graphs $K_{n,L,\mathbf{a},\mathbf{b}}$ are meet irreducible in $\mathfrak{G}(L)$ if and only if the ordinary complete graph on n vertices is meet irreducible? If not, is there a good characterization of lattices and pairs of elements in them for which this is the case?

6   Gaps, Dualities and Trees

The topics of gaps, dualities, trees and related notions have recently, after many years of development mainly by Nešetřil and Tardif, found a very beautiful resolution in the general context of Heyting algebras, see [14], [15], [16], [17] to mention just a few papers of their very substantial work. The references of the indicated papers will lead to other related work. This section contains only a very brief and incomplete outline of their work, relating it to $\mathfrak{L}(I, L)$-structures.

Let L be a lattice. An element $\mathbf{c} \in L$ is *connected* if $\mathbf{c} \leq \mathbf{a} \vee \mathbf{b}$ implies $\mathbf{c} \leq \mathbf{a}$ or $\mathbf{c} \leq \mathbf{b}$. The lattice L has *finite connected decomposition* if for every $\mathbf{c} \in L$ there is a finite set F of connected elements in L with $\mathbf{c} = \bigvee F$. The structures in $\mathfrak{L}_{\text{fin}}(I, L)$ have finite connected decomposition. In addition the elements in $\mathfrak{F}_{\text{fin}}(I, L)$ have a core, as remarked on earlier. A *duality pair* $(\mathbf{l}, \mathbf{r})$ in L is a pair of elements in L so that for all $\mathbf{x} \in L$: $\mathbf{l} \not\leq \mathbf{x}$ if and only if $\mathbf{x} \leq \mathbf{r}$. A pair of elements $(\mathbf{a}, \mathbf{b})$ of L is a *gap* if $\mathbf{a} < \mathbf{b}$ and $\mathbf{a} \leq \mathbf{c} \leq \mathbf{b}$ implies $\mathbf{a} = \mathbf{c}$ or $\mathbf{c} = \mathbf{b}$. The following theorem is a very special case of the general results in [14]:

Theorem 3. *The gaps in a Heyting algebra L with connected decompositions are exactly the pairs $(\mathbf{a}, \mathbf{b})$ such that for some duality $(\mathbf{l}, \mathbf{r})$,*

$$\mathbf{l} \wedge \mathbf{r} \leq \mathbf{a} \leq \mathbf{r} \ and \ \mathbf{b} = \mathbf{a} \vee \mathbf{l}.$$

Let L be a Heyting algebra. Then $\mathfrak{L}_{\mathrm{fin}}(\mathcal{I}, L)$ is a Heyting algebra with connected decompositions and hence we obtain from Theorem 3:

Corollary 2. *The gaps in a $\mathfrak{L}_{\mathrm{fin}}(\mathcal{I}, L)$ with L a Heyting algebra are exactly the pairs $(\tilde{A}, \tilde{B})$ such that for some duality $(\tilde{L}, \tilde{R})$,*

$$\tilde{L} \times \tilde{R} \to \tilde{A} \to \tilde{R} \ and \ \tilde{B} = \tilde{A} + \tilde{L}.$$

Let $(\tilde{L}, \tilde{R})$ be a duality in $\mathfrak{L}_{\mathrm{fin}}(\mathcal{I}, L)$. Then for all $\tilde{X} \in L$:

$$\tilde{L} \nrightarrow \tilde{X} \ \text{if and only if} \ \tilde{X} \to \tilde{R}.$$

That is, given R, the constraint satisfaction problem to determine the structures X with X → R has the solution that there is a structure L such that those X will have a homomorphism into R for which L does not have a homomorphism into X. Of course then replacing R and or L by finitely many structures is an obvious next question. An answer to this and related question can be found in [14].

For which structures A is there a structure B so that (A, B) is a gap and how to calculate the structure B has been answered in [17]. A gap can only be under a "tree like structure". The definitions in [17] of circle and tree generalize in an obvious way to $\mathcal{F}_{\mathrm{fin}}(\mathcal{I}, L)$ structures.

References

1. Maurer, H.A., Sudborough, J.H., Welzl, E.: On the complexity of the general coloring problem. Inform. and Control 51, 123–145 (1981)
2. Maurer, H.A., Salomaa, A., Wood, D.: Colorings and interpretations: a connection between graphs and grammar forms. Discrete Appl. Math. 3, 119–135 (1981)
3. Maurer, H.A., Salomaa, A., Wood, D.: Dense hierarchies of grammatical families. J. ACM 29(1), 118–126 (1982)
4. Maurer, H.A., Salomaa, A., Wood, D.: Dense hierarchies of grammatical families. J. Assoc. Comput. Mach. 29(1), 118–126 (1982)
5. Duffus, D., Sauer, N.: Lattices arising in categorical investigations of Hedetniemi's conjecture. Discrete Math. 152, 125–139 (1996)
6. Balbes, R., Dwinger, P.: Distributive Lattices. University of Missouri Press, Columbia (1974)
7. Birkhoff, G.: Generalized arithmetic. Duke Math. J. 12, 283–302 (1942)
8. Rutherford, D.E.: Introduction to Lattice Theory. Oliver and Boyd (1965)
9. Gierz, G., Hoffmann, K.H., Keimel, K., Lawson, J.D., Mislove, M., Scott, D.S.: Continuous Lattices and Domains. Encyclopedia of Mathematics and its Applications 93 (2003)
10. Kuich, W., Sauer, N., Urbanek, F.: Heyting Algebras and Formal Languages. J. of Universal Computer Science 8(7), 722–736 (2002)

11. Tardif, C.: Hedetniemi's conjecture, 40 years later. Graph Theory Notes of New York LIV, pp. 46–57. New York Academy of Sciences (2008)
12. Zhu, X.: A survey on Hedetniemi's conjecture. Taiwanese Journal of Mathematics 2(1), 1–24 (1998)
13. Sauer, N.: Hedetniemis Conjecture–a survey. Combinatorics, graph theory, algorithms and applications. Discrete Math. 229(1-3), 261–292 (2001)
14. Foniok, J., Nešetřil, J., Pultr, A., Tardif, C.: Dualities and Dual Pairs in Heyting Algebras. Order. arXiv:0908.0428v1 (July 16, 2010)
15. Foniok, J., Nešetřil, J., Tardif, C.: Generalised dualities and maximal finite antichains in the homomorphism order of relational structures. European J. Combin. 29(4), 881–899 (2008)
16. Nešetřil, J., Pultr, A., Tardif, C.: Gaps and dualities in Heyting categories. Comment. Math. Univ. Carolin. 48(1), 9–23 (2007)
17. Nešetřil, J., Tardif, C.: Duality theorems for finite structures (characterising gaps and good characterisations). J. Combin. Theory Ser. B 80(1), 80–97 (2000)

Learning

Transdisciplinary Collaboration and Lifelong Learning: Fostering and Supporting New Learning Opportunities

Gitta Domik[1] and Gerhard Fischer[2]

[1] University of Paderborn, Warburgerstrasse 100, D-33098 Paderborn, Germany
[2] University of Colorado at Boulder, Boulder, CO. 80301-0430, USA

Abstract. The contexts provided by the world of the 21st century require that our societies rethink and reinvent learning, teaching, working, and collaboration. A first basic challenge insufficiently addressed by prior research and practice is that almost all of the significant problems of tomorrow will be *systemic problems*, which cannot be addressed by any one specialty. These problems require *transdisciplinary collaboration* that focuses on opportunities for knowledge workers to work in teams, communities, and organizations that encompass multiple ways of knowing and collaborating. A second basic challenge is that learning can no longer be dichotomized into a place and time to acquire knowledge (school) and a place and time to apply knowledge (the workplace). To educate students today requires that we provide them with opportunities and soft skills to become *lifelong learners*.

This paper (1) discusses the conceptual frameworks that we have developed to address these challenges; (2) describes our implementation and experience teaching a one semester graduate course based on our framework; and (3) discusses implications and future opportunities.

Keywords: 21st century competencies, systemic problems, transdisciplinary collaboration, lifelong learning, self-directed learning, learning on demand, computer science education, breadth-first teaching, Long Tail learning, reflective communities.

1 Introduction

Many real-world problems have become too complex to solve for a single expert out of one discipline. The knowledge relevant to solve complex problems is increasingly distributed among many people requiring *socio-technical environments* [1] that bring together people with different, complementary, and often-controversial points of view to form a community. Despite these widely accepted attributes, contemporary higher education is primarily characterized by receiving knowledge out of one single department (usually synonymous with one single discipline), therefore forming specialists with depth in unidisciplinary knowledge and discipline-dependent characteristics ("stereotype"). We support "tribal behaviour" in our departments, creating "artists", "computer scientists"

C.S. Calude, G. Rozenberg, A. Salomaa (Eds.): Maurer Festschrift, LNCS 6570, pp. 129–143, 2011.

and "urban planners", each group harmonizing their own world and suffering from Groupthink [2].

Another major challenge facing our educational system is that the body of knowledge to be taught in a Computer Science (CS) curriculum expands continuously as testified by the changes in the Computing Curricula recommendations by ACM and IEEE ([3], [4]). Even after our students graduate, the body of knowledge will expand and they will be responsible to acquire knowledge without extrinsic motivation (e.g. mandated assessments) both within their own discipline, but in collaboration with others coming not only from their own discipline.

To respond to these challenges, we are engaged in research activities and educational innovations focused on fostering and supporting new learning opportunities based on inter- and transdisciplinary collaboration and lifelong learning that are aimed at (1) having students practice meaningful collaboration with other disciplines, and (2) transforming students from being educational consumers to become socially competent, responsible, self-directed learners.

This paper first defines and explores transdisciplinary collaboration and lifelong learning. We postulate two strategies in a framework, namely breadth-first and Long Tail, that aid in the learning process, before we describe our implementation and experience teaching a one semester graduate course based on our framework. Finally, we discuss implications and future opportunities.

2   Transdisciplinary Collaboration

Transdisciplinary collaboration is a group process between individuals educated and knowledgeable in different disciplines (such as: computer scientists, biologists, designers of new media, urban planners, etc.). In exploring these collaborations, researchers and educators use the terms *multidisciplinarity, interdisciplinarity,* and *transdisciplinarity,* often without clearly distinguishing among them, though these terms are well defined and distinguished by e.g. Klein [5], Rosenfield [6] and Nicolescu [7]. In short,

- *multidisciplinarity* means that several disciplines are being involved either in a sequential or juxtaposed mode;
- *interdisciplinarity* implies integration or blending of knowledge from different disciplines;
- *transdisciplinarity* places the highest demand with the objective to form new knowledge from available unidisciplinary awareness.

Transdisciplinarity in education requiring the creation of new organizational framework for knowledge out of separate disciplines demands collaboration of researchers and faculty from different disciplines. Therefore, in most standard university courses, interdisciplinary collaboration (feasible with a single educator) will be used to prepare for later transdisciplinary or interdisciplinary collaboration among various disciplines.

Providing students with opportunities in inter- and transdisciplinary education as a preparation for engaging later in transdisciplinary collaboration raises

Table 1. Demands for Transdisciplinary Collaboration in Science Transferred to Education

Demand by Stokols [9]	How educators can be of support:
support members' strong commitment to achieving transdisciplinary goals and outcomes	support students in – finding unique topics they feel passionate about; – team building process
establish common conceptual ground and informal social ties	establish common language and help establish social ties
schedule frequent face-to-face meetings for brain-storming of ideas	encourage and enforce face-to-face meetings; give help with structure of these meetings
establish electronic linkages among participants	encourage the use of free electronic linkages, e.g, Wikis, Skype, or ICQ additionally to Email
constrain unrealistic expectations and ambiguity about shared goals and products; constrain conflicts among alternative disciplinary views of science	participate in selected face-to-face meetings to constrain "tribal behaviour" through own interpersonal and interdisciplinary skills

the issues at what educational level will students be mature enough to blend knowledge or to form new knowledge? Derry and Fischer [8] specifically argue for a transdisciplinary education at the graduate level. Rosenfield [6] also places transdisciplinary training at the early graduate level, because a solid grounding in their own discipline, respect for the contributions that other disciplines can make, and the sensitivity to cooperative endeavour is a prerequisite to perform transdisciplinary research.

Stokols [9] observes in his scientific collaborations the following factors supporting productive and rewarding collaboration between disciplines:

– members' strong commitment to achieving transdisciplinary goals and outcomes;
– interpersonal skills of team leaders;
– history of prior collaboration among team members;
– spatial proximity of team members' offices and laboratories;
– schedule frequent face-to-face meetings for brain-storming of ideas;
– establish electronic linkages among participants;
– foster institutional supports for these objectives.

In addition, he articulates the following factors constraining transdisciplinary collaboration:

– substantial time required to establish common conceptual ground and informal social ties;
– unrealistic expectations and ambiguity about shared goals and products;

- conflicts among alternative disciplinary views of science; and
- bureaucratic impediments to cross-departmental collaboration.

Stokols research is grounded in an analysis of *scientific* collaborations (to improve understanding of nicotine addiction), our research activities transferred these indicators into educational settings. Table 1 transfers educationally relevant indicators to a constructive condition in education.

From Table 1 we can derive two issues that are paramount: (1) students need to find a *common ground* for their communication as early in the course as possible [10]; (2) students need projects that they feel committed to out of *personal interest*. Once these concerns are solved, the other issues (e.g. team building process, enforcing meaningful group meetings and electronic linkage) will be easier to solve.

3   Lifelong Learning

In the 21st century, learning can no longer be dichotomized into a place and time to acquire knowledge (school) and a place and time to *apply* knowledge (the workplace). Todays citizens are flooded with more information than they can handle, and tomorrows workers will need to know far more than they can learn today in school.

Lifelong learning is an essential challenge for inventing the future of our societies; it is a necessity rather than a possibility or a luxury to be considered. It complements and transforms industrial-age with knowledge-age approaches (see Table 2). Lifelong learning is more than adult education and/or training [11]: it is a mindset and a habit for people to acquire. Lifelong learning creates the challenge to understand, explore, and support new essential dimensions of learning such as: (1) self-directed learning, (2) learning on demand, (3) collaborative learning, and (4) organizational learning. These approaches need new media and innovative technologies to be adequately supported.

A significant weakness of current educational systems is that they do not deliberately educate for lifelong learning. Rather, current systems require that at a certain point in their development, learners in all walks of life leave school in which they were mostly consumers of educational material and throw a "big switch" to become socially competent, responsible, self-directed learners who successfully use tools and technologies to enrich their personal and working lives and who collaborate with one another to solve local and global problems. Yet little of their previous educational experiences have prepared them to do any of this.

To enrich the cultures of work and learning and the personal lives of learners by cultivating mindsets and skills for lifelong learning, students must be prepared, not only to excel in traditional academic settings, but to contribute knowledge and effort to a world characterized by change, uncertainty and pressing transdisciplinary problems that will require new forms of scholarship, publication, communication and participation.

Table 2. Contrasting Industrial-Age and Knowledge-Age Approaches

Industrial-Age Approaches		Knowledge-Age Approaches
there is a "scientific", best way to learn and to work (programmed instruction, computer-assisted instruction, production lines, waterfall models)	⇒	real problems are ill-defined and wicked; design is argumentative, characterized by a symmetry of ignorance among stakeholders
separation of thinking, doing, and learning	⇒	integration of thinking, doing, and learning
task domains can be completely understood	⇒	understanding is partial; coverage is impossible
objective ways to decompose problems into standardizable actions	⇒	subjective, situated personal interests; need for iterative explorations
all relevant knowledge can be explicitly articulated	⇒	much knowledge is tacit and relies on tacit skills
teacher / manager as oracle	⇒	teacher / manager as facilitator or coach
operational environment: mass markets, simple products and processes, slow change, certainty	⇒	customer orientation, complex products and processes, rapid and substantial change, uncertainty and conflicts

Against this background, we have articulated the following credo for transdisciplinary collaboration and lifelong learning that grounds the research and education activities discussed in this paper:

"If the world of working and living relies on collaboration, creativity, definition and framing of complex problems and if it requires dealing with uncertainty, change, and intelligence that is distributed across cultures, disciplines, and tools — then education should foster transdisciplinary competencies and mindsets that prepare students for having meaningful and productive lives in such a world."

4 Innovative Teaching and Learning Strategies: Breadth-First and Long Tail

4.1 Teaching Different Disciplines Out of the CS Department

Computer science students are expected to be firmly grounded in their own discipline and possess depth in the body of knowledge as described by the Computing Curricula 2001[3]. Soft skills, as necessary as they are for the success of our graduates in the later work place, are not defined in [3] as a core or optional topic. Nevertheless, computer science students must and will learn essential soft skills during their years at the university: e.g. communication skills (in speech, in writing, visual), or working in teams. "[Soft] skills should not be seen as separate but should instead be fully incorporated into the computer science curriculum and its requirements" as requested in [3]: Educators teach communication skills while giving a seminar or advising a bachelor or master thesis; or use software projects to teach team work in software engineering.

We have to aim at teaching transdiciplinary collaboration and lifelong learning in a similar mode: focusing on the content of our CS curriculum but at the same time preparing students for that important competency. While a seminar is better than a lecture course in teaching the competency of oral presentation, we can identify in [3] areas of knowledge that will hold that promise for transdisciplinary collaboration, e.g. the area of Graphics and Visual Computing, where courses on visualization, augmented reality, animation, or (more recently) game development, deepen the knowledge of graphics architecture or rendering algorithms, but at the same time gain from the presence of students of other disciplines (e.g. media sciences, architecture, physics).

Technical competency is ranked high in the job market, so students of other disciplines are showing sufficient interest in joining computer science courses if the prerequisites are manageable [12]. While an electrical engineering student might be interested in OpenGL programming to better utilize her knowledge on signal processing, a media design student might have interest in Flash scripting or a student of journalism to set up a Wiki.

Acquiring skills in a successful course of mixed disciplines (at the graduate level, as recommended earlier in this paper) will need an appropriate balancing of breadth and depth of participating students. In a suitable project for a visualization course for computer science and physics students using air flow data, computer science students will gain depth in developing and implementing real-time flow visualization algorithms, while physics student will only acquire breadth knowledge in that area. (With a joint lecturer of the physics department involved, computer science students can acquire breadth knowledge of modelling air flows while physics students can deepen their previously theoretical knowledge in fluid dynamics.) There should be no need to take Physics 101 for CS students, or for Physics students to take the CS introductory course to C++, to work jointly on projects.

Sometimes CS educators complain about how long it takes to teach non-technical students the skills of programming before "real" work on joint projects can start, when they should concentrate on developing a *common ground* [10] for *all* students so they could work together on a solution, each grounded in the skills of their own discipline and extending into the other discipline only to build necessary overlaps.

4.2 Breadth-First: Finding a Common Language between Disciplines

Stokols [9] demands to establish a common conceptual ground and informal social ties early on in the project, so that the time left to work *together* is maximized. Finding a common conceptual ground means bridging spatial, temporal, technological, and disciplinary distances [13]. The major issue in a course will be to first empower students of diverse disciplines to communicate with each other. We propose to use a breadth-first strategy, where we start with a holistic view of each topic to teach (breadth) and undermine it with an application; then use depth to the level the students are ready for. The first part (breadth) provides overall understanding of the topic on an entry level. The application should give extra motivation to learn more about this topic. The second part (depth) will built up through sophisticated layers and is designed for a specific discipline. If a topic is prepared breadth-first, then the breadth part of the course can be simultaneously taught to students of various disciplines. Advantages for a breadth-first approach are [14]:

- CS students get a holistic view of a topic before they learn about more complicated details;
- CS students can then move on to any depth-level;
- students of other disciplines learn of the importance of a topic through the goal of the application;
- students of different backgrounds can be taught together at the breadth-level;
- all students are being taught the same "language" to describe problems on and solutions to the topic;
- application oriented approaches are motivational to both men and women.

The result of this approach is that breadth-first leaves students of different disciplines with a common language that they can use to discuss goals and strategies for joint projects.

Let us assume that students of diverse disciplines work together in groups on a visualization project. Language differences will become obvious when students discuss the quality of a visual representation and call it "an effective picture". In the mind of an art major this might mean "aesthetic" picture, a computer scientist will think of a (cost) efficient representation. Introducing the terms "expressive" and "effective" [15] to clearly define quality criteria for visual presentations during the first lectures will later be helpful when students discuss their project goals. "Expressive" and "effective" will then replace their discipline-dependent quality descriptors.

This common language is essentially the most important ingredient for transdisciplinary collaboration, because without it the door stays open for misunderstandings, unrealistic expectations and ambiguity about shared goals. It also opens the opportunity to provide additional depth to CS students either by (1) using learning tools providing breadth in the upper levels, and depth in the lower levels; (2) individually helping CS students find references for depth-topics; or (3) offering a seminar (only for CS students) parallel to an interdisciplinary course.

4.3 Long Tail: Passion-Based and Self-motivated Learning

One of the major roles for new media and new technology from a transdisciplinary collaboration and lifelong learning perspective is not to deliver predigested information to individuals, but to provide the opportunity and resources for engaging them in authentic activities, for participating in social debates and discussions, for creating shared understanding among diverse stakeholders, and for framing and solving personally meaningful problems. Our research is grounded in the fundamental belief that all humans (1) have interest and knowledge in one or more niche domains and (2) are eager to *actively contribute in*

Table 3. Long Tail Concepts in Business and in Learning and Education

Web-Based Businesses	Learning and Education
unlimited shelf-space	unlimited knowledge
megahits (head)	core curriculum (head)
niche markets (tail)	passion for unique topics (tail)
hybrid model of distribution	hybrid model of learning and discovery
many interesting books, movies, songs will not enter the traditional marketplace	many interesting topics and ideas will not be taught in traditional learning environments

personally meaningful activities [16]. The richness of these interests and the passion of the humans involved in them leads to the *Long Tail* [17] of distributed knowledge [18]. The fundamental transformation of a Long Tail perspective refers to at least two aspects: (1) learning and discovery about exotic, but important topics outside the mainstream education curriculum, and (2) the opportunity to communicate with people who share similar *niche interests* anywhere in the world on a regular basis.

The Long Tail theory explores how our economy and culture is shifting from mass markets to million of niches. It analyzes the effect of technologies that have made it easier for consumers to find and buy niche products based on the "infinite shelf-space effect" supported by new distribution mechanisms that eliminate the bottlenecks of broadcast and traditional bricks-and-mortar retail.

The concept of the Long Tail (as developed in business environments) [17] postulates that our culture and economy are increasingly shifting away from a focus on a relatively small number of products and markets at the head of the popularity curve toward a huge number of niches in the tail. The research in our Center for Life Learning & Design (L3D) reinterprets and explores the Long Tail business environments for transforming learning and education [18, 19] as seen in Table 3.

Assessing passion-based, self-motivated learning based on the Long Tail perspective requires fundamentally different assessment approaches compared to what standard educational testing can offer [20]. L3D is currently researching to understand the benefits to the kinds of education that this approach can afford, such as the ability of learners to pursue those topics of interest to them and to take responsibility for their own education (examples of courses can be found at http://l3d.cs.colorado.edu/~gerhard/courses/). By focusing on the tail of the Long Tail, we will not ignore the head but we will create a *synergy* between the two. Interest driven activities are boundary crossing: they move across settings of home, school, work, community, and online. In the context to enhance the competency of transdisciplinary collaboration and education this means that the Long Tail approach will be grounded in the following assumptions [21]:

– The activities of the *head* are the course topics that computer science students will improve their depth in, and students of other disciplines will learn to understand on a breadth level. The motivation for participation is mostly determined by extrinsic motivation (e.g. for credits; to improve job market value).

- The activities of the *tail* (the major contribution of Long Tail learning) should be focused on interest and passion allowing learners of all disciplines to pursue personally meaningful problems. The motivation for participation is mostly determined by *intrinsic motivation*. Learning and discovery are facilitated by passion-based participation on niche topics.

In the following chapter the here presented strategies have been applied at the University of Paderborn to a one semester graduate computer science course with 48 participating students representing three different groups of disciplines: computer science, business information systems and non-technical students (e.g. from media science or the German language department).

5   Implementation and Assessment of our Framework in a Graduate Course

Setting of the course. The University of Paderborn has 14.000 students and is divided into five faculties. The course "Data and Information Visualization" is offered in the CS graduate program as part of a computer graphics module. For the Summer Term 2009 it was opened to graduate students of all disciplines and thus gained 48 participants from three different faculties: 29 CS students (Faculty of Computer Science, Mathematics and Electrical Engineering), 14 business information systems students (Faculty of Business Administration and Economics), 5 non-technical students (media science students and literature students – all from the Faculty of Arts and Humanities). CS students have to be at graduate level, and completed at least a basic computer graphics course and one advanced rendering course. The visualization course included 90 minutes of lecture and 45 minutes of lab time per week over a period of 15 weeks. Students received 4 ECTS (European Credit Transfer and Accumulation System) for the course, which translates to an expected effort of 100-120 hours of work on the students side. In the lectures students learn methods and techniques to visualize information and data in an expressive and effective way. Lab time is being used to practice concepts and techniques. Starting in week 4, students worked on interdisciplinary projects of their choice in teams of their choice (with the restriction that each team had to hold a sufficient disciplinary mix).

Breadth-First: finding a Common Ground. Computer-generated visualization (including visualization of data derived from scientific measurements or scientific computing, or collected by humans or machines) holds multitudes of examples useful for teaching. Most of these are multidisciplinary, owing the context to an application outside CS, while the interactive graphics is clearly of interest to our CS students. Additionally, perception, design, and other areas of disciplines outside CS, play an important role in computer-generated visualization. The core topics to teach computer-generated visualization are: definitions; data;

user and tasks; mapping from data parameters to visual attributes; representation techniques; interaction issues; concepts of the visualization process; and systems and tools. These eight core topics constitute the *head of the knowledge* to be conveyed in a visualization course [22]. Using a "Breadth-First" learning tool (the top levels constitute the breadth that is comprehensible for students of any discipline, [14]) these core topics were taught during lectures. Of the typically four levels for each core topic (increasing level meaning increasing depth) level one and two were presented in class, suitable for all disciplines. This strategy helps both to teach the content of visualization to *all* students, but also to remove misunderstandings in the communication by providing a common language.

Long-Tail: finding topics of personal interest. Starting in the first lecture, each core topic and concept was enforced by visualization examples in an application context. This aided both the breath-first approach in teaching as well as the later search for unique project topics for students. Examples given included: visualization of large, multivariate environmental data; software visualization (e.g. algorithm animation, visualization of large code parts), augmented reality to support surgery; visualization of large information spaces, such as demographic data, etc. In each of these cases visualizations aid in the interpretation of complex data for a specific context (often outside CS), but are only possible through special visualization techniques: e.g. animation, flow visualization, GPU-based volume rendering, etc. These visualizations constituted the tail of *visualization knowledge*.

In week 3 (out of 15 course weeks), students had each to submit a complex data set they desired to visualize as their semester project. They were asked to describe the data in a conceptual form (something they learned to do in the previous lecture), set visualization goals, suggest visualization techniques, and describe possible users. This, we hoped, would bring out the topics that the students personally cared about. The received project proposition brought to light many individual interests (e.g. visualization of 20.000 auctions from the on-line game World-of-Warcraft; visualization of web search results or of traffic analyses) but also of some "hot spots", e.g. visualization of medical, weather or ecological data, that were suggested by several students, but for individually different data sets. In a group effort between all tutors, 7 projects that seemed representative (and interesting) of the 48 data sets were selected: visualizing orthopaedic data on human striding styles utilizing a game engine; visualizing indicators of the very large OECD education data base; visualizing data of the European pollutant emission register; visualizing data of over 70 runs of one student in preparation for a marathon; network performance visualization; flow visualization of a hurricane; and medical volume visualization. Basic knowledge on visualization (by all students) and good graphics programming capabilities (by CS students) were available, but knowledge of new algorithms and/or new Application Programming Interfaces would need to be acquired and design decisions to be made to succeed in the projects.

Supporting the team building process. One major obstacle in interdisciplinary courses is that of building project teams over the first weeks of a course, while students of different disciplines are still unfamiliar with each other. So additionally to providing a common language, the goal was to also facilitate social ties to help in the team building process. While the use of social networks to get to know each other seems a good idea, the practical side of it makes it useless for a one semester course: Once each of the 48 students have become "friends" on a social network, they will slowly get to know each other. This process being too slow, we solved the problem by an early lab assignment, requesting to fill out a "private profile". The form contained information such as "my abilities for the project group", "degree program of student", "former high school", "memberships in clubs or associations", or "favourite films/books". Students were also asked for 1-2 personal pictures (this was not mandatory) and their first name. Every one of 48 students submitted this "private profile". The resulting document was made available on the web (password secured).

When choosing teams in week 4, it was a requirement that students built teams by selecting team members from all three faculties. This ensured a distribution of similar core curriculum knowledge in each team. Students who had submitted the selected 7 projects started the team building process. Support for the selection process was also provided through the "private profiles" collected from all students.

To help students in starting up the communication process in their team, the assignment for the first group meeting included a brainstorming session on the group project. This brainstorming session was a guided role play that made sure that each of the students had a communicative role in the discussion process. This assignment intended to dampen unrealistic expectations of team members, let everyone voice their understanding of the joint project and "break the ice" in their communication. After the first meeting, each team had to meet at least once a week and keep meeting notes using a strict protocol. Meeting notes were also sent to tutors and lecturer. Team members present, action items for the week to come, and the date of the next meetings were obligatory items in the notes. Instructor or tutors would show up at the meetings without notice — both to help on the content of the project and with interpersonal problems, should any arise.

Qualitative and quantitative assessment of course. Admittedly, not every one of the 48 students found the topic with their personal strongest passion because, in order to build teams with different disciplines involved, we reduced the amount of projects from 48 to 7. In all cases but one the team members became personal friends, sometimes even to the point that they would alter personal characteristics as in the case of the "Jogging Group": One runner had suggested providing data tracking over 70 of his runs via cell phone and tracker software, including running length, speed, altitude, temperature, etc. All members of the project group became runners (and very good friends) by the time the project ended. Only in one project (out of seven) the group worked incoherently, splitting into two groups, separating not disciplines but cultures.

A voluntary assessment of students, handed out in the sixth of fifteen weeks, reveals more about the course. Of 48 students, 30 students returned the survey: 18 computer science students; 9 business information systems students; and 3 non-technical students (two media science students and one literature student).

The survey revealed that only 33% of the students had previously participated in interdisciplinary courses at their university, 67% had not. The percentage of computer science students with experience in interdisciplinarity was lower than the average experience in this group. The desire of all students to later work in interdisciplinary teams was up at 90%.

Students were also asked what they would like to know about each other before teaming up in a project group: they showed a strong preference (53%) for "the abilities this person brings to the project" rather than "private information" (10%) or "project interest" (4%).

The number of actual face-to-face meetings for each team was one per week during the first weeks (the obligatory group meeting they had to report about) and 2, 3, or more meetings per week between week 9 and 15. Students used cell phones, Email, ICQ, SVN (a version control system), Wiki, and Skype to communicate between meetings.

The "private profiles" were used by 67% of the students to look up private information of course mates. Business information system and non-technical students used it to a higher percentage than computer science students.

After the project presentations (last week of course), each student was asked to fill out an additional survey (resulting in 46 responses). In one of those questions the percentage of contribution to the project of each individual team member was requested. This was the last chance for students to emphasize their own contribution to the project and thus boost their grade, or to point out failures of other team members in order to find a scapegoat for goals that had not worked out in the project. The closer knit the group had become, the closer these numbers matched. Some groups equally divided the effort by the number of team members, among those the "jogging group". Only one group had widely mismatching numbers — the only group who had turned their project in late and experienced problems throughout the project because of a cultural split as already pointed out above.

In this same — final — survey the question on their desire for interdisciplinary work was repeated. Of the 46 responding students 41 confirmed their desire to later work with interdisciplinary teams — leaving the desire in the same percentage level as before.

Examples of projects for this course and previous interdisciplinary visualization courses can be found in [23].

Did we succeed in preparing students for transdisciplinary collaboration and lifelong learning? The survey shows that students are interested in collaboration with other disciplines, but hardly get a chance to do so in the course of their CS studies. Several indicators (their agreement over individual achievement of team members, interest in personal profiles of other students, stating the desire to work on interdisciplinary teams while and after the interdisciplinary experience, and personal observation) attest to a good collaboration and interest in each other. The strategies employed (personal profiles, early team selection, common language, enforced - but supported - weekly meetings of all team members) gave students much opportunity for face-to-face meetings. Indication for miscommunication was only present in one group out of seven.

Passion for the projects was strongest visible with the "jogging group", but also with a group using a game engine to visually present their data, as well as the groups visualizing education indicators, hurricane data and medical data. In each of these groups people with personal interests on relevant visualization goals were present and could transport their enthusiasm to others on the team. Each team had to acquire new knowledge to succeed in their project. The quality and quantity of all but one of the resulting projects were very pleasing from the subjective standpoint of the educator.

6   Implications and Future Opportunities

In their later work lives, university graduates will need competencies in transdisciplinary collaboration and self-directed learning to cope with the complexity of real-world problems. However, many educational programs in computer science are still dominated by curriculum-driven learning (where educators set the goals and determine the content) and curricula excluding work with other disciplines (supporting tribal behaviour) rather than providing students with the opportunity to become reflective professionals allowing them to acquire the capacity for lifelong learning and respect and ability to work with the perspectives of many, formerly separate disciplines. Opening the curriculum for course work coaching students in educational experiences where they are taught how to collaborate with other disciplines, improvise, innovate, and learn when the answer is not known, is a challenge for the 21st century. In this paper we presented breadth-first and long tail as strategies to use in graduate courses to make our students more creative, imaginative, innovative, and curious beyond their own discipline by teaming up with students of other disciplines to work on a project they feel committed to out of personal interest. The authors are convinced that the competency of transdisciplinary collaboration and self-directed learning, awakened in our students, will support a new climate of problem solving in this century.

Acknowledgments. The themes of this paper reflect some of the many interest and achievements of Hermann Maurer: (1) he has been one of the pioneers to transcend the narrow boundaries of specific disciplines (to name one prominent example: he has been the leading person behind the "The Journal of Universal Computer Science (J.UCS)", a high-quality open access electronic publication dealing with *all* aspects of computer science); and (2) he has been a prime example of a lifelong learner himself by always being at the forefront of exploring new research topics.

Gitta Domik thanks Hermann Maurer for his inspiring lectures during her studies and being a lifelong mentor thereafter. Gerhard Fischer thanks Hermann

Maurer for numerous interesting discussions during the last decade in which he learnt many new ideas.

Both authors thank the members of the Center for LifeLong Learning & Design (L3D) at the University of Colorado at Boulder for providing background information and inspiring debates about the content of this paper. Gerhard Fischers ideas and understanding about transdisciplinary collaboration and education have greatly benefited from collaboration with Sharon Derry (University of Wisconsin) and David Redmiles (University of California at Irvine). Gitta Domik's work was inspired by a research semester at L3D in 2007/2008.

References

1. Mumford, E.: A Socio-Technical Approach to Systems Design. Requirements Engineering 5(2), 59–77 (2000)
2. Janis, I.: Victims of Groupthink. Houghton Mifflin, Boston (1972)
3. Computing Curricula 2001 (2001),
   http://www.acm.org/education/curric_vols/cc2001.pdf
4. Computing Curricula 1991. CACM 34(6), 69–84 (June 1991)
5. Klein, J.T.: A Platform for a Shared Discourse of Interdisciplinary Education. Journal of Social Science Education 5(2), 10–18 (2006), www.jsse.org ISSN 1618-5293,
6. Rosenfield, P.L.: The potential of transdisciplinary research for sustaining and extending likages between the health and social sciences. Social Sciences and Medicine 35, 1343–1357 (1992)
7. Nicolescu, B.: The transdisciplinary evolution of learning (1999),
   http://www.unesco.org/education/educprog/lwf/dl/nicolescu_f.pdf
8. Derry, S., Fischer, G.: Toward a Model and Theory for Transdisciplinary Graduate Education. Paper presented at 2005 AERA Annual Meeting, Symposium, "Sociotechnical Design for Lifelong Learning: A Crucial Role for Graduate Education", Montreal (April 2005), http://l3d.cs.colorado.edu/~gerhard/papers/aera-montreal.pdf
9. Stokols, D.: Towards a Science of Transdisciplinary Action Research. American Journal of Community Psychology 38, 63–77 (2006)
10. Clark, H.H., Brennan, S.E.: Grounding in Communication. In: Resnick, L.B., Levine, J.M., Teasley, S.D. (eds.) Perspectives on Socially Shared Cognition, American Psychological Association, pp. 127–149 (1991)
11. Fischer, G.: Lifelong Learning - More Than Training. Journal of Interactive Learning Research, Special Issue on Intelligent Systems/Tools In Training and Life-Long Learning (Mizoguchi, R., Kommers, P.A.M.(eds.)) 11(3/4), 265–294 (2000)
12. Rushmeier, H.: IEEE Workshop on Visualization Education for Non-Technical Majors: Post Workshop Materials (2006), http://graphics.cs.yale.edu/holly/vis2006/vis-non-tech.html
13. Fischer, G.: Distances and Diversity: Sources for Social Creativity. In: Proceedings of Creativity & Cognition, pp. 128–136. ACM, London (2005)
14. Domik, G., Goetz, F.: A Breadth-First Approach for Teaching Computer Graphics. Education Papers. In: Proceedings of Eurographics 2006, Vienna, Austria, September 4-8, pp. 1–5 (2006)
15. Mackinlay, J.: Automating the Design of Graphical Presentations of Relational Information. ACM Trans. on Graphics 5(2), 110–141 (1986)

16. Fischer, G.: Beyond 'Couch Potatoes: From Consumers to Designers and Active Contributors. In Firstmonday (Peer-Reviewed Journal on the Internet) (2002), http://firstmonday.org/issues/issue7_12/fischer/

17. Anderson, C.: The Long Tail: Why the Future of Business is Selling Less of More. Publisher Hyperion 2006 (2006) ISBN 1401302378

18. Brown, J.S., Adler, R.P.: Minds on Fire: Open Education, the Long Tail, and Learning 2.0 (2008), http://www.educause.edu/ir/library/pdf/ERM0811.pdf

19. Fischer, G.: Cultures of Participation and Social Computing: Rethinking and Reinventing Learning and Education. In: Proceedings of the International Conference on Advanced Learning Technologies (ICALT), pp. 1–5. IEEE Press, Riga (2009)

20. National-Research-Council: Beyond Productivity: Information Technology, Innovation, and Creativity. National Academy Press, Washington, DC (2003)

21. Collins, A., Fischer, G., Barron, B., Liu, C., Spada, H.: Long-Tail Learning: A Unique Opportunity for CSCL? In: Proceedings of CSCL 2009: 8th International Conference on Computer Supported Collaborative Learning, University of the Aegean, Rhodes, Greece, vol. 2, pp. 22–24 (2009)

22. Domik, G.: Do We Need Formal Education in Visualization? Visualization Viewpoint. IEEE Computer Graphics and Applications 20(4) (2000)

23. Domik, G.: Interdisciplinary Collaboration in a Visualization Course, Informatics Education Europe IV, November 5-9, Freiburg, Germany (2009)

Towards an Open Learning Infrastructure for Open Educational Resources: Abundance as a Platform for Innovation

Erik Duval, Katrien Verbert, and Joris Klerkx

Dept. Computerwetenschappen, K.U.Leuven, B3000 Leuven, Belgium
{Erik.Duval,Katrien.Verbert,Joris.Klerkx}@cs.kuleuven.be

Abstract. This paper explains how we have contributed to the development of an open learning infrastructure that manages and makes available Open Educational Resources. By removing friction between people and resources, we can leverage the long tail of learning resources, so that the abundance of learning resources will act as a platform for innovation.

Keywords: open educational resources, learning technology standards.

1 Introduction

This paper briefly presents some of the main outcomes of our work on learning objects, metadata and interoperability. The basic idea is that we are beginning to realize our early vision of an open learning infrastructure that enables scaling up technical facilities for Technology Enhanced Learning (TEL) to a global scale [22].

Our focus for the last 15 years has been on providing easy access to all learning resources, for all teachers and for all students [10]. In a life-long learning context: this means for all of us. Obviously, there are some basic challenges in terms of internet connectivity, but as access to the network proliferates, so will access to digital learning resources. Our vision is very similar to what Hermann Maurer presented in [14].

Making more content and other resources more easily available will not solve all the problems related to education, training and learning in general. However, we do believe that the abundance thus created will act as a motor for innovation, much in the same way that ubiquitous access to music has profoundly changed the way consumers interact with music and, as a consequence, the music industry.

Indeed, there is an assumption underlying much of our work that, at some point, more is not just more, but creates a qualitative tipping point as well. One of the reasons why we pursue global access to all learning resources for everyone is because we believe that there will be a long tail effect [7] of learning material: basically, there may be few students and teachers of more specialized topics like Egyptian hieroglyphs; but on a global scale, there are sufficient people interested in this topic from a learning perspective to create a sustainable community for share and reuse.

C.S. Calude, G. Rozenberg, A. Salomaa (Eds.): Maurer Festschrift, LNCS 6570, pp. 144–156, 2011.

In fact, abundance not only creates new opportunities, but can also create new problems, such as the Paradox of choice [18] that arises when the cognitive and emotional overhead of dealing with abundance overshadows the benefits of a larger number of options. We consider such problems as drivers for innovation, as they encourage us to research novel ways to enable interested parties to find or be alerted about relevant resources in appropriate ways [15].

Since almost 15 years now, we pursue this goal of share and reuse in the ARIADNE Foundation that has developed a network of repositories of learning materials, with associated tools for harvesting and search [2]. More recently, we created a world-wide alliance of similar organizations, a network of networks of repositories: Globe [3] that interconnects about a dozen such networks, using the ARIADNE technology as its technical backbone infrastructure.

This paper is structured as follows: section 2 presents how we are evolving towards an open learning infrastructure. Section 3 illustrates how the resulting abundance is beginning to act as a motor for innovation. Section 4 presents some ongoing and future work. We then present our conclusion and list bibliographical references.

2 Background: Towards an Open Learning Infrastructure

2.1 Introduction

In order to realize an open learning infrastructure, we have contributed to the development of a number of open standards, that enable the interconnection between different infrastructures, or even the development of an integrated infrastructure from heterogeneous independently developed building blocks [13].

The main relevant standards include:

- IEEE LTSC Learning Object Metadata (LOM) [5]: a hierarchical structure of some 70 metadata elements that can be used to describe learning resources;
- CEN WSLT Simple Query Interface (SQI) [6]: a conceptual protocol for searching in repositories with LOM descriptions;
- CEN WSLT Simple Publishing Interface (SPI) [21]: a language for ingesting new metadata and/or resources into a learning object repository;
- Open Archives Initiative Protocol for Metadata Harvesting (OAI-PMH) [23]: a protocol for periodically retrieving all updated or new metadata from a repository.

Most of these standards are conceptual: this means that they are abstract and can be bound to a specific representation, for instance as a SOAP or REST interface for the interfaces or protocols, or as JSON or XML for LOM. The main idea is that they would thus be more resilient to change of technology bindings, an important aspect as the standards are intended to remain relevant for a decade or longer.

2.2   The ARIADNE Infrastructure

The main design principle in ARIADNE is to make everything disappear but the benefits by removing friction when one wants to share and reuse learning resources. For that reason, we have built an infrastructure to make this happen. Figure 1 illustrates the ARIADNE infrastructure.

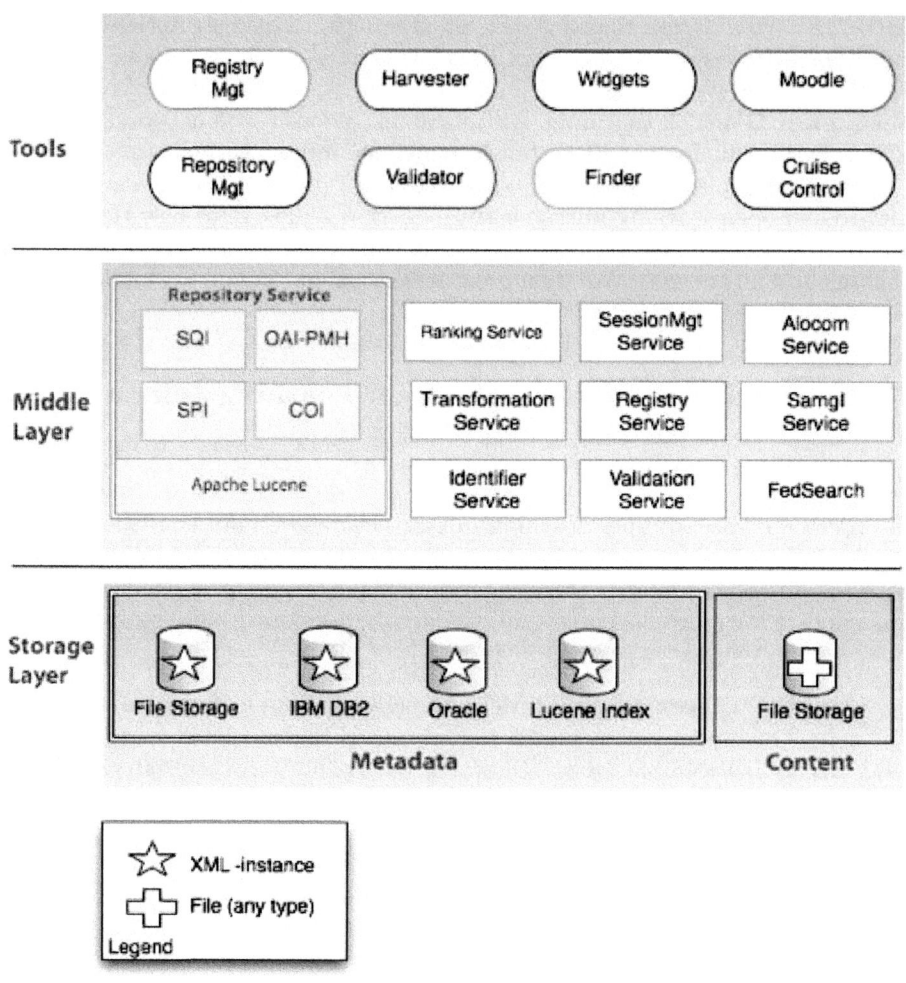

Fig. 1. The layered ARIADNE infrastructure

Basically, the infrastructure is composed of three layers:

1. The Tool layer hides protocols and standards for end users in a toolset that provides access to learning material through web applications, information visualization, mobile information devices, multi-touch displays and mash-up applications (see also below). A more administration oriented application is

the ARIADNE harvester that is able to harvest metadata with OAI-PMH from a content provider into the ARIADNE storage layer.

2. The Middle Layer offers persistent management of learning objects and metadata through a set of services, such as:
   - the repository services that allow for the management of learning objects, relying on standards such as IEEE LTSC LOM [5], CEN WSLT SQI [6], CEN WSLT SPI [21] and OAI-PMH [23];
   - the registry services that manage information on learning object repositories, including the information necessary for other infrastructure components to select protocols supported by a given repository;
   - an identifier service for providing unique identifiers for learning objects managed in the infrastructure,
   - a validation service that checks both the syntactic and semantic validity of metadata instances against multiple standards, specifications and their application profiles,
   - a transformation service that converts metadata from one format, for instance Dublin Core, into another format, for instance the ARIADNE LOM application profile.

3. The Storage Layer allows for storing both content and metadata in diverse repositories depending on the choice of the administrator who deploys the ARIADNE infrastructure.

Detailed information about these services has been published in [13]. In the following section, we show how these services and tools can be orchestrated to add new repositories to the ARIADNE network.

2.3 Adding New Repositories

Figure 2 illustrates how ARIADNE services and tools can be orchestrated to connect the repositories of content providers X (left side of figure) and Y (upper right side) with the ARIADNE network. As an example, we explain how we recently integrated the JorumOpen repository [19] in the ARIADNE network. All resources from JorumOpen are described in the Dublin Core (DC) metadata schema. JorumOpen had already implemented an OAI-PMH target on top of the repository. To connect to ARIADNE, this OAI-PMH target is registered into the ARIADNE Registry (step 1a) where administrative and technical information is added about the repository, such as the title, description, contact person, supported protocols used in his repository (OAI-PMH and DC metadata), etc. The registry uses an RSS feed to alert all (step 1.2) of its client tools about the new repository that has been added.

In response to this alert, the ARIADNE harvester tool issues a query (step 2) to the registry to obtain all relevant information about this repository. In step 3, the harvester performs the following steps:

- The Dublin Core metadata is harvested from JorumOpen using the OAI-PMH protocol (step 3.1).

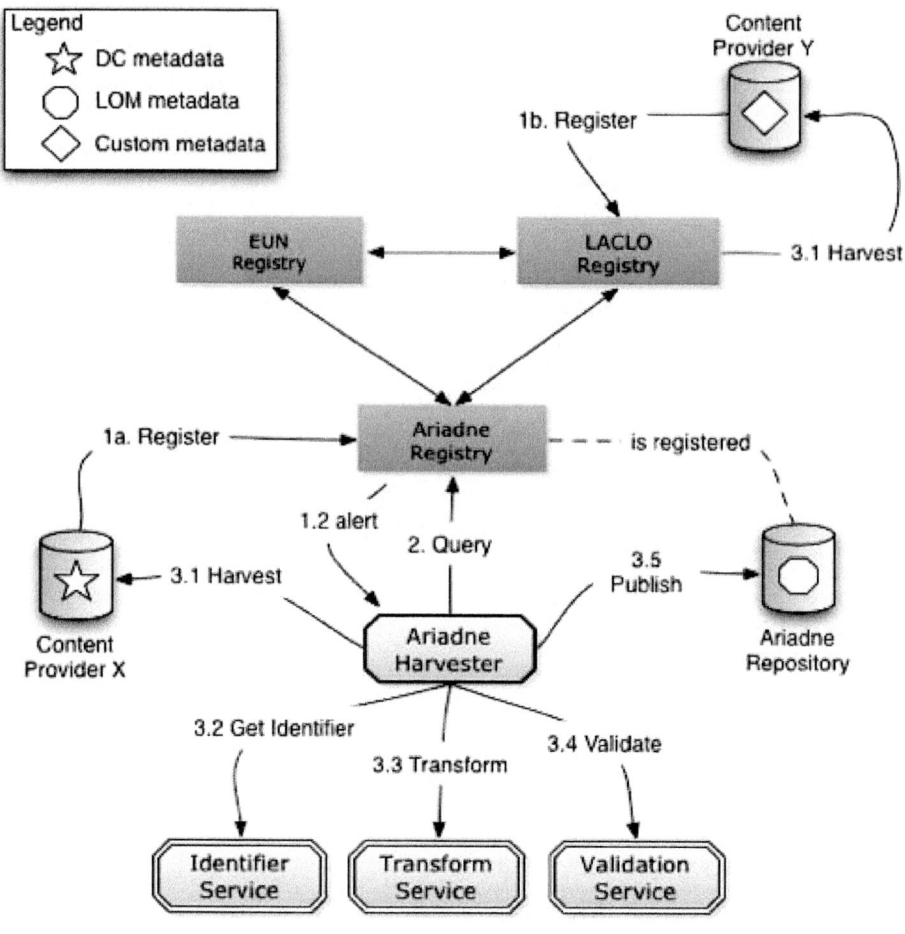

Fig. 2. Adding new repositories

- From experience in various projects, we have learned that we cannot rely on the identifiers that are added by content providers because duplicates may arise. That is why the harvester calls the Identifier service (step 3.2) to generate a unique identifier, which is added to the metadata instances of provider JorumOpen.
- A call to the transform service takes care of the conversion from Dublin Core to the ARIADNE LOM Application Profile (step 3.3).
- Faulty metadata instances often result in errors or inconsistencies in tools and user interfaces. All metadata instances are therefore validated against the validation scheme (step 3.4), and invalid instances are discarded. Mapping metadata from a local metadata scheme to a global one typically happens either by manually editing one record at the time, or in batch with a script written specifically for this mapping. Our experience has shown that both of these methods make this a very error-prone process. For example,

in the eContentplus project MELT, 90% of the original metadata from content providers resulted in validation errors. The reports of the ARIADNE validation service helped the content providers to dramatically decrease this number to less than 5%.
- The harvester uses the Simple Publishing Interface (SPI) specification to publish the harvested and validated metadata into the ARIADNE target that is registered as well in the registry. All content from JorumOpen can thus be found in ARIADNE (step 3.5) after the harvester has completed the cycle from steps 3.1 to 3.5.

It is very important to emphasize the semi-automated nature of this process: all that is required is the registration of some administrative and technical data in the registry. From there on, there may be alerts for manual intervention if metadata does not validate or if the services are not available, but otherwise the process proceeds automatically. This is very important if we want to make this infrastructure scale world-wide.

2.4   From **ARIADNE** to the Rest of the World

Through various projects over the years, the ARIADNE infrastructure has proven to be capable of providing flexible, effective and efficient access to large-scale collections of learning resources. At the time of writing, the ARIADNE registry contains information about 79 repositories that enables access to more than a million learning resources.

In fact, the ARIADNE resources are also available outside of the strict context of the ARIADNE network itself. The registry is interoperable with third-party registries, so that all information added in one registry is automatically synchronized to the other registries. In this way, content that is collected by ARIADNE can automatically be found in other networks as well. This also works the other way around. If another content provider Y is added to the LACLO registry [4], this information is synchronized with the ARIADNE registry. Cycle 3.1 to 3.5 described in the previous section then starts all over again, such that those resources become available for ARIADNE users as well.

All harvested metadata is accessible and open to the world:

1. First of all, the complete LOM/XML dataset can be harvested through the OAI-PMH protocol.
2. Secondly, the LOM/XML dataset can be queried through a SOAP binding that implements the Simple Query Interface (SQI) that supports many types of search technologies.
3. Thirdly, a REST API with a JSON binding of LOM allows you to specify queries and aspects of the result format (like resultListSize, resultformat, languages, etc.). Results can be returned in both XML and JSON result formats.
4. Finally, and a bit more experimental in nature, we have also made available the same data as a SPARQL target on top of an RDF binding of LOM.

2.5   Search and Find

The ARIADNE infrastructure has enabled us to collect more than a million learning resources. To enable efficient and fast search on top of this collection, we make use of the open source Apache Lucene and SOLR frameworks that provide powerful, accurate, efficient and facetted search algorithms.

Because search performance is really essential for a satisfactory user experience, we frequently run a series of benchmarking tests on top of our search services. At the time of writing, we achieve an average 15ms response time during stress testing our services. These stress tests are performed with the help of Apache Jmeter, a Java desktop application designed to load test functional behavior and measure performance of web applications. Although these results are very acceptable, we are currently investigating multiple alternatives for further improving these results when we scale up the number of resources in our network. Options we are currently exploring include:

– In-memory loading of the complete search index,
– Reducing index size by only including a subset of the metadata elements,
– Distributed search over multiple servers.

The ARIADNEFinder is our state-of-the-art web tool for querying: the screenshot in figure 3 shows how we deployed this in the context of GLOBE. The tool enables the end user to issue a keyword search in the top middle part of the interface. The left pane supports facetted search on the results, by selecting

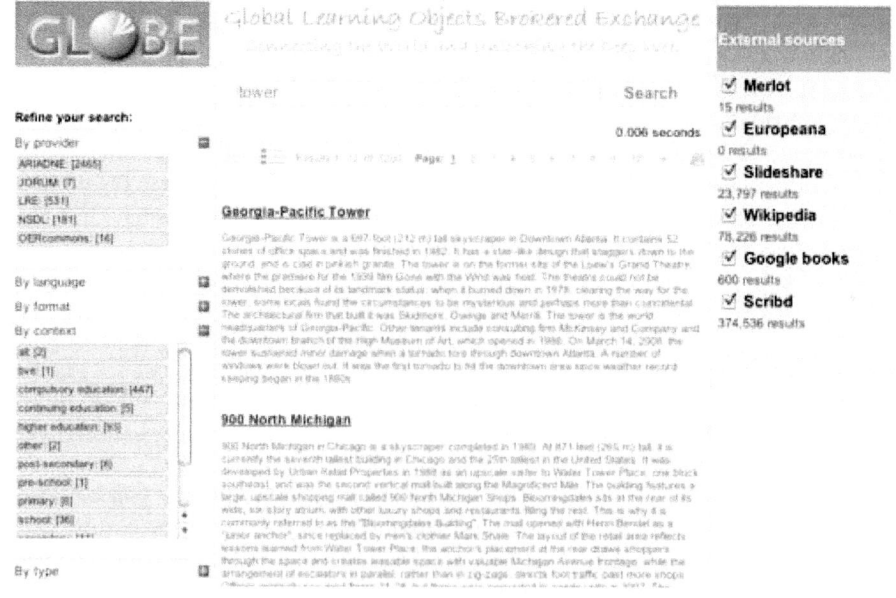

Fig. 3. ARIADNE Finder deployed for GLOBE

facets and values to include relevant results or to exclude results that are of less importance. On the right pane, one can simultaneously issue a query to external sources of material. Typically, for those targets, it does not make sense to harvest all of their resources. In the wikipedia case for example, the resources are very volatile so instead of harvesting those resources every day, we prefer to use their open search API to issue queries to them and federate the results back into the overall search interface.

3   Abundance as a Platform for Innovation

3.1   Introduction

As we mentioned in the introduction, an open learning infrastructure will replace the older problem of scarcity of learning resources by a situation of abundance, so that more effective and efficient ways to make use of that abundance will be required.

We see at least three ways to achieve this goal:

1. integration: rather than providing an external, extra tool for teachers or learners to find relevant resources, we can integrate with their mainstream authoring or teaching or learning workflow and suggest relevant material when appropriate (section 3.2);
2. visualization: in order to provide more sophisticated interaction with learning resources, rich visualizations can be developed where learners and teachers navigate an information space, potentially making use of novel interaction techniques provided by multi-touch large scale displays (section 3.3);
3. analytics: through a careful analysis of detailed tracking of what teachers and learners do, we can obtain a clearer idea of what the user is trying to do and how well he is achieving his goal, which opens up opportunities for advanced user support (section 3.4).

No doubt, there will be other approaches that leverage the emergent abundance in other ways...

3.2   Integration

As mentioned above, teachers and learners can leverage the abundance of learning content in much more flexible ways if we can integrate access to these resources in more subtle ways in their existing workflows, rather than sending them to a dedicated web site or tool.

A successful example of this approach is the component that we have integrated into the Moodle Learning Management System (LMS) [9]. As illustrated by figure 4, when users want to upload a document in their course, our software enables them to search in ARIADNE from within Moodle. In addition to removing friction from the user experience, this also provides us with opportunities to enrich the typical keyword search from the teacher with background knowledge about the course he is working on, including the topic, the student target audience, the technical requirements, etc.

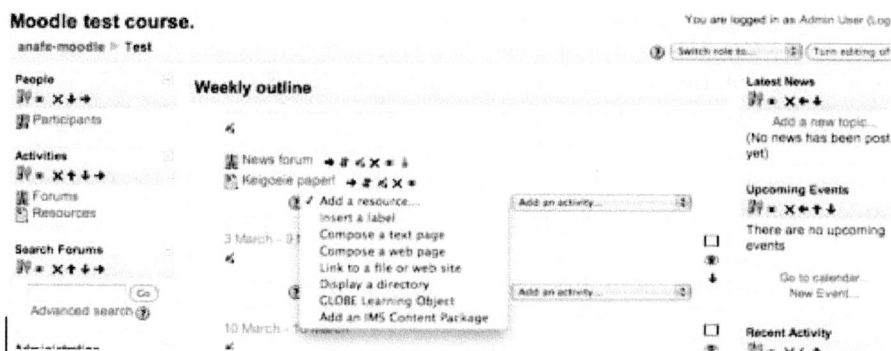

Fig. 4. Searching ARIADNE from within Moodle

Fig. 5. Inserting resources in Moodle and ARIADNE

Similarly, we also enable a teacher to upload a new resource not only in a Moodle course, but also in the ARIADNE repository, without any additional effort or without leaving the familiar learning environment. This is illustrated in figure 5. In this case, we can make use of the contextual information that the LMS provides to enrich the automatic generation of metadata that accompany the resource in the repository.

We have developed similar interfaces from within the Blackboard learning environment, Microsoft Powerpoint and the LAMS authoring tool. A widget for integration into a Personal Learning Environment (PLE) is under development.

3.3   Visualization

When teachers and learners do want to interact explicitly with the abundance of resources available to them, we can use information visualization techniques to provide them with a rich environment for exploration and discussion.

Fig. 6. The Maeve table

A successful example of this approach is the maeve table that provides a large reactable for exploring learning resources about architects, architectural styles, building techniques, etc. [16] - see figure 6. Learners and teachers can manipulate cards that represent the information and put them on an interactive surface to display associated concepts and relations to other information. In this way, learners and teachers can explore a rich information space.

An alternative, more conventional access paradigm is the web portal, shown in figure 6, which uses information visualization techniques such as elastic lists [20], that allows for browsing multi-facetted data structures.

3.4 Analytics

In recent years, researchers are focusing increasingly on the need for better measurement, tracking, analysis and visualization of data about learners. Research on learning analytics [1] evolved that describes the set of activities to help understand and optimize learning and the environments in which it occurs.

The capturing of user activities is often researched as a basis to gather and analyze behavior of learners [11][8]. Several models have been elaborated to track user interactions with tools and resources, such as read and write actions on documents or even keystrokes. Examples of models that are used in a Technology Enhanced Learning context are the Contextualized Attention Metadata [24] and

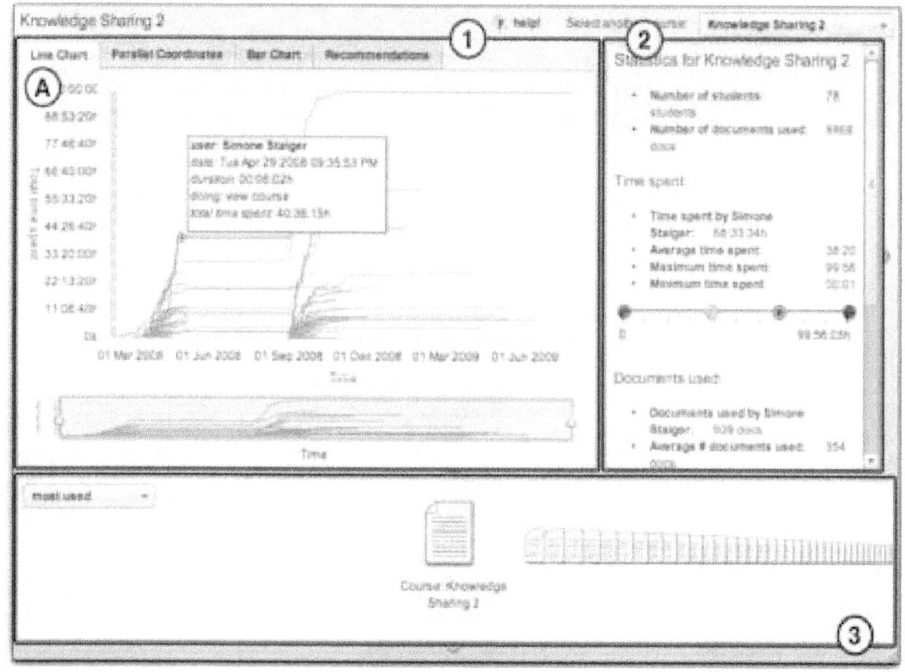

Fig. 7. The Student Activity Meter (SAM)

the UICO [17] models. Both models enable the capturing of user actions within an application, and potentially additional information about her current context, such as location or task related information.

The analysis of such data is a key enabler to gain insights into learning effects achieved and potential impact of technologies on learning. In addition, the visualization of such data has been researched extensively as a basis to support self-reflection, awareness and collaboration among learners or teachers [19]. One of our applications, SAM (Student Activity Meter), visualizes the time learners spent on learning activities [12]. Figure 7 shows some of the visualizations that SAM provides:

– The line chart (vis. A in figure 7) shows a line for every student, connecting all the timestamps when she was working with the cumulative amount of time spent. The inclination of the line shows the effort of the student. A steep line means an intensive working period. A flat line shows inactivity.
– Statistics of global time spent and document use are shown in box 2 in figure 7. Next to the actual numbers, a graphical view is presented with color coding of the minimum, maximum and average time spent and documents used, to give the user a visual comparison. Upon selection of a user in the visualization in box 1, her statistics are also shown.
– The recommendation pane in box 3 allows to navigate through the most used and the most time spent on resources.

Evaluation results indicate that such visualizations can be used successfully to increase awareness for teachers, i.e. of what and how students are doing. Resource usage can show teachers popular learning materials and enables resource discovery.

4 Conclusion

In this paper, we have argued that we are evolving towards an open learning infrastructure, much as originally envisioned in [14]. This evolution will make available an abundance of learning resources that will act as a motor of innovation. In this way, it will help to push further a research interest that permeates much of Hermann Maurers research.

Acknowledgments. Katrien Verbert is a Postdoctoral Fellow of the Research Foundation Flanders - FWO. The research leading to these results has received funding from the European Community Seventh Framework Programme (FP7/2007-2013) under grant agreement no 231396 (ROLE). The work presented in this paper is partially supported by the European Commission eContentplus programme - projects ASPECT (ECP-2007-EDU-417008) and ICOPER (ECP-2007-EDU-417007). The research leading to these results has received funding from the European Community Seventh Framework Programme (FP7/2007-2013) under grant agreements no 231396 (ROLE) and no 257566 (iTEC).

References

1. 1st International Conference on Learning Analytics and Knowledge 2011 (2011)
2. Ariadne Foundation, http://www.ariadne-eu.org
3. GLOBE, http://globe-info.org/
4. LACLO: Latin-American Community of Learning Objects, http://www.laclo.org/
5. IEEE 1484.12.1-2000 Standard for Learning Object Metadata (2000)
6. CEN Workshop Agreement CWA 15454 - A Simple Query Interface Specification for Learning Repositories (2005), ftp://ftp.cenorm.be/PUBLIC/CWAs/e-Europe/WS-LT/CWA15454-00-2005-Nov.pdf
7. Anderson, C.: The Long Tail: Why the Future of Business Is Selling Less of More. Hyperion (2006)
8. Butoianu, V., Vidal, P., Verbert, K., Duval, E., Broisin, J.: User context and personalized learning: a federation of Contextualized Attention Metadata. Journal of Universal Computer Science (2010)
9. Dougiamas, M., Taylor, P.: Moodle: Using Learning Communities to Create an Open Source Course Management System. In: Lassner, D., McNaught, C. (eds.) Proceedings of World Conference on Educational Multimedia, Hypermedia and Telecommunications 2003, pp. 171–178. AACE, Honolulu (2003), http://www.editlib.org/p/13739
10. Duval, E., Forte, E., Cardinaels, K., Verhoeven, B., Durm, R.V., Hendrikx, K., Wentland-Forte, M., Ebel, N., Macowicz, M., Warkentyne, K., Haenni, F.: The ARIADNE knowledge pool system. Communications of the ACM 44(5), 72–78 (2001), http://portal.acm.org/citation.cfm?id=374308.374346

11. Fox, S., Karnawat, K., Mydland, M., Dumais, S., White, T.: Evaluating implicit measures to improve web search. ACM Trans. Inf. Syst. 23(2), 147–168 (2005), http://doi.acm.org/10.1145/1059981.1059982

12. Govaerts, S., Verbert, K., Klerkx, J., Duval, E.: Visualizing Activities for Self-reflection and Awareness. In: Luo, X., Spaniol, M., Wang, L., Li, Q., Nejdl, W., Zhang, W. (eds.) ICWL 2010. LNCS, vol. 6483, pp. 91–100. Springer, Heidelberg (2010)

13. Klerkx, J., Vandeputte, B., Parra Chico, G., Santos Odriozola, J.L., Van Assche, F., Duval, E.: How to share and reuse learning resources: the Ariadne experience. In: Wolpers, M., Kirschner, P.A., Scheffel, M., Lindstaedt, S., Dimitrova, V. (eds.) EC-TEL 2010. LNCS, vol. 6383, pp. 183–196. Springer, Heidelberg (2010), https://lirias.kuleuven.be/handle/123456789/280116

14. Marchionini, G., Maurer, H.: The roles of digital libraries in teaching and learning. Communications of the ACM 38(4) (1995), http://portal.acm.org/citation.cfm?id=205345

15. Morville, P.: Ambient Findability, vol. 11. O'Reilly Media, Inc., Sebastopol (2005), http://www.amazon.ca/exec/obidos/redirect?tag=citeulike09-20\& path=ASIN/0596007655

16. Nagel, T., Pschetz, L., Stefaner, M., Halkia, M., Müller, B.: mæve – An Interactive Tabletop Installation for Exploring Background Information in Exhibitions. In: Jacko, J.A. (ed.) HCI International 2009. LNCS, vol. 5612, pp. 483–491. Springer, Heidelberg (2009), http://dx.doi.org/10.1007/978-3-642-02580-8_53

17. Rath, A.S., Devaurs, D., Lindstaedt, S.N.: UICO: an ontology-based user interaction context model for automatic task detection on the computer desktop. In: Proceedings of the 1st Workshop on Context, Information and Ontologies,CIAO 2009, pp. 8:1–8:10. ACM, New York (2009), http://doi.acm.org/10.1145/1552262.1552270

18. Schwartz, B.: The paradox of choice why more is less. HarperCollins e-books (2007), http://books.google.com/books?id=zutxr7rGc_QC&printsec=frontcover

19. Soller, A., Martínez, A., Jermann, P., Muehlenbrock, M.: From Mirroring to Guiding: A Review of State of the Art Technology for Supporting Collaborative Learning. Int. J. Artif. Intell. Ed. 15(4), 261–290 (2005), http://portal.acm.org/citation.cfm?id=1434935.1434937

20. Stefaner, M., Muller, B.: Elastic lists for facet browsers. In: Wagner, R., Revell, N., Pernul, G. (eds.) DEXA 2007. LNCS, vol. 4653, pp. 217–221. Springer, Heidelberg (2007)

21. Ternier, S., Massart, D., Assche, F.V., Smith, N., Simon, B., Duval, E.: A Simple Publishing Interface For Learning Object Repositories. In: Proceedings of World Conference on Educational Multimedia, Hypermedia and Telecommunications 2008, Chesapeake, VA, pp. 1840–1845 (2008), http://go.editlib.org/p/28625

22. Ternier, S., Verbert, K., Parra, G., Vandeputte, B., Klerkx, J., Duval, E., Ordonez, V., Ochoa, X.: The Ariadne Infrastructure for Managing and Storing Metadata. IEEE Internet Computing 13(4), 18–25 (2009), http://www.computer.org/portal/web/csdl/doi/10.1109/MIC.2009.90

23. Van de Sompel, H., Nelson, M.L., Lagoze, C., Warner, S.: Resource Harvesting within the OAI-PMH Framework. D-Lib Magazine 10(12) (2004), http://www.dlib.org/dlib/december04/vandesompel/12vandesompel.html

24. Wolpers, M., Najjar, J., Verbert, K., Duval, E.: Tracking actual usage: the attention metadata approach. Educational Technology and Society 10(3), 106–121 (2007), https://lirias.kuleuven.be/handle/123456789/158649

Why E-Learning as It Stands Is Not Enough

Narayanan Kulathuramaiyer[1,*] and Hermann Maurer[2]

[1] Faculty of Computer Science and Information Technology,
Universiti Malaysia Sarawak, 94300 Kota Samarahan, Sarawak, Malaysia
nara@fit.unimas.my
[2] Institute for Information Systems and Computer Media,
Graz University of Technology, Graz, Austria
hmaurer@iicm.edu

Abstract. E-Learning today has become widely accepted as a means of
information and knowledge access and sharing for many learning applications. Despite the extensive growth E-learning systems and contents,
it has to be noted that there are still many shortcomings that has led us
to ask the question: Is E-Learning as it stands enough? E-Learning as
it stands today is far from being assimilated fully into everything that
we do. To make things worse, the age of Google is further challenging
E-Learning, through the emergence of phenomena such as Google Copy
Paste Syndrome, the flattening of expertise, short-spanned learner focus
and the emerging culture of mediocrity. The full symbolic power of the
emerging Web dragons together with emerging social trends is expected
to challenge E-Learning much more in future. This paper then highlights
the extent of influence of global Data Mining companies on the current
and future E-Learning. A personalized localized control scenario is given
to serve as an ideal for making E-Learning to become enough for its
envisaged purpose.

1 Introduction

E-Learning has brought about anytime and anywhere learning capability to reach
out to people all over the world. At the same time it has been widely adopted in
institutions across the world by millions of educators. As an example, MOODLE
has around 50,000 sites in 210 countries with over 3.8 million courses, 37 million
users and a growing content repository of 33 million resources and 60 million
quiz questions [1]. This staggering growth and explosive development of learning
contents in a bottom-up fashion may be construed a major success. However, the
question that we pose here is: is this all that we have expected of E-Learning?

E-Learning has been anticipated to become a means to bring about widespread
transformation in empowering citizens to work collaboratively towards a
knowledge-based society. E-Learning as it stands today is however far from being assimilated fully into everything that we do, in order to attempt to achieve
this. To make things worse, the age of Google is further challenging E-Learning,

---

* Corresponding author.

C.S. Calude, G. Rozenberg, A. Salomaa (Eds.): Maurer Festschrift, LNCS 6570, pp. 157–164, 2011.

through the emergence of phenomena such as Google Copy Paste Syndrome, the flattening of expertise, short-spanned focus, culture of mediocrity, etc. The term 'age of Google' is used to describe the era of the Web data mining information supply power houses with extensive highly personal data mining powers. These power houses also cover other big information supply engines such as Microsoft's social networking tools, Facebook and Twitter.

A large number of distributed rationalization agents that make the best sense of available material to suit a particular task will be needed. Although research in this direction has been on the way, a coherent solution consolidating and exploiting available learning resources is far from a reality. Even if these tools emerge, the question of who will have control over such vast resources can also be a major concern. Until an effective organization, rationalization and filtering capability becomes available, E-Learning will continue to expand as isolated bottom up content development for specific purposes.

E-Learning to a large extent is still viewed as an alternative mode of learning; it has not yet matured to take up its anticipated role. For one thing, E-learning cannot be expected to just happen by the mixing of modalities or the mere provision of learning content coupled with multiple easy-to-use communications channels. For E-Learning to remain relevant and play its role effectively it has then to become the mainstream helper for students in their quest for knowledge and life-long learning. This becomes exceedingly important in the emerging mobile learning era.

The difficulty in determining if E-Learning has actually taken place can be illustrated via the following scenario. In a remote, rural, connected E-Learning facility meant to support learning activities, we found computers merely being used for watching recorded TV programmes via CD ROMs. The important lessons learnt were that, without efforts in guiding a learning community adequately and ensuring the proper utilization and application of technology, E-Learning just cannot be expected to happen. There is thus a need to effectively engage a learning community by integrating E-Learning within the local context. Apart from this, there is also a need to integrate mechanisms for the close monitoring of learning activities. The packaging of E-Learning should also duly consider the background of learners (considering capability and needs), their literacy levels and creating opportunities for them to assimilate and apply the knowledge within a local context. There is also a need for human-centred metrics that can help ascertain and keep track of actual learning outcomes. Until E-Learning system can address these concerns effectively, E-Learning cannot become fully assimilated personal learning assistant. The lessons from this scenario are reflective not only of community learning but also of the main stream E-Learning.

2   Challenges to E-Learning

E-learning is faced with numerous challenges that make student learning difficult. Among these are developments associated with the age of Google which have totally undermined the role and relevance of E-Learning. These developments will be discussed here.

2.1   Short Spanned Focus

Anyone can become an instant celebrity in this participative era by creating a popular video; being able to gain even more attention than even a noble prize winner. In the age of Google and Facebook, attention seeking individuals require much less efforts to become note-worthy or even to become recognized as an expert. This of course to a large extent influences learner behavior and their approach to learning.

Emerging cultures includes short message exchanges, integrated environment with aggregated feeds from multiple sources, real-time alerts, indiscriminately competing interrupts, media-rich environment causes a need to constantly stay connected at all times. The packaging of buzz has been neatly assimilated with all forms of contents and information; creating an irresistible charm whereby the younger generation (digitally more native) are getting fully immersed and absorbed within a highly interconnected virtual world. This world then poses great challenges for learners to remain focused and continuously engage in rigorous learning activities. The new media has reduced student focus as Email and emerging communicational means tend to be far too distracting [2]. Another emerging development, as pointed out by [3], is the emergence of a Youtubian generation which would believe a 30 second clip more than a text book. The thinking and questioning ability of people are thus seen as being eroded and compromised.

2.2   Collective Intelligence or Consensus on Ignorance

The web has brought about an environment for 'rapid generation of publications' mainly through the instantaneous access to myriad sources of information. The web, according to Andrew Keen in his book the "Cult of the Amateur"[3] has brought about "less culture, less reliable news and a chaos of useless information". Instead of the promised increase in truth it has filled us with an overload of information of doubtful reliability. Keen points out that we are bogged down by superficial observations rather than deep analysis and shrill opinion rather than considerate judgement. In his words, the internet is being transformed into the sheer noise of 100 million bloggers. When even the keeping track of blogs has in itself become a major challenge, checking for validity will definitely be insurmountable.

This has posed several problems in the actual quality of information from the Web. As Keen puts it, on the internet where everyone has the same voice, the words of a wise man, counts for no more than the mutterings of a fool. This has also been alluded to by Tara Brabazon who calls this phenomenon as the flattening of expertise [4]. Her main concern has been regarding the shallow information acquired from the Web. Brabazon, a professor of media studies in the University of Brighton, describes Google (this includes Wikipedia and other sources) as the "white bread for the mind", whereby the internet is producing a generation of students who survive on a diet of unreliable information. According to her, Google is providing easy answers to difficult questions. Unfortunately students do not pay enough attention to the validity and authenticity of source, and as a result are not able to distinguish between superficial surfing, shallow ideas and well researched serious work.

2.3 Poor Information, Poor Minds

The Web is currently expanding at such a rapid pace, that it becomes a challenge to check the creative expression of learners and to establish the novelty of contents and artifacts created by them. Web contents are being created, exchanged and transferred at lighting speeds making it difficult to determine the degree of originality of efforts.

Students are always on the constant lookout for easier ways of doing things in order to get away with a minimal-effort learning. For example the citation process is being seen as a major chore or painstaking task, where many students don't see the point in complying with such rigorous academic writing practices [5].

Many students tend to take plagiarism lightly and consider a varying degree of copying to be acceptable. This also highlights the lack of responsibility on the part of students who tend to resort to the easiest means of getting work done, without even considering the legibility of their actions. To make the situation worst, there exist numerous readily available sources of information explicitly supporting students in preparation of term papers [5].

The 'Google Copy Paste Syndrome' (GCPS), describes a common activity of performing fast, easy and usually "not diligently researched" copying, through the abduction of passages in text [2]. Acquiring insights is thus performed by 'conveniently searching' as opposed to a rigorous process of learning through scientific discovery. Information on the Web is often used without even considering the validity of source. This syndrome thus endangers creative writing and thinking.

Mediocrity in produced creative works is promoted, as a result of the lack of due deliberation and insightful internalization. This has been aptly summarized by Weber in his words "as the global brain takes shape by providing answers to all queries, a 'text culture without brains' [2] emerges.

2.4 Emerging Models of Dominance that Influence E-Learning

The previous section has described the various challenges to E-learning due to emerging social patterns. Current leading plagiarism detection tools mainly perform shallow similarity check leaving us left with no helpers in effectively dealing with infringements by students. The best plagiarism detection software has also been found to be not as good as Google as shown in [6]. We are thus faced with challenges in the effective control over E-Learning in an age where the best plagiarism software is now owned by global search engines [5].

As people become more and more dependent on the Web and become fully trusting to whatever it says, large search engines will then have the absolute power to influence the views of millions. This form of power is referred to as

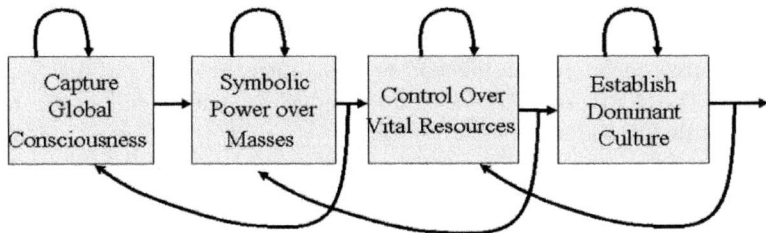

Fig. 1. Model of dominance over information gateways

symbolic power [7], which relates to the ability to manipulate symbols to influence individual life. Web Mining has thus put in the hands of a few large
companies the power to affect the lives of millions by their control over the
universe of information [8].

Despite the fact that arbitrary results are presented by web search engines,
users take their results to be Gospel truth. Users have also shown to be overly
trusting and often rather nave [9]. Typical user behavior also shows that, simple
and efficient search facilitated by search engines is preferred to tedious searches
through libraries or other media.

Reality can be distorted to favour some web sites as opposed to others [10].
Also reality as represented by large information supply companies can be changed
whenever they change their search ranking algorithm. They also have the power
to alter the recording of historical events [9] and to decide on the 'account of
truth' which could well be restricted or product-biased [8]. Having the power to
restrict and manipulate users' perception of reality will then result in the power
to influence lives of people [8]. The full potential of these powers is however yet
to be seen.

The reality presented by the Web is becoming taken to be a substitute for the
hours that would otherwise be spent in inquiry and rationalisation. Weber [2]
aptly states that, 'we are in the process of creating reality by **googeling**'. This
statement emphasizes the utmost reliance on information supply engines such
as Google and Wikipedia that many of us, particularly the younger generation
subject ourselves to.

We describe a model that characterizes the control and influence of data
mining power houses. The model is shown in Figure 1, where the power of
affecting what the masses see enables symbolic power. This power is expected
to be much more than what television has done in the past.

This could then lead to the establishment of de facto gateways enabling control
and authority over vital information resource. Having such a control can over
time bring about cultural shifts in the population, making them even more reliant
on the services of the de facto arbiter of online memory [10].

As illustrated in Figure 1, an influential information supply powerhouse can,
as a result, affect areas of E-Learning as follows:

- Control of the media in determining what learners see at any point in time.
- Control over the memory of the past. Events that do not add value to such a company can be de-emphasized or kept out of user attention.
- Become the "defacto arbiters of knowledge": learners will argue to defend these undisputable authoritative sources.
- Capture and control global consciousness in shaping trends and social norms
- Promote a culture where learners need not concern themselves with memorizing of facts, keeping track of important events, organising documents or even having to make plans about what to do.
- Continuously distract individuals with information, advertisement, 'useful suggestions', etc.
- Influence the life of millions by helping them decide what is 'important' and what is not as important.

3 Scenario for Future

To conclude this paper, we present a teaching scenario from the past that will serve as an ideal for technology-based learning.

A teacher deals with a small class of not more than 15 students (the number here can vary, but has to be small enough to emphasize the personal touch), where the teacher is constantly in touch, personally knowing each and every student. The teacher constantly watches out for the misinterpretation of concepts, lapses in background, absorption levels and uses this information in fine-tuning lesson plans. Distraction and destructive elements are easily noticed and isolated from causing distractions to the learning process. In carrying out the overall learning, the careful direction of ensuring learning goals are met by all students is the main consideration. Learning is not restricted to classroom activities, but also involves guided sessions where informal learning is allowed to take place, assessed and monitored. In measuring student learning, a variety of factors are used; this includes the expert judgment on final submission. Implicit measures of the level of learning then considers the abilities to assimilate and apply concepts and to express ideas on particular issues. Classroom activities would also incorporate remedial activities for ensuring proper learning takes place on a continuous basis.

When technology can become used for enabling such a learning environment E-Learning will definitely be enough. Otherwise, the expected role of E-Learning is bringing about transformation and serving as a useful means will just not happen.

The control over Web Search and its unlimited mining capabilities puts at the hands of few, the power to represent and characterize reality to influence the lives of millions. The immense impact of the Web and a resulting culture poses many more dangers than foreseeable.

The external influence needs to be neutralized, enabling better ways of checking on learning, while supporting learners on the job. As learners become more adept in technology, there is a need to put the knowledge provider in command.

These include the emerging powers and dangers of Data Mining technology and the widening scope of Web search and their expanding influence.

Based on a detailed description of these issues, institutional solutions have been proposed. There has to be a definitive strategic approach by governments and institutions to curb the potential dangers of the control of vital technologies by individual companies. Even if it will be difficult to compete with large mining powers, there is a need to take control over internal data repositories and a need to harness powerful technologies within highly focused localized environments.

At a personal level, the only way to avoid being overpowered by these global search engines is by not over-emphasizing their generic results (could be shallow). Users need to be guided on the importance of seeking reliable sources of information, where search engines are only considered as only a single alternative. The superficial intent mining of search engines should in no way be treated as Gospel truth.

Learner centered metrics need to be specifically defined for E-Learning systems to provide a more humanistic learning. Currently adopted metrics to a large extent tends to be business related or relates to organizational learning efforts. Beyond such measurements, human centered metrics need to be devised.

These measures will thus need to lead towards the enforcing of care into the education process. Without measuring the actual learning efforts, it will be difficult to determine the exact learning needs of learners. These measures need to be modelled in the effective assessment of personal learner efforts.

4   Conclusion

This paper has presented a thought provoking view describing the current state of E-Learning. There is much to be desired in shaping E-Learning to take on the role it has been envisaged to. As ubiquitous learning becomes widely adopted, there is a need to determine exactly what needs to be taught. By having a powerful handy assistant, the need to memorize large amounts of facts is drastically reduced. As such, we do not need to fill the heads of students with unlimited amounts of facts.

It then becomes more important to teach students the art of insightful scholarship, in a quest for knowledge within a dynamic changing world. As such what needs to be taught needs to be evaluated and ratified. In truly supporting lifelong learning, regular upgrade of knowledge (refreshing) should be made compulsory for every learner throughout their life. We will then have to move away fully from just-in-case learning to an effectively just-in-time learning lifelong.

References

1. Moodle.org, http://moodle.org
2. Weber, S.: The Google-Copy-Paste-Syndrome. Telepolis/Hannover, Heise (2007)
3. Keen, A.: The Cult of the Ametuer: How Today's Internet is Killing Our Culture. Doubleday/Currency, New York (2007)

4. Brabazon, T.: The google effect: Googling, blogging, wikis and the flattening of expertise. Libri 56, 157–167 (2006)
5. Maurer, H., Kappe, F., Zaka, B.: Plagiarism: a survey. Journal of Universal Computer Science 12, 1050–1084 (2006)
6. Cont, G.: Googling considered harmful. US Military Academy West Point (2007)
7. Couldry, N.: Media and symbolic power: Extending the range of Bourdieu's field theory. Media@lse Electronic Working Papers, Department of Media and Communications, LSE (2003)
8. Kulathuramaiyer, N., Balke, W.T.: Restricting the view and connecting the dots: Dangers of a web search engine monopoly. Journal of Universal Computer Science 12, 1731–1740 (2006)
9. Kulathuramaiyer, N., Maurer, H.: Addressing Copy-Paste with ICARE. Journal of Research in Innovative Teaching 1, 1–24 (2008)
10. Witten, I.H., Gori, M., Numerico, T.: Web Dragons, Inside the Myths of Search Engine Technology. Morgan Kaufmann, San Francisco (2007)

The Practice of Informatics

Domains: Their Simulation, Monitoring and Control—A Divertimento of Ideas and Suggestions

Dines Bjørner

Fredsvej 11, DK-2840 Holte, Denmark
bjorner@gmail.com

Abstract. This divertimento – on the occasion of the 70th anniversary of Prof., Dr Hermann Maurer – sketches some observations over the concepts of domain, requirements and modelling – where abstract interpretations of these models cover both a priori, a posteriori and real-time aspects of the domain as well as 1–1, microscopic and macroscopic simulations, real-time monitoring and real-time monitoring & control of that domain. The reference frame for these concepts are domain models: carefully narrated and formally described domains. I survey more-or-less standard ideas of verifiable development and conjecture product families of demos, simulators, monitors and monitors & controllers – but now these "standard ideas" are recast in the context of core requirements prescriptions being "derived" from domain descriptions.

A Laudatio: This paper is dedicated to Hermann Maurer and is presented on the occasion of his 70th birthday. Hermann and I both spent years at the legendary IBM Labor in Vienna, Austria. Hermann in the 1960s, I in the early 1970s. Hermann went on to do other things than what the Labor became famous for – and contributed significantly to his chosen, foundational and theoretical science — and then, suddenly, Hermann changed somewhat: into highly applications-oriented and almost exclusively technology-oriented work. Again with very significant contributions and now also with decisive industrial and societal impact. I was deeply influenced – and remain so since my days in the early 1970s – by the Vienna work: formal semantics, first of languages, later of systems understood through the languages they exhibit. I take pride and have joy in developing and presenting, to others, the careful English narration and the formalisation the professional languages, i.e., one, crucial aspect of the domains of air traffic, banking, commodities exchange, container lines, the market, railways, etc., etc. Maurer, I am sure, likewise takes pride in the wonderful universes he and his co-workers create for us inside and on the surface of the computing machine, interacting in sometimes unforeseen but always exciting ways. Congratulation Hermann. We never met at Vienna. But I have enjoyed all the many times that we've met since Vienna – across several continents.

C.S. Calude, G. Rozenberg, A. Salomaa (Eds.): Maurer Festschrift, LNCS 6570, pp. 167–183, 2011.
© Springer-Verlag Berlin Heidelberg 2011

1   Introduction

A background setting for this paper is the concern for professionally developing the right software, i.e., software which satisfies users expectations, and software that is right: i.e., software which is correct with respect to user requirements and thus has no "bugs", no "blue screens".

The present paper must be seen on the background of the main line of experimental research around the topics of domain engineering, requirements engineering and their relation. For details I refer to (6, Chaps. 9–16: Domain Engineering, Chaps. 17-24: Requirements Engineering).

The aims of this paper is to present (1) some ideas about software that (1a) "demo", (1b) simulate, (1c) monitor and (1d) monitor & control domains; (2) some ideas about "time scaling": demo and simulation time versus domain time; and (3) how these kinds of software relate.

The paper is exploratory. There will be no theorems and therefore there will be no proofs. We are presenting what might eventually emerge into (α) a theory of domains, i.e., a domain science (7; 17; 10; 15), and (β) a software development theory of domain engineering versus requirements engineering (16; 9; 11; 14).

The paper is not a "standard" research paper: it does not compare its claimed achievements with corresponding or related achievements of other researchers – simply because we do not claim "achievements" which have been fully, or at least reasonably well theorised – etcetera. But I would suggest that you might find some of the ideas of the paper (in Sect. 3) worthwhile publishing. Hence the "divertimento" suffix to the paper title.

The structure of the paper is as follows.

In Sect. 2 we discuss what a domain description is. Appendix A gives an example.

In Sect. 3 we then outline a series of interpretations of domain descriptions. These arise, when developed in an orderly, professional manner, from requirements prescriptions which are themselves orderly developed from the domain description[1]. The essence of Sect. 3 is (i) the (albeit informal) presentation of such tightly related notions as *demos* (Sect. 3.1), *simulators* (Sect. 3.2), *monitors* (Sect. 3.3) and *monitors & controllers* (Sect. 3.3) (these notions can be formalised), and (ii) the conjectures on a product family of domain-based software developments (Sect. 3.5). A notion of *script-based simulation* extends demos and is the basis for monitor and controller developments and uses. The script used in our example here is related to time, but one can define non-temporal scripts – so the "carrying idea" of Sect. 3 extends to a widest variety of software. We claim that Sect. 3 thus brings these new ideas: a tightly related software engineering concept of *demo-simulator-monitor-controller machines*, and an extended notion of *reference models for requirements and specifications* (22).

---

[1] We do not show such orderly "derivations" but outline their basics in Sect. 3.4.

2   Domain Descriptions

By a domain description we shall mean a combined narrative, that is, precise, but informal, and a formal description of the application domain *as it is:* no reference to any possible requirements let alone software that is desired for that domain. (Thus a requirements prescription is a likewise combined narrative, that is, precise, but informal, and a formal prescription of what we expect from a machine (hardware + software) that is to support simple entities, actions, events and behaviours of a possibly business process re-engineering application domain. Requirements expresses a domain *as we would like ti to be.*)

We bring in Appendix A an example domain description.

We further refer to the literature for examples: (4, *railways* (2000)), (5, *the 'market'* (2000)), (11, *public government, IT security, hospitals* (2006) chapters 8–10), (9, *transport nets* (2008)) and (14, *pipelines* (2010)). On the net you may find technical reports (8) covering "larger" domain descriptions. Recent papers on the concept of domain descriptions are (14; 15; 12; 17; 9; 7; 13).

To emphasize: domain descriptions describe domains as they are with no reference to (requirements to) possibly desired software. Domain descriptions do not necessarily describe computable objects. They relate to the described domain in a way similar to the way in which mathematical descriptions of physical phenomena stand to "the physical world".

3   Interpretations

3.1   What Is a Domain-Based Demo?

A *domain-based demo* is a software system which *"present"* (1) simple entities, (2) actions, (3) events and (4) behaviours of a domain. The *"presentation"* abstracts these phenomena and their related concepts in various computer generated forms: visual, acoustic, etc.

Examples. A domain description might, as that of Appendix A, be of transport nets (of hubs [street intersections, train stations, harbours, airports] and links [road segments, rail tracks, shipping lanes, air-lanes]), their development, traffic [of vehicles, trains, ships and aircraft], etc. We shall assume such a transport domain description below.

(1) Simple entities are, for example, presented as follows: (a) transport nets by two dimensional (2D) road, railway or airline maps, (b) hubs and links by highlighting parts of 2D maps and by related photos – and their unique identifiers by labelling hubs and links, (c) routes by highlighting sequences of paths (hubs and links) on a 2D map, (d) buses by photographs and by dots at hubs or on links of a 2D map, and (e) bus timetables by, well, indeed, by showing a 2D bus timetable.

(2) Actions are, for example, presented as follows: (f) The insertion or removal of a hub or a link by showing "instantaneous" triplets of "before", "during" and "after" animation sequences. (g) The start or end of a bus ride by showing

flashing animations of the appearance, respectively the flashing disappearance of a bus (dot) at the origin, respectively the destination bus stops.

(3) Events are, for example, presented as follows: (h) A mudslide [or fire in a road tunnel, or collapse of a bridge] along a (road) link by showing an animation of part of a (road) map with an instantaneous sequence of (α) the present link , (β) a gap somewhere on the link, (γ) and the appearance of two ("symbolic") hubs "on either side of the gap". (i) The congestion of road traffic "grinding to a halt" at, for example, a hub, by showing an animation of part of a (road) map with an instantaneous sequence of the massive accumulation of vehicle dots moving (instantaneously) from two or more links into a hub.

(4) Behaviours are, for example, presented as follows: (k) A bus tour: from its start, on time, or "thereabouts", from its bus stop of origin, via (all) intermediate stops, with or without delays or advances in times of arrivals and departures, to the bus stop of destination (ℓ) The composite behaviour of "all bus tours", meeting or missing connection times, with sporadic delays, with cancellation of some bus tours, etc. – by showing the sequence of states of all the buses on the net.

We say that behaviours $(3(j)–4(\ell))$ are *script-based* in that they (try to) satisfy a bus timetable $(1(e))$.

Towards a Theory of Visualisation and Acoustic Manifestation. The above examples shall serve to highlight the general problem of visualisation and acoustic manifestation. Just as we need sciences of visualising scientific data and of diagrammatic logics, so **we need more serious studies of visualisation and acoustic manifestation — so amply, but, this author thinks, inconsistently demonstrated by current uses of interactive computing media.**

3.2   Simulations

"Simulation is the imitation of some real thing, state of affairs, or process; the act of simulating something generally entails representing certain key characteristics or behaviours of a selected physical or abstract system" [Wikipedia] for the purposes of testing some hypotheses usually stated in terms of the model being simulated <u>and</u> pairs of statistical data and expected outcomes.

Explication of Figure 1. Figure 1 attempts to indicate four things: (i) Left top: the rounded edge rectangle labelled "The Domain" alludes to some specific domain ("out there"). (ii) Left middle: the small rounded rectangle labelled "A Domain Description" alludes to some document which narrates and formalises a description of "the domain". (iii) Left bottom: the medium sized rectangle labelled "A Domain Demo based on the Domain Description" (for short "Demo") alludes to a software system that, in some sense (to be made clear later) "simulates" "The Domain." (iv) Right: the large rectangle (a) shows a horisontal time axis which basically "divides" that large rectangle into two parts: (b) Above the time axis the **"fat"** rounded edge rectangle alludes to the time-wise behaviour, a *domain trace*, of "The Domain" (i.e., the actual, or real, domain). (c) Below

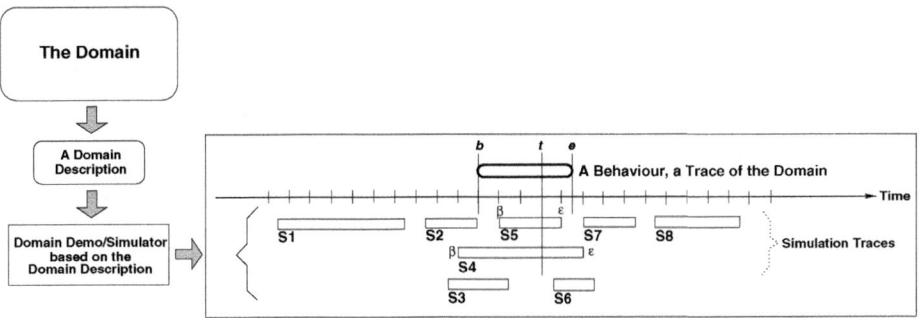

Legend: ⇨ A development; S1, S2, S3, S4, S5, S6, S7, S8: "runs" of the Domain Simulation

Fig. 1. Simulations

the time axis there are eight **"thin"** rectangles. These are labels S1, S2, S3, S4, S5, S6, S7 and S8. (d) Each of these denote a "run", i.e., a time-stamped "execution", a *program trace*, of the "Demo". Their "relationship" to the time axis is this: their execution takes place in the real time as related to that of "The Domain" behaviour.

A *trace* (whether a domain or a program execution trace) is a time-stamped sequence of states: domain states, respectively demo, simulator, monitor and monitor & control states.

From Fig. 1 and the above explication we can conclude that "executions" S4 and S5 each share exactly one time point, t, at which "The Domain" and "The Simulation" "share" time, that is, the time-stamped execution S4 and S5 reflect a "Simulation" state which at time t should reflect (some abstraction of) "The Domain" state.

Only if the domain behaviour (i.e., trace) fully "surrounds" that of the simulation trace, or, vice-versa (cf. Fig. 1[S4,S5]), is there a "shared" time. Only if the 'begin' and 'end' times of the domain behaviour are identical to the 'start' and 'finish' times of the simulation trace, is there an infinity of shared 1–1 times.

In Fig 2 we show "the same" "Domain Behaviour" (three times) and a (1) simulation, a (2) monitoring and a (3) monitoring & control, all of whose 'begin/start' (b/β) and 'end/finish' (e/ϵ) times coincide. In such cases the "Demo/Simulation" takes place in real-time throughout the 'begin $\cdots\cdots$ end' interval.

Let β and ϵ be the 'start' and 'finish' times of either S4 or S5. Then the relationship between t, β, ϵ, b and e is $\frac{t-b}{e-t} = \frac{t-\beta}{\epsilon-t}$ — which leads to a second degree polynomial in t which can then be solved in the usual, high school manner.

Script-based Simulation. A script-based simulation is the behaviour, i.e., an execution, of, basically, a demo which, step-by-step, follows a script: that is a prescription for highlighting simple entities, actions, events and behaviours.

Script-based simulations where the script embodies a notion of time, like a bus timetable, and unlike a route, can be thought of as the execution of a demos where "chunks" of demo operations take place in accordance with "chunks"[2] of script prescriptions. The latter (i.e., the script prescriptions) can be said to represent simulated (i.e., domain) time in contrast to "actual computer" time. The actual times in which the script-based simulation takes place relate to domain times as shown in Simulations S1 to S8 in Fig. 1 and in Fig. 2(1–3). Traces Fig. 2(1–3) and S8 Fig. 1 are said to be *real-time:* there is a one-to-one mapping between computer time and domain time. S1 and S4 Fig. 1 are said to be *microscopic:* disjoint computer time intervals map into distinct domain times. S2, S3, S5, S6 and S7 are said to be *macroscopic:* disjoint domain time intervals map into distinct computer times.

In order to concretise the above "vague" statements let us take the example of simulating bus traffic as based on a bus timetable script. A simulation scenario could be as follows. Initially, not relating to any domain time, the simulation "demos" a net, available buses and a bus timetable. The person(s) who are requesting the simulation are asked to decide on the ratio of the domain time interval to simulation time interval. If the ratio is 1 a real-time simulation has been requested. If the ratio is less than 1 a microscopic simulation has been requested. If the ratio is larger than 1 a microscopic simulation has been requested. A chosen ratio of, say 48 to 1 means that a 24 hour bus traffic is to be simulated in 30 minutes of elapsed simulation time. Then the person(s) who are requesting the simulation are asked to decide on the starting domain time, say 6:00am, and the domain time interval of simulation, say 4 hours – in which case the simulation of bus traffic from 6am till 10am is to be shown in 5 minutes (300 seconds) of elapsed simulation time. The person(s) who are requesting the simulation are then asked to decide on the *"sampling times"* or *"time intervals"*: If 'sampling times' 6:00 am, 6:30 am, 7:00 am, 8:00 am, 9:00 am, 9:30 am and 10:00 am are chosen, then the simulation is stopped at corresponding simulation times: 0 sec., 37.5 sec., 75 sec., 150 sec., 225 sec., 262.5 sec. and 300 sec. The simulation then shows the state of selected entities and actions at these domain times. If 'sampling time interval' is chosen and is set to every 5 min., then the simulation shows the state of selected entities and actions at corresponding domain times. The simulation is resumed when the person(s) who are requesting the simulation so indicates, say by a "resume" icon click. The time interval between adjacent simulation stops and resumptions contribute with 0 time to elapsed simulation time – which in this case was set to 5 minutes. Finally the requestor provides some statistical data such as numbers of potential and actual bus passengers, etc.

Then two clocks are started: a domain time clock and a simulation time clock. The simulation proceeds as driven by, in this case, the bus time table. To include "unforeseen" events, such as the wreckage of a bus (which is then unable to complete a bus tour), we allow any number of such events to be randomly scheduled. Actually scheduled events "interrupts" the "programmed" simulation and leads to thus unscheduled stops (and resumptions) where the unscheduled stop now focuses on showing the event.

---

[2] We deliberately leave the notion of chunk vague so as to allow as wide an spectrum of simulations.

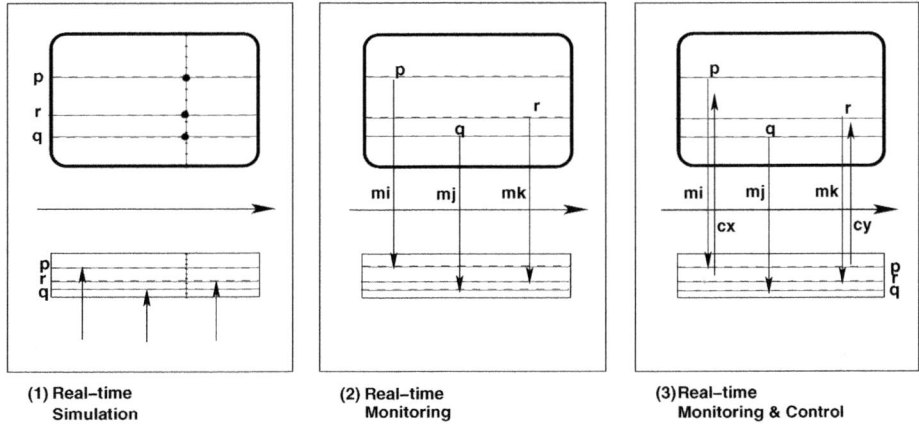

(1) Real–time Simulation   **(2) Real–time Monitoring**   **(3) Real–time Monitoring & Control**

Legend: mi,mj,...,mk: monitorings; cx,...,cy: controls

Fig. 2. Simulation, Monitoring and Monitoring & Control

The Development Arrow. The arrow, ⇨, between a pair of boxes (of Fig. 1) denote a step of development: (i) from the domain box to the domain description box it denotes the development of a domain description based on studies and analyses of the domain; (ii) from the domain description box to the domain demo box it denotes the development of a software system — where that development assumes an intermediate requirements box which has not been show; (iii) from the domain demo box to either of a simulation traces it denotes the development of a simulator as the related demo software system, again depending on whichever special requirements have been put to the simulator.

3.3   Monitoring and Control

Figure 2 shows three different kinds of uses of software systems (where (2) [Monitoring] and (3) [Monitoring & Control] represent further) developments from the demo or simulation software system mentioned in Sect. 3.1 and Sect. 3.2.

We have added some (three) horisontal and labelled (p, q and r) lines to Fig. 2(1,2,3) (with respect to the traces of Fig. 1). They each denote a trace of a simple entity, an action or an event, that is, they are traces of values of these phenomena or concepts. A (named) action value could, for example, be the pair of the before and after states of the action and some description of the function ("insertion of a link", "start of a bus tour") involved in the action. A (named) event value could, for example, be a pair of the before and after states of the entities causing, respectively being effected by the event and some description of the predicate ("mudslide", "break-down of a bus") involved in the event. A cross section, such as designated by the vertical lines (one for the domain trace, one for the "corresponding" program trace) of Fig. 2(1) denotes a state: a domain, respectively a program state.

Figure 2(1) attempts to show a real-time demo or simulation for the chosen domain. Figure 2(2) purports to show the deployment of real-time software for monitoring (chosen aspects of) the chosen domain. Figure 2(3) purports to show the deployment of real-time software for monitoring as well as controlling (chosen aspects of) the chosen domain.

Monitoring. By *domain monitoring* we mean *"to be aware of the state of a domain"*, its simple entities, actions, events and behaviour. Domain monitoring is thus a process, typically within a distributed system for collecting and storing state data. In this process "observation" points — i.e., simple entities, actions and where events may occur — are identified in the domain, cf. points p, q and r of Fig. 2. Sensors are inserted at these points. The "downward" pointing vertical arrows of Figs. 2(2–3), from "the domain behaviour" to the "monitoring" and the "monitoring & control" traces express communication of what has been sensed (measured, photographed, etc.) [as directed by and] as input data (etc.) to these monitors. The monitor (being "executed") may store these "sensings" for future analysis.

Control. By *domain control* we mean *"the ability to change the value"* of simple entities and the course of actions and hence behaviours, including prevention of events of the domain. Domain control is thus based on domain monitoring. Actuators are inserted in the domain "at or near" monitoring points or at points related to these, viz. points p and r of Fig. 2(3). The "upward" pointing vertical arrows of Fig. 2(3), from the "monitoring & control" traces to the "domain behaviour" express communication, to the domain, of what has been computed by the controller as a proper control reaction in response to the monitoring.

3.4   Machine Development

Machines. By a *machine* we shall understand a combination of hardware and software. For demos and simulators the machine is "mostly" software with the hardware typically being graphic display units with tactile instruments. For monitors the "main" machine, besides the hardware and software of demos and simulators, additionally includes *sensors* distributed throughout the domain and the technological machine means of *communicating* monitored signals from the sensors to the "main" machine and the processing of these signals by the main machine. For monitors & controllers the machine, besides the monitor machine, further includes actuators placed in the domain and the machine means of computing and communicating control signals to the actuators.

Requirements Development. Essential parts of Requirements to a Machine can be systematically "derived" from a Domain description. These essential parts are the *domain requirements* and the *interface requirements*. Domain requirements are those requirements which can be expressed, say in narrative form, by mentioning technical terms only of the domain. These technical terms cover only phenomena and concepts (simple entities, actions, events and behaviours) of the domain. Some domain requirements are *projected, instantiated,* made more *deterministic* and *extended*[3].

---

[3] We omit consideration of *fitting*.

(a) By *domain projection* we mean a sub-setting of the domain description: parts are left out which the requirements stake-holders, collaborating with the requirements engineer, decide is of no relevance to the requirements. For our example it could be that our domain description had contained models of road net attributes such as "the wear & tear" of road surfaces, the length of links, states of hubs and links (that is, [dis]allowable directions of traffic through hubs and along links), etc. Projection might then omit these attributes.

(b) By *domain instantiation* we mean a specialisation of entities (simple, actions, events and behaviours), refining them from abstract simple entities to more concrete such, etc. For our example it could be that we only model freeways or only model road-pricing nets – or any one or more other aspects.

(c) By *domain determination* we mean that of making the domain description cum domain requirements prescription less non-deterministic, i.e., more deterministic (or even the other way around!). For our example it could be that we had domain-described states of street intersections as not controlled by traffic signals – where the determination is now that of introducing an abstract notion of traffic signals which allow only certain states (of red, yellow and green).

(d) By *domain extension* we basically mean that of extending the domain with phenomena and concepts that were not feasible without information technology. For our examples we could extend the domain with bus mounted GPS gadgets that record and communicate (to, say a central bus traffic computer) the more-or-less exact positions of buses – thereby enabling the observation of bus traffic.

Interface requirements are those requirements which can be expressed, say in narrative form, by mentioning technical terms both of the domain and of the machine. These technical terms thus cover shared phenomena and concepts, that is, phenomena and concepts of the domain which are, in some sense, also (to be) represented by the machine. Interface requirements represent (i) the initialisation and "on-the-fly" update of simple machine entities on the basis of *shared* domain entities; (ii) the interaction between the machine and the domain while the machine is carrying out a (previous domain) action; (iii) machine responses, if any, to domain events — or domain responses, if any, to machine events cum "outputs"; and (iv) machine monitoring and machine control of domain phenomena. Each of these four (i–iv) interface requirement facets themselves involve projection, instantiation, determination, extension and fitting.

Machine requirements are those requirements which can be expressed, say in narrative form, by mentioning technical terms only of the machine. (An example is: visual display units).

3.5   Verifiable Software Development

An Example Set of Conjectures. (A) From a domain, $\mathcal{D}$, one can develop a domain description $\mathbb{D}$. $\mathbb{D}$ cannot be verified. It can at most be validated. Individual properties, $\mathbb{P}_{\mathbb{D}}$, of the domain description $\mathbb{D}$ and hence, purportedly, of the domain, $\mathcal{D}$, can be expressed and possibly proved

$$\mathbb{D} \models \mathbb{P}_{\mathbb{D}}$$

and these may be validated to be properties of $\mathcal{D}$ by observations in (or of) that domain.

(B) From a domain description, $\mathbb{D}$, one can develop requirements, $\mathbb{R}_{\text{DE}}$, for, and from $\mathbb{R}_{\text{DE}}$ one can develop a domain demo machine specification $\mathbb{M}_{\text{DE}}$ such that

$$\mathbb{D}, \mathbb{M}_{\text{DE}} \models \mathbb{R}_{\text{DE}}.$$

The formula $\mathbb{D}, \mathbb{M} \models \mathbb{R}$ can be read as follows: in order to prove that the Machine satisfies the Requirements, assumptions about the Domain must often be made explicit in steps of the proof.

(C) From a domain description, $\mathbb{D}$, and a domain demo machine specification, $\mathbb{S}_{\text{DE}}$, one can develop requirements, $\mathbb{R}_{\text{SI}}$, for, and from such a $\mathbb{R}_{\text{SI}}$ one can develop a domain simulator machine specification $\mathbb{M}_{\text{SI}}$ such that

$$(\mathbb{D}; \mathbb{M}_{\text{DE}}), \mathbb{M}_{\text{SI}} \models \mathbb{R}_{\text{SI}}.$$

We have "lumped" $(\mathbb{D}; \mathbb{M}_{\text{DE}})$ as the two constitute the extended domain for which we, in this case of development, suggest the next stage requirements and machine development to take place.

(D) From a domain description, $\mathbb{D}$, and a domain simulator machine specification, $\mathbb{M}_{\text{SI}}$, one can develop requirements, $\mathbb{R}_{\text{MO}}$, for, and from such a $\mathbb{R}_{\text{MO}}$ one can develop a domain monitor machine specification $\mathbb{M}_{\text{MO}}$ such that

$$(\mathbb{D}; \mathbb{M}_{\text{SI}}), \mathbb{M}_{\text{MO}} \models \mathbb{R}_{\text{MO}}.$$

(E) From a domain description, $\mathbb{D}$, and a domain monitor machine specification, $\mathbb{M}_{\text{MO}}$, one can develop requirements, $\mathbb{R}_{\text{MC}}$, for, and from such a $\mathbb{R}_{\text{MC}}$ one can develop a domain monitor & controller machine specification $\mathbb{M}_{\text{MC}}$ such that

$$(\mathbb{D}; \mathbb{M}_{\text{MO}}), \mathbb{M}_{\text{MC}} \models \mathbb{R}_{\text{MC}}.$$

Chains of Verifiable Developments. The above illustrated just one chain of development. There are others. All are shown in Fig. 3. The above development is shown as the longest horizontal chain (third row).

Figure 3 can also be interpreted as prescribing a widest possible range of machine cum software products (18; 25) for a given domain. One domain may give rise to many different kinds of DEmo machines, SImulators, MOnitors and Monitor & Controllers (the unprimed versions of the $\mathbb{M}_{\text{T}}$ machines (where T ranges over DE, SI, MO, MC)). For each of these there are similarly, "exponentially" many variants of successor machines (the primed versions of the $\mathbb{M}_{\text{T}}$ machines).

What does it mean that a machine is a primed version? Well, here it means, for example, that $\mathbb{M}'_{\text{SI}}$ embodies facets of the demo machine $\mathbb{M}_{\text{DE}}$, and that $\mathbb{M}'''_{\text{MC}}$ embodies facets of the demo machine $\mathbb{M}_{\text{DE}}$, of the simulator $\mathbb{M}'_{\text{SI}}$, and the monitor $\mathbb{M}''_{\text{MO}}$. Whether such requirements are desirable is left to product customers and their software providers (18; 25) to decide.

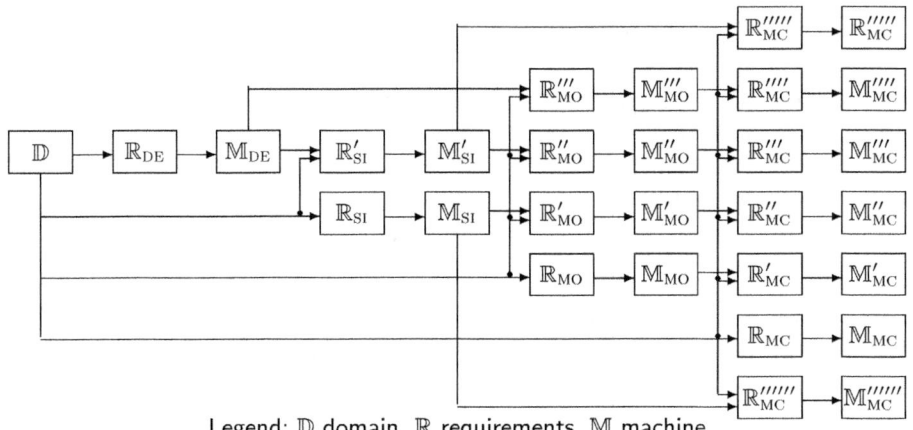

Legend: $\mathbb{D}$ domain, $\mathbb{R}$ requirements, $\mathbb{M}$ machine

DE:DEMO, SI: SIMULATOR, MO: MONITOR, MC: MONITOR & CONTROLLER

Fig. 3. Chains of Verifiable Developments

4 Conclusion

Our divertimento is almost over. It is time to conclude.

4.1 Discussion

The $\mathbb{D}, \mathbb{M} \models \mathbb{R}$ ('correctness' of) development relation appears to have been first indicated in the Computational Logic Inc. Stack (1; 21) and the EU ESPRIT ProCoS (2; 3) projects; (22) presents this same idea with a purpose much like ours, but with more technical details and full discussion.

The term 'domain engineering' appears to have at least two meanings: the one used here (7; 13) and one (23; 20; 19) emerging out of the Software Engineering Institute at CMU where it is also called *product line engineering*[4]. Our meaning, is, in a sense, more narrow, but then it seems to also be more highly specialised (with detailed description and formalisation principles and techniques). Fig. 3 illustrates, in capsule form, what we think is the CMU/SEI meaning. The relationship between, say Fig. 3 and *model-based software development* seems obvious but need be explored.

What Have We Achieved. We have characterised a spectrum of strongly domain-related as well as strongly inter-related (cf. Fig. 3) software product families: *demos, simulators, monitors* and *monitor & controllers*. We have indicated varieties of these: simulators based on demos, monitors based on simulators, monitor & controllers based on monitors, in fact any of the latter ones in the software product family list as based on any of the earlier ones. We have sketched temporal relations between simulation traces and domain behaviours:

---

[4] http://en.wikipedia.org/wiki/Domain_engineering

a priori, a posteriori, macroscopic and *microscopic*, and we have identified the real-time cases which lead on to monitors and monitor & controllers.

What Have We Not Achieved — Some Conjectures. We have not characterised the software product family relations other than by the $\mathbb{D}, \mathbb{M} \models \mathbb{R}$ and $(\mathbb{D}; \mathbb{M}_{\mathrm{XYZ}}), \mathbb{M} \models \mathbb{R}$ clauses. That is, we should like to prove conjectured type theoretic inclusion relations like:

$$\wp([\![\mathcal{M}_{\mathrm{X}_{\underline{\mathbf{mod}}}\ \mathrm{ext.}}]\!]) \sqsupseteq \wp([\![\mathcal{M}'^{\cdots'}_{\mathrm{X}_{\underline{\mathbf{mod}}}\ \mathrm{ext.}}]\!]), \qquad \wp([\![\mathcal{M}'^{\cdots'}_{\mathrm{X}_{\underline{\mathbf{mod}}}\ \mathrm{ext.}}]\!]) \sqsupseteq \wp([\![\mathcal{M}''^{\cdots'}_{\mathrm{X}_{\underline{\mathbf{mod}}}\ \mathrm{ext.}}]\!])$$

where X and Y range appropriately, where $[\![\mathcal{M}]\!]$ expresses the meaning of $\mathcal{M}$, where $\wp([\![\mathcal{M}]\!])$ denote the space of all machine meanings and where $\wp([\![\mathcal{M}_{x_{\underline{\mathbf{mod}}}\ \mathrm{ext.}}]\!])$ is intended to denote that space modulo ("free of") the y facet (here *ext.*, for extension).

That is, it is conjectured that the set of more specialised, i.e., n primed, machines of kind x is type theoretically "contained" in the set of m primed (unprimed) x machines $(0 \le m < n)$.

There are undoubtedly many such interesting relations between the DEMO, SIMULATOR, MONITOR and MONITOR & CONTROLLER machines, unprimed and primed.

What Should We Do Next. This paper has the subtitle: *A Divertimento of Ideas and Suggestions*. It is not a proper theoretical paper. It tries to throw some light on families and varieties of software, i.e., their relations, and. It focuses, in particular, on so-called DEMO, SIMULATOR, MONITOR and MONITOR & CONTROLLER software and their relation to the "originating" domain, i.e., that in which such software is to serve, and hence that which is being *extended* by such software, cf. the compounded 'domain' $(\mathbb{D}; \mathbb{M}_i)$ of in $(\mathbb{D}; \mathbb{M}_i), \mathbb{M}_j \models \mathbb{D}$. These notions should be studied formally. All of these notions: requirements projection, instantiation, determination and extension can be formalised; and the specification language, in the form used here (without CSP processes, (24)) has a formal semantics and a proof system — so the various notions of development, $(\mathbb{D}; \mathbb{M}_i), \mathbb{M}_j \models \mathbb{R}$ and $\wp(\mathbb{M})$ can be formalised.

References

[1] Bevier, W.R., Hunt Jr., W.A., Strother Moore, J., Young, W.D.: An approach to system verification. Journal of Automated Reasoning 5(4), 411–428 (1989); Special Issue on System Verification

[2] Bjørner, D.: A ProCoS Project Description. Published in two slightly different versions: (1) EATCS Bulletin (October 1989), (2) Plander, I.(ed.): Proceedings: Intl. Conf. on AI & Robotics, Strebske Pleso, Slovakia, November 5-9. North-Holland, Publ., Amsterdam (1989), Dept. of Computer Science, Technical University of Denmark (October 1989)

[3] Bjørner, D.: Trustworthy Computing Systems: The ProCoS Experience. In: 14th ICSE: Intl. Conf. on Software Eng., Melbourne, Australia, May 11-15, pp. 15–34. ACM Press, New York (1992)

[4] Bjørner, D.: Formal Software Techniques in Railway Systems. In: Schnieder, E. (ed.) 9th IFAC Symposium on Control in Transportation Systems, Technical University, Braunschweig, Germany, June 13-15, pp. 1–12 (2000); VDI/VDE-Gesellschaft Mess– und Automatisieringstechnik, VDI-Gesellschaft für Fahrzeug– und Verkehrstechnik (invited talk)

[5] Bjørner, D.: Domain Models of "The Market" — in Preparation for E–Transaction Systems. In: Kilov, H., Baclawski, K. (eds.) Practical Foundations of Business and System Specifications, The Netherlands. Kluwer Academic Press, Dordrecht (2002)

[6] Bjørner, D.: Software Engineering, vol. 3: Domains, Requirements and Software Design. Texts in Theoretical Computer Science, the EATCS Series, vol. 3. Springer, Heidelberg (2006)

[7] Bjørner, D.: Domain Theory: Practice and Theories, Discussion of Possible Research Topics. In: Jones, C.B., Liu, Z., Woodcock, J. (eds.) ICTAC 2007. LNCS, vol. 4711, pp. 1–17. Springer, Heidelberg (2007)

[8] Bjørner, D.: Domain Descriptions (technical reports):
   1. On Development of Web-based Software. A Divertimento of Ideas and Suggestions, http://www2.imm.dtu.dk/~db/wfdftp.pdf
   2. XVSM: A Narrative and a Formalisation, http://www2.imm.dtu.dk/~db/xvsm-p.pdf
   3. The Tokyo Stock Exchange, http://www2.imm.dtu.dk/~db/todai/tse-1.pdf and http://www2.imm.dtu.dk/~db/todai/tse-2.pdf
   4. What is Logistics, http://www2.imm.dtu.dk/~db/logistics.pdf
   5. A Domain Model of Oil Pipelines, http://www2.imm.dtu.dk/~db/pipeline.pdf
   6. A Container Line Industry Domain, http://www2.imm.dtu.dk/~db/container-paper.pdf
   7. A Railway Systems Domain, http://www.railwaydomain.org/PDF/tb.pdf
   8. CoMet: Comparative Methodology, A Technical Note. Transport Systems, http://www2.imm.dtu.dk/~db/comet/comet1.pdf
   R&D Experiments, Bjørner, Fredsvej 11, DK-2840 Holte, Denmark (2007-2010)

[9] Bjørner, D.: From Domains to Requirements. In: Degano, P., De Nicola, R., Bevilacqua, V. (eds.) Concurrency, Graphs and Models. LNCS, vol. 5065, pp. 1–30. Springer, Heidelberg (2008)

[10] Bjørner, D.: An Emerging Domain Science – A Rôle for Stanisław Leśniewski's Mereology and Bertrand Russell's Philosophy of Logical Atomism. Higher-order and Symbolic Computation (2009)

[11] Bjørner, D.: Domain Engineering: Technology Management, Research and Engineering. Research Monograph (# 4); JAIST Press, 1-1, Asahidai, Nomi, Ishikawa 923-1292 Japan (2009); This Research Monograph contains the following main chapters:
   1. On Domains and On Domain Engineering – Prerequisites for Trustworthy Software – A Necessity for Believable Management, pp. 3–38
   2. Possible Collaborative Domain Projects – A Management Brief, pp. 39–56
   3. The Rôle of Domain Engineering in Software Development, pp. 57–72
   4. Verified Software for Ubiquitous Computing – A VSTTE Ubiquitous Computing Project Proposal, pp. 73–106
   5. The Triptych Process Model – Process Assessment and Improvement, pp. 107–138

6. Domains and Problem Frames – The Triptych Dogma and M.A.Jackson's PF Paradigm, pp. 139–175
7. Documents – A Rough Sketch Domain Analysis, pp. 179–200
8. Public Government – A Rough Sketch Domain Analysis, pp. 201–222
9. Towards a Model of IT Security — – The ISO Information Security Code of Practice – An Incomplete Rough Sketch Analysis, pp. 223–282
10. Towards a Family of Script Languages – – Licenses and Contracts – An Incomplete Sketch, pp. 283–328

Bjørner will post this 507 page soft cover book (with 77 fine photos of "all things Japanese", in full colours, taken by Dines in 2006) to you provided you e-mail your name and address and post international reply postage coupons, in the total amount of: Denmark 60.50 Kr., Europe 126.00 Kr., elsewhere 209.00 Kr, http://en.wikipedia.org/wiki/International_reply_coupon

[12] Bjørner, D.: On Mereologies in Computing Science. In: Roscoe, B. (ed.) Festschrift for Tony Hoare, London, UK. History of Computing, Springer, Heidelberg (2009)
[13] Bjørner, D.: Domain Engineering. In: Boca, P., Bowen, J. (eds.) BCS FACS Seminars, London, UK. LNCS (the BCS FAC Series), pp. 1–42. Springer, Heidelberg (2010)
[14] Bjørner, D.: Domain Science & Engineering – From Computer Science to The Sciences of Informatics, Part I of II: The Engineering Part. Kibernetika i sistemny analiz (2) (May 2010)
[15] Bjørner, D.: Domain Science & Engineering – From Computer Science to The Sciences of Informatics Part II of II: The Science Part. Kibernetika i sistemny analiz (2) (May 2010)
[16] Bjørner, D.: Believable Software Management. Encyclopedia of Software Engineering 1(1), 1–32 (2011)
[17] Bjørner, D., Eir, A.: Compositionality: Ontology and Mereology of Domains. In: Dams, D., Hannemann, U., Steffen, M. (eds.) Concurrency, Compositionality, and Correctness. LNCS, vol. 5930, pp. 22–59. Springer, Heidelberg (2010)
[18] Bosch, J.: Design and Use of Software Architectures: Adopting and Evolving a Product-line Approach. ACM Press/Addison-Wesley, New York/NY (2000)
[19] Buschmann, F., Henney, K., Schmidt, D.C.: Pattern-Oriented Software Architecture: On Patterns and Pattern Languages. John Wiley & Sons Ltd., England (2007)
[20] Falbo, R., Guizzardi, G., Duarte, K.C.: An Ontological Approach to Domain Engineering. In: Proceedings of the 14th International Conference on Software Engineering and Knowledge Engineering, SEKE 2002, Ischia, Italy, July 15-19, pp. 351–358. ACM, New York (2002)
[21] Good, D.I., Young, W.D.: Mathematical Methods for Digital Systems Development. In: Prehn, S., Toetenel, H. (eds.) VDM 1991. LNCS, vol. 552, pp. 406–430. Springer, Heidelberg (1991)
[22] Gunter, C.A., Gunter, E.L., Jackson, M.A., Zave, P.: A Reference Model for Requirements and Specifications. IEEE Software 17(3), 37–43 (2000)
[23] Harsu, M.: A Survey on Domain Engineering. Review, Institute of Software Systems, Tampere University of Technology, Finland (December 2002)
[24] Hoare, C.A.R.: Communicating Sequential Processes. C.A.R. Hoare Series in Computer Science. Prentice-Hall International, Englewood Cliffs (2004); Published electronically: http://www.usingcsp.com/cspbook.pdf (2004)
[25] Pohl, K., Bockle, G., van der Linden, F.: Software Product Line Engineering. Springer, Heidelberg (2005)

A   An Example Domain Description

A domain description is a specification of the domain **as it is**, without any reference to requirements, let alone required software.

A.1   Nets

We first describe abstraction of nets, hubs (street intersections, train stations, airports, harbours) and links (street segments, rail tracks, air lanes, sea lanes):

Hubs and Links

1. There are nets, hubs and links.
2. A net contains zero, one or more hubs.
3. A net contains zero, one or more links.

type
  1. N, H, L
value
  2. obs_Hs: N → H-set
  3. obs_Ls: N → L-set
axiom
  2. ∀ n:N • **card** obs_Hs(n) ≥ 0
  3. ∀ n:N • **card** obs_Ls(n) ≥ 0

Hub and Link Identifiers

To express the mereology (12): how parts compose into a whole, the connections of hubs and links, we introduce the abstract concepts of hub and link identifiers.

4. There are hub identifiers and there are link identifiers.
5. Hubs of a net have unique hub identifiers.
6. Links of a net have unique link identifiers.

type
  4. HI, LI
value
  5. obs_HI: H → HI
  6. obs_LI: H → LI
axiom
  5. ∀ n:N, h,h′:H • {h,h′}⊆obs_Hs(n) ∧ h≠h′ ⇒
          obs_HI(h)≠obs_HI(h′)
  6. ∀ n:N, l,l′:L • {l,l′}⊆obs_Ls(n) ∧ l≠l′ ⇒
          obs_LI(l)≠obs_LI(l′)

Observability of Hub and Link Identifiers

We postulate reasonable observer functions: such which a person with a reasonably good sight could "implement".

7. From every hub (of a net) we can observe the identifiers of the zero, one or more distinct links (of that net) that the hub is connected to.
8. From every link (of a net) we can observe the identifiers of the exactly two (distinct) hubs (of that net) that the link is connected to.

value
  7. obs_LIs: H → LI-set
axiom
  7. ∀ n:N,h:H•h ∈ obs_Hs(n) ⇒ ∀ li:LI•li ∈
          obs_HIs(l) ⇒ L_exists(li)(n)
value
  8. obs_HIs: L → HI-set
axiom
  8. ∀ n:N,l:L•l ∈ obs_Ls(n) ⇒
  8. **card** obs_HIs(l)=2 ∧ ∀ hi:HI•hi ∈
          obs_HIs(l) ⇒ H_exists(hi)(n)

value
  L_exists: LI → N → **Bool**
  L_exists(li)(n) ≡ ∃ l:L•l ∈ obs_Ls(n)∧obs_LI(l)=li
  H_exists: HI → N → **Bool**
  H_exists(hi)(n) ≡ ∃ h:H•h ∈ obs_Hs(n)∧obs_HI(h)=hi

If we had chosen an ability to observe from a hub its connected links and from a link it connected hubs, then it would follow that from any hub (or any link), without "moving" one could observe the entire net; we find that kind of "observability" to be problematic and to, potentially leading to inconsistencies.

Net Descriptors

9. A net descriptor, ND, associates to each hub identifier
10. a possibly empty link-to-hub identifier map, LHIM, from the identifier of a link emanating from a hub to the identifier of the connected hub.

type
  9. ND = HI ₘ LHIM
  10. LHIM = LI ₘ HI

The hub identifiers of the definition set of net descriptors are called the defining occurrences of hub identifiers. The hub identifiers of the range of link-to-hub identifier map are called the using occurrences of hub identifiers.

11. Wellformedness of a net descriptor is simple.
    a) The set of using occurrences of hub identifiers must be a subset of he set of defining occurrences of hub identifiers.
    b) If in nd:ND an hi maps into some li which in turn maps into hi′, then in nd:ND hi′, amongst other link identifiers maps into li which in turn maps into hi.

value
  11. wf_ND: ND > **Bool**
  11. wf_ND(nd) ≡
  11a. {(nd(hi))(li)|hi:HI,li:LI•hi ∈ **dom** nd∧li
              ∈ **dom** nd(hi)}⊆**dom** nd
  11b. ∧ ∀ hi,hi′:HI,li:LI • hi ∈ **dom** nd ∧ nd(hi)=li ⇒
  11b.   (nd(hi))(li)=hi′ ⇒ (nd(hi′))(li)=hi

12. From a net one can extract its net descriptor.

value
  12. xtr_ND: N → ND
  12. xtr_ND(n) ≡
  12. [hi↦[li↦hi′]|l:L,li,li′:LI,hi,hi′:HI•
  12.   l ∈ obs_Ls(n)∧li=obs_LI(l)∧{hi,hi′}
              =obs_HIs(l)]
  12. ∪ [hi↦[]|h:H•h ∈ obs_Hs(n)∧obs_LIs(h)={}]

Routes

We first define a concept of paths.

13. A path is a triple:
    a) a hub identifier, h_i, a link identifier, l_j, and another hub identifier, h_k, distinct from h_i,
    b) such that there is a link ℓ with identifier l_j in a net n such that {h_i, h_k} are the hub identifiers that can be observed from ℓ.

type
  13. Pth = HI × LI × HI
axiom
  13a. ∀ (hi,li,hi′):Pth • ∃ n:N,l:L • l ∈ obs_Ls(n) ⇒
  13b.   obs_LI(l)=li ∧ obs_HIs(l)={hi,hi′}

14. From a net one can extract all its paths:
    a) if l is a link of the net,
    b) l_j its identifier and
    c) $\{h_i, h_k\}$ the identifiers of its connected hubs,
    d) then (h_i, l_j, h_k) and (h_k, l_j, h_j) are paths of the net.

value
14. paths: N → Pth-**set**
14a. paths(n) ≡
14d.   {(hi,lj,hk),(hk,lj,hi)|l:L,lj:LI,hi,hk:HI•l ∈
14b.   obs_Ls(n) ∧ lj=obs_LI(l) ∧
14c.   {hi,hk}=obs_HIs(l)}

15. From a net descriptor one can (likewise) extract all its paths:
    a) Let h_i, h_k be any two distinct hub identifiers of the net descriptor (definition set),
    b) such that they both map into a link identifier l_j,
    c) then (h_i, l_j, h_k) and (h_k, l_j, h_j) are paths of the net.

value
14. paths: ND → Pth-**set**
14. paths(nd) ≡
15a.   {(hi,lj,hk),(hk,lj,hi)|hi,hk:HI,lj:LI • hi≠hk ∧
15b.   {hi,hk}⊆**dom** nd ⇒ lj ∈ **dom** nd(hi)∩ **dom** nd(hk)}

Now we can define routes.

16. A route of a net is a sequence of zero, one or more paths such that
    a) all paths of a route are paths of the net and
    b) adjacent paths in the sequence "share" hub identifiers.

type
16. R = Pth*
axiom
16. ∀ r:R, ∃ n:N •
16a.   elems r ⊆ paths(n) ∧
16b.   ∀ i:**Nat** • {i,i+1}⊆**inds** r ⇒
16b.   **let** (_,_,hi)=r(i), (hi′,_,_)=r(i+1) **in** hi=hi′ **end**

17. From a net, n, we can generate the possibly infinite set of finite and possibly infinite routes:
    a) $<>$ is a route (*basis clause 1*);
    b) if p is a path of n then $< p >$ is a route of n (*basis clause 2*);
    c) if r and r' are non-empty routes of n
    d) and the last h_i of r is the same as the first h_j of r' then the concatenation of r and r' is a route (*induction clause*).
    e) Only such routes which can be formed by a (finite, respectively infinite) application of basis clauses Items 17a and 17b and induction clause Items 17c–17d are routes (*extremal clause*).

value
17. routes: N|ND → R-**infset**
17. routes(nond) ≡
17a. **let** rs = {⟨⟩} ∪
17b.   {⟨p⟩|p:Pth•p ∈ paths(nond)} ∪
17c.   {r⌢r′|r,r′:R•{r,r′}⊆rs ∧
17d.   ∃ hi,hi′,hi″,hi‴:H,li:LI,r″,r‴:R •
17d.   {r″,r‴}⊆rs ∧
17d.   r=r″⌢⟨(hi,li,hi′)⟩∧r′=⟨(hi″,li′,hi‴)⟩⌢r‴
                      ∧ hi′=hi″} **in**
17e. rs **end**

A.2 Buses, Bus Stops and Bus Schedules

Buses
We now consider buses and routes and schedules related to buses.

18. Buses have unique identifiers and are further undefined.
19. Bus identifiers can be observed from buses.

type
18. B, BI
value
19. obs_BI: B → BI

Bus Stops

20. A link bus stop indicates the link (by its identifier), the from and to hub identifiers of the link,
21. and the fraction "down the link" (from the hub of the from to the hub of the to hub identifiers) of the bus stop position.

type
20. BS = mkL_BS(sel_fhi:HI,sel_li:LI,sel_f:F,sel_thi:HI)
20. F = {|f:**Real**•0<f<1|}

Bus Stop Lists and Routes

22. A bus stop list is a sequence of two or more bus stops, bsl.
23. A bus route, br, is a pair of a net route, r, and a bus stop list, bsl, such that route r is a route of n and such that bsl is embedded in r.
24. bsl is embedded in r if
    a) there exists an index list, il, of ascending indices of the route r and of the length of bsl
    b) such that the ith path of r
    c) share from and to hub identifiers and link identifier with the $il(i)$th bus stop of bsl.
25. We must allow for two or more stops along a bus route to be adjacent on the same link — in which case the corresponding fractions must likewise be ascending.

value
  n:N
type
22. BSL = {|bsl:BS*•**len** bsl≥2|}
23. BR = {|(r,bsl):(R×BSL)•r ∈
      routes(n)∧is_embedded_in(r,bsl)|}
value
24. is_embedded_in: BR → **Bool**
24. is_embedded_in(r,bsl)(n) ≡
24a.   ∃ il:**Nat*** • **len** il=**len** bsl ∧
24a.   **inds** il⊆**inds** r ∧ ascending(il) ⇒
24b.   ∀ i:**Nat** • i ∈ **inds** il ⇒
24b.   **let** (hi,lj,hk) = r(il(i)),
24c.   (hi′,lj′,f,hk′) = bsl(i) **in**
24c.   hi=hi′ ∧ lj=lj′ ∧ hk=hk′ **end** ∧
25.   ∀ i:**Nat** • {i,i+1}⊆**inds** il ⇒
25.   **let** (hi,lj,f,hk)=bsl(i), (hi′,lj′,f′,hk′)
25.   =bsl(i+1) **in**
25.   hi=hi′ ∧ lj=lj′ ∧ hk=hk′ ⇒ f<f′ **end**

24a. ascending: **Nat*** → **Bool**
24a. ascending(il) ≡ ∀ i:**Nat***{i,i+1}⊆**inds** il ⇒
                il(i)<il(i+1)

Bus Schedules

26. Let us introduce a net. It is referred to in some subsequent wellformedness predicates.
27. A timed bus stop is a pair of a time and a bus stop.
28. A timed bus stop list is a sequence of timed bus stops.
29. A bus schedule is a pair of a route and an embedded timed bus stop list where
30. position-wise "earlier" bus stops occur at earlier times that Position-wise "later" bus stops.

value
26.   n:N
type
27.   TBS :: sel_T:T sel_bs:BS
28.   TBSL = TBS*
29.   BusSched = {|(r,tbsl):(R×TBSL)•r ∈
          routes(n)∧wf_BusSched(r,tbsl)|}
30.   SimBusSched = {|tbsl:TBSL•wf_TBSL(tbsl)|}
value
29.   wf_BusSched: BusSched → **Bool**
29.   wf_BusSched(r,tbsl) ≡
29.   is_embedded_in(r,(sel_BS(tbsl(i))|i:[1..**len** tbsl])) ∧
30.   wf_SimpleBusSched(tbsl)

30.   wf_SimpleBusSched: TBSL → **Bool**
30.   wf_SimpleBusSched(tbsl) ≡
30.   ∀ i:**Nat**•{i,i+1}⊆**inds** tbsl ⇒
            sel_T(tbsl(i))<sel_T(tbsl(i+1))

A.3   Timetables

31.   A bus b that plies a bus schedule starting at time t
      has a unique bus number, b_t; colloquially it is bus b
      at departure time t, or, even more colloquially: the t
      o'clock bus b — but henceforth we do not "encode"
      such bus "numbers".
32.   A [time]table maps bus numbers to bus schedules.
33.   A bus timetable is a pair of a net descriptor and a
      table.

type
31.   BNo
32.   TBL = BNo $\overrightarrow{m}$ BusSched
33.   BTT = ND × TBL

Denotations

What are routes and bus timetables scripting (i.e., prescribing) ? Routes (lists of connected link traversal desig-
nations) script that one may transport people or freight
along the sequence of designated links. Bus timetable
scripts denote (at least) two things: the set of bus traffics
on the net which satisfy the bus timetable, and information that potential and actual bus passengers may, within
some measure of statistics (and probability), rely upon for
their bus transport. Here, we shall now develop the idea
of bus timetables denoting certain traffics.

A.4   Bus Traffic

34.   Bus traffic is here considered a discrete function
      from time into bus positions on the net.
35.   From (such) a bus we can observe its bus number.
36.   A bus is at any time positioned either at a hub or
      a fraction of a distance along a link.
37.   Fractions are reals in the open interval between 0
      and 1.
38.   We shall not define necessary bus traffic wellformed-
      ness conditions.

type
34.   BTF = T $\overrightarrow{m}$ (B $\overrightarrow{m}$ BP)
35.   BP == atH(hi:HI) | onL(li:LI,f:F,li':LI)
37.   F = {|f:**Real**•0<f<1|}
value
36.   obs_BNo: B → BNo
38.   wf_BTF: BTF → **Bool**

Bus Traffic versus Bus Timetable

In expressing generation of bus traffics and whether a bus
traffic satisfies a bus timetable, we shall make the following assumptions: buses must not depart from a bus stop
earlier than its scheduled time; and buses, when "late"
must not be "too late", that is, must not be further away
than the nearest previous hub or approaching the bus
stop along its link. These assumptions are encoded by the
"multiplier" and "fraction increment" constants m and δ
introduced now.

39.   Let m be a positive natural number (a time interval
      multiplier, say, of value 2,3,4).
40.   Let δ be a "tiny" (position) fraction increment.
41.   Satisfaction of a bus traffic with respect to a bus
      timetable is expressed in terms of
a)   a predicate over buses, represented by their bus
     numbers bn;
b)   we consider only the timed bus schedule;
c)   for all bus stops we express a predicate over
     bus traffic positions;
d)   namely that there exists a time, t', of the traf-
     fic which is equal to or some small time interval
     before the time of the scheduled stop,
e)   at which time (t') some buses have traffic po-
     sitions bp such that
f)   the bus being considered, namely bn, is
     recorded in the traffic;
g)   among those bus positions as having
h)   being either at the appropriate hub or
i)   on the appropriate link, either at the bus stop
     ($f' = f$) or shortly before that bus stop ($f'-δ$).

value
39.   m:**Nat, axiom** 0<m≤5
40.   δ:**Real, axiom** 0<δ≪1
41.   satisfy: BTF × BTT → **Bool**
41.   satisfy(btf,btt:(nd,tbl)) ≡
41a.   ∀ bn:BNo•bn ∈ **dom** tbl ⇒
41b.   **let** (_,tbsl) = tbl(bn) **in**
41c.   ∀ (t,bs:mkL_BS(hi',li',f',hi'')):TBS•(t,bs)∈
>   **elems** tbsl ⇒
41d.   ∃ t':T•t' ∈ **dom** btf∧t−m∗ti<t'≤t∧
41e.   **let** bp = btf(t') **in**
41f.   bn ∈ **dom** bp ∧
41g.   **case** bp(bn) **of**
41h.   atH(hi) → hi=hi',
41i.   onL(hi,li,f,li') → li=li'∧hi=hi'∧f'−δ≤f≤f'
41.   **end end end**

In the above satisfaction relation we do not consider
where the buses are at times properly "between" bus
stop times (other than when very "close" – as expressed
by the proposition t−m∗ti<t'≤t).

Roots and Stimuli to a New Perception of Informatics

Jozef Gruska*

Faculty of Informatics, Masaryk University,
Botanická 68a, 602 00 Brno, Czech Republic
gruska@fi.muni.cz

When you reach for the stars you may not get one, but you won't come up with a handful of mud either.
Leo Burnett

If men cease to believe that they will one day become gods then they will surely become worms.
Henry Miller

Abstract. In the recent paper, "A perception of Informatics" [9],a new view of Informatics, visionary and philosophical in the essence, has been presented in quite general terms and ways[1]. This new perception of Informatics has been then illustrated and put more "down to earth" in [9] through the presentation of some of the grand challenges of "new Informatics".

In the present paper some of the main impulses/needs or drives for and roads towards such a new perception of Informatics are summarized and discussed in more details. To see them well is also of large importance for a full understanding and acceptance of such a new view of Informatics. All of them are also closely related to some of the major problems of current science and technology.

---

* Support of the grant MSM0021622419 is to be acknowledged.

[1] One should note that the new perception of Informatics, as presented and discussed in [9], could have been emerged already quite a few years ago because it is, in some sense, a natural deduction from and generalisation of various views already cautiously, more or less, indicated some years ago, here and there, by several visionaries. However, until quite recently, there have not been really sufficiently strong reasons explicitly visible to see well that such a maximal (total) upper bound on the perception of Informatics could be not only proper, but also much needed and prosperous, for both the discipline and society.

Three events had started to change much the situation. The first one was the development of an understanding that (quantum) information processing processes are, and have always been, the driving forces in our physical, biological and social worlds. The second one, due to the existence of so powerful internet and web, was an understanding that the field drives from a concentration on information processing (computation) through a concentration on information transmission to a concentration on information management. The third one was an understanding that the Informatics based methodology extends much, in depth and scope, the Mathematics based methodology. To perceive the scope and aims of Informatics in much deeper and broader sense started to be therefore inevitable.

C.S. Calude, G. Rozenberg, A. Salomaa (Eds.): Maurer Festschrift, LNCS 6570, pp. 184–199, 2011.
© Springer-Verlag Berlin Heidelberg 2011

1   A New Perception of Informatics

> Imagination is more important than knowledge.
>
> *Albert Einstein*

One of the basic standpoints leading to a new perception of Informatics, in [9], has been that the overall development of science, technology, medicine, economy and practically of all major areas of the activities of mankind, much depends on the progress in Informatics, provided this field is sufficiently deeply and broadly understood and developed. Therefore, it has to be much in the interest not only of Informatics itself, but actually of the whole society, that this discipline is perceived, supported, developed, and also projected into all levels and forms of education, in a way that leads to its proper development, largest outcomes and broadest impacts.

This new perception of Informatics sees Informatics as the oldest technology and science discipline consisting of four very closely interrelated components: scientific, engineering, methodological and application.

As a scientific discipline, Informatics is seen as being both a deeply fundamental and a broadly applied science. The most fundamental goals of the scientific Informatics are to discover and explore the principles, laws, limitations, phenomena and processes of information processing worlds and, in particular, to develop an information processing understanding of the universe, evolution, life, brain, mind, intelligence, complexity and security, as well as to develop a deep scientific understanding of the problems related to the specification, design, validation, reliability, security, structure, analysis and efficiency of huge and complex information managing, processing, communication and imaging tools and systems[2].

Current computation, communication and imaging revolution is seen, at this perception, only as one of the very important milestones in the development of both scientific and engineering Informatics, as well as of the Informatics-driven methodology. However, the scientific goals of Informatics go far beyond what this technology developments and its applications do and are expected to motivate, imply and require.

As a scientific discipline, Informatics is seen as being, in some sense, currently the leading scientific discipline - due to its enormous impacts on all other academic disciplines, as discussed below, and far beyond that[3].

---

[2] Systems that are of crucial importance for functioning of society and may be even global from one point of view and up to the exascale from another point of view.

[3] Sciences used to have a "Queen of science", guiding and serving other sciences, with very broad impacts on the overall development of sciences and also on education at all levels. This role was played, for example, see [5] by Medicine in Padua and at the same time Theology in Paris in 17th century; by Philology during the Renaissance; by Mathematics after Galileo's time due to its methodological impacts and partly also by Physics in the 20th century, mainly due its involvements with very basic elements of the nature as well as its impacts on the industrial revolution. Informatics is quite fast replacing (expanding/extending) Mathematics (that is seen here as being one of the grounding stones of scientific Informatics, and the same holds for Logic) in its Queen/servant or servant/Queen role with respect to other scientific and technological disciplines.

To achieve its scientific goals, Informatics has to develop a huge variety of paradigms, principles, concepts, models, theories, methods and tools. Some of them are very abstract and may seem to be far from the needs of the narrowly seen computer science. However, most of them have very deep goals, though curiosity may be sometimes seen as the main or the only driving force of them. They are, however, in most of the cases actually much needed in order to develop powerful concepts, paradigms, theories and tools to deal with basic problems of the understanding of principles, laws, limitations, phenomena and processes of information processing worlds, as well as for the development of powerful information processing and transmitting systems designing and processing methods and tools.

As an engineering discipline, Informatics concentrates on the development of paradigms, principles, concepts, models, methods and tools for specification, design, validation, analysis and maintenance of natural and especially human-made (hardware) devices and (software) systems used for acquiring, mining, structuring, storing, processing, imaging and transmitting data, information and knowledge, as well as for the development of tools and methods (for example, operating systems, data bases, specification and programming languages and corresponding methodologies and so on) to make efficient use of such devices and systems. To increase much power, intelligence, reliability, robustness and security of information processing, communication and imaging tools are some of the big tasks of engineering informatics. Low-energy systems and miniaturization - to move to nano- atto- and quantum-levels - is one way to go to enable long life for the Moore law and to have systems with more than petaflops performance and exabytes data stores.

Engineering Informatics concentrates also much on the design of intelligent information processing systems and robots that could either simulate or even outperform those of living beings and especially of humans in various (especially brain and behavioural) activities. The goal is not only to have powerful and intelligent collaborators, but also to use designs and performance of such artifacts to get a deeper understanding of the nature and human/brain/mind activities. Cell-, bio- and brain-inspired computing is one of its grand challenges with already amazing partial achievements.

As an engineering discipline, Informatics is seen as the leading engineering discipline with enormous impacts on all other engineering disciplines, as well as on humanities and liberal art, especially on their methodologies and tools, as the very powerful servant of all of them.

Scientific and engineering Informatics create and develop also the basis for a new and very powerful, Informatics-driven, methodology for science, engineering and mankind in general. The methodology that puts also two basic old methodologies, experimental and theoretical, to new heights. The Informatics-driven methodology can also be seen as extending much mathematics-driven methodology and creating platforms for a successful application of the holistic approach to science as an alternative to the reductionism dominating so far. The new methodology is based on, and leads to, a vision of the nature, society and virtual worlds as being written in the information processing terms, extending by that Galileo's view that nature is written in the mathematical language[4].

The main components of this new methodology are: ("digital") modelling and simulation (both being of another dimension than before), visualisation, virtualization, abstraction, algoritmization, complexity considerations, tools to apply holistic approach to complex problems, mechanisation of reasoning and deduction, design of systems beating intellectual performance of humans and so on. For details and illustrations see [9].

Informatics is also quite specific in taking a very special care to facilitate its applications by developing a variety of methods, tools and systems that allow to use easily its application potential in a variety of ways and to use information processing resources and tools by everyone, from everywhere and anytime, and often in almost no-time. The design of a global Internet, Web and computer (network) and of the "intelligent dust" are some of the extreme highlights in this direction.

For a more detailed description and analysis of the four main components of "new Informatics" see [Gruska 2010], where also several grand challenges of scientific and engineering Informatics have been listed and discussed.

2   Roots of a New Perception

> At the heart of everything is the question,
> not the answer.
>
> *John Archibald Wheeler*

There are several main reasons why a new perception of Informatics, as presented in [9], is badly needed. A perception that is much broader and deeper than the current view of computer science - as of the science dealing with *a broad range of phenomena related to computers and their use*. These reasons are actually closely related to some of the most basic global problems of the current academic disciplines and society.

1. It starts to be understood that in the foreseeable future, in the 21st century, most, if not almost all, of the major technological innovations and big innovative projects in science, economy, finances, health and environmental care and in almost all other areas of societal activities will require to use, and in an essential way, more or less sophisticated Informatics paradigms, principles, methodologies or/and information storing, structuring, processing, communication and presentation tools[5]. The overall development of society, science, technology, health and

---

[4] Observe that the use of Mathematics and deduction can be seen as a very old methodology for science. However, it has actually been only after the scientific revolution in the 17th century, after a new and very powerful Mathematics has been developed, especially through mathematical analysis, that Mathematics has indeed started to play, as methodology, a really very important role.

[5] By Bill Gates, see also [16], *The percentage of college freshmen planning to major in computer science dropped by 70% between 2000 and 2005. In an economy in which computing has become central to innovation in nearly every sector, this decline poses a serious threat to American competitiveness. Indeed, it would not be an exaggeration to say that every significant technological innovation of the 21st century will require new software to make it happen.*

environmental care, economy, finances, but also of politics, care for our cultural heritage and art will therefore much depend on the character and pace of the progress in Informatics, in all of its four components. This can hardly be achieved unless Informatics develops with a very broad and deep view of the discipline, and of its grand challenges, and to all this the research agendas, creation of the institutional settings for research, as well as channeling of the research support are fully adjusted.

2. Society starts to understand, or at least to believe, that one, perhaps the main, of the ways to go in the coming future is to drive, and fast, toward so-called *knowledge society* at which knowledge, its production, dissemination, and utilisation are peacemakers and remote dynamos of the progress. Informatics-based tools and the Informatics-driven methodology clearly play at these knowledge production, dissemination and application a very important and many sided role and all that requires again a very broad and deep development of Informatics.

3. Informatics, its concepts, paradigms, methods and tools, are helping, more and more, to bridge various areas of science and technology, as well as to cross-fertilize them. It is therefore of large importance for society that Informatics develops as broadly and deeply as possible.

Indeed, it starts to be understood that science and technology, as the main producers and consumers of knowledge, are to play the key role in the transformation of our society to a knowledge society. However, it starts to be also understood that to achieve all that is far from trivial and a simple idea of putting more money into science in order to get proportionally more practical dividends out of it does not work well, see [6]. In order to achieve the above goals, a deeper understanding and a better view of the relation between the fundamental (basic or pure) or knowledge oriented science on one side, and the use or application (national goals or grand-challenges) oriented science on the other side, is much needed. A new understanding is also needed of the relation between the potential of science and technology to produce new knowledge and to put this knowledge to use. In addition, it starts to be also understood, and much emphasised, that the goal of the basic research is not only (a) *to produce knowledge*, but also (b) *to disseminate knowledge* and, what is quite a recent wisdom, (3) *to put knowledge into use*. It also starts to be understood that the relations between the pure- or basic- or fundamental-research on one side and the applied- or engineering- or technology-oriented research on the other side, are very complex and strong influences go in all directions, see also [15].

A closer look to the features of the Informatics-driven methodology reveals that this methodology contains a variety of very important features to bridge, in both directions, and very significantly, these two areas of research. The areas that used to be seen, for good reasons, in the pre-modern-Informatics era, as being far from each other and actually so far, and as so antagonistic, that one of the most basic position of Vanevar Bush in his so immensely influential report "Science, the endless frontiers", from 1945, was that "applied research invariably drives out pure" [4].

The old view of the relation between knowledge oriented pure and use oriented applied science was much related to the well observed understanding,

corresponding to the goals, methods and tools these two areas of science used, that
not only the goals of the pure and applied research, but also of science and engineering, are so different, but that to work in these different areas requires actually
very different type of skills and therefore also of people. However, nowadays when
all these areas of science and technology are done by researchers who starts to master main features of the Informatics-driven methodology and the outcomes of science and technology are to a significant degree and in the limit manifested through
various Informatics-oriented products,[6] differences between these, seen as so different, or even antagonistic before, disciplines slowly start to blur out. That is a
phenomenon society has to be very pleased with. There are therefore nowadays
again, as many times in the history, good reasons to assume that there is only one
science, very closely related to technology, and that science should be divided only
to a good and a bad one. In order to support even much more this new phenomenon
in the development of science and technology - that makes also science to be engineering driven, to a certain degree, and engineering to be science driven, again to
a certain scale - it is much needed that Informatics, as the basis of the Informatics-
driven methodology, develops really in full broadness and sufficient depth.

Moreover, the fundamental science, equipped, supported and guided by the
paradigms, concepts, systems and methodology of Informatics, has now many
new tools and know-how to put knowledge in use in the way that makes also the
fundamental science richer and can much profit out of it. For example, through
the design, analysis and optimization of algorithms and protocols, through the
design of models and their exploitation through the analysis, simulations, visualisation, through an adoption of holistic approach and so on. On the other side,
the use-oriented and technology research can nowadays much faster and better
make use of the basic-research outcomes because they come in a more ready to
use form. Bridges, to a large extent due to the powerful Informatics concepts,
models and tools, play by that again the key role. All that implies that the
progress in the development of all basic branches of science and technology and
their mutual fertilisation and impacts, what seems to be of so large importance
for society, much depends on the overall progress in Informatics and on the depth
and broadness of its scope and aims.[7]

---

[6] For example, results of science and technology are often presented through methods
transferred to algorithms that are implemented through software products. Moreover,
it is getting understood that the attempts to come with the best, for example the most
efficient, algorithms and software can bring a deeper understanding of the underlying
problems and therefore to have an important discovery value. In a similar way one can
illustrate the bridging role of other features of the Informatics-driven methodology.

[7] At this point it is perhaps good to note that two big failures, in practically all major
documents of IT, are continuously made. (1) Too narrow views of the field, that is
seen as being driven mainly by the progress in technology, and that need later to be
replaced by new ones due to new developments that extend the scope and deepen
fundamentals of the discipline; (2) Underestimation of the problems related to the
efficient design of correct and efficient software - due to the old technology view of
new software "technology".

4. For an overall proper development of both individuals and the whole society, it is much needed that education concerning Informatics thinking[8] and a permanent capability to master ever more sophisticated information processing, communication and imaging technology and methodology, penetrates and is embedded, in an adequate way, into all stages and orientations of the main (life long) education processes. In order to introduce and to develop such a new paradigm deeply and broadly into the education processes, requires that the whole society sees convincingly the depth, scope, challenges, goals and tools of Informatics in such an appropriate and challenging way that it will be broadly believed that an introduction of such a new and fundamental features into the education processes will stand the scrutiny of time. All that is hardly possible unless Informatics is perceived as a discipline with highly comparable depth and broadness.[9]

5. Two of the recent and closely related paradigms of the current science and technology, which are believed/hoped to have magic impacts, are *multidisciplinarity* and *collaboration*. It is getting strongly believed, and there are good reasons for that, that one of the ways to increase the progress in science and technology is through a better and faster transfer of concepts, models, ideas, methods and tools from one academic discipline to another and to deal with problems that require multidisciplinary expertise. These ideas are in some way not really new, but only nowadays there are good ways and very powerful tools to make these two paradigms to be the ones really to focus on. The main reason behind is the fact that Informatics, as the area of science, technology and the basis of the Informatics driven methodology, offers a variety of concepts, models, theories, methods and especially powerful tools to facilitate much interdisciplinarity and collaboration.

There are many reasons and ways modern Informatics should be seen as facilitating multidisciplinarity and collaboration in science and technology. These reasons are as a whole such that much deeper and broader development of Informatics is much desirable to support Informatics contributions to multidisciplinarity and collaboration: (a) Information gathering, storing and processing processes are in the heart of many important phenomena and problems of a variety of academic disciplines and therefore similar, Informatics thinking motivated, approaches can be a basis of their solutions; (b) Informatics thinking leads to asking a new type of fundamental questions concerning fundamental phenomena of a variety of academic disciplines - questions that motivate approaches that lead to new and deeper

---

[8] This is seen here and in [9] as a more proper platform for so-called *Computational thinking*, [10].

[9] A significant change in the whole educational process, that is conservative in principle and have always been - for good reasons - can hardly get really through unless it is fully understood by society that such a change will well meet societal needs and that what is behind is of really lasting, broad and deep importance. This can hardly be achieved with the computer-centered view of the field, but more likely in case Informatics is seen as the leading discipline of sciences and technologies and even as the discipline of broader and deeper importance.

insights into the problems, or nontrivial, but answerable questions, which put old puzzles in a new light even if they fall short of answering them. (c) Informatics concepts, languages and reasoning create a common framework to express problems and their (algorithmic) solutions from a variety disciplines in a way that allows to see similarities between them and makes transfer of tools and outcomes from one discipline to another much easier.

Concerning collaboration, an important additional fact is the existence of powerful and global communication networks that allow to share and make use of geographically distributed devices and to transfer almost in no time not only information and knowledge, but also powerful information processing devices. This makes feasible the task to create efficiently working and geographically much distributed virtual collaboratories.

Let us observe, in this connection, that the founders of the modern science, in the 17th century, used to be mostly multidisciplinary scientists par excellence. One reason for that was their strong background in Mathematics and a belief that the laws of nature are written in the language of Mathematics. Their important methodology was to transfer problems from different sciences into a common mathematical language and then to use a common pool of knowledge in mathematics to solve them. That allowed them to work successfully in several areas of science. Such a situation was actually almost to the Second World War.[10] Afterwards, the situation has started to change and specialisation has started to dominate. Knowledge has started to accumulate and methodologies have started to develop so fast and so far and their applications required so much of the key resources, and not only of intellectual resources, but also computational, that it was no longer in the competence even of the brightest minds to embrace several areas of science. The existence of the Informatics-driven methodology and mechanisation of various intellectual, creative and computational processes and science making activities in general, have started again to change the situation. To bring this development to additional heights, with big impacts, requires much progress in the overall understanding of the Informatics developments and challenges in all their depth and breadth as well as of the Informatics-driven methodology. At the same time, the progress in the development of the Informatics-driven methodology requires progress in scientific and engineering Informatics and in the development of tools to facilitate application of this methodology.

6. It starts to be understood that information processing plays so important role in nature, and especially in living beings, that we can say that one of the ways to understand universe, evolution, life, brain, mind, intelligence, complexity and so on is through the study of the underlying information processes, their principles, laws and limitations, see also [8]. In short, one can say that natural, earth, behavioral and social sciences are, in their fundamentals, information

---

[10] At that period it was sufficient for a small group of the very top scientists to keep close contacts in order to be almost fully informed about the key developments in science and technology in general.

processing driven.[11] It starts to be also understood that information processing is for living beings of such importance as eating and breathing.

For example, there are good reasons to consider Informatics and Physics as two windows to see, explore and understand the world(s). Physics can be seen as dealing with the laws, limitations, phenomena and processes of the physical worlds - Informatics, in turn, as dealing with the laws, limitations, phenomena and processes of the information processing worlds. To explore the relation between the physical worlds and the information processing worlds is one of the grand challenges of science in general. The question which of these two types of worlds is more basic may be one of those eternal questions that can give long life to Philosophy as it is the *mind versus matter puzzle*.[12]

The existence of powerful information processing in nature, and also a natural idea to explore its primitives and fundamentals in order to develop new information storing and processing technologies that could far overcome current technologies, requires that Informatics takes a much broader view of the field and see it also as the one that is very deep and fundamental.

7. History of science and technology teaches us that it is very important to search for a proper perception and fundamentals of a scientific discipline and that the outcomes of such a search lead often to a much broader view of the discipline with far reaching consequences. History also teaches us that a discovery/development of a new perception of a discipline, if correct, can change almost everything in the discipline. History of Physics is an excellent example how

---

[11] This, of course, does not mean that by studying information driven processes one can get the whole scientific truth. For example, in spite of the fact that on the most basic level molecular Biology can be seen as the most fundamental one with the largest potential for far reaching discoveries for life sciences, this does not mean that it is not of importance, from a very different point of view, to explore other problems of life sciences. As one of many examples, let us mention the study of the behaviour of various species such as ants and whales, or species that are in the danger of extinction. Moreover, incredibly intelligent behaviour and surprising cooperation of some species can be much inspiring for both scientific and engineering Informatics.

[12] In this context of interest are the following two quotations of famous physicists. The first one is from W. Heisenberg, one of the founders of quantum mechanics:

- I think that modern Physics has definitely decided in favour of Plato. In fact the smallest units of matter are not physical objects in the ordinary sense: they are forms, ideas which can be expressed unambiguously only in mathematical language.

and second one from John Archibald Wheeler, one of the founders of modern cosmology:

- I think of my lifetime in physics as divided into three periods. In the first period I was in the grip of the idea that *everything is particle*. I call my second period *everything is field*. Now I am in the grip of a new vision, that *everything is information*.

who named black holes and created slogan *It from bit* summarizing his previous thoughts, which has been later updated by David Deutsch as *It from qubit*.

important it is to challenge the "obvious, or common sense, views of the field". Around the 17th century Physics was seen as a discipline that deals "with the stuff one can put between fingers". Quantum physics and the relativity theory are some of the main examples of the developments that have changed Physics for ever concerning its depth and scope, all with very important practical implications.

8. The possibility to formulate and try to deal with so grand challenges that even a partial successes in dealing with them may be very important for the development of a discipline and for its recognition by other academic disciplines and society. If an area of science and technology does not have such indeed grand challenges that need huge research force to deal with, then it can lose a momentum and an interest of the brightest minds in science and technology as well as potential students, as well as of society and research money providing agencies[13] Really grand challenges can hardly exist in a discipline that is not very deep and has not very broad scope. Physics could hardly develop really grand challenges when seeing its goal as to deal with *things one can handle between fingers*. To understand the essence of time and space is really a grand challenge for physics, as well as to develop a *theory of everything*.

9. Development of (meta)science and engineering of science making activities can be seen as one of the grand challenges of Informatics. To meet this challenge requires naturally to perceive and develop Informatics very broadly and deeply.

There have already been developments that justify consideration and formulation of such a grand challenge. For example, results in artificial intelligence have already indicated that the border line between creativity and mechanized reasoning is much thinner that we have thought not very long time ago.

For example, theorem proving used to be seen as one of the highlights of creative thinking and as a technical basis of the theoretical methodology. There are already results in theorem proving that overcome human mind, and all that with theorem provers that work in a very simple and general way. Once million times faster computers are available, theorem proving could be, to a large extent mechanized. At least to such an extent that it would reduce, to a significant extent, the task of mathematicians to make hypothesis.

Also in the area of engineering numerous highly intellectual activities, at least as we could see them not so many years ago, have been mechanized to a remarkable degree and often the level was obtained that is hardly achievable by humans in a reasonable time. Developing engineering of the science making activities, at least to a remarkable degree, and, of the corresponding meta-science and engineering is therefore a reasonable and really grand challenge that will sooner or later be met by one or another way.

---

[13] Mathematics seems to be currently in such a stage. One can see it from its grand challenges, or big problems/challenges, as formulated by the Clay institute. This is a list of very interesting and old problems that for years resisted all efforts to solve them. However, at least some of them can be, potentially, solved in such a way that this may not have actually too much impact on Mathematics and its potential to come with grand discoveries. Moreover, some of them can hardly be even easily explained to non-specialists.

10. One can observe an increasing convergence of many academic disciplines to Informatics and their mutual fertilization, for benefit of all sides. For this process to be fully successful, it is desirable to have very broadly and deeply developed Informatics to meet all needs and potentials.

The fact that natural, behavioural and social sciences are, in their fundamentals, much information processing driven is far from the main reason why these areas of science, and not only they, start to be more and more (inter)connected with Informatics. Another important facts are that Informatics concepts, paradigms, methods, results and tools provide a new quality microscopes and also telescopes for mind and lead to new deep questions and new ways of approaching deep old questions, as well as to new ways of understanding of deep problems of these sciences. Moreover, Informatics concepts, models and tools allow also to bring into new heights the holistic approach for these sciences and in this new way to get deep insights into their complex phenomena and to complement in this way the reductionist approach to them as well as to overcome its limitations.

Because of strong impacts of Informatics, especially of its methodology, on all academic disciplines, one can indeed talk about their convergence to and increasingly strong relation with Informatics. As a consequence, a significantly new perception of Informatics, of its wideness and depth, would likely have a strong general impact on all academic disciplines, scholarship, art, technologies concerning also their research agenda, on the creation of the institutional settings for research and also for channeling of the research support, as well as on the education at all its levels and targets. All that may lead to a new framing of the science, technology and education policies.

3   Impulses of a New Perception

> The only limits to our realization of tomorrow will be our doubts of today. Let us move forward with strong and active faith.
>
> *Franklin D. Roosevelt*

The first important impulse came from the observations that several areas of (computer) science, which were to a large extent originally motivated by computer technology or computing methodology, started to liberate themselves from the role of serving mainly computer and computing technologies, and that they actually needed that liberalisation for their healthy and vigorous development and outcomes of new quality and generality. For example, combinatorics on words; formal languages, automata, computational, communication and descriptional complexity theories, semantics, concurrency, various logical systems and so on. It started also to be clear that the more powerful computing systems we have and the more complex problems can be solved with them, the more general, deep and broad theories are needed to help to develop useful concepts, insights and tools to deal with the underlying problems of these systems and their applications.[14]

---

[14] For example, the larger and more important software systems are being designed, the much better, deeper and broader science of designing correct software and verifying its correctness, as well as for analysing it deeply is needed.

Moreover, rapid increase of the performance and decrease of the cost and size of computing systems, as well as their increasing reliability and enormous consequences of all that, are fully in accord with the old wisdom that a new technology can develop rapidly only in the case an intellectual framework has been already available for its development and that one of the major impacts of the new technology is to bring the original intellectual framework to new heights. This applies in this case especially to the development of formal and logical systems, but actually to all other areas the origin of which can be traced to the pre-computer era.

The second main impulse came from the three basic discoveries in natural sciences.

The first one was the discovery, by Francis Crick and James Watson, in 1953, of the twin-corkscrew structure of DNA and how genetic information is encoded into DNA - followed by the demonstration, due to [1] at first, how DNA can be used as a form of computation and that such DNA-computing has a potential for a remarkable efficiency. All that created huge and important areas of research.

The second one was the discovery of quantum teleportation and of unconditionally secure quantum generation of shared random classical key, [2,3], followed by the demonstration, by [11,12,13], that quantum computing could be performed and has a potential for remarkable efficiency. That led also to a huge increase of the research in quantum information processing and communication.

Both of these basic discoveries changed the views on physics and biology that started to be seen and explored as being, to a significant extent at least, in their fundamentals, information processing driven sciences. From that it has been only a natural and logical step to see other natural sciences, especially chemistry, in this way, as being, to an important degree again, information processing driven - and a new revolution in the study of natural and also other, especially behavioural and social sciences, has emerged. All that, supported by an immense development of the power and miniaturization of information processing technology, has initiated various new attempts to deal with perhaps the main frontier of science - mind - and the attempts to understand it through a "reverse engineering of the brain" - what could, perhaps, lead also to dealing with such phenomena as consciousness that have been so far considered as being out of the reach of (current) science.

The third major discovery was that there are one or very few cells organisms, as paramecium (from 50 to 350 μm in length), that do information processing par excellence in order to find foods, to avoid predators, to learn to find a mate and to have sex - and also without having any synapses. Cells are therefore information processing devices par excellence. All that led to a deep observation that information processing is extremely important for life in general. In this way it got clear that in order to search for the beginning of the history of powerful information processing systems we need to go to the very beginning of the history of life.

The third main impulse came from the emerging observations that a new, very broadly applicable and successful methodology, based on the development of the discipline, had been emerging and its proper essence, foundation and potential developments and applications started to be explored. All that led to the need to back this new methodology by a proper development of the discipline.

Another impulse came from the observation that paradigms, theories and technologies behind the field have applications practically in all fields and areas of activities of the society and by that the need arose to find the "largest common denominator" of the field and to come with a perception of the field that would match perceptions of the fundamental sciences in its deepness, clarity and intellectual simplicity. A perception that would, likely, stand the scrutiny of time and new developments and discoveries would likely only enforce its validity.

In particular, one should realize that the emrging discipline actually brings a new dimension to the centuries old efforts to derive knowledge from information, to formalize knowledge and to formalize as well as to mechanize reasoning. It is also to bring a new dimension to the centuries old attempts to understand, match and beat performance of bodies and minds of living beings.

Also on a more philosophical level, it started to be realized that information processing superparadigm is the one that is to dominate in the current science and technology, replacing the machine/clock paradigm that used to dominate for a long time, since the 14th century. For such a new paradigm to be really a superparadigm with big impacts, it needs the support of a science that keeps being vigorously developed and is deeper and broader in scope than what has been offered with the computer-centric view of the field.

It started to be also realized that the old vision of the field makes it increasingly difficult to get proper financial support for the most of the attractive visionary challenges. Other areas of science and technology started to be more successful in "taking the cream" of the Informatics challenges, in spite of the fact that they lack sufficient expertise for dealing with such challenges.

Finally, decreasing enrollment of students in computer science in some countries, see [van Leeuwen and Tanca, 2007], and continuing problems to embed basics of the field in a proper form into the high school education, finally started to force the computer science community "to open the eyes" and to start to investigate why the field stopped to attract the best student minds and how to deal with this problem.

4   What Can Informatics Learn from the Development of Other Sciences?

Another way to justify such a new, deeper and broader in scope, perception of Informatics is to analyse the development of other sciences and technology disciplines and to show that new steps suggested to be taken by this new perception have already been taken in the past, very successfully and with big dividends, by some other, actually all, major academic disciplines.

In this paper we will only very briefly discuss what Informatics can learn from the development of the Physics. In more details such issues will be discussed in the full version of the paper to be presented on the author's site at the portal of the Academia Europaea, Informatics section [9].

4.1   What Can Informatics Learn from Physics?

Physics is a natural science par excellence. Deepness and broadness of its laws and limitations; understanding of the phenomena and processes and impacts of all that knowledge led a famous physicists, E. Rutherford, to say (in 1912) that *In Science there is only Physics: all the rest is stamps collecting.* a well known exaggeration having its deep point.

What is actually Physics about? Some say, Physics is about matter and energy; others that it is about space and time and the rest is stamps collecting. Exaggerations that have again their points.

There have been, of course, other views of Physics. Originally, Physics used to be developed within *Natural philosophy.* In the 17th century Physics was seen as "dealing with the stuff one can handle between fingers". At the end of the 19th century it was believed that the laws of Newton and Maxwell were correct and complete laws of physics. That led lord Kalvin to claim "There is nothing essentially new to be discovered in Physics".

However, the discovery of quantum Physics and the relativity theories have shown how deeply wrong previous views were and new discoveries changed the Physics radically. Moreover, they put it into another depth and broadness - all that with enormous impacts also on our understanding of the "stuff we can handle between fingers". For example, the quantum theory is nowadays needed for understanding properties of superfluids, functioning of laser, the substance of chemistry, the structure and function of DNA, the existence and behaviour of solid bodies, color of stars, ...

In addition, Physics, as the fundamental science, started to explore space, time, black holes, black matter and energy, and so on. It started to explore the universe from the Big Bang to the ever expanding horizons and to see galaxies that are more than 10 milliards of light years away. The Planck scale and superstrings are some of the hot problems on the agenda. Large Hadron Collider (LHC) is currently the main experimental tool to explore deep nature and related to that is the LCD grid network of more than 100 000 processors in 130 organizations across 34 countries.[15] The idea of the Internet was also born from the needs to improve communication in order to explore nature better in its deepness.

By [14], five main problems (grand challenges) of the current Physics are:

- (*Problem of the theory of everything.*) To unify the general relativity theory and the quantum theory into a single theory (that could be then seen as a complete theory of nature).
- (*Problem of the interpretation of quantum theory.*) To solve the problem of foundation of quantum theory either by finding a clear interpretation of the current theory or by finding a new theory without current inconsistencies.
- (*Problem of the unification of particles and forces.*) To find out whether all particles and forces could be described by a single theory that could explain all of them as following from a single fundamental entity.

---

[15] This network is now able to process 1.25GB of data produced by LHC detectors per second.

- (*Problem of the constants.*) To explain how nature chooses values of constants in the standard model of nature.
- (*Problem of the black matter and energy*) Explain the nature of black matter and black energy or, if they do not exist, explain how and why is gravitation modified for huge sizes.

It is also of interest to look into the methodologies Physics has been used to deal with its problems. In short, one can say that Physics has been using all available methodologies that could promise to produce interesting/important results. Let us mention two particular cases.

In the 17th century Physics solved the long standing and key problem of understanding of the direct motion by geometrizing the problem. That is by going into a (virtual) mathematical/geometrical friction-less space. In the process of doing this, Physics was able to replace the mysterious concept of *impetus*, that assumed to have some (mysterious) spirit behind each motion, by the modern concept of *inertia* and to come this way to the modern theory of motion. By achieving this Physics *drove spirits out from scientific thoughts* and opened the door to see the universe as running as a piece of clockwork, [5].

Discovery of the quantum theory and attempts to understand its relation to reality have brought another radically new view on the essence of the underlying science and its methodologies. One of the key observations, much connected with the peculiarities and randomness of quantum measurement, is that we understand nature only through information obtained via measurements. That resulted in the views by Bohr that *It is wrong to think that the task of Physics is to find out how nature is. Physics concerns with what we can say about nature* and led to such slogans as *It from bit* due to Wheeler that was later modified by Deutsch to *It from qubit*. That led to the view, not shared by all, of course, that *Everything is information* and to the formulation of so-called principle of *quantization of information*, [17]. Namely that *An elementary [physical] system is a manifestation of one bit of information.*

Current highlight of Physics - superstrings theory - operates with objects in 10 dimensional space. This theory has very high standing, in spite of the fact that it does not seem to be a testable theory - what used to be seen as a must feature of any theory to be accepted as a physical theory.

There are many other things Informatics can and should learn from the development of Physics. Here are some of them.

Physics, as the science, has had so far practical applications exceeding that of any science before. In spite of that, the need to deal with immediate problems of the practice can hardly be seen as the main, or as the only, driving force of its development[16]. It has been rather curiosity and the need to extend our knowl-

---

[16] In this connection of interest is the following position of J. Robert Oppenheimer, who directed Los Alamos Scientific Laboratory [15], *The things we learned [during the war] are not very important. The real things were learned in 1890 and 1905 and 1920, in every year leading up to the war, and we took this tree with a lot of ripe fruit on it and shook it hard and out came radar and atomic bomb...*

edge and understanding of the physical world, far beyond the one our senses can capture, that was behind Physics main discoveries and contributions.

Physics has made big progress even by exploring properties of particles that are not sure to exist (in some reasonable sense) or in developing theories we see no way to verify experimentally. Beauty, compactness, simplicity and surprising conclusions have been often enough in case no conflict with experiments have been recorded or predictable.

It has been to a very large extent due to the capability of Physics to keep making its research space broader and broader, deeper and deeper and to look for its most fundamental elements that made not only knowledge Physics produced, but also the impacts this new knowledge had, so remarkable.

References

1. Adleman, L.M.: Molecular computation of solutions to combinatorial problems. Science 206(11), 1021–1024 (1994)
2. Bennett, C.H., Brassard, G.: Quantum cryptography: public key distribution and coin tossing. In: Proceedings of IEEE Conference on Computers, Systems and Signal processing, Bangalore, India, pp. 175–179 (1984)
3. Bennett, C.H., Brassard, G., Crépeau, C., Jozsa, R., Peres, A., Wootters, W.K.: Teleporting an unknown quantum state via dual classical and Einstein-Podolsky-Rosen channels. Physical Review Letters 70, 1895–1899 (1993)
4. Bush, V.: Science - The Endless Frontiers; A report to the President on a Program for Postwar Scientific Research. National Science Foundations (1945)
5. Butterfield, H.: The origin of modern science. The Free Press, New York (1997)
6. Griffiths, P.A. (Chair of the Committee). Science, technology and the Federal Government: national Goals for a new Era. National Academy Press, Report of Committee on Science, Engineering and Public Policy of the National Academy of Sciences (1993)
7. Gruska, J.: Quantum computing. McGraw-Hill, New York (1999)
8. Gruska, J.: A broader view on limitations of information processing by nature. Natural Computing 6, 75–112 (2007)
9. Gruska, J.: A perception of informatics (2010), http://www.AE-Info.org/ae/User/Gruska.Jozef
10. Linn, M.(Committee chair): The scope and nature of computational thinking. Report of a Workshop, national Research Council of the National Academies, USA (2010)
11. Shor, P.W.: Algorithms for quantum computation: discrete log and factoring. In: Proceedings of 36th IEEE FOCS, pp. 124–134 (1994)
12. Shor, P.W.: Scheme for reducing decoherence in quantum computer memory. Physical Review A 52, 2493–2496 (1995)
13. Shor, P.W.: Fault-tolerant quantum computation. In: Proceedings of 37th IEEE FOCS, pp. 56–65 (1996)
14. Smolin, L.: The trouble with physics. The rise of string theory, the fall of science and what comes next. Spin Networks Ltd. (2006)
15. Stokes, D.E.: Pasteur's quadrant. Basic science and technological innovation. Brookings Institution Press, Washington (1997)
16. van Leeuwen, J., Tanca, L. (eds.): Student enrolment and image of the informatics discipline. Tech. Rep. UU-CS-2007-024, Utrecht University (2007)
17. Zeilinger, A.: A foundational principle for quantum mechanics. Foundation of Physics

Towards a New Shape Description Paradigm Using the Generative Modeling Language

Sven Havemann[1] and Dieter W. Fellner[1,2]

[1] Institute of ComputerGraphics and KnowledgeVisualization (CGV),
Graz University of Technology, Graz, Austria
s.havemann@cgv.tugraz.at
www.cgv.tugraz.at
[2] Fraunhofer IGD and GRIS, Darmstadt University of Technology,
Darmstadt, Germany
d.fellner@igd.fraunhofer.de
www.igd.fraunhofer.de

Abstract. A procedural description of a three-dimensional shape has undeniable advantages over conventional descriptions that are all based on the exhaustive enumeration paradigm. Although it is a true generalization, a procedural description of a given shape class is not always easy to obtain. The main problem is that procedural descriptions are typically Turing-complete, which makes 3D shape design formally (and practically) a programming task. We describe an approach that circumvents this problem, is efficient, extensible, and conceptually simple. We demonstrate the broad applicability with a number of examples from different domains and sketch possible future applications. But we also discuss some practical and theoretical limitations of the generative paradigm.

Keywords: generative modeling, procedural shapes, programming language, interactive shape design, 3D computer graphics.

1 What Is Generative Modeling?

It is not a trivial problem to find a good digital representation for describing the shape of a three-dimensional object. Maybe the most basic approach is to resort to sampling: The surface of the object is digitized, e.g., using a laser scanner that quickly produces millions of sample points on the surface of the object, as seen from a specific viewpoint. A 3D scanner acts very much like a photographic camera that produces a bitmap containing not only color, but also depth information. Consequently, the resulting depth image is called a *range map*. For the purpose of this paper, we are concerned with the shape alone, not with the color or material of a 3D object.

A range map faithfully captures all detail (as much as the *sampling density* permits), but it is highly redundant: A scan of a flat surface produces points that all lie in the same plane. So the next idea is to resort to tesselations: Every manifold, e.g., a 2D surface embedded in 3D space, admits a simplicial decomposition, in this case a triangulation. This solves the problem of flat surfaces,

C.S. Calude, G. Rozenberg, A. Salomaa (Eds.): Maurer Festschrift, LNCS 6570, pp. 200–214, 2011.

but curved surfaces still require a vast amount of triangles, depending on the required error tolerance.

The search for more powerful shape descriptions has produced over the last 30 years a large variety of geometrical primitives, ranging from freeform surfaces (parametric and iso-valued) over meshes (triangles, B-reps) to rather special ones (union of spheres, *moving least squares* surfaces). With NURBS, the dominant surface representation in industrial applications, it is only a matter of positioning the control points in the right place to create a spoon, a chair, or a car wing. But a spoon has an inner logic beyond control points, and this logic is not reflected in any representation following the enumerative paradigm. They all share the same problem, namely that there is no real reduction in complexity: n spoons require n times the space of one spoon, as point cloud or as NURBS model.

1.1 The Generative Modeling Paradigm

One way out of this dilemma is a paradigm change towards procedural shape descriptions. The idea of *generative modeling* is to understand a shape not as a huge list of elementary geometric objects, but as a **list of object generating operations**. While enumerative shape representations encode the result of a geometric construction process, a generative representation encodes the construction process itself. Note that this is in fact a true generalization: a triangle becomes a constant operation producing this triangle. So a generative description always works in a layered fashion on top of a conventional shape description:

- **L2:** Shape programming language MEL, MaxScript, Python – or **GML**
- **L1:** Shape operators   create triangle, move vertex, extrude
- **L0:** Shape data structure   triangles, B-reps, NURBS, point clouds

Generative modeling works best for man-made objects since it can capture very well regularites of all sorts. Man-made shapes exhibit regularities for a variety of reasons, only to mention aesthetics and style, manufacturing constraints and cost efficiency. Brick walls are less expensive when the bricks are equal. Consequently, the number of *shape design patterns* is in fact rather limited [5].

Despite clear advantages of procedural modeling, enumerative representations are still predominant. A major concern is robustness: When transmitting a generative model, the receiving system must behave identically as the sender to obtain the identical result. And this identity must hold on all three levels lised above. So the central question is: Considering all three levels L0, L1, L2, can there ever be a general exchange standard for procedural models?

1.2 GML, the Generative Modeling Language

The *Generative Modeling Language* (GML) belongs to the simplest class of programming languages, stack-based languages. The language core is identical to that of Adobe's *PostScript* [1]. PostScript is the 'invisible' programming language: When pressing the Print button, e.g., in Microsoft Word, the PostScript printer driver generates a computer program that is executed by the printer. PostScript has two outstanding advantages over other languages: It is designed for automatic code generation and for execution on modest hardware.

GML ranges on the language level (L2), so it acts on top of certain shape operators to manipulate a certain low-level shape representation. These are detailed in sections 3 and 4. But before, we need to look at possible alternatives.

2   Related Approaches

Procedural and generative modeling are gaining importance for several reasons. First of all, there is a need for more dynamic computer applications. With increasing computer power (Moore's law), more and more data can be processed on the fly. Advantages are that (a) a process description is typically tiny, and (b) process parameters can be varied later on. There is an enthusiastic Generative Design community around the *Processing* framework from Casey Reas and Ben Fry [13,12]. The majority of interactive art installations today are realized with it. The Processing approach is to streamline the programming task so that art-directed people can use it without too much frustration. Processing has considerable success with this approach, and some of the results are stunning.

However, it is doubtful that the approach scales to industrial applications. Not all artists are good coders. GML is not optimized for ease of coding; instead, like PostScript, it shall be generated invisibly by an interactive 3D application.

Shape grammars are another flavor of procedural modeling. They have gained considerable attention due the CityEngine [11] software that is based on the grammar language *CGA Shape* from Müller et al. [9]. It follows the principle of recursively splitting up a larger shape (box) into smaller shapes, each shape carrying a symbol. The rules of a context-free *split grammar* determine the split direction and size. Terminal boxes are filled with nice pre-modeled architectural elements. This approach works extremely well for very regular classical buildings.

Grammar evaluation requires a stack, so it may not be surprising that GML is well suited for the task. Section 5.2 shows some grammar-based GML models.

Maybe the most important class of procedural approaches are highend 3D modeling systems. The mid-90s witnessed a silent revolution in industrial design. Pro/Engineer from Parametric Technologies was the first CAD software to allow engineers constructing, e.g., a complete car rear axle as one parametric model; whole product families could be generated by changing a few high-level parameters. The approach was soon adopted by the other major CAD vendors. Apparently, today more than 90% of all consumer goods are created parametrically using software such as Pro/E, CATIA, SolidWorks, Unigraphics. But of course, each vendor defends his proprietary approach, and the exchange of intelligent *MCAD* models is a huge problem [10]: A parametric model created in Pro/E can usually be imported to CATIA only as a static model, i.e., as single instance of the shape family. This is a comfortable situation for the vendors.

We think that GML is suitable as a general exchange format for intelligent CAD models. Its versatility is demonstrated in sections 4 and 6. After all, the big trend is towards more customizable CAD applications, since the big gain is in the domains: Ship hull design, engine design, design of supermarkets or of coffee machines. – Exactly this is the idea behind, e.g., GML for Maya (sec. 6).

3   GML Fundamentals

GML follows the simple and general *stream of tokens* approach: A stream of individual tokens is processed, token after token. A token either contains data, in which case it is put on a stack, or a processing instruction, an *operator*. Operatorsuse the *operand stack*: Input parameters are poppsed, then processed, and results are pushed. Many pure data formats can be trivially converted to a stream of tokens: A string with a sequence of numbers separated by white spaces is already a valid GML program. The GML parser does not build up a parse tree, so it is actually only a tokenizer that treats each token independently.

GML provides only two compound data structures, (heterogenous) arrays and dictionaries. When executing ["x" /a 5] the opening marker [is pushed just like string, literal name, and integer. But the closing] is actually an operator. It searches on the stack for the marker, pops the values in between to create an array, and pushes an array token. Functions are created the same way using curly braces; *all* tokens are considered literals (and are pushed) until the closing } creates an *executable array*. So GML functions are in fact just ordinary token arrays, and all array operations can be applied to them (concat, get/set).

Besides (a) syntactic simplicity and (b) token arrays as functions, code generation is facilitated by (c) the stack. Values are passed anonymously without explicitly declared parameter lists (no *signatures*). All in all, *12 language rules* are completely sufficient to describe the language ([4], Fig. 5.5, p. 217).

A first GML example. The code in Fig. 1 works in an assembly-line fashion. The quad operator (line 1) takes two corners of a rectangle and a mode flag and pushes an array of 4 points. The 3D runtime engine renders objects on the stack, e.g., point arrays as open polygons. Line 2 converts the polygon to a mesh and pushes a halfedge of the double-sided quad (rendered as half arrow). It is the consumed by the extrude operator (line 3) together with a vector (w,h,m) describing width w, height h and mode m of the extrusion. In line 4, (1,0,1) normalize 0 describes

1: (0,0,-2) (1,1,0) 2 quad
2: /cyan setcurrentmaterial 5 poly2doubleface
3: (0,1,1) extrude
4: (0,0,1) (1,0,1) normalize 0 project_ringplane
5: (2,0,0) (0,1,-1) 2 quad
6: /yellow setcurrentmaterial 5 poly2doubleface
7: 0 bridgerings

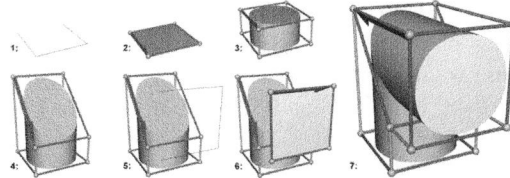

Fig. 1. GML works in an assebmly line fashion: Each operation takes its input(s) from the stack and leaves its result(s) on the stack for the next (Details: see text)

a plane by normal vector and distance from origin, onto which the extruded face (halfedge from line 3) is projected in vertical direction (0,0,1). Lines 5 and 6 create another double-sided quad. Line 7 finds two halfedges on the stack, which are then connected vertex-wise. bridgerings works only when both faces have the same degree, in this case four. – So each line processes the results of one or more previous lines; intermediate results wait on the stack until they are needed.

4   Procedural Shape Design with GML

It is straightforward to generalize a given parametric model like the one from Fig. 1 by replacing concrete values by parameters. However, a shape family does not come for free. It can be a challenging intellectual endeavour to determine the similarity and the difference of a class of given shapes. The parametric car rim model in Fig. 3 is the result of a baccalaureate thesis. We were given about 30 individual models of triangulated car rims from Volkswagen, which were manually partitioned into three different classes with distinctively different properties. One parametric model was created for each class, sharing as much functionality as possible. The main difference was the shape of the spokes. However, all rim classes shared some parameters, e.g., the number of spokes. So some of the parameters could be exposed as sliders in 3D, so that a new car rim within the design space of a class can be generated within a fraction of a second.

A wealth of examples. The range of possible applications of the same principle is shown in Fig. 2. The engine is a didactic model exposing a number of fundamental design parameters such as number of cylinders, piston height, and crank shaft radius. Most importantly, the opening angle of the housing connects a continuum of V-engine, boxer engine and in-line engine. – Gothic architecture is a prime example of parametric design from the 12th and 13th century [6]. Gothic constructions use exclusively compass and ruler. The standard *pointed arch* has a recursive structure with a circular rosette and two pointed sub-arches. Every parameter change requires a re-construction from scratch, the amount of geometry generated is substantial. The *Procedural Cathedral*, a model of Cologne cathedral, contains about 100 KB GML code.– The graph-like pipe structures (left) are an example of a style library. All styles permit a hierarchical structure with sub- and sub-sub-pipes that can be opened up. This is also a domain-specific modeling tool, as it allows editing of pipe graphs [8]. – The *CAVE configurator* is for planning a complex projection system (projector cones with arrows) in a room with complex geometry. – Five points are sufficient to define the structure of a chair, but a bed and a sofa have the same structure. This example hints at the separation of structure from appearance. – Finally, the *Castle Construction Kit* [3] enables also non-expert users to create complex geometry; its purpose is to study whether GML technology is suitable for computer games.

4.1   Six Main Fields of Application for the GML Technology

- **Enhance existing applications by 3D component.** Since our reality is three-dimensional, most software products should have a 3D module.

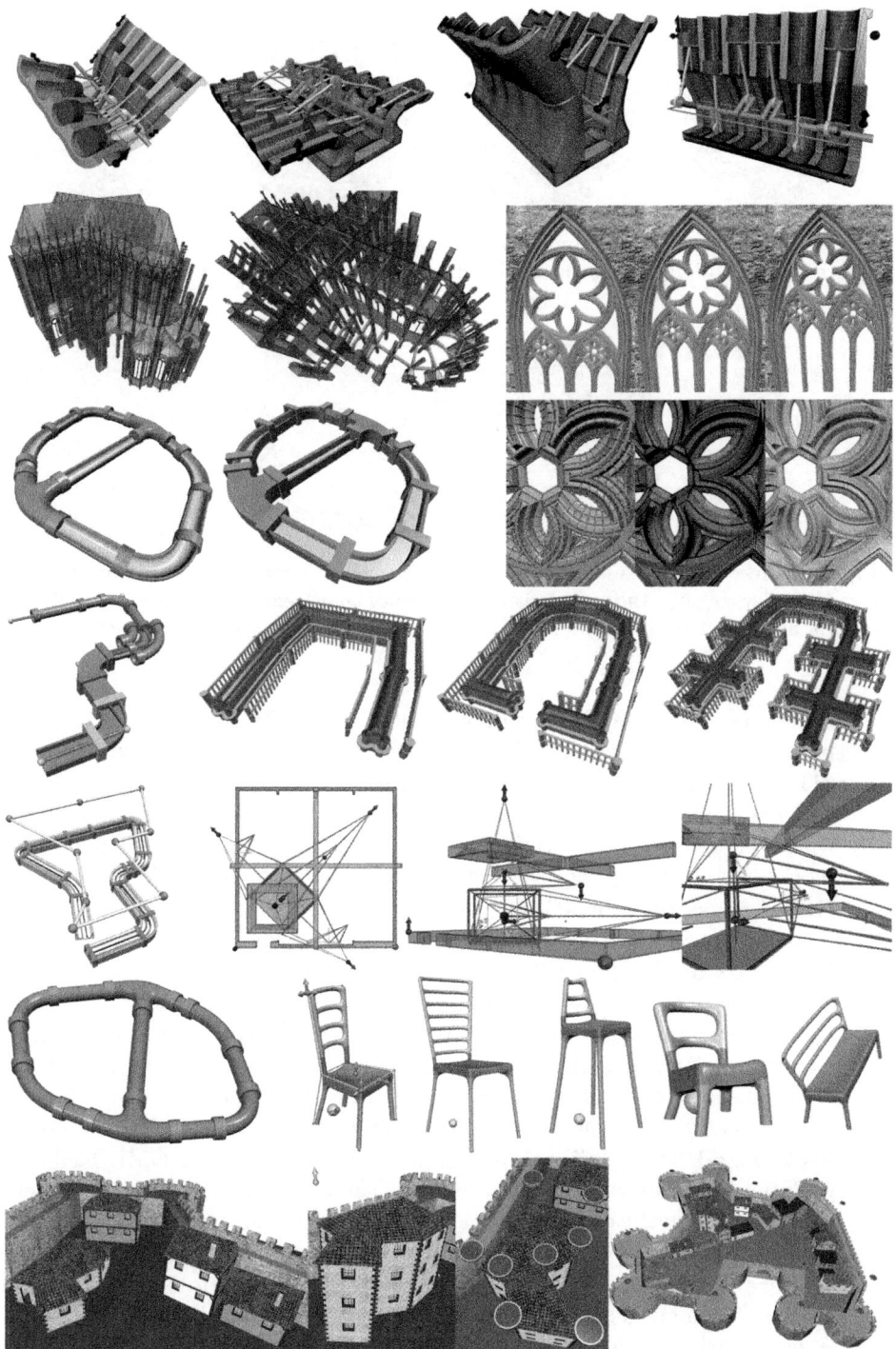

Fig. 2. GML examples. A concrete model can easily be generalized to a shape family.

Fig. 3. Three classes of car rims. The spokes of the three rims types are generated by different 'overridding' functions. Right image: Changing the number of spokes.

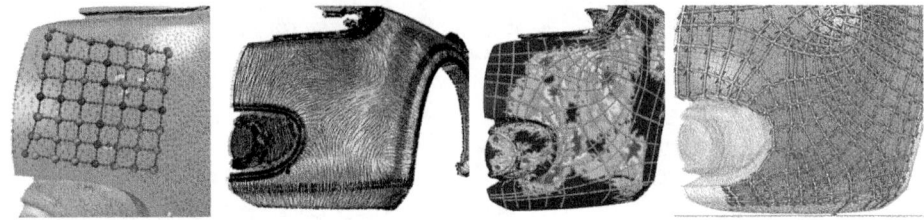

Fig. 4. Interactive high-quality surface reconstruction. A scanned triangle mesh is analyzed in order to guide the user-assisted creation of an as-regular-as-possible subdivision control mesh (pcB-Rep, see section 5.1). Fully automatic approaches are not accepted.

Examples: Logistics, facility management, SAP. By integrating GML, full parametric 3D modeling and viewing functionality becomes available.

– **3D Modeling for specialized domains.** Each domain has its domain-dependent shape building blocks. Examples: Bridges, buildings, street networks, pipe networks, car rims, furniture. Careful parametrization of building blocks can efficiently yield a great variation in shape by combinations.

– **Rapid mass instantiation.** Model collections even with thousands of 3D models (*Google Warehouse*) offer not too much variation in each category: 3 hands, 50 cars, 7 cupboards etc. Generative shape families can cover a whole continuum of similar but different shapes, and avoid repetition.

– **Systematic parameter variation.** In order to optimize constructions in engineerin, simulation software can automactically highlight problematic regions in the model. If automatic analysis is complemented by automatic model creation, the optimization feedback loop can hopefully be closed.

– **Web-based 3D applications.** As a modeling language, GML facilitates updating the construction history on the server whenever a modeling operation is issued on the client (see [2]). Possible applications: Web-based product configuration, collaborative 3D-editing, virtual worlds (a la SecondLife)

– **General exchange format for intelligent 3D models.** The great potential of domain-dependent 3D modeling tools can not be leveraged today. A new market could evolve if specialized engineering companies could sell *solutions to 3D modeling problems*, instead of just 3D models and renderings.

5   Three Low-Level Shape Representations (L0/L1)

GML as such is only a programming language (level L2 from sec. 1.1). But a shape description requires also a low-level shape representation (L0) and operators to manipulate it (L1). The first representation used was the pcB-Rep; but recently the concept was extended to Convex Polyhedra (CPs) and Volumetric Bitmaps (VBs) for reasons described in the following.

5.1   Progressive Combined B-Reps (pcB-Reps)

The generative models shown in Figs. 1-5 all use *progressive combined B-Rep meshes*, short pcB-Reps. The concept is shown in Fig. 5, where the coarse *control mesh* is in the top right. Like any B-rep, the faces of a pcB-rep can have any degree (e.g., octagons) but its edges carry an additional flag: they are either *sharp* or *smooth*. If all edges are sharp, the pcB-rep is rendered as a polygonal object, but faces with a smooth edge are rendered as Catmull/Clark subdivision surface. The setup and render routine is highly optimized to allow for progressive refinement over several frames, and adaptive level-of-detail; for details see [4].

Since not everything must be recomputed at once, even very complex models such as the Gothic window (Fig. 2) can be changed at interactive rates, i.e., with a complete regeneration between two mouse ticks when dragging a slider.

On the conceptual level, the innovation was to use a well-defined operator interface, the *Euler operators*, for mesh manipulation. They act as a middleware for all higher modeling operations such as **extrude** or **bridgerings**, but are also available as GML operators. GML therefore allows fine-grained mesh editing on the halfedge level. A single new GML type, the *halfedge token*, was added as a mesh reference. It uniquely idenifies one vertex/face combination of the mesh.

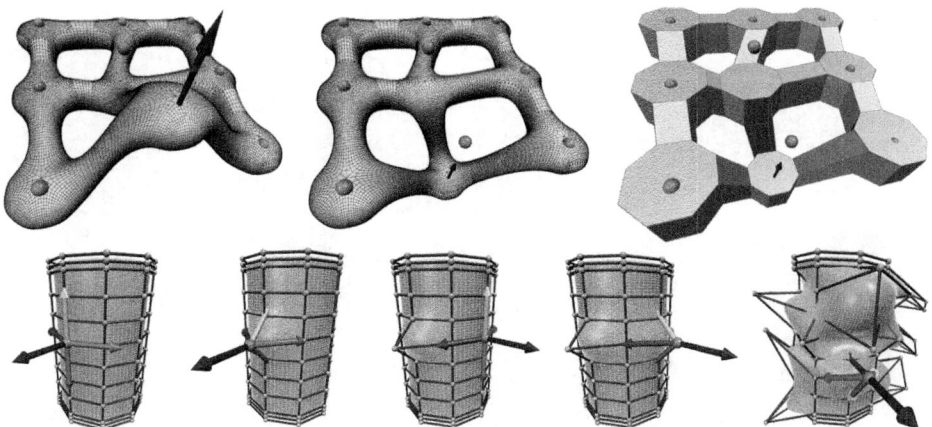

Fig. 5. Product mass customization. Concept study for customizable consumer products. Top: Organic network. Bottom: End-user customizable free-form lamp shade.

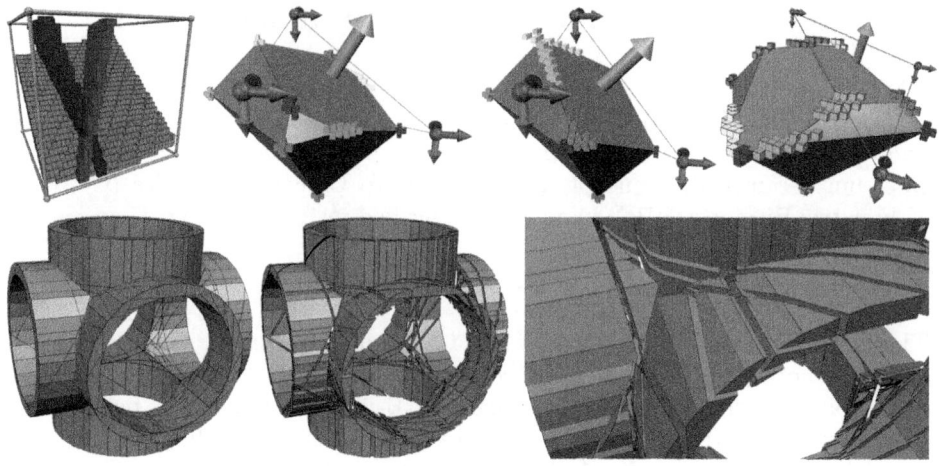

Fig. 6. Computing Convex Polyhedra. Plane intersection (top) and robustness test.

Meshes are great for local modifications, but their global consistency can be a problem. Inserting a vertex into an edge splits up both respective halfedges. This might break the repeatability of a subsequent mesh operation that uses these halfedges as *anchor*. – Halfedges can be brittle references.

5.2   Convex Polyhedra (CPs)

Very robust with respect to split operations are *convex polyhedra*. Fig. 6 (top) shows an oriented plane defined by three (ordered) points. It partitions 3-space in two infinite half-spaces, 'interior' and 'exterior'. A convex polyhedron (CP) is the intersection of several such 'interiors'. The challenge is to compute its corners, which can be done in a fast and robust way on the integer grid.

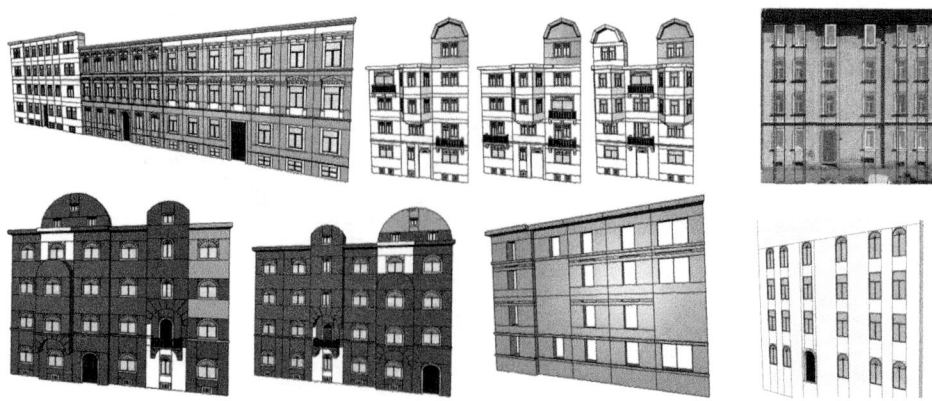

Fig. 7. CITYFIT examples. A GML shape grammar for Convex Polyhedra is generated automatically from the results of an image analysis pass (images to the right).

With a robust CP evaluation method also CSG, i.e., Boolean set operations, become possible. The robustness is demonstrated by moving inwards the planes of all CPs by a fixed amount. This produces gaps, and many CPs correctly vanish because the halfspace intersection is now empty.

CPs can be considered a generalization of rectangular boxes, so they can also be used as primitive for shape grammars. Fig. 7 shows some facades created by CP-split grammars. They allow greater expressiveness since architectural elements like columns, rounded arches, rounded roofs etc. can now be expressed *within* the grammar, rather than using pre-modeled geometry. Another challenge is to use grammars also for building interiors. This was successfully demonstrated with the compouter science building in Graz (Fig. 8, also see [7]). An important advantage of such a procedural model is that different views can be generated on the fly by re-defining the grammar rules; furthermore, default parameters can be replaced anytime later by measured values to produce a more accurate model.

Another interesting implication is that CP-grammars can much better represent modern styles, e.g., *deconstructivism*, that use intersections and not classical splits. The interactive building configurator in Fig. 9 runs on an Apple iPhone and can be operated using touch gestures. Another step further goes the House-Configurator software (Fig. 10), which allows the user to move walls, windows, and doors etc., but also to specify constraints that need to be maintained.

Convex Polyhedra have also proven useful for CAD applications beyond architecture. Fig. 11 shows the model of a mechanical device that is composed of several moving parts. Optimizing the dimensions of the parts has proven difficult because of the many interdependencies. After a number of CAD drawings, a GML model using CPs was created that allowed much shorter turnaround times in optimization (cf. section 4.1).

5.3 Volumetric Bitmaps (VBs)

The latest addition to the set of GML supported shape representations is the Volumetric Bitmap (VB). The goal of the METADESIGNER project is to provide (like Processing [13]) a tool for artists and shape designers to create parametric procedural models. This requires a shape representation with really minimal requirements in terms of data structure consistency.

A volumetric representation has the great advantage that in principle, each individual voxel can be switched on or off. More efficient is to render whole

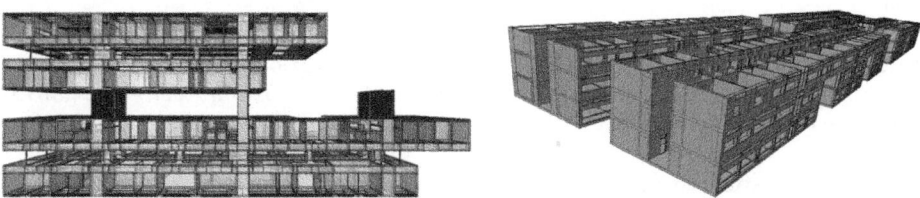

Fig. 8. Box grammar example. The computer science building of TU Graz is not as regular as it seems. Parametric grammar rules are used, e.g., a *corridor-wall-office* split.

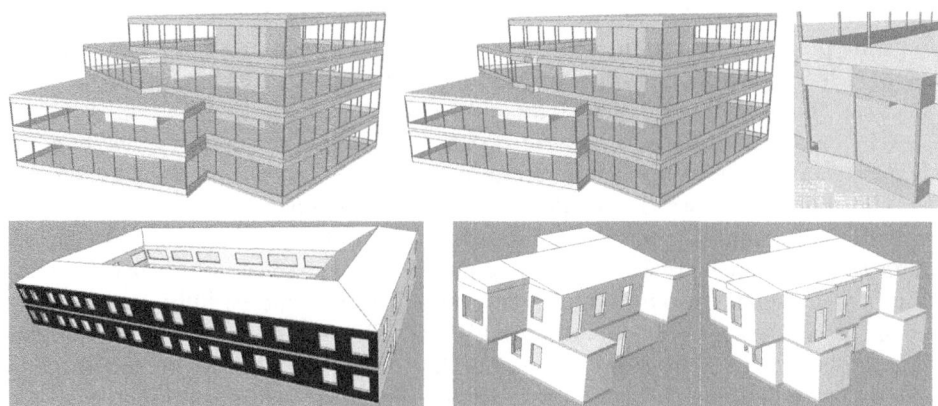

Fig. 9. Gandis project: Conceptual 3D modeling of office buildings as iPhone application. Top: Intersections are faithfully computed using CSG, the *curtain wall* facade follows the outline of the union of the three independent box-shaped parts. Bottom: Touch-optimized user interaction and parametric non-standard residential building.

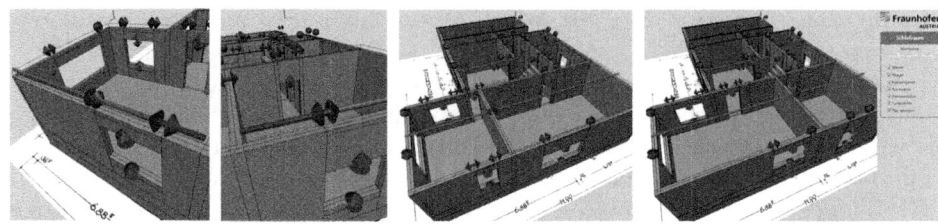

Fig. 10. Interactive Interiors. Left images: The user can fix distances (red portion of slider). Right images: When dragging the wall, the fixed distances remain unchanged.

```
Mechanical−main−dict begin
  / clearance       0.3              def
  /p14−thick−t      1.3              def
  /p11−radius       2.5              def
  /p12−radius       p11−radius       def
  /p12−thick        p14−thick−t
                    clearance add    def
  ...
end
```

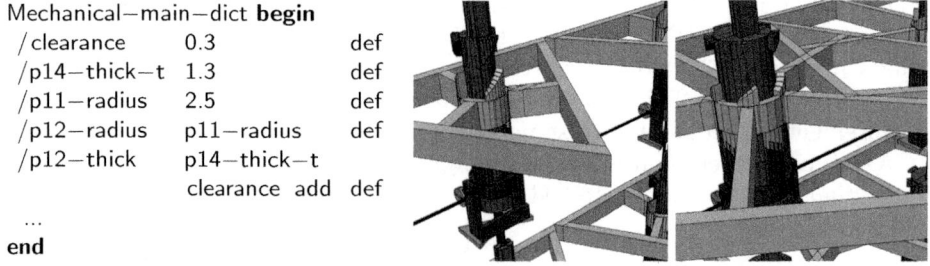

Fig. 11. Optimizing assemblies. Left: Mechanical constructions have a long parameter list. Some are free, others are computed (e.g., $p12Thick = p14ThickT + clearance$). By convention, they are stored in a *model dictionary*, essentially a property list.

objects like a sphere to the volume. More complex shapes can simply be created by moving a solid object through the volume, which is continuously rendered into the volume. This reduces shape design to motion design, which is easier to control for artists and designers than, e.g., mesh consistency.

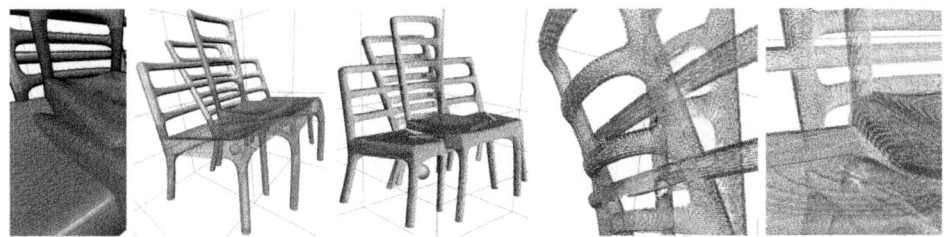

Fig. 12. Volumetric Bitmaps. Left: Three intersecting chair models. Right: Self-intersections are automatically removed when rendering the chairs to the volumetric grid.

6   The GML Technology Portfolio

GML comes in various flavors, Fig. 14 shows the range of applications and usage scenarios. The reason for this versatility is that GML does not comes as GUI-based application, but only as a C++ library (or DLL). Its size is very small (2.5 MB); the minimal GUI-based application, TestGML, has less than 3 MB. Another reason for the versatility is that the GML library can be operated basically using three commands:

- GMLApplet::call(std::string command)   to execute a GML command string;
- GMLApplet::render()   for OpenGL output; and
- GMLApplet::handle(...)   for mouse and keyboard input.

This API can easily be wrapped, e.g., to JavaScript for a web browser plugin; to COM for an ActiveX control (ActiveGML); to Java for a Processing extension; as well as to MEL for a plugin to the high-end 3D modeling software Maya, which also uses OpenGL for rendering.

Using this API, GML can also easily be integrated with any GUI-based application, using whichever GUI library is provided. Typically, the GUI callback function, e.g., of a button or a manu item, triggers the GMLApplet::call method with a fixed GML command that executes a function of a GML library that is

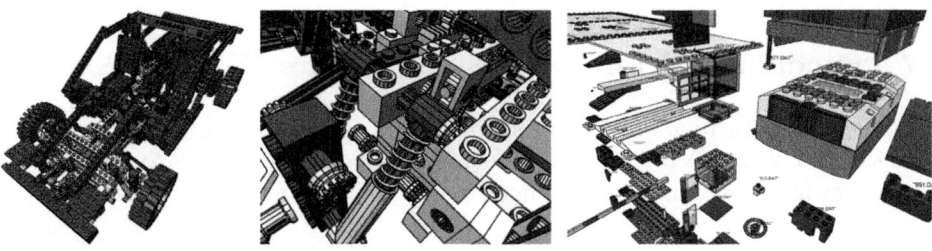

Fig. 13. Scriptable LEGO. The GML LEGO resource holds a hierarchy of transformations (a *scene graph*). It follows the move-and-drop approach; parts can be added, removed, and translated. The grid semantics can be scripted on the GML level.

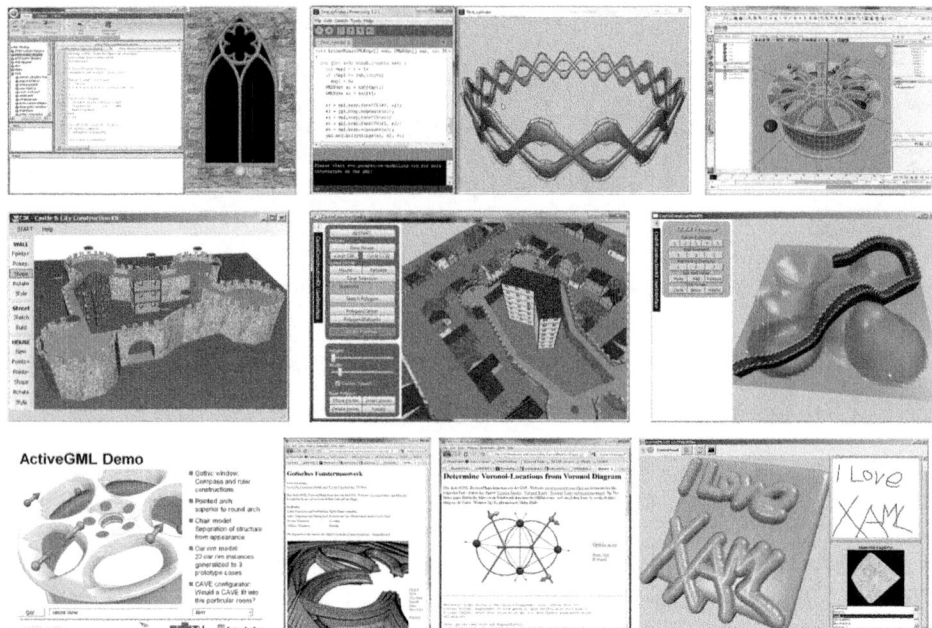

Fig. 14. GML technology portfolio. Top: GMLStudio IDE, GML for Processing, GML for Maya. Middle: Castle Construction Kit as C# application, in a WPF/XAML canvas, with a plugin for height-sensitive walls. Bottom: GML on a Powerpoint slide, on a web page, and steered by a WPF applet for pen-assisted drawing.

loaded in the beginning. Of course, the command string can be created dynamically, e.g., to transmit a slider value to the GML applet.

A more sophisticated environment using Microsoft WPF/Silverlight is currently being developed. It supports also *data binding*, i.e., the value of a slider in the 2D GUI can be bound to the value of a GML variable. This way, a bi-directional connection between 2D GUI and GML can be realized, e.g., to trigger a re-configuration of the 2D GUI in response to a selection event in the 3D view. This will enable a new generation of very dynamic applications with tight integration of 2D and 3D content.

7 Fundamental Limitations and Future Work

There are three fundamental problems of the generative modeling approach, which also apply to procedural modeling in general. Strategies to avoid or circumvent htem are among the difficult research problems of the future:

The Persistent Naming Problem. Whenever a modeling operation is executed, it is applied with respect to a reference, sometimes called *anchor*. When the anchor is moved or vanishes, the operation cannot be reliably performed any more. In that case the reference (*'name'*) does not persist, hence the name. This

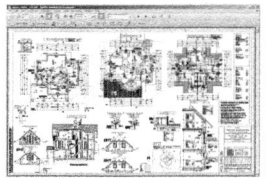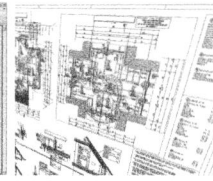

Fig. 15. GML from data. Left: To convert PDF to GML, the plan is printed to a PostScript file. GML commands are inserted using text search/replace. Right: The export of a GIS system in CSV format was also converted to GML using text tools.

is especially an obstacle for automating GUI-based operations. When the user modifies a specific step of a stairway, a column of an arcade, a vertex of a mesh – what was the reason for selecting this item? If the user does not provide a selection rule, but only a mouse click, the action can not be retargeted, i.e., later re-used with a different stairway, arcade, or mesh. – The persistent naming problem occurs in many different variants.

The Kolmogorov Complexity is uncomputable. GML programs are tiny compared to the amount of data they produce. The Gothic window in full resolution produces a 262 MB .obj file out of 44 KB GML code. So it is tempting to us it as compression scheme. But this amounts to the question: Given a shape, which (small/smallest) GML program can produce this shape? This is equivalent to asking for the Kolmogorov complexity of a shape. The *Kolmogorov complexity* of a bit sequence is the size (in bytes) of the smallest computer program (in a given language) that produces exactly this sequence. Unfortunately, from information theory it is known that the Kolmogorov complexity is uncomputable.

Generative Surface Reconstruction is an ill-posed problem. A weaker form of the inverse problem is the question: Given a GML model of a chair with free parameters, and a scanned model of a chair, what is the parameter set that fits best the template to match the scan? Parameter fitting is an inverse problem, and in general it cannot be decided either. Fitting often fails because the distance measure is misguided by unimportant details since the fitting algorithm can a priori not distinguish between imporant and unimportant feature.

8 Summary and Conclusion

- **Generative 3D Modeling is a paradigm change** in the description of 3D objects: Not as lists of geometric primitives, but as sequence of operations. Any GML model can immediately be parameterized to create a whole shape family of similar shapes.
- **Automatic code generation** is the feature that makes the difference: Procedural modeling requires a file format that is a programming language. In GML, literal manual programming is replaced by Lego-like plugging together of code fragments in background.

- **Full range from static to intelligent data:** GML is very close to pure data formats for non-procedural data, e.g., XML. Data refactoring by gradually introducing loops and function calls allows exploiting regularities to decrease data size and increase high-level control.

Acknowledgements

The authors gratefully acknowledge the generous support from the European Commission for the FP7 IP 3D-COFORM (grant ICT 231809), and from the Austrian Research Promotion Agency (FFG) for the Fit-IT VisualComputing projects CITYFIT (grant 815971/14472), METADESIGNER (grant 820925/18236), and GANDIS.

But and foremost we thank the GML group in Graz: René Berndt, Ulrich Krispel, Wolfgang Thaller, Christoph Schinko, Volker Settgast, Torsten Ullrich, Manfred Krieger, Martin Hecher, Alex Falkensteiner, Bernhard Hohmann, Björn Gerth, Harald Csaszar.

References

1. Adobe Inc.: PostScript Language Reference Manual, 3rd edn. Addison-Wesley, Reading (1999)
2. Berndt, R., Havemann, S., Fellner, D.: 3d modeling in a web browser to formulate content-based 3d queries. In: Proc. Web 3D 2009, pp. 111–118. ACM Press, New York (2009)
3. Gerth, B., Berndt, R., Havemann, S., Fellner, D.W.: 3d modeling for non-expert users with the castle construction kit v0.5. In: Proc. VAST 2005, pp. 49–57. Eurographics/ACM Siggraph, Eurographics Press (November 2005)
4. Havemann, S.: Generative Mesh Modeling. Ph.D. thesis, Braunschweig Technical University, Germany (November 2005)
5. Havemann, S., Fellner, D.: Patterns of shape design. In: Proc. I-Know 2009, pp. 93–106. J. UCS Journal of Universal Computer Science, Graz (2009)
6. Havemann, S., Fellner, D.W.: Generative parametric design of gothic window tracery. In: Proc. VAST 2004, pp. 193–201. Eurographics, Brussels (2004), http://www.eg.org/EG/DL/WS/VAST/VAST04/193-201.pdf
7. Hohmann, B., Havemann, S., Krispel, U., Fellner, D.: A gml shape grammar for semantically enriched 3d building models. Computers and Graphics 34, 322–334 (2010)
8. Mendez, E., Schall, G., Havemann, S., Junghanns, S., Fellner, D., Schmalstieg, D.: Generating semantic 3d models of underground infrastructure. IEEE Computer Graphics and Applications 28(3), 48–57 (2008)
9. Müller, P., Wonka, P., Haegler, S., Ulmer, A., Gool, L.V.: Procedural modeling of buildings. In: ACM SIGGRAPH, vol. 25, pp. 614–623 (2006)
10. Pratt, M.: Extension of iso 10303, the step standard, for the exchange of procedural shape models. In: Proc. Intern. Conf. on Shape Modeling and Applications (SMI 2004), Genova, Italy, pp. 317–326 (June 2004)
11. Procedural Inc.: CityEngine (2009), http://www.procedural.com/
12. Processing website, www.processing.org
13. Reas, C., Fry, B.: Processing: A Programming Handbook for Visual Designers and Artists. MIT Press, Cambridge (2007)

Name Resolution by Rewriting in Dynamic Networks of Mobile Entities[*]

Jan van Leeuwen[1] and Jiří Wiedermann[2]

[1] Department of Information and Computing Sciences, Utrecht University,
P.O. Box 80.089, 3508 TB Utrecht, The Netherlands
j.vanleeuwen@cs.uu.nl

[2] Institute of Computer Science, Academy of Sciences of the Czech Republic,
Pod Vodárenskou věží 2, 182 07 Prague 8, Czech Republic
jiri.wiedermann@cs.cas.cz

Abstract. In link-free networks of communicating entities in motion like mobile ad hoc networks there is no central authority for naming and communications management. The set-up of new nodes is managed by autoconfiguration, using so-called zero configuration protocols. These protocols tend not to scale very easily and have difficulty with network partitioning and merging. We propose a number of techniques for assigning unique identifiers to entities in zero configuration protocols that are more flexible and yet lead to name extensions of smallest possible length, assuming that the entities in motion mix sufficiently. The methods use simple rewrite rules, viewing names as words over a finite alphabet.

1 Introduction

In networks one distinguishes between the *name* of an entity and its *address*, where the former identifies the entity and the latter is used in the lower-layer routing protocols. We consider the problems of naming and name conflict resolution in 'on the fly' networks of communicating entities where the entities travel and randomly meet in some space, like mobile ad hoc networks (MANETs) and dynamic multi-agent systems. In these networks, entities can only communicate with neighbouring entities and there is no central control. The networks require special protocols (cf. [3,4]) to provide and maintain a communications infrastructure in which entities can enter and leave at arbitrary times.

In traditional IP networks, name and address assignment are handled by the DHCP servers in the network. In the case of ad hoc networks of moving entities we need *autoconfiguration protocols* that run in every node, like the so-called 'zero configuration' protocols [8,23]. In these protocols the naming problem is non-trivial because all decision making is done locally. Given a decentralized mechanism for assigning initial names, how can the network-wide uniqueness of names be ensured? How can name conflicts be averted? Solutions in existing

[*] This research was partially supported by institutional research plan AV0Z10300504 and Czech National Science Foundation grant No. P202/10/1333.

C.S. Calude, G. Rozenberg, A. Salomaa (Eds.): Maurer Festschrift, LNCS 6570, pp. 215–227, 2011.
© Springer-Verlag Berlin Heidelberg 2011

autoconfiguration protocols tend not to scale easily and also have difficulty coping with network partitioning and merging. We will design some techniques for name resolution that are attractively simple and yet give more flexibility. The techniques use simple rewrite rules on names.

Although uniqueness of names is an ultimate goal of any decentralized naming system, in certain applications the requirements are less stringent. For example, it may be sufficient if names are unique in all sufficiently large *neighbourhoods*. This is ensured by *lazy protocols* which only resolve name conflicts when they arise and prevent the correct functioning of the (local) communications structure. Also, entities may be part of different 'subnets' and one may only be interested in uniquely naming entities within every subnet, allowing entities of the same name to exist in different subnets simultaneously. All this can also happen under a *dynamic scenario* in which entities enter and leave and subnets form and merge. It is the scenario we adopt.

Autoconfiguration protocols should not be demanding on local memory. Following the design of Internet Protocol Version 6 [17], a common form of automatic configuration is *stateless* autoconfiguration. Here it is immaterial which names are assigned, as long as they are unique and of use for identification purposes. (In stateful autoconfiguration some information is remembered and e.g. a database of names and addresses may be employed.) Note that name resolution most likely leads to longer names 'in the limit'. Thus we want to pack name spaces as best as we can when resolving conflicts. We will be especially interested in the *size* of names in large ad hoc networks. The simple methods we propose are (nearly) stateless and keep names as short as possible, assuming that the entities mix sufficiently. A complete lazy autoconfiguration protocol based on these techniques is given in [21].

The paper is organized as follows. In Section 2 we describe some existing approaches to name resolution in mobile ad hoc networks and dynamic networks of mobile agents. In Section 3 we give a simple protocol which starts with an unknown number of entities with initially given names, and which resolves name conflicts whenever entities meet, i.e. come within each other's transmission range. In Section 4 the method is tuned to obtain a protocol which leads to 'optimally packed' names of length bounded by $H + \lfloor \log n \rfloor$ for distinguishing among n entities, where H is a bound on the size of the initial names. In this Section we also consider the robustness of the protocol under the dynamic scenario.

2   Preliminaries

In ad hoc networks of communicating entities, the entities (devices, agents) must collaborate in the absence of a supporting network infrastructure. Each network node can directly communicate with the nodes within a certain radius only, given by the reach of its communications hardware and possibly limited also by the presence of obstacles. We assume that nodes do not know the entities in their neighbourhood beforehand and that there are no implicit hierarchical orderings or clusterings to be taken into account in the naming protocol (see e.g. [10]).

The problems of naming and name management are well-studied in networks of communicating processes, e.g. in distributed operating systems ([7], Ch. 7). Naming assigns to each process a unique label, which is generated algorithmically. Ensuring name uniqueness is complex when new processes can appear arbitrarily, not one by one and without a unique *server* that could name them. We study naming in the scenario in which entities keep joining or leaving, individually or in batches, without central control. We want methods that keep names *as short as possible*, in the interest of memory efficiency.

While entity names are easily generated locally, one needs techniques for *duplicate name detection* (like 'duplicate address detection' or DAD [20]) and *name conflict resolution*. As duplicate detection involves probing, the techniques are often combined with neighbour discovery or even reconstruction of the entire topology of the ad hoc network. (Known algorithms as in [1] or [6] are based on network traversal.) Standard approaches to naming include (cf. [16]):

- assignment of (a unique range of) names by a global (or external) naming authority [9,14],
- taking a unique 'name' stored in the hardware of the respective mobile entity (e.g. the MAC number of the wireless access card) [20],
- generating a name randomly, using a (pseudo-)random number generator with suitable ranges in the nodes [15,19,24].

The first approach is often not applicable or uses extra information, and the second may not be in the interest of the entity. The third approach is most commonly used but does not guarantee unique names and thus needs conflict resolution. When a conflict is detected, the entities involved must somehow choose other names and hope that no new conflicts are introduced.

Autoconfiguration could require *symmetry breaking* between entities and thus, as leader entities are neither available nor desired in our context, we assume that entities possess a simple *random number generator* for choosing initial names randomly and for *coin-tossing* when symmetry must be broken. In e.g. [2] a good account is given of the available techniques and their shortcomings.

2.1   Interpreting Names as Words

In some models, randomly assigned names are long enough to practically exclude the possibility of having doubles. We consider the case in which relatively *short* initial names are generated e.g. randomly, and conflict resolution is used to *scale* to a network of any size. Initial entity names can also be generated by *hashing* unique but private entity identifiers to a small domain of (short) words.

Let an entity c have a current name $h = h_c$. One can view h as the encoding of a whole set of names owned by c. Most proposals for name resolution follow this viewpoint. A typical example is the use of the buddy system from dynamic storage allocation for dynamic name space allocation [11]. If a new but unnamed entity x enters the network and finds a named entity c, then c assigns to x a (unique) name from its name space and subsequently splits off half of it name space and gives it to x. A similar approach using sets of integer intervals $\subseteq [0, 2^k]$

as subspaces was described in [24] and used also in [18]. Another version using disjoint initial address spaces, is given in [9].

In this paper we interpret every name h_c as a word in $\Sigma^\star$ with $\Sigma = \{0, 1\}$. A name h_c represents the entire set $h_c\Sigma^\star$ of potential names beginning with h_c, 'owned' by c. In Section 3 we will show that this leads to a simple and flexible method for name resolution, without the need for much administration. We will prove that it gives a close to optimal solution for the naming problem, assuming that nodes move around and mix suitably in each other's ranges. In Section 4 we improve it further to a name-length optimal protocol.

3   A Simple Name Resolution Protocol

Consider an ad hoc network of mobile communicating entities which move around. Every entity c that wants to join the network, is assumed to generate an initial name $h = h_c \in \Sigma^\star$ for itself when it joins, using e.g. the random generator it possesses. We assume that all initial names are *equally long*, so no initial name is a proper prefix of another name. This is reasonable, although the validity of our protocols will not depend on it. Let $|x|$ denote the length of word x.

We assume that every initial h is small (e.g. $|h| = 8$). The initial choice of h_c implies that there are likely to be name conflicts ('collisions') and thus name resolution may be required. We want a name resolution method that does *not* depend on knowledge of N, the number of current or future nodes in the network, and that allows the number of entities to grow and shrink freely.

For the analysis of our protocols we will adopt a suitable model for mobile entities which we call the *encounter model*. In this model the entities mix in each other's ranges such that eventually all entities will encounter in pairs of two and are able to check each other's names. The entities are said to 'mix well' if they encounter uniformly at random. If entities mix well, any name resolution method will use an expected number of at least $\Omega(N)$ encounters.

3.1   Basic Protocol

The basic version of the proposed name resolution method simply divides the name spaces between entities of the same name, quite similar to the buddy system in [11]. However, the chosen representation makes this easy to implement and scalable to networks of any size.

> **Protocol A**
> 1. *(initialize)* if entity c enters, then it generates an initial name $h = h_c$.
> 2. *(encounter)* if two entities of equal name h meet, then one of them is renamed to $h0$ and the other to $h1$.

Rule 2 in Protocol A clearly requires symmetry breaking between the two entities, if they find themselves having the same name h. This can be done by coin-tossing, using the random generators which the entities possess.

Note that every encounter of two equally named entities may lead to a further name conflict: names $h0$ and $h1$ may already exist. Thus, by resolving one conflict we may create two more. Protocol A may be seen as a form of *distributed hashing* if the initial names are assigned by a hash function, with distributed collision detection and conflict resolution. Assume that the set of entities in the network stabilizes. We first show that Protocol A converges.

Proposition 1. *On the assumption that entities mix well, Protocol A eventually leads to unique names for all entities.*

Proof. Entities with different names remain differently named, no matter how their names are extended in later encounters. Two entities that have the same name when they meet, resolve their name-conflict in the encounter and are thus named differently forever from that moment on. The assumption implies that all pairs will eventually meet and thus that all names become unique in the long run. This happens with probability tending to 1 as time goes to infinity.   □

Proposition 2. *Suppose the number of entities with the same initial name h has grown to some (unknown) number n. Then the unique names that will eventually result for these entities using Protocol A will all have length $\leq |h| + \lfloor \log n \rfloor$.*

Proof. As the n entities mix, $\lfloor \frac{n}{2} \rfloor$ of them are named $h0$ and $\lfloor \frac{n}{2} \rfloor$ of them become named $h1$, eventually. Precisely $n - 2\lfloor \frac{n}{2} \rfloor \leq 1$ entities will remain with name h, which is then unique. The argument simply continues recursively. Let an entity be in *level i* if it has obtained a name $h\alpha$ of length $|h| + i$. To analyse the result, write $n = a_m 2^m + \cdots + a_1 2^1 + a_0$ in binary notation, with $m = \lfloor \log n \rfloor$. The protocol eventually resolves names level after level such that in the end:

$a_i = 0 \rightarrow$ no word $h\alpha$ of length $|h| + i$ is the name of an entity in the network, and

$a_i = 1 \rightarrow$ every word $h\alpha$ of length $|h| + i$ is the name of an entity, each of precisely one entity that permanently resides in level i.

This implies that the longest names that result in Protocol A will be those corresponding to the nodes in level $m = \lfloor \log n \rfloor$.   □

Proposition 3. *Suppose the number of entities with the same initial name h has grown to some (unknown) number n. The entities obtain their unique name with Protocol A after a total of $\mathcal{O}(n \log n)$ name changes.*

Proof. If level i is full in the end, the 2^i names in the level are all used and account for $2^i \cdot i$ name-changes in the process. The total number is thus at most $\sum_{a_i=1}^{m} i \cdot 2^i = \mathcal{O}(m2^m) = \mathcal{O}(n \log n)$.   □

If n remains *small*, the protocol is simple and efficient. For larger n the proof shows that in the long run a large number of extensions of length $\leq \lfloor \log n \rfloor$ will not be used, although they are used in intermediate stages. To be more precise, let $\bar{n} = b_m 2^m + \cdots + b_1 2^1 + b_0$ be the 1-*complement* of n, with $b_m = 0$ and $b_i = \bar{a}_i$. Then precisely the extensions in the levels i with $b_i = \bar{a}_i = 1$ (i.e. $a_i = 0$) will not be used in the end, if no new entities enter the network. In case $n = 1 \cdot 2^m$ this amounts to $1 + 2 + \cdots + 2^{m-1} = 2^m - 1$ names, thus about 50% of the available name space remains unused here.

3.2   Expected Number of Encounters

An entity c needs to undergo up to $\log n$ name changes to attain its unique final name, with n as above. However, an entity needs the specific encounters to make this happen. If entities are mobile and mixing arbitrarily, they encounter randomly and thus many more than $\log n$ encounters may be needed before the resolutions have the desired effect.

To estimate this properly, assume that we have a fixed set of N mobile entities initially and that there are $n = n_c$ entities c with initial name $h = h_c$. By the assumption that entities mix well, entity c encounters other entities in the set uniformly at random, step after step. We will say that entities mix *aggressively* if the probability of meeting an equal-named counterpart is greater than 0 in every step, as long as the name resolution process has not finished. Assume also that $n = 2^m$ for some integer $m \geq 2$. (For $m = 0$ there is no name conflict and for $m = 1$ the expected number of encounters is precisely $N - 1$.)

Proposition 4. *An entity c with initial name $h = h_c$ attains its unique final name in Protocol A after an expected number of at least $\frac{10}{9}(N - 1)$ and at most $(2n - \log n)(N - 1)$ encounters, the latter under the assumption that entities mix aggressively.*

Proof. Suppose entity c has reached the ith level in the name resolution process and thus has just gotten a name $h\alpha$ with $|\alpha| = i$, for some i with $0 \leq i < m$. There will be $n_i = \frac{n}{2^i}$ nodes in level i that eventually have name $h\alpha$, and they have to encounter with another entity of name $h\alpha$ (after they were named $h\alpha$) in order to resolve the name conflicts. This applies to entity c in particular. Because the other entities with name $h\alpha$ only appear gradually and also disappear again after their conflict is resolved, the probability of c to encounter another entity of name $h\alpha$ may be much smaller than $p_i = \frac{n_i - 1}{N - 1}$ in every trial.

We model the name resolution process of entity c in level i by a *Poisson trial* with success probabilities $r_1, r_2, \cdots$. Here r_k denotes the probability that c encounters an entity of name $h\alpha$ in the kth try. (A Poisson trial is a Bernoulli trial with varying probabilities of success, cf. [5].) We clearly have $0 \leq r_k \leq p_i$. The expected number of encounters before c can resolve its name conflict and move to the next level, is equal to the expected number of trials to obtain a success in the Poisson trial for the first time. We can bound this from below by first omitting all steps with $r_k = 0$ and then considering the resulting Poisson trial, thus effective assuming that $\frac{1}{N-1} \leq r_k \leq p_i$. The expected number of trials to reach a first success in this trial is at least

$$\sum_{k=1}^{\infty} k \prod_{j=1}^{k-1} (1-r_j)\, r_k \geq \frac{1}{N-1} \sum_{k=1}^{\infty} k \prod_{j=1}^{k-1} (1-r_j) \geq \frac{1}{N-1} \sum_{k=1}^{\infty} k(1-p_i)^{k-1} =$$

$$= \frac{1}{N-1} \frac{1}{p_i^2} = \frac{N-1}{(n_i-1)^2}.$$

With this bound we can estimate the expected number of encounters in order for c to go from level 0 to level m, the level at which it will have finally resolved all its name conflicts. By linearity of expectation and using that $m \geq 2$, this number is at least equal to

$$\sum_{i=0}^{m-1} \frac{N-1}{(n_i-1)^2} = (N-1) + \frac{1}{9}(N-1) + \sum_{i=0}^{m-3} \frac{N-1}{(n_i-1)^2} \geq \frac{10}{9}(N-1).$$

In order to derive an upper bound, we return to the original Poisson trial. Let us assume that the entities mix aggressively, i.e. that $r_k > 0$ and thus $\frac{1}{N-1} \leq r_k \leq p_i$ for all $k \geq 1$. The expected number of trials to reach a first success in the trial is then equal to

$$\sum_{k=1}^{\infty} k \prod_{j=1}^{k-1} (1-r_j)\, r_k \leq p_i \sum_{k=1}^{\infty} k \prod_{j=1}^{k-1} (1-r_j) \leq$$

$$\leq p_i \sum_{k=1}^{\infty} k(1 - \frac{1}{N-1})^{k-1} = p_i(N-1)^2 = (n_i-1)(N-1).$$

By linearity of expectation, the total expected number of encounters in order for c to go from level 0 to level m and have its name fully resolved is then bounded by

$$\sum_{i=0}^{m-1} (n_i-1)(N-1) = \left(\sum_{i=0}^{m-1} \frac{1}{2^i} n - m \right)(N-1) \leq (2n - \log n)(N-1)$$

which was to be shown. $\square$

If all entities start with initial names that have at most $n = \mathcal{O}(1)$ conflicts, the given argument shows that under reasonable assumptions *the conflicts are all resolved in an expected number of* $\Theta(N)$ *rounds of encounters*. The basic protocol thus satisfies the basic requirement of any name resolution protocol.

Under the same assumption on the mixing behaviour as above, the expected number of encounters also has a limited deviation from its mean. Let X_i be the random variable denoting the number of trials needed by entity c in order to move from level i to level $i+1$ according to the given model.

Proposition 5. *Using protocol A and assuming that the entities mix aggressively, we have for every $t > 0$*

$$Prob(|X_i - E(X_i)| \geq t\sqrt{n_i}\,(N-1)) \leq \frac{2}{t^2}.$$

Proof. Model the random process for entity c in level i as before by a Poisson trial with success probabilities $r_1, r_2, \cdots$. Assuming that the entities mix aggressively means that $r_k > 0$ and thus $\frac{1}{N-1} \leq r_k \leq p_i$ for all $k \geq 1$. $E(X_i)$ was estimated in the proof of Proposition 4. The variance of X_i can be estimated as follows:

$$Var(X_i) = E(X_i^2) - E(X_i)^2 \leq \sum_{k=1}^{\infty} k^2 \prod_{j=1}^{k-1} (1 - r_j) r_k \leq p_i \sum_{k=1}^{\infty} k^2 (1 - \frac{1}{N-1})^{k-1} =$$

$$= p_i (2 - \frac{1}{N-1})(N-1)^3 = (2 - \frac{1}{N-1}) n_i (N-1)^2 \leq 2n_i (N-1)^2,$$

where we use that $\sum_{k=1}^{\infty} k^2 x^{k-1} = \frac{1+x}{(1-x)^3}$. The estimate for $Prob(|X_i - E(X_i)| \geq t\sqrt{n_i}\,(N-1))$ now follows from Chebyshev's Inequality. $\qquad \square$

If the set of entities in the network does not stabilize but continues to grow, Protocol A works properly and all entities eventually become uniquely named if they mix sufficiently well in the pool of entities.

4   Name Length-Optimal Resolution

Protocol A did not make optimal use of the available name space and could leave up to 50% of the available names unused. This does not have a great effect on the maximum name length, but it can be avoided. The key is not to destroy the entity names in the encounter rule but keep all existing names in use.

One approach is to split rule '$h\ h \to h0\ h1$' into two rules '$h\ h \to h\ h0$' and '$h\ h \to h\ h1$', and to let two entities of equal name h apply one of these rules *at random* when they encounter. One can show that this leads to names of *expected* length at most $\mathcal{O}(H + \log n)$. To achieve it as a worst case and obtain balanced name lengths, we must eliminate the randomness. Introduce a companion name $h^\dagger$ with every name h and change Protocol A as follows.

Protocol B
1. *(initialize)* if entity c enters, then it generates an initial name $h = h_c$.
2. *(encounter)* if two entities of name h or $h^\dagger$ meet, then the name conflict is resolved according to the following rules:
    $h\ \ h\ \ \to h^\dagger\ h0$
    $h\ \ h^\dagger \to h\ \ h1$
    $h^\dagger\ h^\dagger \to h^\dagger\ h1$
    ($h^\dagger\ h$ is treated as $h\ h^\dagger$).

In all other encounters, names $h^\dagger$ are treated as names h. (The name $h^\dagger$ can be implemented using a single indicator bit.) Rule 2 again requires that arising symmetries are broken by coin-tossing, using the random generators that all entities possess.

Names now carry up to one bit of extra semantics: names h stand for an equal number of entities that were renamed to $h0$ and to $h1$, and names $h\dagger$ stand for an equal number of entities that were renamed to $h0$ and to $h1$ plus one more entity that was renamed to $h0$. Assume that the number of entities in the network stabilizes. We first show that Protocol B converges.

Proposition 6. *On the assumption that entities mix well, Protocol B eventually leads to unique names for all entities.*

Proof. Objects whose initial names differ, will have different names forever. We thus consider an arbitrary initial name h and show that the name conflicts between all entities with initial name h are resolved properly in the limit. As the protocol leads to entities with names $h0$ and $h1$ (the latter only if there are more than 2 entities with name h), the result then follows by induction. Define the following counters for the entities that enter the network with name h, where we assume their total number is eventually n:

$a =$ the number of entities with name h,
$b =$ the number of entities with name $h^\dagger$,
$c =$ the number of entities with name $h0$,
$d =$ the number of entities with name $h1$.

Protocol B can be seen to maintain the following invariants:

(I1) $a + b + c + d = n$,
(I2) $c = b + d$,
(I3) $a + b$ decreases by 1 in each encounter of two entities named h or $h\dagger$.

The result now follows from invariant I3. With probability tending to 1 as time goes to infinity, all entities with name h meet and we obtain that $a + b = 1$ and thus either $a = 1$ and $b = 0$ or vice versa. Also $c + d = n - 1$ and, whatever c and d are, they are $< n$. Thus the protocol converges by induction. □

Proposition 7. *Suppose the number of entities with the same initial name h has grown to some (unknown) number n. Then the unique names that will eventually result for these entities using Protocol B will all have length $\leq |h| + \lfloor \log n \rfloor$.*

Proof. Observe the following additional invariant for the protocol. Let s count the number of steps in the process of resolving a name conflict involving h or $h^\dagger$:

(I4) $d = a + c - n + s$.

Note that the resolution leads to a single name h in $s = n - 1$ name changes: the result will be a name h without a † if n is odd and a name $h^\dagger$ with a † if n is even. From the invariant it follows that at this point the following occurs:

− if n is *odd*, then $a = 1, b = 0, s = n - 1$ and thus $d = c = \lfloor \frac{n}{2} \rfloor$.
− if n is *even*, then $a = 0, b = 1, s = n - 1$ and thus $d = c - 1$ and $c = \lfloor \frac{n}{2} \rfloor$.

Proceeding recursively we obtain a name tree T_n which has an entity named h or $h^\dagger$ in its root, $T_{\lceil \frac{n-1}{2} \rceil}$ as its left subtree, and $T_{\lfloor \frac{n-1}{2} \rfloor}$ as its right subtree, with the subtrees filled recursively. Write $n = (2^m - 1) + l$ for some $0 \leq l < 2^m - 1$. Then T_n is a binary tree with its first m levels completely filled and the $(m+1)$-st level filled with l nodes. The bound on the name-lengths implied by using Protocol B follows, as $\lfloor \log n \rfloor$ is the lowest level of T_n. □

Proposition 8. *Name resolution using Protocol B leads to names with extensions of minimum possible length.*

Proof. This follows because T_n is a minimum-depth binary tree with n nodes. Names of length $|h| + \lfloor \log n \rfloor$ (in the bottom level) are only used insofar as names in this level are needed. $\qquad\qquad\square$

4.1   Joining, Leaving, and Migrating Entities

Joining a network is easy. A joining entity generates a name immediately and it can communicate right away with the entities in the neighbourhood, even if name conflicts are to be expected. This is similar to the protocols in [20] and [13] where a joining entity must check immediately whether its randomly chosen address is not used by another entity.

The advantage of Protocol B is the use of name extensions of minimum possible length, its scalability and its flexibility under the dynamic scenario. Entities can *join* at any time and name conflicts are automatically resolved in due course, in a reasonable number of steps. Entities that *leave* or *fail* do not obstruct the protocol either.

Clearly entities that leave take their name with them and thus make 'holes' in the name space. These holes are automatically filled up if the corresponding names are generated again in a name resolution step. If they are not filled up, the effect of leading to longer names is limited due to the smoothing $\log n$ term. Thus, an explicit 'name reclaiming protocol' is not really necessary.

Migrating entities are easily handled as well. Assume that an entity migrates from one subnetwork to another. Suppose that protocol B is used in both subnetworks. Obviously, the appearance of a new entity with a given name is no problem. There is no mechanism by which encountering entities can sense that one of them is foreign, and the protocol just works. The minimality of names in the networks can be disturbed, though.

Only when many entities join a network at the same time, a proliferation of conflict resolutions can occur. This seems to happen in any decentralized, leader-free protocol (cf. [16]). However, thanks to the lazy technique, there is no message flooding when assigning names or resolving duplicates, in contrast to protocols that are geared to detect all possible naming conflicts beforehand (cf. [12]). The absence of leaders in our protocol has a further advantage in making it more robust against the failure or temporary absence of nodes. Failing nodes are accommodated in the same way as nodes that are leaving. Neighbouring entities will eventually detect that the failed or migrated entity is no longer responding and cease to communicate with it.

4.2   Network Partitioning and Merging

Suppose two subnetworks, of sizes n_1 and n_2 respectively, merge. Assume that both subnetworks have been using Protocol B. As the entities of the two subnetworks mix, the protocol simply continues to resolve the name conflicts without change. The protocol works as if the entities belonged to the same subnetwork but have not met until now.

Assume that names of maximal length have been used in each subnetwork, i.e. of length $H + \lfloor \log n_1 \rfloor$ and $H + \lfloor \log n_2 \rfloor$, respectively. Now observe that, since $\max\{\lfloor \log n_1 \rfloor, \lfloor \log n_2 \rfloor\} \leq \lfloor \log(n_1 + n_2) \rfloor$, the names in the subnetwork are not too long at the moment of the merge and Protocol B will simply resolve names with a minimal extension again. Clearly it does not matter how many subnetworks merge.

Proposition 9. *If Protocol B was used from the very beginning in the given subnetworks, then it continues to yield name extensions of minimum possible length after the subnetworks merge.*

If the entities in an ad hoc network get partitioned, the entities can keep their names and protocol B can continue to operate without intervention in each part. However, it is clear that partitioning may lead to holes again in the set of names in a subnetwork. On the positive side, when entities return they can use their original names as if nothing happened, i.e. as if in the meantime they have not encountered any entity.

5   Conclusion

The given name resolution methods can be incorporated into any automatic configuration protocol, given a local naming algorithm that is used at the creation of any entity. The techniques work in any dynamic scenario.

Name resolution protocols always seem prepared for the worst case, in which every entity will communicate with every other entity. However, for local message routing in ad hoc networks, short names that are locally unique are sufficient. This is where *lazy duplicate detection* comes in. Our basic protocols offer a smooth transition from the initial state when hardly any entity communicates, to the intermediate but very probable state when groups of communicating entities have more or less stabilized and changes occur only sporadically.

The protocols show that lazy autoconfiguration in dynamic, ad hoc networks of communicating entities in motion is entirely feasible. Starting from a basic lazy version which resolves name conflicts only when they arise in an encounter, an optimization of this protocol lead to a version which uses name extensions of minimum possible length. The protocol scheme easily scales and is resilient to the joining, leaving (including failure), and migration of entities. Last but not least, the protocol is completely decentralized, making use of no leader nodes and no global information.

References

1. Beauquier, J., Gastin, P., Villain, V.: A linear fault-tolerant naming algorithm. In: van Leeuwen, J., Santoro, N. (eds.) WDAG 1990. LNCS, vol. 486, pp. 57–70. Springer, Heidelberg (1991)

2. Bernardos, C., Calderon, M.: Survey of IP address autoconfiguration mechanisms for MANETs, internet draft, http://bgp.potaroo.net/ietf/idref/draft-bernardos-manet-autoconf-survey/#ref-1

3. Fan, Z.: IPv6 Stateless Address Autoconfiguration in Ad Hoc Networks. In: Conti, M., Giordano, S., Gregori, E., Olariu, S. (eds.) PWC 2003. LNCS, vol. 2775, pp. 665–678. Springer, Heidelberg (2003)

4. Fan, Z., Subramani, S.: An address autoconfiguration protocol for IPv6 hosts in a mobile ad hoc network. Computer Comm. 28(4), 339–350 (2005)

5. Feller, W.: An introduction to probability theory and its applications, 3rd edn., vol. 1. J. Wiley & Sons, New York (1968)

6. Fraigniaud, P., Pelc, A., Peleg, D., Pérennes, S.: Assigning labels in unknown anonymous networks. Distrib. Computing 14, 163–183 (2001)

7. Goscinski, A.: Distributed operating systems: The logical design. Addison-Wesley Publ. Comp., Sydney (1991)

8. Guttman, E.: Autoconfiguration for IP networking: enabling local communication. IEEE Internet Computing, 81–86 (May-June 2001)

9. Indrasinghe, S., Pereira, R., Haggerty, J.: Conflict free address allocation mechanism for mobile ad hoc networks. In: 21st Int. IEEE Conference on Advanced Information Networking and Applications (AINA 2007), Workshops Proceedings, pp. 852–857. IEEE Computer Society, Los Alamitos (2007)

10. Li, L., Cai, Y., Xu, X.: Cluster-based autoconfiguration for mobile ad hoc networks. Wireless Personal Communications 49(4), 561–573 (2009)

11. Mohsin, M., Prakash, R.: IP address assignment in a mobile ad hoc network. In: Proc. 2nd IEEE Military Comm. Conf., MILCOM 2002, pp. 856–861 (2002)

12. Nesargi, S., Prakash, R.: MANETconf: Configuration of hosts in a mobile ad hoc network. In: Proc. 21st Joint IEEE Conf., INFOCOM 2002, IEEE, Los Alamitos (2002)

13. Perkins, C.E., Malinen, J.T., Wakikawa, R., Belding-Royer, E.M., Sun, Y.: IP address autoconfiguration for ad hoc networks, IETF Internet draft (November 2001)

14. Steenstrup, M.E.: Neighbor discovery among mobile nodes equipped with smart antennas. In: 3rd Scandinavian Workshop on Wireless Ad-hoc Networks (ADHOC 2003), Proceedings (2003), http://www.wireless.kth.se/adhoc03

15. Sun, Y., Belding-Royer, E.M.: Dynamic address configuration in mobile ad hoc networks, UCSB Tech. Rep. 2003-11, Dept. of Computer Science, University of California at Santa Barbara (June 2003)

16. Sun, Y., Belding-Royer, E.M.: A study of dynamic addressing techniques in mobile ad hoc networks. Wireless Communications and Mobile Computing 4, 315–329 (2004)

17. Thomson, S., Narten, T.: IPv6 stateless address autoconfiguration, RFC 2462, Network Working Group (1998), http://www.faqs.org/rfcs/

18. Thoppian, M.R., Prakash, R.: A distributed protocol for dynamic address assignment in mobile ad hoc networks. IEEE Trans. Mobile Computing 5, 4–19 (2006)

19. Toner, S., O'Mahony, D.: Self-Organising Node Address Management in Ad Hoc Networks. In: Conti, M., Giordano, S., Gregori, E., Olariu, S. (eds.) PWC 2003. LNCS, vol. 2775, pp. 476–483. Springer, Heidelberg (2003)

20. Vaidya, N.H.: Weak duplicate address detection in mobile ad hoc networks. In: Third ACM International Symposium on Mobile Ad Hoc Networking and Computing (MobiHoc 2002), pp. 206–216. ACM Press, New York (2002)

21. van Leeuwen, J., Wiedermann, J.: Lazy autoconfiguration in mobile ad hoc networks and dynamic sets of mobile agents, Technical Report UU-CS-2006-018, Department of Information and Computing Sciences, Utrecht University (2006)
22. Ye, F., Peng, R.: A survey of addressing algorithms for wireless sensor networks. In: 5th Int. Conference on Wireless communications, networking and mobile computing, pp. 3605–3611. IEEE, Los Alamitos (2009)
23. Zeroconf Working Group: Internet Engineering Task Force, IETF (1999), `http://www.zeroconf.org`
24. Zhou, H., Ni, L.M., Mutka, M.W.: Prophet address allocation for large scale MANETs. Ad Hoc Networks 1, 423–434 (2003)

Maintaining the Personal Style and Flair of Handwriting in Presentation Recordings

Khaireel A. Mohamed and Thomas Ottmann

Institut für Informatik, Albert-Ludwigs-Universität Freiburg,
D-79110 Freiburg, Germany
{khaireel,ottmann}@informatik.uni-freiburg.de

Abstract. We present a new technique for approximating handwritten traces sampled from a digital graphics tablet, via a digital pen, during a computer presentation. Our goal is not only to maintain the personal style and flair of the encoded handwriting, but also to provide an efficient and practical approximation of the handwritten traces that does not deteriorate when resized at arbitrary scales. We adopt known polyline simplification algorithms and utilize second-order rational Bézier curves in our "active" methodologies. The proposed active smoothing algorithm solves its task while data is still being received.

1   Introduction

In systematic sciences like Mathematics, Physics, Informatics, Engineering disciplines, and others, ex-cathedra lectures held by an expert in the field still comprise an essential part of any higher educational program. The lecturer and students regularly meet in a lecture theatre and the lecturer may use the standard equipment like the blackboard and chalk to communicate his lesson. Or, he may prepare (perhaps PPT or PDF) slides beforehand, which he then uses to present, explain, and annotate using a computer and a large screen projector. Already some 40 years ago, pioneers like Hermann Maurer tried to decouple the time and space constraints inherently involved in this teaching method by video-taping lectures and replaying them on demand. We will not, however, discuss the well-known didactical problems associated with this method of teaching. Instead we will concentrate on the technical aspects involving the recording and replaying of *live* lectures, which we think are essential for satisfying students and lecturers alike. Nowadays there are a number of available tools that support the seamless production and consumption of lecture recordings. Thus, it is by no means a coincidence that many departments at institutes of higher learning routinely incorporate the so called "e-lecture services" as part of their programs to record elaborate and content-rich presentations and then afterwards make them available online. This in turn has led to the establishment of large repositories which are used extensively by on-site as well as remote students [7,10].

We assume that the recording of a live lecture is done in such a way that some or all data streams generated during the presentation are digitally recorded.

C.S. Calude, G. Rozenberg, A. Salomaa (Eds.): Maurer Festschrift, LNCS 6570, pp. 228–244, 2011.
© Springer-Verlag Berlin Heidelberg 2011

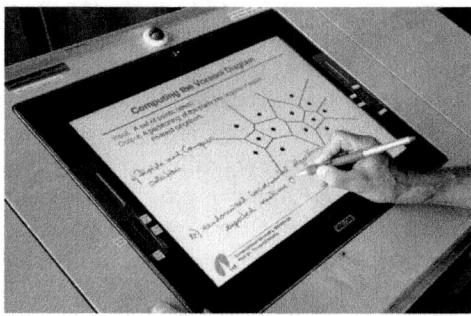

Fig. 1. A lectern with a Wacom Cintiq Interactive Pen Display tablet

These data streams comprise the presented slides, the handwritten annotations or the text (when using a digital whiteboard, or a graphics tablet with a digital pen), the audio and video streams of the lecturer and of the audience alike. The streams also include any further related material like animations or simulations running on the computer or web pages loaded into the presentation device. At the Faculty of Engineering of the University of Freiburg, each lecture theatre is equipped with a special lectern installed with a Wacom Cintiq Interactive Pen Display (tablet) which the lecturer uses for presentations and annotations, cf. Fig. 1. The lecturer can bring either his own laptop or load the slides for his lecture to the local computer of the lectern. Both the whiteboard action stream and the audio stream of the lecturer's voice are then recorded using a tool running on his own laptop or on the computer in the lectern. Sometimes the video stream of the lecturer is also captured by a built-in CCD camera of the presentation computer or by an external digital camera. At the end of the lecture the recorded data streams are automatically bundled, transformed into various replay formats, enriched with metadata (like lecture series, lecturer's name, date, length of recording, keywords, etc.), and included into the electures portal of the department. In this way a comprehensive coverage of the lectures comprising the educational program of the Faculty of Engineering in Freiburg has been established [6].

Well aware of the risk of oversimplification and not taking into account that there are hybrid forms, we distinguish three major categories of presentation recording systems currently in use for producing electures.

1.1 Screen Grabbing Systems

The most prominent example for this category is the screen video capture program Camtasia Studio [14]. The user can define an area of the screen or a window that is to be captured by taking some 25 digital copies per second of the screen pane and transforming this picture stream into a video which can be combined with the audio stream of the lecturer and the stream of a video cam. Camtasia uses a special codec tailored to screen capture videos which is more efficient and produces more compact video streams than the ones produced by video cams taking real world videos. The advantage of using a screen grabbing system is that everything shown on the screen is captured and standard video output formats can be produced which can be replayed by most computers even if the screen grabbing software is not installed. However, the object-based source of the presentation is destroyed by the recording. Thus, structuring and editing of and (text) retrieval in the recorded stream is difficult, if not impossible. Screen grabbing also implies that, sometimes, unwanted messages appearing on the screen as well as commands for navigating through the presentation and other data detracting from the content of the presentation are also recorded. Moreover, resizing the video to adapt it to either larger or smaller displays may deteriorate its quality considerably.

1.2   VCR Recording

The core idea behind this recording technology is to tab and record the data sent from the presentation computer and to replay these data on demand. A number of different tools have been developed following this general idea over the years. Among the early ones is the MBone VCR - Video Conference Recording tool developed at the University of Mannheim [4]. The MBone VCR allows to record and play back teleconferences held over the Multicast Backbone (MBone) on the Internet by capturing and recording all Mbone data packets (audio, video, and whiteboard actions) generated during the presentation. The MBone VCR does not need to know which particular application a data stream originates from or what the exact content of the data stream is; it suffices that the data stream conforms to one of the supported protocols. A similar idea is behind the Tele-TASK kit developed at the HPI in Potsdam [2]. It basically consists of a box jammed between the presentation computer and the data projector with further input channels for the presenters audio and video. This allows for recording, storing, and transforming the combined data, such that they can be replayed or streamed over the internet on demand. The advantage is that the recording is done completely in the background such that the presenter (and his computer) is not affected in any way. He may not even notice that his presentation is recorded at all! On the other hand, this mode of recording suffers from similar deficiencies as the screen grabbing method. The symbolic representation of the source data is lost. Though many of the desirable features may be reconstructed from the captured data, the problems of fading out unwanted (system and control) information appearing on the screen as well as deteriorating its quality when resizing the replay screen remain.

1.3   Object-Based Recording

Here, all data streams, in particular the whiteboard action stream, are recorded separately in the best possible quality without destroying their symbolic representation. Eventually, this (visual) stream is merged with its base source, like the PowerPoint or PDF file, in the final output. So far, the only example of this object-based recording method that is commercially available today is Lecturnity [5]. For replay, the recorded data streams are synchronized and rendered on demand. The rendering (of the whiteboard action stream) is adapted to the size of the replay screen. Object-based recording has a lot of further advantages. Editing and automatically structuring of the recording as well as full text retrieval in the recorded data stream is possible. Recording unwanted information popping up on the screen can easily be avoided. Of course, replay requires installing special replay software. However, the data stream can also be transformed to common video and streaming formats and post processed such that it can be optimally adapted even to unusual displays like handheld computers or mobile phones and be replayed using standard tools.

A disadvantage not solved so far is the fact that the handwritten annotations of the lecturer, produced during the presentation on the interactive graphic display using the digital pen, are currently stored as a series of simplified time-stamped pixels. This has the undesired effect that those recorded/replayed annotations generally do not reflect the personal style of writing of its author. They appear spidery and deteriorate when resized. On the other hand, an advantage of the object-based recording technique is that it is easy to record the (time stamped) pixel trace of the pen separately from the other data streams. Note that the problem of extracting handwritten annotations made on a tablet PC or a graphics tablet used during the live presentation is more difficult, if not infeasible, for the two modes of recording discussed in the previous sections. The major part of this paper is devoted to bring forth a possible solution to overcome the problem of improving the quality of handwriting both during presentation as well as during replay.

2 Roadmap: From Discrete Traces to Smoothed Curves

The visible trails left behind by the handmade expressions of markings, strokes, and lines created on the interactive display using a digital pen (a stylus) created by the presenter during a live lecture should look smooth on the presentation screen and should be stored compactly in such a way that they can be synchronized with the other data streams and rendered without deterioration at any resolution/size during replay. In order to allow for greater flexibility and applicability we shall assume that a digital trail, or *Trace*, produced by the stylus is made up of a series of time-stamped points with respect to its position on the 2D screen. Other parameters such as tilt, pressure, pen-brush, and the likes delivered as outputs by some digital tablets shall not be taken into account. The Traces should be displayed, stored, and replayed in such a way that they look "legibly desirable" and that they faithfully represent the personal style and flair contained in the original handwriting.

Definition 1. [Trace] *A Trace $T_a = \langle p_{a_1}, p_{a_2}, \ldots, p_{a_n} \rangle$ is a collection of n time-ordered points, where two adjacent points $p_{a_i}, p_{a_{i+1}} \in T_a$ are joined by a single Edge $E_{a_i} = \overline{p_{a_i} p_{a_{i+1}}}$, for $1 \leq i \leq n - 1$. The unique time-stamp of the starting point at p_{a_1} identifies T_a.*

In other words, a Trace here refers to a single raw entity, sampled from a transducer device, starting at a pen-down event and ending with a pen-up event. These two pen-events coincide with p_{a_1} and p_{a_n}, respectively. If convenient, we suppress the time stamps and simply refer to the ordered sequence of x- and y-coordinates in the Trace. What concerns us the most is to discover how we can properly represent Traces by continuous, smooth curves. The solution must

- be efficient in runtime,
- be within an acceptable error bound,
- 'smooth' out the uneven pixelated lines and any noise of the input data,
- maintain precise resolution in deep zoom levels, and above all,
- preserve the extraordinary features of the raw Trace that are the defining style and flair contained in the original handwriting.

Forcing a single algebraic polynomial curve of order n to pass through all the n points of the given Trace is certainly not a choice. If n is large, then this may lead to unpredictable fluctuations of the polynomial curve approximating the given Trace. Even breaking down the Trace into arbitrary smaller chunks is not a feasible solution. For it is not clear where to break the Trace and how to glue the piecewise approximations back together. We will instead approximate the Traces by algebraic curves of low order, like second or third order spline curves, Bezier curves, or ellipses which can be represented by a few parameters only. For that purpose we have first to identify the *crucial* points of a given Trace that are characteristic for the style and flair of any handwriting. We claim that it is sufficient just to maintain sharp-edge vertices, inflection points, and a few tangential points in a given Trace in order to have it symbolically represented. That is, we throw away all the other points from the original Trace and approximate the set of remaining points by second-order curves glued together appropriately. Note, however, that this idea is subject to a number of inherent difficulties.

2.1   Analogues of Derivatives and Curvature for Traces

First, because Traces are just sequences of discrete points, notions like derivative, curvature, inflection points, etc. are not well-defined. Secondly, how can we show that second order-curves are sufficient to approximate and symbolically represent Traces produced by a digital pen?

To solve both problems, we follow two plausible heuristics. First, we approximate the first and second derivatives defined for algebraic curves by discrete measurements taken from the input data only. And second, we give a "visual" proof of our approach – the reader may convince himself that our approach of identifying crucial points in the given Trace, then simplifying the Trace and approximating the simplified Trace by a quadratic curve within certain error bounds leads to an acceptable result.

Let us assume that the set of n points in a given Trace T is in the form $p_i = (x_i, y_i) = (x_i, f(x_i))$, for $1 \le i \le n$, in which we take y_i to be expressed as a function of $f(x_i)$. Then in analogy to the standard definition of the first derivative for differentiable functions, we define the first derivative at the point p_i as dp_i.

$$dp_i = f'(x_i) \approx \frac{f(x_{i+1}) - f(x_{i-1})}{h_{i+1} + h_i} \text{ , where } h_i = x_i - x_{i-1} \tag{1}$$

$$= \frac{y_{i+1} - y_{i-1}}{x_{i+1} - x_{i-1}} \quad \text{, for } 1 \leq i \leq n. \tag{2}$$

Defining the derivatives at the endpoints p_1 and p_n of T can also be done in analogy to differentiable functions defined over a closed interval.

By measuring the rate of change of the first derivative through applying the same approximation method, we even out the estimates in the resultant measures of the second derivative. Recall the second-order (symmetrical) differential approximation of a point $p \equiv (x, f(x))$,

$$f''(x) \approx \frac{f'(x+h) - f'(x-h)}{2h}. \tag{3}$$

The above definition presupposes that the $f(x)$ representation of T is twice differentiable. This condition does not, of course, hold for a Trace of discrete points sampled from the input device. However, using five consecutive neighbouring points, we can similarly approximate the second derivative of the point p_i and denote it simply as $d^2 p_i$.

$$d^2 p_i = f''(x_i) \qquad \approx \frac{f'(x_{i+1}) - f'(x_{i-1})}{h_{i+1} + h_i} \tag{4}$$

$$= \frac{1}{x_{i+1} - x_{i-1}} \left(\frac{y_{i+2} - y_i}{x_{i+2} - x_i} - \frac{y_i - y_{i-2}}{x_i - x_{i-2}} \right), \text{ for } 2 < i < n - 1. \tag{5}$$

We can now use these values computed for every point on the Trace in order to define an analogue of the curvature for Trace points. In the general sense, *curvature* refers to the change of direction per unit length. The curvature of a straight line is zero everywhere. A circle with radius r has constant curvature $1/r$ on all of its points. In general, for arbitrary plain curves the curvature changes from point to point. The computation of the curvature for plain curves depends on the way in which the curve is given. Let us assume that the curve is given as the graph of a function f. Then the curvature in a point $p_x = (x, f(x))$ can be computed as follows:

$$k(p_x) = \frac{f''(x)}{(1 + (f'(x))^2)^{3/2}} \tag{6}$$

The expression above is applicable to proper continuous curves which are given in explicit form and which are at least twice differentiable, see, e.g., p. 230 in [13]. In our approach with the indeterministic points in the trace T, we approximate the curvature in each point of T by the approximations of the first and second derivatives and add an additional step to further even out the curvature reading at p_i with its neighbour p_{i-1}:

$$\widehat{k_i} = \frac{1}{2}(k_i + k_{i-1}). \tag{7}$$

By monitoring the curvature values computed at every point p_i, we can determine the characteristics of those points with respect to the underlying curve of the Trace T. The curvature at a point tells us whether the curve is locally convex, a circular arc, or a straight line.

2.2 Classification of Points in a Trace

Definition 2. [Inflection point] *An inflection point on a well-defined curve $f(x)$ is a point $p_i \equiv (x_i, f(x_i)) \in f(x)$ at which the curvature $k(p_i)$ changes sign from $k(p_{i-1})$.*

Definition 3. [Sharp-edge vertex] *A sharp-edged vertex is detected at $p_i \in T$ when the absolute difference between two consecutive curvature measurements $k(p_{i-1})$ and $k(p_i)$ is unusually high, with respect to the readings of the average curvature differences of all other neighbouring points in T.*

Our definitions on derivatives and curvature for Traces in Section 2.1 allow us to apply Definition 2 directly to each point in a Trace. However, if we encounter a huge jump in values (known as a "spike") when tracking from $k(p_{i-1})$ to $k(p_i)$, then the curve we are travelling on has just made an abrupt sharp turn. That is, we have just come across a sharp-edge vertex at the point p_i, as per indicated in Definition 3.

3   Polyline Simplification

The main goal of the polyline simplification problem is to reduce the line data substantially, while still preserving its appearance with respect to the original. In other words, we keep only the *critical* points in the input polygonal path that are vital to the overall shape of the polyline. The rest of the points are removed (or not) depending on the desired level of simplification. Note that the critical points identified by a polyline simplification algorithm may be different from the *crucial* points which are considered as being characteristic for handwritten Traces. Classical polyline simplification is the selective removal of 'unwanted' points, based on a predefined tolerance value, that is made to serve two main objectives, to reduce data volume, and to maintain the quality of polylines when scale is reduced.

Quantifying the goodness of simplified polylines is not a straight-forward preconception, if the polylines have characteristics of handwritten Traces. A good approximation of a polyline is the simplified polyline where only the important points in the original are kept. This suggests that we are measuring some sort of an error signal. We look to the eliminated points of the original polyline and calculate their euclidean distances with respect to the line-segments in the simplified polyline that replaced those points.

Let $T = \{p_1, \ldots, p_n\}$ be a polyline containing n points. Also, for any eliminated point $p_i \equiv (x_i, y_i) \in T$, let $p'_i \equiv (x'_i, y'_i)$ be a corresponding point on the line-segment $\overline{p_r p_s}$ connecting two *kept* points $p_r, p_s \in T$, where $r < i < s$. Then,

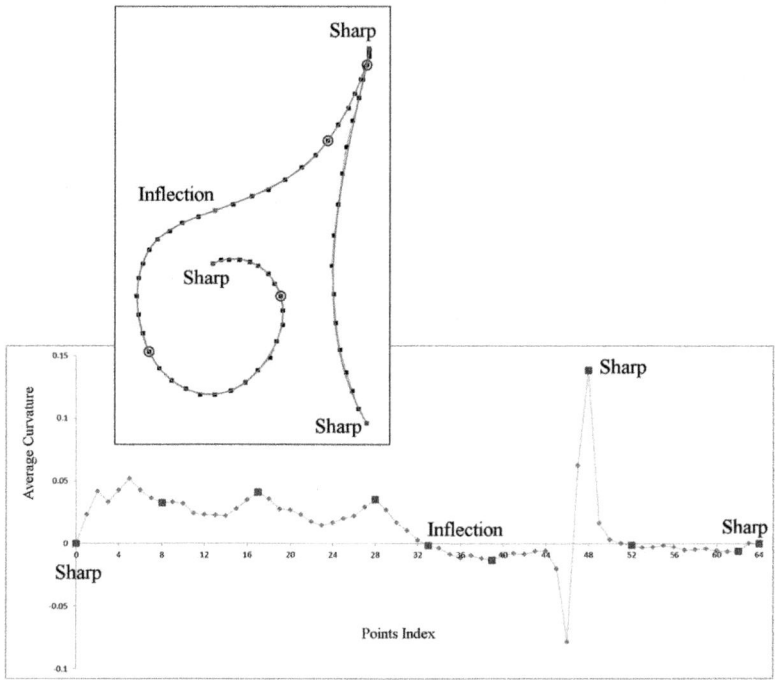

Fig. 2. Classifying discrete points from curvature readings. *Top:* Input Trace T, smoothed. *Bottom:* The Points index, running from 0 to N on the horizontal axis coincides with the point p_0 to p_N on the Trace. For each point p_i, its curvature $k(p_i)$ is plotted on the graph.

the square of the error measure err_T of the simplified polyline, with respect to the original T, is computed as

$$\text{err}_T^2 = \frac{1}{n} \sum_{i=0}^{n} (x_i - x_i')^2 + (y_i - y_i')^2. \tag{8}$$

This way, we obtain an error measurement that is independent of the length of the polyline T, and is analogous to the standard deviation in probability theory. It prevents a simplification from deviating too much from the original line in any point (thus strengthening the choice of critical points), and secondly, it punishes strong deviations in few points more severely than small deviations in many points.

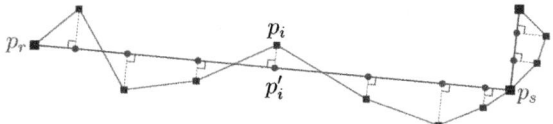

Fig. 3. Measuring error of a simplified polyline

3.1   The Douglas-Peucker (DP) Algorithm

The Douglas-Peucker (DP) algorithm is the most popular among the many classical simplification routines in the literature [1]. It is, however, an *offline* algorithm in the geometric sense. That is, the DP algorithm requires the full knowledge of all the points in a given polyline in order for it to deduce the near-optimal *critical* points' positions. This is as opposed to the *local* routine algorithms that we shall discuss in Reumann-Witkam's [12] and Opheim's [9] algorithms. Using a 'divide-*refine*-and-conquer' approach, the DP algorithm begins by building a very rough approximation of the original line, connecting the endpoints. Let us, in general, term these two endpoints as p_A and p_B. Subsequently, all the intermediate points lying in the trajectory between p_A and p_B are tested until a single point p_i is found and marked as critical, if and only if it satisfies the following two conditions:

1. that p_i is the farthest point away from the line $\overline{p_A p_B}$; and
2. that the orthogonal distance between p_i and $\overline{p_A p_B} > \epsilon$, where ϵ is a predetermined corridor distance.

If such a p_i exists, then the DP algorithm repeats the above step with two divided segments with the new endpoints p_A and p_i, and p_i and p_B. Otherwise, it terminates. The worst-case runtime of the naïve DP algorithm is $O(n^2)$, while on average it takes $O(n \log n)$ time. Hershberger and Snoeyink [3] developed a more sophisticated version of the DP algorithm that reduces the worst-case runtime.

3.2   The Reumann-Witkam (RW) Algorithm

A Local Processing Routine technique, the intuitive Reumann-Witkam (RW) algorithm [12] needs only a single pass to identify all points in a given polyline that it deems critical. Starting at the critical endpoint p_1, the RW algorithm runs by recursively building a 'tolerance' corridor using the input width ϵ.

Let p_i be the latest critical point identified by the RW algorithm. Then the tolerance corridor is built on top of p_i, based on the *trend* of the line at p_i.

Typically, the *trend* at p_i refers to the gradient (or the approximation of the gradient) of the line at p_i. The corridor itself is parallel to this trend and it is pointed in the direction of p_{i+1}. All points after p_i lying inside the corridor are eliminated, until the traversal reaches the first point p_j where it no longer follows the trend and subsequently lies outside the corridor. The point p_j is then identified as the next critical point, and the RW algorithm repeats again from there. This process continues until all n points in the polyline are processed. As evidenced from the example in Fig. 4, there is a special case when the RW algorithm returns an incorrect simplification (when thinking of simplifying handwriting Traces). Here, we see that an obvious critical point at the top of the figure has been left out. This error only happens whenever there exists a *sharp* turning point (or points) within the boundaries of the tolerance corridor. And because those sharp-edge points did not violate the corridor condition stated above, they were eliminated by the RW algorithm and deemed as non-critical.

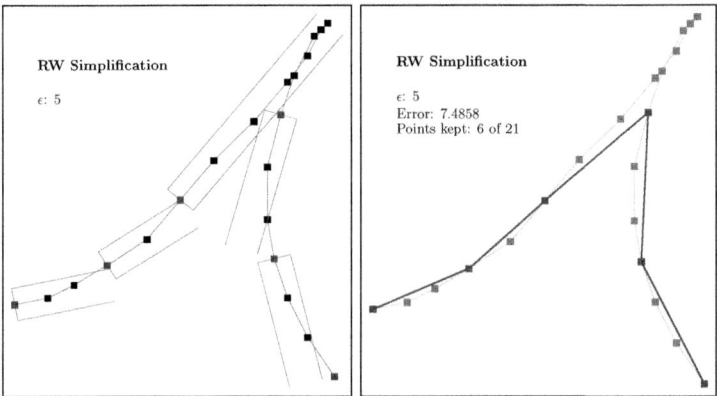

Fig. 4. The Reumann-Witkam (RW) algorithm

3.3   Improving the Solutions of Reumann-Witkam's

The problem of missing all sharp-edge points in the polyline can be avoided by imposing an additional constraint which has been proposed by Opheim. Opheim [9] used exactly the same routine as the RW algorithm, except that his algorithm is constrained by an extra maximum distance check s_{max} [9]. After constructing the tolerance corridor at the latest critical point p_i, all points p_k after p_i are eliminated if and only if the following two conditions hold:

1. The point p_k lies inside the tolerance corridor; and
2. the length of the chord $\overline{p_i p_k} \leq s_{max}$.

A critical point p_j is found if it violates at least one of the two conditions, and the Opheim algorithm repeats again from there. This process continues until all n points in the polyline are processed.

3.4   The RW-DP Algorithm

The combined RW-DP, like the Opheim algorithm, also uses the original RW routine to first *locally* identify the critical points. However, unlike Opheim's approach with the additional s_{max} constraint, we apply the *global* DP subroutine during the traversal on to every segment of the polyline identified between the previous critical point p_i and the newly identified critical point p_j.

In essence, we only need to run once more through all m points in the segment between p_i and p_j, before locating the elusive sharp-edge point, if one does exist. Thus, we maintain the overall runtime of the RW-DP algorithm to stay within $O(n)$ bounds, while improving the quality of simplification if such erroneous situations arise, as seen in the resultant Fig. 5 compared to the original RW simplification in Fig. 4.

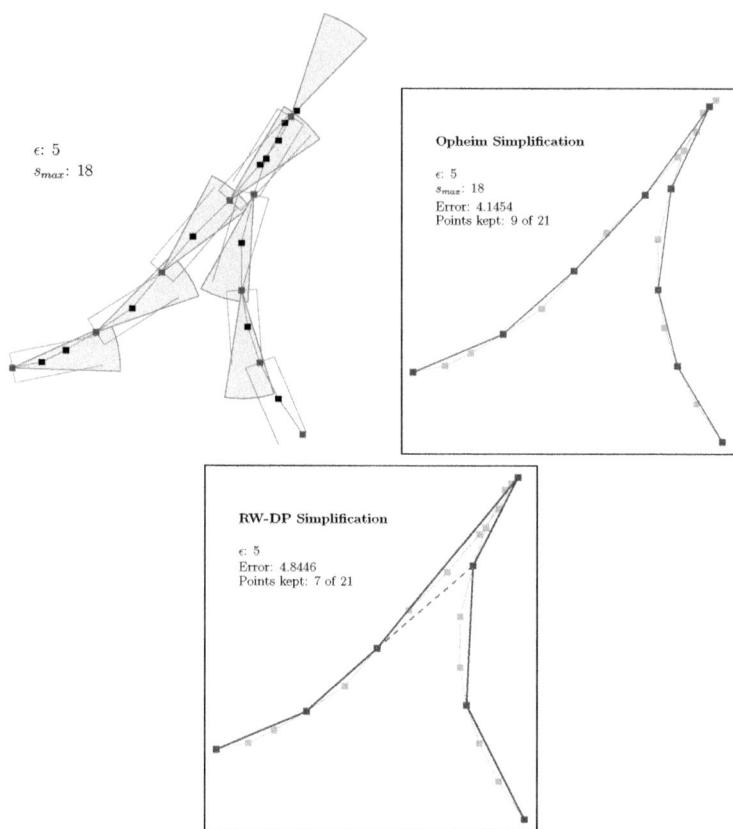

Fig. 5. The Opheim and RW-DP algorithms. From top-left, clockwise: Tolerance corridors (blue rectangles) and additional s_{max} constraints (yellow cones); resultant Opheim simplification; resultant RW-DP simplification.

3.5   The Optimal Polyline Simplification

Let $T = \{p_1, \ldots, p_n\}$ be a polyline containing n points. We may think of T as the handwritten Trace produced by the pen input. Then, from the quality measure we proposed in the beginning of this section, it is possible to compute an optimal simplification of T for a given reduction rate. Suppose we want to have a simplified T keeping only m points, where $m < n$. Then the naïve approach to get the optimal simplification of T is to try out all possible point subsets of size m, determine the error for each such approximation, and then select one that minimizes this error. However, we can do this in a more elegant manner.

The problem of finding an approximation with minimal error exhibits the characteristic of the "optimal substructure", one where an optimal solution comprises the optimal solutions to subproblems.

Lemma 1. *Let $E[i,j,k]$ be the minimal error of a simplification that approximates T between p_i and p_j, using exactly k intermediate points. Then for $k \geq 1$ and $1 < i < j < n$,*

$$E[i,j,k] = \min_{i<l<j-k}\{ \ E[i,l,0] + E[l,j,k-1] \ \}. \tag{9}$$

Proof. Let p_l be the first point after p_i that we decide to keep. Then the total error made by this approximation is the error made between p_i and p_l, plus the error made between p_l and p_j. An optimal approximation must minimize this sum, given that the two subsegments are also optimal. Thus, for all possible choices of p_l, we know the minimal errors $E[i,l,0]$ and $E[l,j,k-1]$, and we can determine the point p_l contributing to the minimal error and compute $E[i,j,k]$ using the equation above. □

Let T' be the optimal simplified version of the original polyline T. If T' is to retain only m points from T, then the optimal approximation of T will have an error of $E[1,n,m-2]$ with T'. A simplification routine always retains the two original endpoints p_1 and p_n, and so we are only left to find $m-2$ intermediate points in T to keep. By Lemma 1, we need to compute $E[1,l,0]$ and $E[l,n,m-3]$ for all p_l between p_1 and p_{n-m-2}. The first of the two terms is a straight-forward computation, since there is only one way to approximate the line between p_1 and p_l using zero intermediate points. The second term, on the other hand, requires recursive computations, where in each recursion, the third parameter of the second term is reduced by one – until it reaches zero, in which case the final term can then be directly computed as above.

Clearly, from the recursion steps, one can see that the general singular terms $E[i,j,0]$ need to be calculated $O(n)$ times each. We can speed up this computation by avoiding to calculate the subproblems more than once using the scheme of Dynamic Programming, where we only need to store calculated values once in a table and look them up if we need them again. That is, we start by calculating $E[i,j,0]$ for all possible values of i and j directly, and store them in the top row of the table. From these, we compute the next row using the equation in Lemma 1; i.e. computing $E[i,j,1]$ for all possible values of i and j. We continue until all k rows of the table are filled. We can then extract from the completed table an approximation that yields the optimal error by tracing back which terms that were summed to construct it.

The space requirement for this dynamic calculation is cubic in the number of points n, because of the size of the table. The runtime is $O(n^4)$, since to compute one table entry, we first have to minimize all entries in the row above. While this is far better than the naïve runtime of $\frac{n!}{m!(n-m)!} = O(n!)$, this algorithm is still unacceptable for regular use. It does, however, become a very useful benchmark for evaluating the quality of non-optimal algorithms.

3.6 Simplified Polylines for Smoothing Routines

Up until this juncture, we have maintained a strict distinction between the *critical* points identified and maintained by a polyline simplification algorithm and

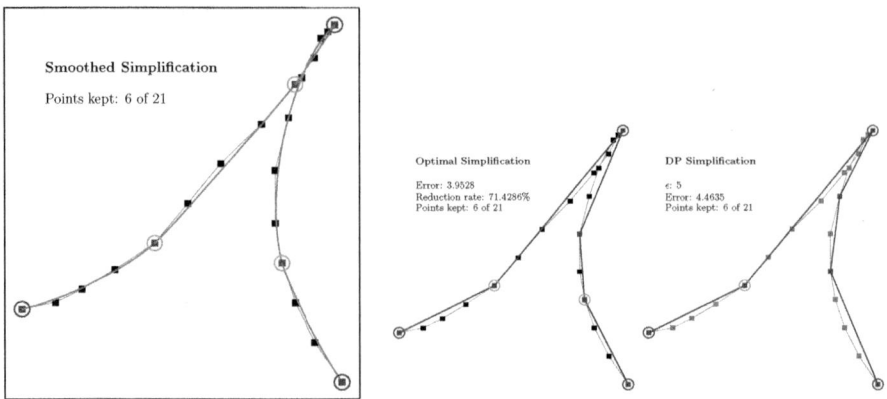

Fig. 6. Smoothed simplification versus polyline simplifications

the *crucial* points characterising the personal style and flair of handwritings. To better realise the significance of this distinction, let us look at the example shown in Fig. 6. The figure depics the result of our smoothing algorithm to be explained below alongside the results of two other polyline simplications that we have discussed. We have purposely chosen the examples where there are exactly six points kept from the original 21 for the purpose of our comparative arguments.

The *crucial* points marked red in the smoothed simplification are the sharp-edge vertices characterized by Definition 3, and they coincide with the *critical* sharp-edge vertices identified by the Optimal and DP algorithms. The other three crucial blue points are either tangent joints or inflection points, two of which match the critical points from the optimal simplification. These crucial points are the necessary proponents that approximate and define the (orange) curve segments accurately. As a direct consequence of this, the smoothed simplification correctly reveals a tiny loop at the top of the original trace, which was an intended preconception of our example – an important feature which is not evident in the two resultant simplified polylines.

4   Active Online Smoothing

Our online method to approximate the incoming Trace delivered by the pen input from the transducer device can now be roughly described as follows. Looking only a few points back, each incoming point is computer for its first and second derivatives, as well as for its curvature. Then based on the curvature measurements, the points are classified into one of the three categories: *normal, inflection,* or *sharp-edge.*

At the same time the combined RW-DP line simplifacion algorithm is used to eliminate the non-crucial normal points. That is, starting at the first point of a Trace which is considered to be critical and, hence, kept for the subsequent smooth approximation we proceed to find the next critical point, and while we are still in the process of sampling points from the transducer device, the simplified Trace is approximated by a parametric curve between these critical points. The next critical point may be the end of the Trace, an inflection point, a sharp-edge vertex, or normal point enduring the polyline simplification. In order to approximate the simplified Trace by segments of quadratic curves glued together in such a way that the resulting curve is continuous and the left and right tangents at the glued points are identical, we have, however, to break the sequence of incoming points even further. We split the simplified Trace T into segments, whose trajectory of internal points contains only a single extremum, so that it is possible to approximate T evenly with a single second-order curve K. For that purpose we consider the last chosen critical point P_A as one point of a proper *contact triangle* and the currently active incoming point P_B as the other. P_A and P_B form the baseline of the contact triangle $\triangle ABC$, and the intersection point P_C between the two tangent lines through the points P_A and P_B forms its third vertex. If the interior of $\triangle ABC$ contains all points between P_A and P_B, then the Trace segment between these two points is convex and has at most one local extremum. The segment can now be approximated by a second-order rational Bézier curve. As far as the smoothing routine goes, we gather as many points as possible, as we traverse from P_A to P_B until we come to the point where the condition that the contact $\triangle ABC$ containing all intermediate points in its interior is violated.

Definition 4. *A second order rational Bézier curve $K(t)$ comprises the three vertices of its contact triangle $\triangle ABC$ and three weights w_0, w_1, and w_2 that correspond to the vertices P_A, P_C, and P_B, respectively. The curve is completely inscribed in $\triangle ABC$ and is defined by its quadratic equation*

$$K(t) = \frac{(1-t)^2 w_0 P_A + 2t(1-t)w_1 P_C + t^2 w_2 P_B}{(1-t)^2 w_0 + 2t(1-t)w_1 + t^2 w_2}. \tag{10}$$

Let $\overline{AB}$ be the baseline of the constraint-triangle $\triangle ABC$. Let M be the midpoint of the baseline $\overline{AB}$. Then we determine the point $p_i = L \in T$ on the trace that lies on $\overline{CM}$. If no such point exists, then we pick the point L that is the intersection of the line-segment $\overline{p_i p_{i-1}}$ and the line $\overline{CM}$. We choose the weights $w_0 = 1$ and $w_2 = 1$ and compute the weight w_1 of the rational quadratic Bézier curve $K(t)$ as follows:

$$w_1 = \frac{\|ML\|}{\|LC\|} \tag{11}$$

In this way we generate an approximated curve $K(t)$ for T. Of course, this estimate may not necessarily be *desirable*, as the only thing that we can guarantee from this exercise is that $K(t)$ will pass through the three points P_A, L, and P_B and the lines $\overline{AC}$ and $\overline{BC}$ are tangents to $K(t)$ in the points P_A and P_B.

Let us now explain what we mean by a *desirable* approximation. Let $K(t)$ as depicted in Fig. 7 be the approximated curve for T obtained from computing the weight w_1 as explained above. Let p and q be the points on the edges $\overline{AC}$ and $\overline{CB}$, respectively, such that the line $\overline{pq}$ is parallel to $\overline{AB}$ and passes through the point

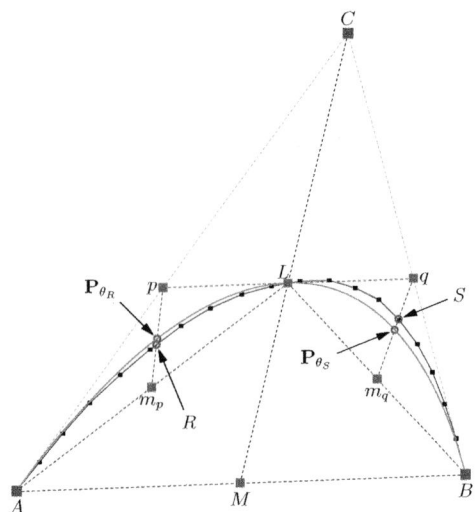

Fig. 7. Measuring error at the partition corridors

L. Let m_p and m_q be the midpoints of $\overline{AL}$ and $\overline{LB}$, respectively. Also, let R be the intersection between $\overline{pm_p}$ and T, and let S be the intersection between $\overline{qm_q}$ and the trace T. Then, for $P_{\Theta_R} = K(0.25)$ and $P_{\Theta_S} = K(0.75)$, the partition error-corridor at P_{Θ_R} and P_{Θ_S} are $\epsilon_R = \|RP_{\Theta_R}\|$ and $\epsilon_S = \|SP_{\Theta_S}\|$, respectively, and that, for a predetermined tolerance corridor value ϵ, the curve $K(t)$ is a *desirable* approximation of T if and only if both the following conditions are met:

$$\epsilon_R \leq \epsilon, \text{ and } \epsilon_S \leq \epsilon. \tag{12}$$

Let us draw a similarity to the two split conditions in the DP algorithm discussed in Section 3.1. If both ϵ_R and ϵ_S are within the bounds of the predetermined tolerance corridor value ϵ, then all other points in T are also within the bounds of ϵ with respect to their corresponding points in $K(t)$. The curve K is then considered a desirable estimate of the Trace segment T. Otherwise the trace segment is split at the identified point L and the two parts are recursively approximated in the same way until the error condition is met.

We do not need to physically instantiate the curve $K(t)$ in order to perform the error measurements. That is, once we have found the point L, we can immediately deduce w_1 based on the constraint-triangle $\triangle ABC$, and obtain our expression for $K(t)$. Identifying the points R and S is a straight-forward geometrical computation on $\triangle ABC$ and T, and that the points P_{Θ_R} and P_{Θ_S} are the results of evaluating the curve's expression by substituting $t = 0.25$ and $t = 0.75$, respectively, into $K(t)$. We can also show that identifying the point L does not require traversing $O(n)$ points in a trace segment T of n points – in fact, we only need $O(1)$ time to accomplish this. In summary, the approximation can be computed very efficiently *while data is still being received* to produce output renditions of high-quality smooth curves that do not deplete at any resolutions, cf. [8] for further details.

Fig. 8. Active-smoothing example output quality

Fig. 9. Active-smoothing example output quality

5   Conclusion

There are many ways of approximating discrete sets of points, i.e. traces obtained from the pen input of a transducer device. We have utilized second order rational Bézier curves in such a way that the approximation can already be computed while input data is still beeing received. Other approaches may use quadratic Bézier curves or elliptic arcs, see [8]. Our choice of second order rational Bézier curves was motivated by the fact that the resulting active smoothing algorithm can be implemented very efficiently. It preserves computational ressources and leaves enough potential for other purposes like recording a presentation, animating an algorithm, or running a simulation while smoothing the Trace. At the end we present a few examples to show the output quality of the active smoothing routine. We illustrate them in Figures 8 and 9.

References

1. Douglas, D.H., Peucker, T.K.: Algorithms for the reduction of the number of points required to represent a digitized line or its caricature. Cartographica: The International Journal for Geographic Information and Geovisualization 10(2), 112–122 (1973)
2. Hasso Plattner Institut, Potsdam, Germany, http://www.tele-task.de/
3. Hershberger, J., Snoeyink, J.: Speeding up the douglas-peucker line simplification algorithm. Tech. rep., University of British Columbia, Vancouver, BC, Canada, Canada (1992)
4. Holfelder, W.: MBone VCR - Video Conference Recording on the MBone. In: Proceedings of ACM Multimedia 1995, pp. 237–238. ACM, New York (1995)
5. IMC AG, Saarbrücken, Germany, http://www.lecturnity.de/de/lecturnity/uebersicht/

6. Institut für Informatik, Technische Fakultät, Universität Freiburg, `http://electures.informatik.uni-freiburg.de/portal/web/guest/home`
7. Lauer, T., Trahasch, S.: Begriffsbesprechung: Vorlesungsaufzeichnung. i-com – Zeitschrift für interaktive und kooperative Medien 4, 61 (2005)
8. Mohamed, K.A.: Concepts and Solutions for Efficient Handling of the Digital Ink, Ph.D. dissertation, Freiburg (2009), `http://www.freidok.uni-freiburg.de/volltexte/7361/`
9. Opheim, H.: Smoothing a digitized curve by data reduction methods. In: Encarnacao, J.L. (ed.) Proceedings of the International Conference and Exhibition, Eurographics 1981, pp. 127–135. North-Holland Publishing Company, Amsterdam (1981)
10. Ottmann, T.: Von Menschen und Computern: Über mehr als 10 Jahre Erfahrungen mit Präsentationsaufzeichnungen an Universitäten. In: von Kortzfleisch, H.O., Bohl, O. (eds.) Wissen, Vernetzung, Virtualisierung, pp. 175–186. Eul Verlag, Köln (2008)
11. Pottmann, H., Wallner, J.: Computational Line Geometry, 1st edn. Springer, Heidelberg (2001)
12. Reumann, K., Witkam, A.P.M.: Optimizing curve segmentation in computer graphics. In: Gunther, A., Levrat, B., Lipps, H. (eds.) Proceedings of the International Computing Symosium, New York, NY, USA, pp. 467–472. Elsevier, Amsterdam (1974)
13. Richter, M.: Grundwissen Mathematik für Ingenieure. Auflage, vol. 2. Vieweg und Teubner, Wiesbaden (2009)
14. TechSmith Corporation, `http://www.techsmith.com/`

TGV-Fusion

Thomas Pock[1], Lukas Zebedin[2], and Horst Bischof[1]

[1] Inst. for Computer Graphics and Vision,
Graz University of Technology
{pock,bischof}@icg.tugraz.at
[2] Microsoft Photogrammetry
lucas.zebedin@microsoft.com

Abstract. Location awareness on the Internet and 3D models of our habitat (as produced by Microsoft (Bing) or Google (Google Earth)) are a major driving force for creating 3D models from image data. A key factor for these models are highly accurate and fully automated stereo matching pipelines producing highly accurate 3D point clouds that are possible due to the fact that we can produce images with high redundancy (i.e., a single point is projected in many images). Especially this high redundancy makes fully automatic processing pipelines possible. Highly overlapping images yield also highly redundant range images. This paper proposes a novel method to fuse these range images. The proposed method is based on the recently introduced total generalized variation method (TGV). The second order variant of this functional is ideally suited for piece-wise affine surfaces and therefore an ideal case for buildings which can be well approximated by piece-wise planar surfaces. In this paper we first present the functional consisting of a robust data term based on the Huber-L^1 norm and the TGV regularization term. We derive a numerical algorithm based on a primal dual formulation that can be efficiently implemented on the GPU. We present experimental results on synthetic data as well as on a city scale data set, where we compare the method to other methods.

1 Introduction

Recovery of realistic models of urban environments from aerial imagery has been an important research topic in computer vision for more than 20 years. Recently, large scale efforts from large enterprises like Microsoft are underway, aiming at building a virtual equivalent of our planet including realistic models of thousands of cities worldwide. The enormous scale of such a project, encompassing tens of thousands of the largest cities worldwide, makes any manual attempt to solve the arising problems prohibitively expensive. The only way to tackle such an undertaking is by a fully automatic processing pipeline. Such a workflow would start with the raw images collected by a digital aerial camera mounted on an aircraft and would automatically produce a virtual, digital representation of the covered area. For a recent overview on producing 3D models and other information from aerial images see [1]. The other papers in this special issue cover other

C.S. Calude, G. Rozenberg, A. Salomaa (Eds.): Maurer Festschrift, LNCS 6570, pp. 245–258, 2011.
© Springer-Verlag Berlin Heidelberg 2011

aspects of producing 3D models of our virtual habitat. Using digital cameras, we can produce highly overlapping and thus redundant images of no additional cost. This high redundancy enables fully automatic methods for high quality *3D* reconstruction (e.g. [2]). An important step towards the *3D* reconstruction is computing the range images. Due to the high redundancy in the input data, also the range images are highly redundant. The robust fusion of several range images to a single high quality range image - also called digital surface model (*DSM*) - is the main topic of this paper.

Basically, the fusion can be done in full *3D* (e.g. [3]) or in $2\frac{1}{2}D$ (e.g. [4]). Our target application is *3D* modeling of buildings from very large aerial images where it is simply not possible (and also not necessary) to have a full *3D* representation of the buildings. Hence, we will consider the $2\frac{1}{2}D$ case in this paper.

The range image fusion approach we are going to present in this paper is based on variational approaches for image regularization [5,6,7]. The basic idea of the variational approach is that the solution of the model is given by the minimizer of an energy-functional. The energy functional usually is composed of two basic terms. A regularization term, which reflects the a-priori assumption about the smoothness properties of the solution and a data term which forces the solution to be similar to the input data. Clearly, different choices of the regularization and data terms will lead to different solutions. Variational models can be further divided into two fundamental classes: Convex and non-convex problems. The obvious advantage of convex problems over non-convex problems is that one has the guarantee to find a global optimum. This means that the quality of the solution of a convex functional solely depends on the accuracy of the variational model. On the other hand, for non-convex problems, the quality of the solution is subject to both the model and the optimization algorithm, since in general only a local minimizer can be computed. We will therefore restrict ourselves to convex models in this paper.

State-of-the-art variational image regularization techniques [6,7] are typically based on a first-order smoothness assumption. While this assumption might be reasonable for general images, it is less useful for regularizing range images. The reason is that first-order smoothness leads to a preference of piecewise constant solutions (*a.k.a.* staircaseing effect), which is not appropriate to regularize range images containing slanted surfaces such as roofs. Total generalized variation (*TGV*) as recently introduced in [8] has some desired properties for regularizing range images. The key property of TGV^K regularization is, that it favors piecewise polynomial signals of order $k-1$ (e.g. TGV^2 favors piecewise affine functions). Therefore, TGV^2 regularization is perfectly suited to regularize range images. The main contributions of this paper are:

- A new convex variational model for robust fusion of range images, which combines TGV^2 regularization with a robust Huber-L^1 data term.
- A novel efficient numerical algorithm based on a new first-order primal-dual algorithm which can be efficiently parallelized on graphics processing units.

– The demonstration of the favorable properties of the proposed method on a large scale city dataset.

The paper is organized as follows. In section 2 we review convex variational methods for image regularization and highlight possible advantages and disadvantages. As most existing methods are formulated to deal with only one observation, we will also consider (straight-forward) generalizations of these models to multiple observations. In section 3 we present the proposed TGV^2 model for range image fusion. For minimization we present an efficient first-order primal-dual algorithm, which will be detailed in section 4. In section 5 we show experimental results using synthetic and real images. In the last section we draw conclusions and show directions for future research.

2   Related Work

In this section we review some basic variational image denosing models. While in their original formulations, the models include a data term which takes only one observation into account, we will already consider the case with multiple observations.

2.1   Quadratic Model

The quadratic model (or Tikhonov model) [5] is one of the earliest - dating back to 1943 - and simplest regularization method used for ill-posed problems. It is defined as the quadratic variational problem

$$\min_{u} \left\{ \alpha \int_{\Omega} |\nabla u|^2 dx + \sum_{l=1}^{K} \int_{\Omega} (u - f_l)^2 dx \right\} , \qquad (1)$$

where $\Omega \subset \mathbb{R}^2$ is the image domain, K is the number of observed range images, $f_l : \Omega \to \mathbb{R}$ denotes a single observation, and $u : \Omega \to \mathbb{R}$ is the sought solution. The free parameter $\alpha \geq 0$ is used to control the amount of smoothing in u. The left term is the regularization term which reflects the smoothness assumption. The right term measures the distance of the solution to the observed data. Note that it is very common for range images that the number of observations may vary over the image domain (e.g. invalid ranges due to occlusions). Since image locations with a larger number of observations imply a higher confidence in the input data, we do not normalize the data term with respect to the number of observations in our models.

   In view of our range image fusion problem, the quadratic model tries to find a smooth solution u which minimizes the squared distance to the single observations f_l. Being quadratic in u, the Tikhonov model poses a simple optimization problem, but it does not perform very well for our purpose. The main reason is that the quadratic regularization term leads to an oversmoothing of edges and the quadratic data term is not robust against strong outliers in the observed data.

2.2   *ROF* Model

L^1 estimation procedures have shown to be an effective tool for many different problems. The first who introduced L^1 estimation methods for image restoration were Rudin, Osher and Fatemi (*ROF*) in their seminal paper on edge preserving image denoising [9]. In its unconstrained form, the *ROF* model is defined as the variational model

$$\min_u \left\{ \alpha \int_\Omega |\nabla u|\, dx + \frac{1}{2} \sum_{l=1}^K \int_\Omega (u - f_l)^2\, dx \right\} . \tag{2}$$

The first term is the so called total variation semi-norm of u. We point out that in this definition, the *TV* norm is only valid for sufficiently smooth function u (e.g. $u \in C^1(\Omega)$). Fortunately, there exists also a duality based formulation of the total variation which enables a valid definition for any integrable function $u \in L^1(\Omega)$.

$$TV^\alpha(u) = \sup \left\{ - \int_\Omega u \operatorname{div} \varphi dx \ : \varphi \in \mathcal{C}_c^1(\Omega, \mathbb{R}^2), \|\varphi\|_\infty \le \alpha \right\} , \tag{3}$$

where $\mathcal{C}_c^1(\Omega, \mathbb{R}^2)$ is the space of continuously differentiable functions with compact support in Ω. Note that this formulation also allows to overcome the non-differantiability of the *TV* norm. Besides its convexity, the main advantage of the *ROF* model of the quadratic model is, that it allows for sharp discontinuities in the solution. This is an important feature, since we assume to have sharp depth discontinuities in our range images. However, due to the quadratic data term the *ROF* model is still very sensitive to strong outliers (e.g. caused by occlusion) in the observed range images.

2.3   *TV-L¹* Model

The TV-L^1 model [10,7,11] is obtained from the *ROF* model by replacing the L^2 norm in the data term with the L^1 norm.

$$\min_u \left\{ \alpha \int_\Omega |\nabla u| dx + \sum_{l=1}^K \int_\Omega |u - f_l|\, dx \right\} . \tag{4}$$

Due to the L^1 norm in the data term, it turns out that the TV-L^1 model is much more effective than the *ROF* model at removing strong outliers [7].

2.4   Huber Model

Although the TV-L^1 model has the nice properties to preserve sharp discontinuities in the solution and to be robust against outliers, it has two problems: First, it suffers from the so-called staircasing effect - an effect which describes the formation of artificial discontinuities in the solution [12]. Second, the L^1 norm is not the optimal choice for the expected noise. In real range images the observed noise is the sum of Gaussian noise and outliers.

It turns out that the Huber norm helps in reducing the staircasing effect and also better reflects the noise model of real range images. The Huber norm [13] is defined as

$$|x|_\gamma = \begin{cases} \frac{|x|^2}{2\gamma} & \text{if} \quad |x| \leq \gamma \\ |x| - \frac{\gamma}{2} & \text{if} \quad |x| > \gamma \end{cases}, \tag{5}$$

where γ is a free parameter that defines the threshold between quadratic and L^1 penalization. Using (5) for both the regularization term and the data term in (4), we obtain the Huber model

$$\min_u \left\{ \alpha \int_\Omega |\nabla u|_\varepsilon \, dx + \sum_{l=1}^K \int_\Omega |u - f_l|_\delta \, dx \right\}, \tag{6}$$

where ε, end δ are the parameters of the respective Huber norms. Note that by appropriate choices of ε and δ, the Huber model unifies the quadratic model, the ROF model and TV-L^1 model into a single model. However, while the Huber norm reduces the staircasing effect to some extent, it still favors flat solutions. In the next section we will see that the incorporation of higher-order derivatives plays a key role in obtaining a model which does not suffer from this problem.

3   Total Generalized Variation

In [8] Bredies, Kunisch and Pock proposed the mathematical model of total generalized variation (TGV). The main property of TGV regularization is that it allows to reconstruct piecewise polynomial functions of arbitrary order (piecewise constant, piecewise affine, piecewise quadratic, ...) . As the TV regularizer, the TGV regularizer has the nice property of being convex. This allows to compute a globally optimal solution.

The TGV semi-norm of order $k \geq 1$ with regularization parameters $\alpha = (\alpha_0, ..., \alpha_{k-1}) > 0$ is defined as

$$TGV_k^\alpha(u) = \sup \left\{ \int_\Omega u \, \text{div}^k \varphi \, dx : \varphi \in \mathcal{C}_c^k(\Omega, \text{Sym}^k(\mathbb{R}^2)), \right.$$
$$\left. \|\text{div}^l \varphi\|_\infty \leq \alpha_l, l = 0, .., k-1 \right\}, \tag{7}$$

where $\mathcal{C}_c^k(\Omega, \text{Sym}^k(\mathbb{R}^2))$ denotes the space of continuously differentiable symmetric k-tensors with compact support in Ω. It is obvious that for $k = 1$, (7) corresponds to the dual definition of the total variation semi-norm (3), i.e. TGV is indeed a generalization of the TV regularizer. The definition of the total generalized variation restricts the function v to be in a complicated convex set. This leads to computationally complex minimization algorithms [8]. Using Legendre

- Fenchel duality, we can transform the dual problem (7) to a primal formulation [8]:

$$TGV_k^\alpha(u) = \inf_{\substack{u_l \in C_c^{k-l}(\Omega, \mathrm{Sym}^l(\mathbb{R}^2)) \\ l=1,\ldots,k-1 \ , \ u_0=u \ , \ u_k=0}} \sum_{l=1}^{k} \alpha_{k-l} \int_\Omega |\mathcal{E}(u_{l-1}) - u_l| dx \ , \qquad (8)$$

where $\mathcal{E}(u)$ denotes the symmetrized gradient operator

$$\mathcal{E}(u) = \frac{\nabla u + \nabla u^T}{2} \ .$$

Note that this representation has converted functional (7), which depends on higher order derivatives to a functional of recursive expressions depending only on first order derivatives. Using this representation one can intuitively assess how the total generalized variation is working. Before measuring the L^1 norm of the expression $\mathcal{E}(u_{l-1})$ a vector field u_l is subtracted which itself should have low variation. That is, if low variations are present in some areas of u_{l-1} (e.g. smooth gradients), the vector field u_l will cover these areas, and therefore will decrease the L^1 norm of $\mathcal{E}(u_{l-1})$ in these areas. Hence, $TGV_k^\alpha(u)$ automatically balances the first and higher order derivatives instead of using any fixed combination. For the application to range images from our habitat, it turns out that TGV regularization of second order ($k = 2$) is sufficient since buildings can be well approximated by piecewise planar surfaces.

3.1   The Proposed Model

We are now ready to state the proposed variational model for range image fusion.

$$\min_{u,v} \left\{ \alpha_1 \int_\Omega |\nabla u - v| dx + \alpha_0 \int_\Omega |\mathcal{E}(v)| dx + \sum_{l=1}^{K} \int_\Omega |u - f_l|_\delta \, dx \right\} \ . \qquad (9)$$

This model combines TGV regularization of second order (8) with the Huber-L^1 norm in the data term. Note that it significantly differs from the TGV^2 denosing model proposed in [8], where a quadratic data term is used. Therefore we can not make use of the minimization algorithm proposed in [8]. In addition, the original algorithm used in [8] is quite slow, since it is based on the dual formulation (7) which requires an additional inner loop to project onto a very complex set. The algorithm we are going to describe in the next section is based on the primal formulation (8) which does not require such an inner loop.

4   Numerical Algorithm

In order to implement an algorithm to minimize (9) on a digital computer, we have to introduce the discrete version of (9).

4.1 Discretization

We consider a regular Cartesian grid of size $M \times N$:

$$\Omega^h = \{(x_i, y_j) = (ih, jh) : 1 \leq i \leq N, 1 \leq j \leq M\} \ ,$$

where h denotes the size of the spacing and (i, j) denote the indices of the discrete locations $(ih, jh) \in \Omega^h$. From now on, we will denote the quantities of the discrete setting by the superscript h. Let $U^h = \mathbb{R}^{MN}$ and $V^h = \mathbb{R}^{2MN}$ be finite dimensional vector spaces equipped with scalar products

$$\hat{u}^h, \bar{u}^h \in U^h : \langle \hat{u}^h, \bar{u}^h \rangle = \sum_{i,j} \hat{u}^h_{i,j} \bar{u}^h_{i,j} \ ,$$

$$\hat{v}^h, \bar{v}^h \in V^h : \langle \hat{v}^h, \bar{v}^h \rangle = \sum_{i,j} (\hat{v}^h_1)_{i,j} (\bar{v}^h_1)_{i,j} + (\hat{v}^h_2)_{i,j} (\bar{v}^h_2)_{i,j} \ .$$

Furthermore, let $u^h \in U^h$ and $v^h = (v^h_1, v^h_2) \in V^h$ be discrete versions of the unknown functions u and v in (9) and let $f^h = (f^h_1, \ldots, f^h_K)^T \in \mathbb{R}^{KMN}$, $l = 1 \ldots K$ be the discrete observations. For discretization of the gradient operator ∇^h we use standard finite differences with Neumann boundary conditions

$$(\nabla^h u^h)_{i,j} = \begin{pmatrix} (\delta^h_x u^h)_{i,j} \\ (\delta^h_y u^h)_{i,j} \end{pmatrix} \ ,$$

where

$$(\delta^h_x u^h)_{i,j} = \begin{cases} \dfrac{u^h_{i+1,j} - u^h_{i,j}}{h} & \text{if } 0 < i < M \\ 0 & \text{if } i = M \end{cases} \ , \quad (\delta^h_y u)_{i,j} = \begin{cases} \dfrac{u^h_{i,j+1} - u^h_{i,j}}{h} & \text{if } 0 < j < N \\ 0 & \text{if } j = N \end{cases} \ ,$$

are standard first order finite differences. Similarly, the discrete variant of the symmetriced gradient operator is defined as

$$(\mathcal{E}^h v^h)_{i,j} = \begin{pmatrix} (\delta^h_x v^h_1)_{i,j} & \dfrac{(\delta^h_y v^h_1)_{i,j} + (\delta^h_x v^h_2)_{i,j}}{2} \\ \dfrac{(\delta^h_y v^h_1)_{i,j} + (\delta^h_x v^h_2)_{i,j}}{2} & (\delta^h_y v^h_2)_{i,j} \end{pmatrix} \ . \tag{10}$$

The discrete variant of (9) can now be written as

$$\min_{u^h, v^h} \left\{ \alpha_1 \|\nabla^h u^h - v^h\|_1 + \alpha_0 \|\mathcal{E}^h v^h\|_1 + \sum_{l=1}^{K} \sum_{i,j} |u^h_{i,j} - (f^h_l)_{i,j}|_\delta \right\} \ . \tag{11}$$

This minimization problem poses a large scale non-smooth optimization problem. Hence one can not expect that any black box solver will find the solution in a reasonable time. Instead we will make use of first-order primal-dual algorithms which have been shown to be a good choice for large-scale convex optimization problems [14] in imaging.

252 T. Pock, L. Zebedin, and H. Bischof

4.2 Primal-Dual Formulation

Let us rewrite minimization problem (11) as a convex-concave saddlepoint problem [14]. By applying the Legendre-Fenchel transform to (11) we obtain

$$\min_{u^h, v^h} \max_{p^h, q^h, r^h} \left\{ \langle \nabla^h u^h - v^h, p^h \rangle + \langle \mathcal{E}^h v^h, q^h \rangle + \sum_{l=1}^{K} \langle u^h - f_l^h, r_l^h \rangle - \frac{\delta}{2} \|r_l^h\|^2 \right\}$$

$$\text{subject to} \qquad \|p^h\|_\infty \leq \alpha_1, \ \|q^h\|_\infty \leq \alpha_0, \ \|r_l^h\|_\infty \leq 1, \qquad (12)$$

where p^h, q^h and r_l^h are the dual variables. The obvious advantage of the primal-dual formulation (12) over the primal formulation (11) is, that the non-differentiable L^1 terms have been transformed to linear terms with simple ball constraints on the dual variables. Note that for clarity of the presentation, we did not exploit the obvious symmetry in (10). In any practical implementation, one can easily make use of the symmetry to reduce the memory footprint of the algorithm.

4.3 Numerical Algorithm

Our algorithm is based on the first-order primal-dual algorithm introduced in [14], where also convergence of the algorithm is proven. Before we start to describe the algorithm, let us define some useful quantities. The convex sets P^h, Q^h and R^h are defined as

$$P^h = \{ p^h \in \mathbb{R}^{2MN} : \|p^h\|_\infty \leq \alpha_1 \} ,$$
$$Q^h = \{ q^h \in \mathbb{R}^{4MN} : \|q^h\|_\infty \leq \alpha_0 \} ,$$
$$R^h = \{ r^h \in \mathbb{R}^{MN} : \|r^h\|_\infty \leq 1 \} .$$

$$(13)$$

Furthermore, let the convex function $F(r_l^h)$ be defined as

$$F(r_l^h) = \mathcal{I}_{R^h}(r_l^h) + \frac{\delta}{2} \|r_l^h\|^2 , \quad \mathcal{I}_{R^h}(r_l^h) = \begin{cases} 0 & \text{if} \ r_l^h \in R^h \\ \infty & \text{else} \end{cases} .$$

The primal-dual algorithm is now as follows. We choose the primal and dual steps widths $\tau > 0$, $\sigma > 0$. We let $(u^h)^0 \in U^h$, $(v^h)^0 \in V^h$, $(p^h)^0 \in P^h$, $(q^h)^0 \in Q^h$ and $(r_l^h)^0 \in R_l^h$, $l = 1, \ldots, K$. Furthermore we let $(\bar{u}^h)^0 = (u^h)^0$ and $(\bar{v}^h)^0 = (v^h)^0$. Then for any $n \geq 0$ the iterations are given by

$$\begin{cases} (p^h)^{n+1} = \mathcal{P}_{P^h} \left((p^h)^n + \sigma \nabla^h (\bar{u}^h)^n \right) \\ (q^h)^{n+1} = \mathcal{P}_{Q^h} \left((q^h)^n + \sigma \mathcal{E}^h (\bar{v}^h)^n \right) \\ (r_l^h)^{n+1} = (I + \sigma \partial F)^{-1} \left((r_l^h)^n + \sigma((\bar{u}^h)^n - f_l^h) \right), \ l = 1 \ldots K \\ (u^h)^{n+1} = (u^h)^n - \tau \left((\nabla^h)^T (p^h)^{n+1} + \sum_{l=1}^{K} (r_l^h)^{n+1} \right) \\ (v^h)^{n+1} = (v^h)^n - \tau \left((\mathcal{E}^h)^T (q^h)^{n+1} \right) \\ (\bar{u}^h)^{n+1} = 2(u^h)^{n+1} - (u^h)^n \\ (\bar{v}^h)^{n+1} = 2(v^h)^{n+1} - (v^h)^n \end{cases} \qquad (14)$$

The Euclidean projectors $\mathcal{P}_{P^h}(\hat{p}^h)$ and $\mathcal{P}_{Q^h}(\hat{q}^h)$ are given by

$$\left(\mathcal{P}_{P^h}(\hat{p}^h)\right)_{i,j} = \frac{\hat{p}^h_{i,j}}{\max\left\{1, \|\hat{p}^h_{i,j}\|/\alpha_1\right\}} \;, \quad \left(\mathcal{P}_{Q^h}(\hat{q}^h)\right)_{i,j} = \frac{\hat{q}^h_{i,j}}{\max\left\{1, \|\hat{q}^h_{i,j}\|/\alpha_0\right\}} \;.$$

The solution of the resolvent operator $(I + \sigma\partial F)^{-1}(\hat{r}^h_l)$ is defined through the minimization problem

$$(I + \sigma\partial F)^{-1}(\hat{r}^h_l) = \arg\min_{\rho^h} \frac{\|\rho^h - \hat{r}^h_l\|^2}{2\sigma} + F(\rho^h) \;. \qquad (15)$$

This problem poses a simple quadratic problem with pointwise ball constraints. The solution of (15) is given by

$$\left((I + \sigma\partial F)^{-1}(\hat{r}^h_l)\right)_{i,j} = \frac{(\hat{r}^h_l)_{i,j}/(1 + \sigma\delta)}{\max\left\{1, \left|(\hat{r}^h_l)_{i,j}/(1 + \sigma\delta)\right|\right\}} \;.$$

Note that the basic iterations of the algorithm are extremely simple. Indeed, the main computational effort of each iteration consists of computing the discrete gradient operations which are resembled by matrix vector products with very sparse matrices. The algorithm is therefore easy to implement and can efficiently be accelerated on parallel hardware such as graphics processing units. Finally, note that by using $K = 1$ and δ large enough our model reduces to a TGV^2 model with quadratic data term and only one input image. Hence, the proposed primal-dual algorithm can be used to efficiently minimize the original TGV^2-based denoising model of [8].

5   Results

In this section we present experimental results for the proposed TGV^2-based range image fusion model. The robustness of the method is evaluated on synthetic data and its practical applicability is justified by applying the proposed method to a large scale city dataset.

5.1   Synthetic Data

In our first experiment we apply the proposed fusion model to synthetically generated data to study the effects of noise and in particular the impact of redundancy. The synthetic dataset consists of an idealized building block with roof shapes, fairly common in urban environments. On the left hand side there is a gabled roof, whereas on the right hand side a hip roof is modeled. The dynamic range of this synthetic signal is $[50, 200]$, in the experiments this signal is sampled on a regular grid of 256×256 pixels. Real world range images usually contain a small amount of additive noise but contain a large number of gross outliers. In order to simulate this noise characteristics we use the following procedure to generate the degraded images. First, we add zero mean Gaussian noise with a

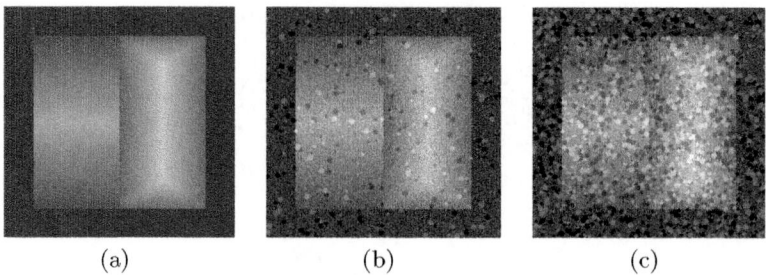

(a)   (b)   (c)

Fig. 1. Illustration of the synthetic dataset used to evaluate the performance of the proposed TGV^2-based fusion model. Image (a) depicts the ground truth, (b) and (c) show degraded observations samples by adding Gaussian noise of $\sigma = 10$ and 10% and 50% outliers, respectively.

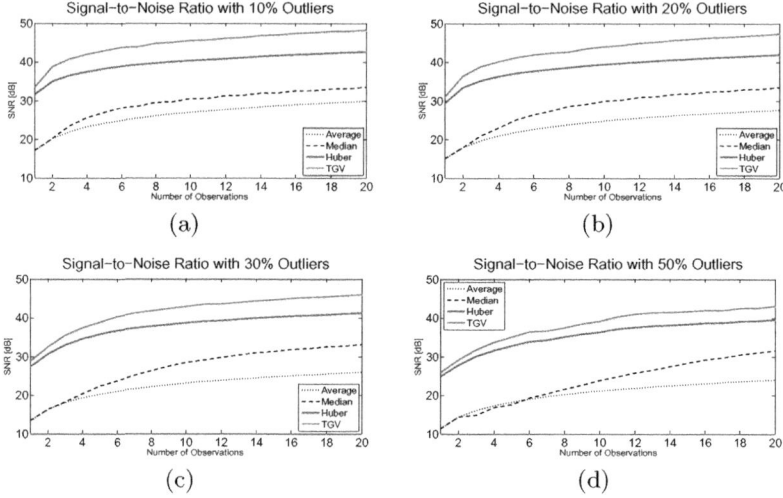

Fig. 2. Signal-to-noise ratio (SNR) for different degrees of degradation and a different number of observations. While for all methods the SNR increases with an increasing number of observations, the proposed TGV^2 model performs best in all situations.

standard deviation of 10. Second, a certain amount of pixel groups with variable sizes are replaced with outliers having an offset of ± 50. Fig. 1 shows the ground truth range image and the degraded versions with an increasing number of outliers. Fig. 3 (a) shows a *3D* rendering of the ground truth range image.

We compared our method against three methods: The first two methods are two very simple methods - computing the point-wise average and computing the point-wise median. The third method is the Huber model (6) which serves as the baseline model. For minimization of the Huber model we use an adapted version of the proposed primal-dual algorithm (14). For each method and experiment, we determined the optimal parameter settings. Note that for the Huber model, this implies that also the quadratic, ROF and $TV\text{-}L^1$ models are included in the

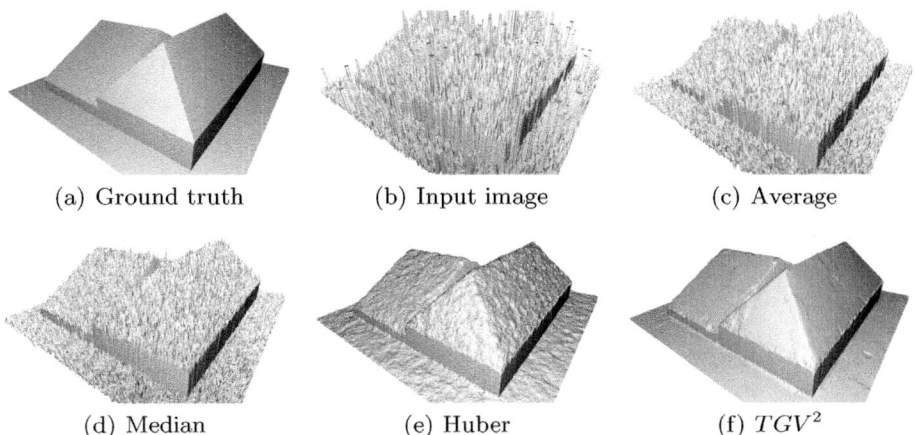

(a) Ground truth   (b) Input image   (c) Average

(d) Median   (e) Huber   (f) TGV^2

Fig. 3. *3D* renderings of an experiment with 10% outliers and 5 observations. The proposed TGV^2-based fusion model significantly outperforms the Huber model. It very well captures the piecewise affine nature of the *3D* model and hence leads to a natural reconstruction of the *3D* building. Also note that the simple methods (Average and Median) completely fail to reconstruct the *3D* building.

parameter optimization. Performance of each method is evaluated with respect to both the degree of noise and the number of observations.

Fig. (2) shows the results of the performance evaluation. For evaluation purpose, we computed the signal-to-noise ratio (SNR)

$$SNR = 10 \log_{10} \frac{\left\| g^h \right\|^2}{\left\| u^h - g^h \right\|^2} \, ,$$

between the ground truth image g^h and the solution of the method u^h. Note that the proposed TGV^2 model performs best in all situations. Interestingly, the advantage of the TGV^2 model over the Huber model increases with an increasing number of observations. From Fig. 3, one can further see that the TGV^2 model captures the piecewise affine nature of the synthetic *3D* building very well. On the other hand, the Huber model inherently imposes a bias towards piecewise constant solutions and hence exhibit small staircases on the roof.

5.2   Real Data

In our second experiment we apply the proposed TGV^2 model to a large real-world dataset of Graz The data set consist of 155 aerial images each of 11500 × 7500 pixels covering an area of 7.6 km^2. The images have an average along-strip overlap of 85% and across-strip overlap of 65% at a ground sampling distance of 8 cm which amounts to about twenty observations per ground pixel on average. The input range images were produced by applying a state-of-the-art dense image matching algorithm based on scanline optimization and backmatching similar to [15]. For each image a pixel-synchronous range image is computed by stereo

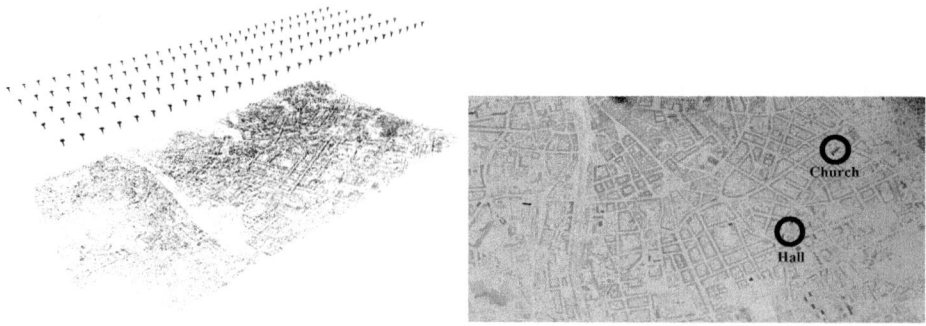

Fig. 4. Large aerial data set of Graz (a) shows a sparse reconstruction together with the camera positions. (b) shows the final digital surface model. The black circles mark two buildings for which detailed views are presented in Fig. 6 and Fig. 5.

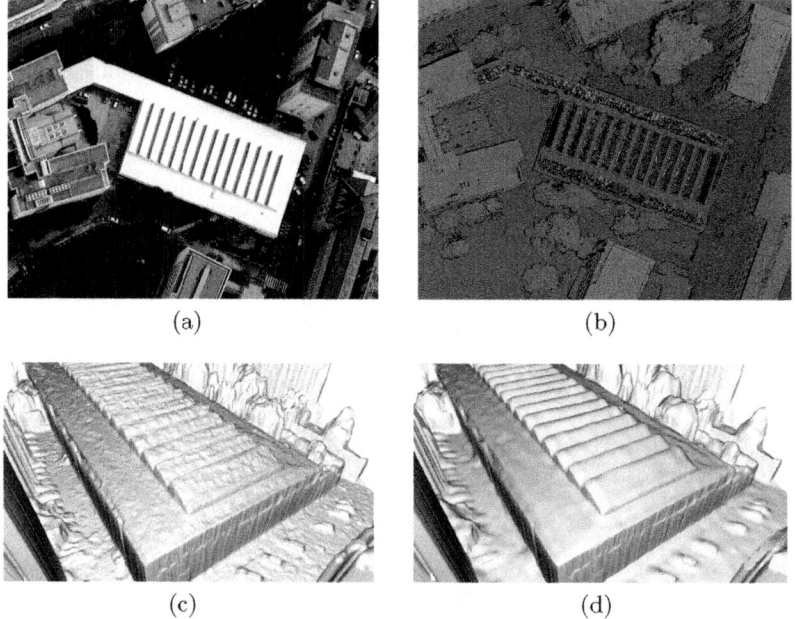

Fig. 5. Hall: (a) shows one input image, (b) shows one corresponding range image (black pixels denote invalid ranges), (c) shows the result of range image fusion using the Huber model and (d) shows the result using the TGV^2 model

matching of two adjacent images. See Fig. 6 (a)-(b) and Fig. 5 (a)-(b) for some sample images. The range images are then converted into a point cloud, which is projected onto the ground plane, thus giving multiple observations per pixel on the ground. Fig. 4 (a) shows a sparse reconstruction of the city together with the regular pattern, the images have been taken from the plane.

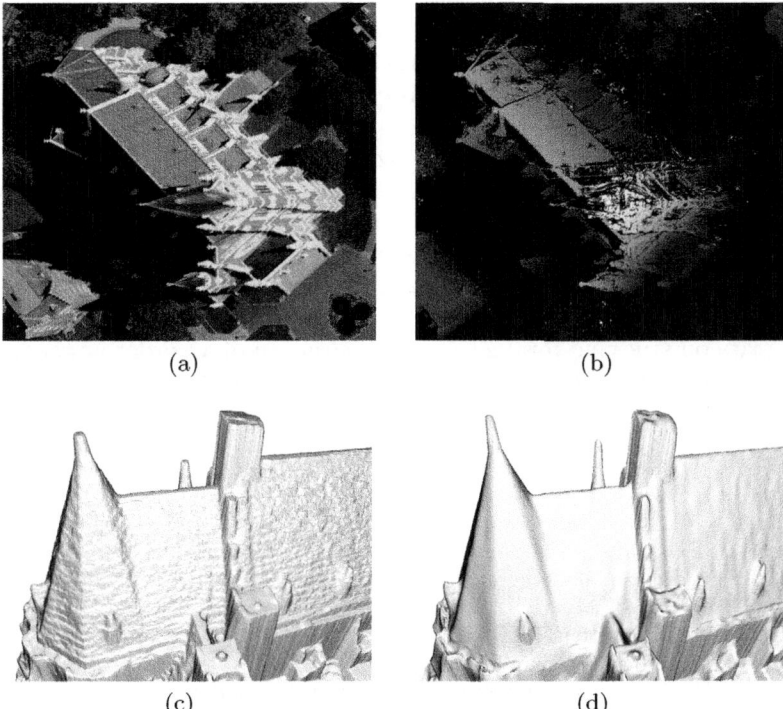

(a)   (b)

(c)   (d)

Fig. 6. Church: (a) shows one input image, (b) shows one corresponding range image (black pixels denote invalid ranges), (c) shows the result of range image fusion using the Huber model and (d) shows the result using the TGV^2 model

We applied the proposed TGV^2-based range image fusion method to compute one single digital surface model (DSM) out of the range images. Clearly, the complete data does not fit the memory of any graphics card. Thus we divided the complete image domain into 282 tiles each of 2048×2048 pixels and applied the algorithm to each of the tiles. In order to eliminate boundary effects we used a sufficiently large overlap between the tiles. Thanks to a GPU-implementation of the primal-dual algorithm and a workstation equipped with 4 Nvidia Tesla GPUs, we were able to process 4 tiles at once. The overall processing time for the city data set was about 45 minutes for the stereo matching and 18 minutes for the fusion.

Fig. 4 (b) depicts the final DSM model. The black circles mark two interesting buildings, for which we provide detailed *3D* renderings. Fig. 5 shows a large hall with a roof that consist of a regular pattern of planes. Note that due to reflections, the range images are very sparse in these areas. The proposed TGV^2 model leads to much smoother results and keeps the details of the 3D building. Fig. 6 shows a detailed *3D* view of a church with very steep roofs. One can see that the TGV^2 model leads to much smoother results while keeping the important details in the reconstruction. On the other hand, the Huber model exhibits strong staircasing on slanted surfaces such as the roof.

6   Conclusion

In this paper we proposed a convex variational approach for the fusion of several range images to a single high quality digital surface model. The variational model is based on total generalized variation regularization of second order and a robust Huber-L^1 data term. For minimization we proposed an simple first-order primal-dual algorithm, which can be efficiently parallelized on graphics processing units. In experimental results on synthetic data we showed the robustness of the method against noise and - most importantly - showed that the method efficiently exploits redundancy in the data. Results on real data, showed that the proposed method can be applied to large scale data sets. Future work will concentrate on studying total generalized variation of an order larger than two. The proposed solution is another step towards realistic 3D models of our habitat.

References

1. Leberl, F., Bischof, H., Pock, T., Irschara, A., Kluckner, S.: Aerial computer vision for a 3d virtual habitat. Computer 43, 24–31 (2010)
2. Agarwal, S., Snavely, N., Simon, I., Seitz, S.M., Szeliski, R.: Building rome in a day. In: International Conference on Computer Vision, ICCV (2009)
3. Zach, C., Pock, T., Bischof, H.: A globally optimal algorithm for robust TV-L^1 range image integration. In: Proceedings of the 11th International Conference Computer Vision, Rio de Janeiro, Brazil, pp. 1–8 (2007)
4. Curless, B., Levoy, M.: A volumetric method for building complex models from range images. In: Proceedings of SIGGRAPH 1996, pp. 303–312 (1996)
5. Tikhonov, A.N.: On the stability of inverse problems. Dokl. Akad. Nauk SSSR 5, 195–198 (1943)
6. Rudin, L., Osher, S., Fatemi, E.: Nonlinear total variation based noise removal algorithms. Physica D 60, 259–268 (1992)
7. Nikolova, M.: A variational approach to remove outliers and impulse noise. J. Math. Imaging and Vision 20, 99–120 (2004)
8. Bredies, K., Kunisch, K., Pock, T.: Total generalized variation. Technical report, Institute for Computer Graphics and Vision (2010)
9. Rudin, L., Osher, S., Fatemi, E.: Nonlinear total variation based noise removal algorithms. Physica D 60, 259–268 (1992)
10. Aujol, J.F., Gilboa, G., Chan, T., Osher, S.: Structure-texture image decomposition–modeling, algorithms, and parameter selection. Int. J. Comp. Vision 67, 111–136 (2006)
11. Chan, T., Esedoglu, S.: Aspects of total variation regularized L^1 function approximation. SIAM J. Appl. Math. 65, 1817–1837 (2004)
12. Chan, T., Esedoglu, S., Park, F., Yip, A.: Total Variation Image Restoration: Overview and Recent Developments. In: Mathematical Models in Computer Vision. Springer, Heidelberg (2005)
13. Huber, P.: Robust Statistics. Wiley, New York (1981)
14. Chambolle, A., Pock, T.: A first-order primal-dual algorithm for convex problems with applications to imaging (2010),
   http://hal.archives-ouvertes.fr/hal-00490826
15. Hirschmüller, H.: Stereo vision in structured environments by consistent semi-global matching. In: Conference on Computer Vision and Pattern Recognition, pp. 328–341 (2006)

Secure and Privacy-Preserving eGovernment—Best Practice Austria

Karl Christian Posch, Reinhard Posch, Arne Tauber, Thomas Zefferer, and Bernd Zwattendorfer

Institute for Applied Information Processing and Communications, Graz University of Technology, Inffeldgasse 16a, A-8010 Graz, Austria

Abstract. In the past, contact with public authorities often appeared as winding way for citizens. Enabled by the tremendous success of the Internet, public authorities aimed to react on that shortcoming by providing various governmental services online. Due to these services, citizens are not forced to visit public authorities during office hours only but have now the possibility to manage their concerns everywhere and anytime. Additionally, this user friendly approach also decreases costs for public authorities.

Austria was one of the first countries that seized this trend by setting up a nation-wide eGovernment infrastructure. The infrastructure builds upon a solid legal framework supported by various technical concepts preserving security and privacy for citizens. These efforts have already been awarded in several international benchmarks that have reported a 100% online availability of eGovernment services in Austria.

In this paper we present best practices that have been followed by the Austrian eGovernment and that have paved the way for its success. By virtually following a traditional governmental procedure and mapping its key stages to corresponding online processes, we provide an insight into Austria's comprehensive eGovernment infrastructure and its key concepts and implementations. This paper introduces the most important elements of the Austrian eGovernment and shows how these components act in concert in order to realize secure and reliable eGovernment solutions for Austrian citizens.

1 Introduction

The Austrian eGovernment has been awarded with top ranks in several European-level eGovernment studies during the past couple of years. Among the key concepts for this success were the solid treatment of the citizen's right for privacy and data protection, together with best-practice procedures for identification when necessary. It is thus no surprise that Austria's eGovernment has influenced the European development to a significant extent. The advances with the Digital Agenda prove that this avenue was rightly taken. eID and electronic signature play an outstanding role within this new European Commission effort now.

In this paper, we look at the overall scope of Austria's eGovernment services. We will virtually follow an eGovernment process from the application stage towards back-office processing and final delivery. Moreover, we will also point out

C.S. Calude, G. Rozenberg, A. Salomaa (Eds.): Maurer Festschrift, LNCS 6570, pp. 259–269, 2011.

typical potential security risks and measures taken to counter these risks to guarantee a secure and reliable eGovernment process. It becomes apparent that the quality of administrative services can be significantly improved with eGovernment processes while, at the same time, these services can also be delivered at a much lower cost than with traditional procedures.

Most often in the past, contact with public authorities has typically been tedious for citizens. People were often forced to spend hours queuing in front of counters or filling complex forms without helping assistance. More recently, public authorities have been positively influenced by the private sector, where customer friendliness is key for success. By improving traditional procedures in terms of efficiency and customer orientation, citizens have developed from pure suppliants to emancipated customers. In this context, public authorities have evolved to customer-oriented service providers satisfying the needs of their customers.

In parallel to this development we could observe significant advances in information technology. Especially the success story of the Internet has had a significant impact on various areas of life during the past decades. Public authorities reacted to this trend and started to offer different online services for citizens too. Driven by the aspiration to continuously improve existing procedures in terms of efficiency and customer friendliness, public authorities aimed to employ the Internet in order to spare citizens personal visits at administrative offices.

The online processing of procedures involving citizens and public authorities has the potential to improve common paper-based procedures significantly. Austria was one of the first countries that recognized this potential and started to build a comprehensive eGovernment infrastructure early on. Nevertheless, the new electronic approach also raised many new challenges. Considering the fact that various procedures are potentially dealing with data which are sensitive with respect to privacy and security, it is crucial that they are at least as reliable and as secure as their traditional non-electronic pendants. In order to guarantee the integrity and security of eGovernment infrastructures, these aspects need to be defined not only on technical level, but also on legal level. Therefore, in Austria the E-Government Act [7], which has come into effect in 2004 and has been amended in 2008, defines the legal framework for all eGovernment procedures in Austria.

Basing on the given legal framework, Austria has taken the challenge to develop a comprehensive and future-proof eGovernment framework. Austria's early investments in eGovernment and future technologies have already paid off: In the past years, several international benchmark [5] [4] [3] have reported a 100% online availability of eGovernment services in Austria.

In this article, we describe key components of the Austrian eGovernment. We present best practices which have contributed to its success. The article guides the reader through a typical eGovernment procedure and introduces basic concepts and building blocks of the Austrian eGovernment infrastructure. By reading this paper, the reader will get an understanding of the overall technical setup that has paved the way for the success of the Austrian eGovernment.

In section 2 we describe an exemplary procedure and identify its three basic stages. With this we briefly introduce a typical administrative procedure. In subsequent sections we provide details on these three fundamental stages and show how their different requirements have been met. In this way, we provide the reader with an overview of the Austrian eGovernment with its relevant core components and basic concepts, as well as concrete implementations. Finally, we draw conclusions and give a brief outlook towards future developments and trends.

2   Common Structure of Administrative Procedures

Procedures at public administrative offices have been purely paper-based for centuries. Those procedures involving citizens and public authorities can generally be subdivided into three basic stages, as illustrated in Figure 1. These stages are *Application, Back-office processing* and *Delivery.* In this section we identify these main stages by looking in some detail at the issuance of a criminal-record certificate.

Administrative procedures are guided by legal requirements. When mapping traditional paper-based administrative procedures to electronic web-based services, basically the same requirements as for paper-based approaches hold true. In the remainder of this section we identify some key requirements relevant for each of these three stages.

In order to request the issuance of a criminal-record certificate, a citizen has to formally apply in order to trigger the adequate administrative procedure. Thus, *Application* is the initial phase of many governmental processes. In traditional governmental processes, usually a paper-based application form has to be filled by the applicant. This is quite often only possible during office hours of the responsible public authority. The case officer in charge verifies the provided application data and the citizen's identity by checking an ID document presented by the citizen. Authentication of the applicant and verification of the citizen's application data are thus the key elements of this first stage.

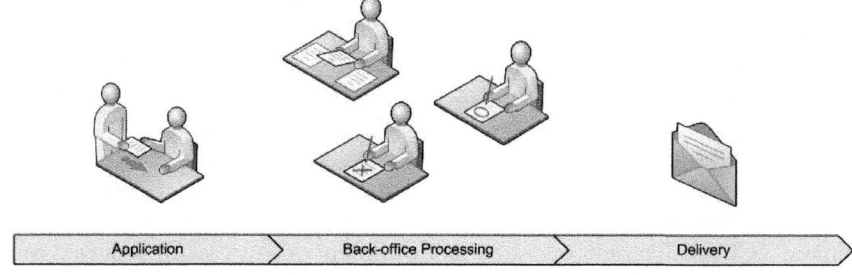

Fig. 1. Three stages of administrative procedures

Then follows *Back-office processing*. In this phase, case officers manage all necessary processes for responding to the applicant's request. In order to issue a criminal-record certificate, for instance, the case officer has to examine whether there are any crimes registered for the particular citizen. When all required data has been collected, an appropriate paper-based criminal-record certificate is finally generated. In order to prove the authenticity of this certificate, the document is signed by the public authority. The key elements of this second stage are thus the efficient and reliable processing of internal files and data records, and the signing of documents by the public authority.

In the final phase, *Delivery*, the case officer in charge delivers the requested certificate to the applying citizen. In traditional paper-based procedures, the certificate is usually delivered either directly to the citizen during office hours or via registered mail. Thus, reliable and evidential delivery of documents is of major importance in order to close the electronic process in a proper manner.

Depending on the service and the degree of user interaction, eGovernment services are usually subdivided according to a maturity model consisting of five classes: *Information, one-way interaction, two-way interaction, transaction*, and *targetisation/automation*. This model has also been applied by Capgemini for the eGovernment benchmark reports [5]. The example procedure discussed in this paper—Issuance of a Criminal-Record Certificate—is a fully transactional service, and thus falls into the class *transaction*.

In the following sections, we show how the three phases of classical administrative procedures have been implemented within the Austrian eGovernment. In doing so, we describe the core elements, the key concepts, and some methods of the awarded Austrian eGovernment.

3   Electronic Application

Similar to traditional governmental processes, identification, authentication and signatures play an important role within electronic government, too. When applying for certain services, for instance, a citizen often needs to be uniquely identified. This holds true for traditional paper-based procedures as well as for their electronic equivalents. Austria's eGovernment solution for mapping identification, authentication, and signatures into the digital world is the so-called *Austrian citizen-card concept* [8]. The idea behind this concept is to provide both, citizens as well as administrative online-service providers, secure and reliable means for identification and authentication in online eGovernment processes. Generally, this concept is independent from technology and platform, and supports various functions such as the creation and verification of electronic signatures or the encryption and decryption of electronic documents.

Figure 2 illustrates the Austrian citizen-card concept. Basically, three parties are involved in this concept: The citizen who wants to use a certain service, the relying party and—acting as intermediary—the so-called citizen-card environment (CCE). The citizen-card environment decouples all security-related functions from the underlying citizen-card technology. For example, the citizen card can be a smartcard, e.g. bank card, student card or health-insurance

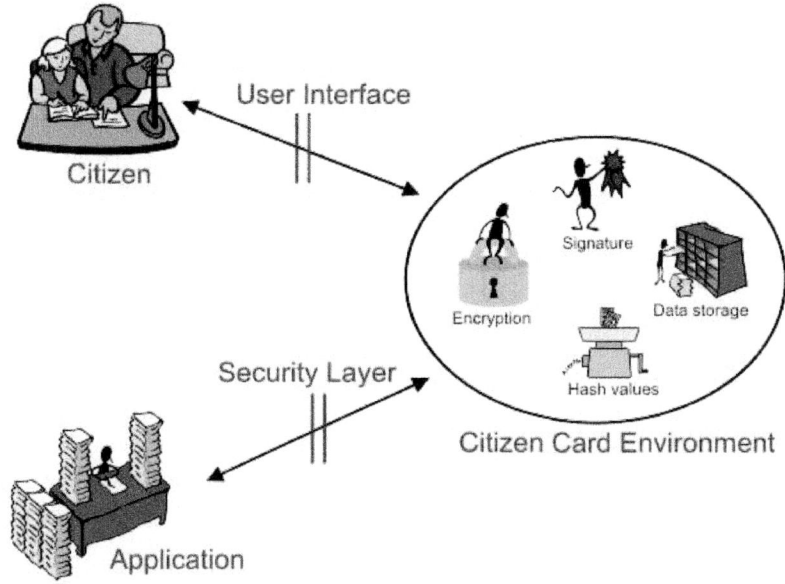

User Interface

Citizen

Security Layer

Application

Signature

Encryption

Hash values

Data storage

Citizen Card Environment

Fig. 2. The Austrian Citizen Card Concept [1]

card[1] or also a mobile phone. Thus, applications that want to access a certain functionality of the citizen card just need to communicate with the citizen-card environment. The citizen-card environment handles all technology-specific operations, e.g. secure smartcard communication. The communication between the application and the citizen-card environment is based on a defined interface, the so-called security-layer interface [1]. This interface is XML-based and its protocol messages can be transported over HTTP or TCP.

According to the citizen-card concept, the citizen-card environment can either run on the citizen's local computer or on a remote server accessible via the Internet. Currently, several proprietary and open-source implementations for a local citizen-card environment exist. An open-source implementation based on Java-Applet technology for a server-based citizen-card environment has been discussed in [6]. In this case, only a minimal piece of software needs to be installed on the local system to handle the communication with the smartcard – namely the Java Applet in the user's web browser. An alternative for server-side signature creation uses mobile phones as secure devices for authentication. This option has been discussed in [11]. In this latter approach, security functions are implemented by a server-side hardware security module, but authorized via a mobile transaction number (mobile TAN) sent via SMS to the user.

In 1999 the European Union has published the so-called EU Signature Directive [12] which focuses on qualified electronic signatures. Such qualified electronic signatures are legally equivalent to hand-written signatures. Thus, almost any

---

[1] Currently, each Austrian citizen possesses such a health-insurance card where the citizen-card functionality can be simply activated.

governmental process where a citizen's signature is required can also be processed online. Qualified signatures according to this directive can be generated by an Austrian citizen card. However, qualified electronic signatures can also be used for secure authentication in eGovernment processes. Authentication is an important process to verify that a citizen is the certain person she claims to be. To simplify the authentication process for online-service providers, an open-source module for identification and authentication has been developed. A server-side middleware named MOA-ID (Module for Online Applications – Identification) [10] acts as intermediary between the citizen-card environment and the actual online application. In this way, the online application does not need to communicate directly with the citizen-card environment, but instead receives all data required for identification and authentication via a standardized interface (SAML [15]). Initially, MOA-ID reads the citizen's identification data via the citizen-card environment from the citizen's smartcard or another equivalent device. This identification data is stored within an XML data structure. After this first step, i.e. identification, the citizen is asked to sign an appropriate text to confirm her authentication request towards the online application. Finally, the citizen's signature is verified and an authentication token containing relevant identification and authentication information is assembled and transmitted to the online application.

An fundamental aspect of authentication in administrative processes is delegation. Austria is the only country in Europe having automated mechanisms for delegation. In paper-based procedures, mandates are used to attest that a person is empowered to represent another person. We can find the application of mandates in several scenarios, e.g. in court proceedings. Other examples are the procuration in commercial transactions when acting on behalf of a company, or a postal mandate when receiving deliveries on someone else's behalf. Electronic mandates belong to the core of the Austrian eGovernment strategy. Empowerment is established through electronic mandates based on XML structures stored on the citizen card. This approach has been discussed in detail in [14]. In the course of an identification process based on MOA-ID, electronic mandates are read out and validated together with the citizen's electronic signature.

After completion of the *Application*, the citizen-related information that has been collected in this first step is handed over to appropriate *Back-office processes*.

4   Back-Office Processes

Citizens trigger administrative procedures by making a formal application. In Austrian eGovernment services, this is usually done by means of appropriate web forms in connection with the citizen card. The applicant's citizen card allows a secure and reliable remote user authentication and it allows the citizen to sign applications online. As soon as the electronic application form is transmitted to the responsible public authority, related back-office processes are started. The objective of these processes is the appropriate processing of the applicant's request. In case of our example process here, i.e. issuance of a criminal-record certificate, back-office processes involve the collection of the particular applicant's criminal records and the preparation of an electronically signed criminal-record certificate.

The *efficient* processing of back-office processes is an important requirement for public authorities not only in Austria, but in the entire European Union. According to the Services Directive [13], which has been published by the European Parliament and the Council on 12 December 2006, and which had to be implemented by EU Member States by 28 December 2009, procedures and formalities need to be simplified. In this way, the establishment of businesses and the provision of services within the European Union is aimed to be facilitated for both, natural and legal persons.

In the remainder of this section, we show how efficient back-office processing according to the requirements defined by the EU Service Directive is accomplished within the Austrian eGovernment. Thereby, we put the focus on the internal processing of electronic files and data records, and the application of electronic signatures by public authorities.

The internal processing of files and data records is one of the key challenges of administrative back-office processes. While paper-based files have built the basis of such processes until now, information technologies have significantly enhanced theses processes in terms of efficiency during the past decades. In Austria, public authorities make use of the so-called electronic file system (Elektronischer Akt, ELAK) that allows for processing of electronic records free of media breaks. The ELAK is a key element of the Austrian eGovernment strategy. As a workflow management system for internal work processes, it supports a seamless cooperation free of media breaks between different administrations and enables a one-stop administration for citizens. All Austrian ministries are connected to the electronic file system of the federal administration (ELAK im Bund, EiB). The EiB is operated by the Federal Data Processing Center and, since its start in 2001, about 9500 workstations have been connected to this system. Both, public administrations and citizens, benefit from the electronic file system. Besides the benefits mentioned, case officers can easily access, search for, and timely edit documents. Since all documents are digital, there are no unnecessary delivery delays when sharing or disseminating them. Citizens can thus receive documents and notifications 24 hours a day, 7 days a week.

Besides the efficient internal processing of files and data records, the preparation of electronic documents is the second key requirement for back-office processes in the Austrian eGovernment. In order to ensure data-origin authentication, for example in official notifications, documents being issued by public authorities need to be signed. Signatures applied by public authorities are usually referred to as *official signatures*.

The Austrian solution for electronic official signatures has been discussed in [9] and addresses two basic objectives. First, Austrian official signatures allow citizens to reliably verify that the signer actually is a public authority or a public official. This has been achieved by defining an registered X.509 object identifier

(OID) as extension to the signature certificate. The OID reliably identifies signatures being applied by public authorities, and allows citizens to verify whether or not obtained documents originate from public authorities.

The second objective that has been addressed by the Austrian solution for official signatures is resistance against media breaks. This means that the electronic signature of digital documents remains verifiable even if this document has been printed to paper. This objective has been achieved by relying on pure text-based electronic signatures. This means that all signed content needs to be based on text and must be visible on the document in order to allow a manual reconstruction from printouts. Furthermore, all information covered by the applied electronic signature must be printed out on the document as well. Amongst others, this includes the signature value, information about the signatory, and a link to a signature verification service that can be used to verify the document's signature.

Another key benefit of the Austrian official signature is its technology independence. The method used is applicable to various document formats including XML, PDF, and Microsoft Office documents. This allows for a widespread and flexible use of official signatures according to the needs of the particular application.

The electronic file system and official signatures represent the basic building blocks of back-office processes in the Austrian eGovernment. By guaranteeing an efficient processing of digital data records and allowing for reliable data-origin authentication, these two concepts contribute to the awarded quality of Austrian eGovernment.

5   Electronic Delivery

Governments and public administrations deliver important documents (e.g. subpoenas) in a reliable and evidential way. Registered and certified mail are useful vehicles serving this purpose in the postal world. Registered mail gives senders extended tracking possibilities and evidence of having submitted a particular delivery at a certain point in time. Certified mail provides a further proof of receipt signed by the recipient or a delegate. Document delivery is usual the last phase of an administrative procedure. Within eGovernment, an electronic equivalent is required to ensure a process free of media breaks. Standard mailing systems like e-mail have a poor evidential quality. They can rather be compared to sending a postcard, which lacks integrity, confidentiality, sender-identity information, authenticity, and non-repudiation.

In the Austrian eGovernment a certified mail system (CMS) is being used. As one of the first systems, the Austrian *document delivery system* (DDS) has been established in 2004 to facilitate reliable and evidential communications with public bodies over the Internet. The legal basis of this system is laid down by the Law on the Delivery of Official Documents [2]. The Austrian DDS defines four types of participants: Senders, recipients, delivery agents, and a central lookup service (CLS). Delivery agents operate certified mail services by providing the following two mail handling functionalities: Mail delivery agents (MDA) for senders, and mail transfer agents (MTA) for recipients. Delivery agents must be approved by the Federal Chancellery for compliance with technical, organizational and legal requirements. So far, three providers have been approved. Two private sector companies[2] and the Federal Data Processing Center[3]. The system is free of charge for all recipients. Recipients can register with any delivery agent, even with multiple. Registration is based on the Austrian citizen card. This ensures qualified authentication and identification procedures in order to provide a high service quality for senders. A hallmark of the Austrian DDS is its communication architecture. In contrast to e-mail-based architectures, senders are not required to register with delivery agents. They must register with the central lookup service (CLS) instead. The CLS is a register, operated by the Federal Chancellery, holding the data of all recipients registered with any delivery agent. This is necessary because the Austrian DDS has no domain-based communication architecture like e-mail. It is not possible to determine a recipient's delivery agent just on the basis of the recipient's address data. The main delivery process steps are as follows:

1. Senders query the CLS to find out with which delivery agent a recipient is registered with. Due to data privacy protection the CLS returns only a minimalistic set of data sufficient to correctly address a recipient: an encrypted delivery token holding the recipient's unique identifier, the URLs of recipient's delivery agent(s), supported MIME types by the sender and an optional encryption certificate.
2. Senders directly transmit a delivery to the recipient's delivery agent. The communication protocol is based on web-services technology using the simple object access protocol (SOAP).
3. The delivery agent informs the recipient that a delivery is ready for pick-up.
4. The recipient authenticates at the delivery agent and confirms the reception of a new delivery by creating a qualified electronic signature (QES) using her citizen card.
5. As a result, the delivery agent returns this non-repudiation of receipt (NRR) evidence back to the sender.

The Platform Digital Austria has developed an open-source module called MOA-ZS (Modules for Online Applications – ZuStellung) to facilitate the integration of the certified-mail functionality into senders' back-office applications. MOA-ZS defines a middleware implementing the four key functionalities required for using the Austrian DDS: CLS query, payload encryption, document delivery, and reception of returning NRR evidences. The module is provided as an open-source module to foster the take-up by public administrations and the adoption and extension by private businesses. With some minor restrictions, the Austrian DDS can also be used by private businesses to deliver documents with the quality of certified mail. Security and privacy for recipients have been strengthened in the case of private senders to ensure a high level of trust in this system. With

---

[2] https://www.meinbrief.at, https://zustellung.telekom.at
[3] https://www.brz-zustelldienst.at

this public-private sector shared system, the Austrian DDS has demonstrated its abilities on a national level to be deployable on the large scale. A next challenge for the Austrian DDS, especially within the context of the European service, is interoperability on the European level. The use of open standards, interfaces and technologies is a key factor for a sustainable system and facilitates upcoming interoperability efforts. Due to its openness and flexibility, the Austrian DDS is well prepared to face this challenge.

6   Conclusions and Outlook

In the past years, information technologies have increasingly made their way into traditional adminstrative procedures. Favored by the success of the Internet, eGovernment has improved many of these procedures in terms of efficiency and usability. In this paper we have introduced the Austrian way to overcome the various challenges of eGovernment. We have introduced the basic building blocks of the Austrian eGovernment infrastructure that are used to build up secure and reliable solutions for both, citizens and public administrations.

While this paper has primarily focused on Austrian approaches, similar attempts to enhance eGovernment have been made in other EU Member States as well. Since these solutions are most often specific to the particular Member State, they are usually able to satisfy the needs of the particular country only. Thus, interoperability between these systems is often an issue. To bear this challenge, several international research projects have been launched in order to support the ecosystem of key policy areas like eID, eHealth, eProcurement, and the Services Directive. Austria participates in several of these large scale pilots and contributes its experiences in design and implementation of secure and reliable eGovernment infrastructures to the development of cross-border solutions on an European level.

References

1. Federal Chancellery Austria. The Austrian Citizen Card (May 2004), http://www.buergerkarte.at/konzept/securitylayer/spezifikation/aktuell/index.en.html
2. Bundesgesetz. Bundesgesetz über die Zustellung behördlicher Dokumente (April 1982), http://www.ris.bka.gv.at/GeltendeFassung.wxe?Abfrage=Bundesnormen&Gesetzesnummer=10005522
3. Capgemini. EU eGovernment-Studie 2006 (2006)
4. Capgemini. EU eGovernment Report 2007 (2007)
5. Capgemini. eGovernment Benchmark 2009 (2009)
6. Centner, M., Orthacker, C., Bauer, W.: Minimal-Footprint Middleware for the Creation of Qualified Signatures. In: INSTICC Institute for Systems, and Portugal Communication Control Technologies of Information (eds.) Proceedings of the 6th International Conference on Web Information Systems and Technologies, pp. 64–69. INSTICC - Institute for Systems and Technologies of Information, Control and Communication, Portugal (2010)

7. Bundesgesetzblatt für die Republik Österreich BGBl. I Nr. 10/2004. The Austrian E-Government Act (2004)
8. Leitold, H., Hollosi, A., Posch, R.: Security Architecture of the Austrian Citizen Card Concept. In: ACSAC 2002: Proceedings of the 18th Annual Computer Security Applications Conference, Washington, DC, USA, p. 391. IEEE Computer Society, Los Alamitos (2002)
9. Leitold, H., Posch, R., Rössler, T.: Media-break resistant eSignatures in eGovernment: an Austrian experience. In: Gritzalis, D., Lopez, J. (eds.) SEC 2009. IFIP-AICT, vol. 297, pp. 109–118. Springer, Heidelberg (2009)
10. ARGE Spezifikation MOA: Spezifikation Module für Online Applikationen - ID (August 2007), http://egovlabs.gv.at/projects/moa-idspss
11. Orthacker, C., Centner, M., Kittl, C.: Qualified Mobile Server Signature. In: Hinchey, M., Meyer, B., Turner, J.A., et al. (eds.). IFIP-AICT. Springer, Heidelberg (2010) (in press)
12. European Parliament and the Council: Directive 1999/93/ec on a community framework for electronic signatures (December 1999)
13. The European Parliament and the Council of the European Union: Directive 2006/123/EC of the Eurpean Parliament and of the Council on services in the internal market (2006)
14. Rössler, T.: Empowerment through Electronic Mandates – Best Practice Austria. In: Godart, C., Gronau, N., Sharma, S., Canals, G. (eds.) I3E 2009. IFIP-AICT, vol. 305, pp. 148–159. Springer, Heidelberg (2009)
15. OASIS Security Services (SAML) TC. Security Assertion Markup Language (SAML), http://www.oasis-open.org/committees/tc_home.php?wg_abbrev=security

The Quest for Uncertainty

Jörg Zimmermann and Armin B. Cremers

Institute of Computer Science,
University of Bonn, Germany
{jz,abc}@iai.uni-bonn.de

Abstract. The question of how to represent and process uncertainty is of fundamental importance to the scientific process, but also in everyday life. Currently there exist a lot of different calculi for managing uncertainty, each having its own advantages and disadvantages. Especially, almost all are defining the domain and structure of uncertainty values a priori, e.g., one real number, two real numbers, a finite domain, and so on, but maybe uncertainty is best measured by complex numbers, matrices or still another mathematical structure. Here we investigate the notion of uncertainty from a foundational point of view, provide an ontology and axiomatic core system for uncertainty, derive and not define the structure of uncertainty, and review the historical development of approaches to uncertainty which have led to the results presented here.

1 Introduction

The quest for a theory of inductive logic, i.e., a logic defining the relationship between observations and hypotheses, lies at the heart of the scientific process. Accordingly, there is a plethora of research aiming at the clarification of this relationship (probability theory as Bayesian theory [9], possibility theory [3], Dempster-Shafer theory [16], revision theory [4], ranking theory [19], non-monotonic logic [5], ...). The application of probability theory to the problem of inductive logic is known as Bayesian inference. Despite its intuitive appeal and many successful applications, it was never considered as a solution to the problem of induction because of technical and philosophical problems. In fact, the 20th century witnessed a strong rejection of probability theory as a theory for induction. Probability theory was developed to describe the randomness of observable events, not the plausibility of unobservable hypotheses. The randomness of events can be seen as an objective property of a physical system, whereas the plausibility of hypotheses is intrinsically subjective, depending on the knowledge of an "observer". A first attempt to directly axiomatize the intuition of reasoning under uncertainty was made by Richard T. Cox in 1946 [2], but despite its important role as a starting point for a new branch of mathematical, subjective uncertainty theory, Cox's axiom system has drawbacks which have prevented it from becoming a generally accepted axiomatization of uncertainty measures, most notably its assumption that uncertainty values must be measured by real numbers. Addressing this issue, it is an important goal to define

C.S. Calude, G. Rozenberg, A. Salomaa (Eds.): Maurer Festschrift, LNCS 6570, pp. 270–283, 2011.

alternative axiom systems with a reduced number of controversial assumptions and investigate their implications. One important contribution to this endeavor is the axiom system by S. Arnborg and G. Sjödin [1], which has inspired the axiom system introduced in this article.

2 An Ontology of Uncertainty

In the realm of empirical knowledge, uncertainty is unavoidable. A piece of information is in general not known to be true or false, but must be annotated by shades of certainty. But what exactly is the structure of these "shades of certainty"? Are there ontologically different types of uncertainty, and, after all, how to assess, process and communicate uncertainty? One early distinction of types of uncertainty was introduced by Frank Knight in his seminal book "Risk, Uncertainty, and Profit" [10] on page 19:

"Uncertainty must be taken in a sense radically distinct from the familiar notion of risk, from which it has never been properly separated.... The essential fact is that 'risk' means in some cases a quantity susceptible of measurement, while at other times it is something distinctly not of this character; and there are far-reaching and crucial differences in the bearings of the phenomena depending on which of the two is really present and operating.... It will appear that a measurable uncertainty, or 'risk' proper, as we shall use the term, is so far different from an unmeasurable one that it is not in effect an uncertainty at all."

In today's language one would describe "risk" as the uncertainty about the occurrence of events *within* a fully specified stochastic model. The "Knightian Uncertainty" is the uncertainty with regard to the correct model, what is today sometimes called model risk, especially in financial mathematics.

In the next paragraph we introduce an ontology of uncertainty, and, even more general, an ontology of indefiniteness, accompanied by a suitable terminology.

2.1 Indefiniteness

The advance of research in artificial intelligence, knowledge representation and expert systems has led to a plethora of new approaches to represent and process information: for example possibility theory, certainty factors, and non-monotonic logics. This has led to confusion about the exact differences and commonalities between the different calculi, and where they are competing approaches and where they are complementary. One striking example is fuzzy logic, which is still regarded as an alternative calculus for processing uncertain information, where in fact it is a generalization of the notion of an event. This is clearly stated by Judea Pearl in [14]: "Fuzzyness is orthogonal to probability theory - it focuses on the ambiguities in describing events, rather than the uncertainty about the occurrence or non-occurrence of events." Classical events are called crisp, in order to express that they are definitely defined: in a specific situation the event has occurred or not – there are no "degrees of occurrence". The standard approach to represent a set of crisp events is a Boolean algebra. In this sense, one can say that a crisp event is an element of a Boolean algebra.

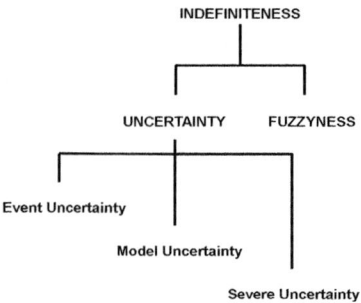

Fig. 1. Ontology of Indefiniteness

We suggest the notion "indefiniteness" for describing all sorts of non-certain, non-crisp information. This leads to the following ontology of indefiniteness:

2.2   Types of Uncertainty

Here we propose three types of uncertainty, extending the Knightian ontology:

1. Event Uncertainty (quantitatively known unknowns)
2. Model Uncertainty (qualitatively known unknowns)
3. Severe Uncertainty (unknown unknowns)

We want to illustrate these three types of uncertainty – and their principal differences – with an example taken from Bernoulli processes:

Event Uncertainty: Consider the coin model with $p = \frac{1}{2}$. The question what will be the next outcome of an observation can be answered by a definite probability. In this case the probability is $\frac{1}{2}$, meaning that we are maximally unsure what will happen next, even under a specific, complete stochastic model, but other questions can be answered with more certainty by the coin model. For example, the probability that we will observe 450 to 550 heads out of 1000 tosses of the coin is greater than 0.998. So, for this specific question the coin model delivers an answer with near certainty.

Model Uncertainty: Here we assume that the observations are generated by a Bernoulli process, but with unknown success probability p. Without introducing a prior distribution for the model parameter, this implies that we only can infer probability intervals for events, for example the probability that we will observe between 45 and 55 successes out of 100 experiments is in the interval $[0, .71]$, regardless of the value of p.

Severe Uncertainty: This is the "black swan" case, the possibility, that the true model is not even approximately in the set of considered models. An example would be that the true process is a deterministic switch between successes and failures, leading to a probability of 1 for the above example.

The case of severe uncertainty leads to the question of how to describe all possible models. If one requires that a model has to be an algorithmic object, the answer to this question is the set of all programs, also called program space. R. Solomonoff pioneered learning in program space in the 1960s, employing a Bayesian framework for describing model uncertainty and a prior distribution on programs inspired by Occam's razor [17,18]. Unfortunately, despite the fact that all models have to be represented by programs, the learning process devised by Solomonoff for the whole program space is not computable. The question of how to essentially retain the generality of Solomonoff's approach, but render the learning process computable has spawned a research area of its own, which is today called universal induction or algorithmic probability [8,15].

3   Formalizing Uncertainty

First we have to discuss a subtle issue of terminology. Above we have used the notion "uncertainty values" to denote generalized truth values. Unfortunately, there is the following problem when using this term in a formalized context: no uncertainty about a proposition can be identified with sure knowledge, but maximal uncertainty about a proposition is *not* certainty with regard to the negation of the proposition. The domains of truth values we want to axiomatize contain a greatest and a least element, where the greatest element should represent certainty and the least element impossibility, i.e. certainty of the negated proposition. For this reason, we adopt the notion "confidence measure" instead of uncertainty measure in the following definitions and axioms.

3.1   The Algebra of Truth Bearers

Before delving into the structure of uncertainty, we have to define the objects and their relations which are capable to take on truth values, the *truth bearers*. In a context of crisp events, i.e., after the fact it is unambiguously decidable if the event has occurred or not, the algebra of truth bearers is normally considered to be a Boolean algebra, but when truth bearers are not crisp, then another algebra has to be used, i.e., a fuzzy algebra where the law of the excluded middle is not valid: $x \lor \neg x \neq 1$.

However, for the purpose of the present article we focus on Boolean algebras as the structure of propositions. The investigation of uncertainty measures for non-Boolean proposition algebras is open to future research.

3.2   Uncertainty: The Boolean Case

A *conditional confidence measure* for a Boolean Algebra $\mathbf{U}$ and a domain of confidence values $\mathcal{C}$ is a mapping $\Gamma : \mathbf{U} \times \mathbf{U} \setminus \{\bot\} \to \mathcal{C}$. Let $A, B \in \mathbf{U}$, then the expression $\Gamma(A|B)$ reads: "the confidence value of A given B (wrt. Γ)". The domain of confidence values is partially ordered and has a greatest ($\top$) and a least ($\bot$) element. A *confidence space* is a triple $(\mathbf{U}, \Gamma, \mathcal{C})$. One of the following axioms (Extensibility) for confidence measures deals with relations between confidence spaces defined over different Boolean algebras. Thus it is necessary to introduce a *set of confidence spaces* all sharing the same domain of confidence values. Such a set of confidence spaces we will call a *confidence universe*, and the following axiom system is concerned with such confidence universes, and not single confidence spaces. This seemingly technical shift in perspective is essential for the formalization of natural properties like extensibility, which plays a crucial role as an intuitive axiom complementing Cox's assumptions (see section 5).

We now state seven axioms, which can be grouped in three "connective axioms" and four "infrastructure axioms", where the connective axioms concern properties of the logical connectives and the infrastructure axioms deal with basic properties of the order relations, the combinability of confidence spaces and a closure property.

3.3   The Core of Uncertainty

In the following, we use $\Gamma(A)$ as an abbreviation for $\Gamma(A|\top)$.

(Not)   For all $(\mathbf{U_1}, \Gamma_1, \mathcal{C})$ and $(\mathbf{U_2}, \Gamma_2, \mathcal{C})$:

If $\Gamma_1(A_1) = \Gamma_2(A_2)$, then $\Gamma_1(\bar{A}_1) = \Gamma_2(\bar{A}_2)$.

The axiom **Not** expresses that the information in the confidence value of a statement A is sufficient to determine the confidence value of $\bar{A}$. This is justified by the requirement that every piece of information which is relevant for the confidence value of A is relevant for the confidence value of $\bar{A}$ and vice versa.

(And₁)   For all $(\mathbf{U_1}, \Gamma_1, \mathcal{C})$ and $(\mathbf{U_2}, \Gamma_2, \mathcal{C})$:

If $\Gamma_1(A_1|B_1) = \Gamma_2(A_2|B_2)$ and $\Gamma_1(B_1) = \Gamma_2(B_2)$,

then $\Gamma_1(A_1 B_1) = \Gamma_2(A_2 B_2)$.

The axiom **And₁** states that the information in the confidence values of the partial propositions determine the confidence value of the conjunction. Otherwise the confidence value of the conjunction would contain information which is not reflected in the partial propositions, although this information would be clearly relevant for at least one of them.

(And₂)   For all $(\mathbf{U_1}, \Gamma_1, \mathcal{C})$ and $(\mathbf{U_2}, \Gamma_2, \mathcal{C})$:

If $\Gamma_1(A_1 B_1) = \Gamma_2(A_2 B_2)$ and $\Gamma_1(B_1) = \Gamma_2(B_2) \neq \bot\!\!\!\bot$,

then $\Gamma_1(A_1|B_1) = \Gamma_2(A_2|B_2)$.

The axiom **And₂** ensures that all the information contained in a conditional confidence value $\Gamma(A|B)$ will be preserved in the confidence value of the conjunction $\Gamma(AB)$ when combined with the confidence $\Gamma(B)$ (unless $\Gamma(B) = \bot\!\!\!\bot$, in which case the value of $\Gamma(A|B)$ is irrelevant). Otherwise relevant information about the partial propositions would not be contained in the confidence value of the conjunction.

(Order$_1$) For all $(\mathbf{U}, \Gamma, \mathcal{C})$ and all $A, B \in \mathbf{U}$: If $A \leq B$, then $\Gamma(A) \leq \Gamma(B)$.

(Order$_2$) For all confidence values $v, w \in \mathcal{C}$ with $v \leq w$ there is a confidence space $(\mathbf{U}, \Gamma, \mathcal{C})$ with $A, B \in \mathbf{U}$ and $A \leq B$, $\Gamma(A) = v$, $\Gamma(B) = w$.

These two axioms connect the natural ordering of the Boolean algebra ($A \leq B$ iff $A \wedge B = A$) with the ordering on the confidence domain, where **Order$_1$** specifies the forward direction and **Order$_2$** specifies the backward direction (figure 2).

(Extensibility) For all $(\mathbf{U_1}, \Gamma_1, \mathcal{C})$ and $(\mathbf{U_2}, \Gamma_2, \mathcal{C})$ there is a confidence space $(\mathbf{U_3}, \Gamma_3, \mathcal{C})$, so that $\mathbf{U_3} \cong \mathbf{U_1} \otimes \mathbf{U_2}$, and for all $A_1, B_1 \in \mathbf{U_1}$, $A_2, B_2 \in \mathbf{U_2}$:

$$\Gamma_3(A_1 \otimes \top_2 \,|\, B_1 \otimes B_2) = \Gamma_1(A_1|B_1) \quad \text{and} \quad \Gamma_3(\top_1 \otimes A_2 \,|\, B_1 \otimes B_2) = \Gamma_2(A_2|B_2).$$

This axiom requires the extensibility of domains of discourse, i.e., two independently defined confidence spaces shall be embeddable into one frame of reference.

(Background) For all $(\mathbf{U}, \Gamma_1, \mathcal{C})$ and all $C \in \mathbf{U}$ there is a confidence space $(\mathbf{U}, \Gamma_2, \mathcal{C})$, so that for all $A, B \in \mathbf{U}$:

$$\Gamma_1(A|BC) = \Gamma_2(A|B).$$

This closedness under conditioning assures that for every conditional confidence measure Γ_1 which is specialized by conditioning on some "background knowledge" C, there is a conditional confidence measure Γ_2 yielding the same valuations without explicitly mentioning C.

For the justification of the axioms it is important to interpret the expression $\Gamma(A|B)$ as: "*all* that can be said about the confidence of A given B (wrt. Γ)." Given this interpretation, the common justification of the connective axioms is that a violation of these axioms will necessarily lead to a loss of relevant information. Note that the axioms use only equations and inequalities between

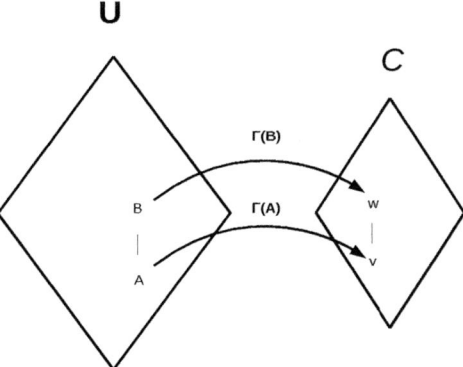

Fig. 2. Ordered confidence values v and w with corresponding propositions in a suitably chosen confidence space $(\mathbf{U}, \Gamma, \mathcal{C})$

confidence values, because there are no algebraic operations defined on the domain of confidence values yet.

In order to designate this and similar axiom systems, we propose a nomenclature based on the connnective axioms. Extensionality of negation, conjunction, and disjunction is denoted as axiom N, C_1, and D_1, respectively. The reconstructibility of the confidence value of an argument of a conjunction or a disjunction, given the compositional confidence value and the confidence value of the other argument, is denoted as axiom C_2 and D_2, respectively. Using this terminology, the above introduced axiom system can be referenced as NC_{12}.

4   The Structure of Uncertainty

A first important implication of the NC_{12} axioms is stated in the following theorem.

SFG-Theorem: There exist functions $S : \mathcal{C} \to \mathcal{C}$, $F : \mathcal{C}^2 \to \mathcal{C}$ and $G : \{(x, y) \in \mathcal{C}^2 | x \leq S(y)\} \to \mathcal{C}$ with:

$$\Gamma(\bar{A}) = S(\Gamma(A)), \tag{1}$$

$$\Gamma(A \wedge B) = F(\Gamma(A|B), \Gamma(B)), \tag{2}$$

$$\Gamma(A \vee B) = G(\Gamma(A), \Gamma(B)), \qquad \text{if } AB = \bot. \tag{3}$$

Proof: First we prove a lemma stating that for every pair of confidence values there is a confidence measure and two independent propositions such that the confidence measure assigns the given confidence values to these propositions.

Independence Lemma: For all $v, w \in \mathcal{C}$ there is a confidence space $(\mathbf{U}, \Gamma, \mathcal{C})$ with $A, B \in \mathbf{U}$, such that:

$$\Gamma(A|B) = \Gamma(A) = v \quad \text{and} \quad \Gamma(B|A) = \Gamma(B) = w.$$

Proof: According to **Order**$_2$, there are confidence spaces $(\mathbf{U_1}, \Gamma_1 \mathcal{C})$, $(\mathbf{U_2}, \Gamma_2, \mathcal{C})$ and propositions $A \in \mathbf{U_1}$ and $B \in \mathbf{U_2}$ with $\Gamma_1(A) = v$ and $\Gamma_2(B) = w$. Then axiom **Extensibility** guarantees the existence of a confidence space $(\mathbf{U_1} \otimes \mathbf{U_2}, \Gamma_3, \mathcal{C})$ with:

$$\Gamma_3(A|B) = \Gamma_1(A) = v \quad \text{and} \quad \Gamma_3(B|A) = \Gamma_2(B) = w.$$

$\square$

Next we show that axioms **Not** and **And**$_1$ imply the existence of the functions S and F.

Let $v \in \mathcal{C}$ be a confidence value, so that there is a confidence space $(\mathbf{U_1}, \Gamma_1, \mathcal{C})$ and $A_1 \in \mathbf{U_1}$ with $\Gamma_1(A_1) = v$. Then define:

$$S(v) = \Gamma_1(\bar{A}_1).$$

This function is well-defined, because whenever there is another confidence space $(\mathbf{U_2}, \Gamma_2, \mathcal{C})$ having v as value of the confidence measure Γ_2, say $\Gamma_2(A_2|B_2) = v$, then axiom **Not** assures that $\Gamma_2(\bar{A}_2|B_2) = \Gamma_1(\bar{A}_1)$. That is, the value of S does not depend on the specific choice of confidence space having v as a value. The totality of S follows from axiom **Order**$_2$, which enforces that for every $v \in \mathcal{C}$ there is at least one confidence space taking v as a value. Additionally, one can show that S is an antitone function, i.e., $x \leq y \Rightarrow S(x) \geq S(y)$, and that $S(\mathbb{T}) = \perp\!\!\!\perp$ and $S(\perp\!\!\!\perp) = \mathbb{T}$.

The analog will be proved for conjunction by introducing a binary function F. Note that a proposition B and a *conditional* proposition $A|B$ are related by F.

According to the independence lemma, for all $v, w \in \mathcal{C}$ there is a confidence space $(\mathbf{U_1}, \Gamma_1)$ with $\Gamma_1(A_1|B_1) = \Gamma_1(A_1) = v$ and $\Gamma_1(B_1) = w$. Define F as follows:

$$F(v, w) = \Gamma_1(A_1 B_1).$$

The well-definedness is implied by axiom **And**$_1$, the value of $F(v, w)$ does not depend on the confidence space and events having v and w as confidence values. The totality of F is assured by the independence lemma, too, which is valid for all $v, w \in \mathcal{C}$.

Lemma: F is associative.

Proof: Let $x, y, z \in \mathcal{C}$ and $(\mathbf{U}, \Gamma, \mathcal{C})$ a confidence space with $A, B, C \in \mathbf{U}$ and $\Gamma(A|BC) = \Gamma(A) = x$, $\Gamma(B|C) = \Gamma(B) = y$ and $\Gamma(C) = z$. Such a confidence space always exists according to the independence lemma. Then it follows:

$$F(F(x, y), z) = F(F(\Gamma(A), \Gamma(B)), \Gamma(C)) = F(F(\Gamma(A|BC), \Gamma(B|C)), \Gamma(C)) =$$
$$= F(\Gamma(AB|C), \Gamma(C)) = \Gamma(ABC) = F(\Gamma(A|BC), \Gamma(BC)) =$$
$$= F(\Gamma(A), F(\Gamma(B|C), \Gamma(C))) = F(\Gamma(A), F(\Gamma(B), \Gamma(C))) = F(x, F(y, z)).$$

$\square$

In the same way, by using the independence lemma to construct the appropriate confidence spaces, one can show that F is commutative and has $\mathbb{T}$ as a neutral element. Next we derive the cancellation property for F on $\mathcal{C}^+ = \mathcal{C} \setminus \{\perp\!\!\!\perp\}$.

Lemma: F is cancellative on $\mathcal{C}^+$, i.e., $F(x, z) = F(y, z)$ implies $x = y$.

Proof: Let $x, y, z \in \mathcal{C}^+$ and $(\mathbf{U}, \Gamma, \mathcal{C})$ be a confidence space with $A, B, C, D \in \mathbf{U}$ and $\Gamma(A|C) = \Gamma(A) = x$, $\Gamma(B|D) = \Gamma(B) = y$, and $\Gamma(C) = \Gamma(D) = z$, again using the independence lemma to show the existence of such a confidence space. Then we have $F(x, z) = \Gamma(AC)$ and $F(y, z) = \Gamma(BD)$. Thus, $F(x, z) = F(y, z)$ implies $\Gamma(AC) = \Gamma(BD)$. Invoking And$_2$ (without worrying about the case $z = \perp\!\!\!\perp$, because we are talking about $\mathcal{C}^+$), we get $\Gamma(A|C) = \Gamma(B|D)$, i.e., $x = y$.

$\square$

The next step is the extension of the monoid $(\mathcal{C}^+, F)$ to a group. This can be done analogously to the classical algebraic construction of $\mathbb{Z}$ from $\mathbb{N}$, a construction which works for all cancellative commutative monoids.

Using S, F, and F^{-1}, the partial function G on $\{(x, y) \in \mathcal{C}^2 | x \leq S(y)\}$ is defined as follows:

$$G(x, y) = S(F(S(F(x, F^{-1}(S(y))))), S(y))), \qquad \text{if } y \neq \mathbb{T},$$
$$G(\bot, \mathbb{T}) = \mathbb{T}, \qquad \text{else.}$$

In order to illustrate this definition, we note that G can be seen as a solution of the problem to represent addition with the functions $x * y$, $1 - x$, and $1/x$. Using these functions, G translates into:

$$1 - (1 - \tfrac{x}{1-y})(1 - y) ,$$

which reduces to addition.

First we have to show that this is a well-defined function. For this, we have to establish that on the domain of G the expression $F(x, F^{-1}(S(y)))$ is in $\mathcal{C}$, because the S-function is still only defined on $\mathcal{C}$, and not on the group extension.

Lemma: $\forall x, y \in \mathcal{C}$, $y \neq \mathbb{T} : x \leq S(y) \Rightarrow F(x, F^{-1}(S(y))) \in \mathcal{C}$.

Proof: With Order$_2$ and $x \leq S(y)$ it follows that there is a confidence space $(\mathbf{U}, \Gamma, \mathcal{C})$ with $A, B \in \mathbf{U}$, $A \leq B$, $\Gamma(A) = x$, and $\Gamma(B) = S(y)$. Now, because of $A \leq B$, it holds that $\Gamma(AB) = \Gamma(A) = x$. Let $\Gamma(A|B) = z$, which is uniqely determined according to And$_2$. z satisfies the equation $x = F(z, S(y))$, which is equivalent to $z = F(x, F^{-1}(S(y)))$. Because z is, by definition, in the range of a confidence measure, we have $z \in \mathcal{C}$ and hence $F(x, F^{-1}(S(y)) \in \mathcal{C}$. $\qquad\square$

Having the well-definedness of G established, it is easy to show that G has the desired property. Let $\Gamma(B) \neq \mathbb{T}$ and $AB = \bot$:

$$\Gamma(A \vee B) = S(\Gamma(\bar{A} \wedge \bar{B})) = S(F(S(\Gamma(A|\bar{B})), S(\Gamma(B))))) =$$
$$= S(F(S(F(\Gamma(A \wedge \bar{B}), F^{-1}(S(\Gamma(B)))))), S(\Gamma(B)))) .$$

Now $A \wedge \bar{B}$ is equal to A, because we assumed $AB = \bot$. Hence G has the stated property for $\Gamma(B) \neq \mathbb{T}$. In the case of $\Gamma(B) = \mathbb{T}$, we invoke Order$_1$ to show that $\Gamma(A \vee B) = \mathbb{T}$, too. Furthermore, because $AB = \bot$ implies $A \leq \bar{B}$, we have, again by Order$_1$, $\Gamma(A) \leq \Gamma(\bar{B}) = S(\Gamma(B)) = \bot$. Hence $\Gamma(A) = \bot$, and we can apply the second part of the definition of G, which yields $\Gamma(A \vee B) = G(\Gamma(A), \Gamma(B)) = G(\bot, \mathbb{T}) = \mathbb{T}$. This finishes the proof of the SFG-theorem.

$\qquad\square$

Arnborg and Sjödin proved in [1] a theorem clarifying the algebraic structure of $\mathcal{C}$ resulting from their axioms: it is the $[0, 1]$-interval of a totally ordered field. Analyzing their proof, we find that the construction of a field from a ring will fail if one does not assume a total order on $\mathcal{C}$. In lemma 13 of [1] they state that the ring they have constructed is a totally ordered integral domain, i.e. a ring without zero divisors. Then they use a theorem from S. MacLane and G. Birkhoff in [12] which states that every totally ordered integral domain can be embedded in a totally ordered field. But this will not work in the case of partial order because without the total order assumption one cannot prove that the constructed ring will not contain zero divisors. So, lemma 13 of [1] cannot be transferred to the partial order case, which blocks the application of the MacLane-Birkhoff theorem. This is an interesting example of the interplay between order properties and algebraic properties: a total order assumption has strong algebraic implications, while partial order has not. Accordingly, order properties and algebraic properties cannot, as one might have hoped, treated separately. Based on these observations we formulate the following conjecture:

Ring Conjecture: The domain of confidence values $\mathcal{C}$ of a confidence universe satisfying the axiom system NC_{12} can be embedded in a partially ordered ring $(\hat{\mathcal{C}}, 0, 1, \oplus, \odot, \leq)$. Let $\hat{\cdot} : \mathcal{C} \to \hat{\mathcal{C}}$ be the embedding map, then the following holds:

$$\hat{\perp\!\!\!\perp} = 0, \quad \hat{\top\!\!\!\top} = 1, \quad \forall v, w \in \mathcal{C} : v \leq w \Leftrightarrow \hat{v} \leq \hat{w}.$$

Furthermore, all confidence measures Γ of the confidence universe satisfy:

$$\hat{\Gamma}(\top) = 1, \tag{4}$$

$$\hat{\Gamma}(A \vee B) = \hat{\Gamma}(A) \oplus \hat{\Gamma}(B), \qquad \text{if } AB = \perp, \tag{5}$$

$$\hat{\Gamma}(A \wedge B) = \hat{\Gamma}(A|B) \odot \hat{\Gamma}(B). \tag{6}$$

We state this as a conjecture, because a full proof is beyond the scope of this article. A proof outline can be found in [20], which documents work in progress. If it can be confirmed, it will yield an algebraic characterization of uncertainty based on NC_{12}: *Uncertainty can be represented by elements of the $[0,1]$-interval of partially ordered rings.*

Furthermore, with regard to the ring operations, the uncertainty measures satisfy the same axioms as probability measures satisfy with regard to the real numbers. But in contrast to the real numbers, a ring may be only partially ordered or may contain infinitesimal elements, like the hyperreal numbers. Possible applications of the above results to other uncertainty calculi are discussed in section 6.

5   The Lineage of NC_{12}

Our approach of axiomatizing uncertainty measures extends a line of thinking started by R. T. Cox in 1946. In [2], based on axioms which should hold for all uncertainty measures, Cox derived a theorem stating that uncertainty measures are essentially probability measures, although his axioms are very different from the axioms of probability theory. A recent exposition of his result can be found in [9].

The approach used by Cox was one of the first attempts to justify the use of probabilities as a representation of uncertainty by directly axiomatizing the intuition on uncertainty measures and then *deriving* that uncertainty measures have the same mathematical structure as probability measures. This was a surprising result, given the fact that Cox's axioms look totally different from the Kolmogorov axioms of probability theory. But despite its new and far reaching conclusions, Cox's theorem was not widely acknowledged. This can be attributed to at least two factors: first, it became clear that Cox's derivation of his theorem was not complete. The assumptions he made were not sufficient to reach the conclusion in its full generality. This was noted by several authors, and J. Halpern showed in detail where Cox's proof failed by constructing a counterexample in [6]. It was not before 1994 that J.B. Paris completed Cox's proof by introducing a new axiom [13]. This axiom closes the loopholes in Cox's proof, but is very technical in nature. Thus it is not acceptable as an axiom which should hold for all reasonable uncertainty measures. This leads to the second factor contributing to the slow adoption of Cox's result: there is at least one axiom which is too strong to be considered as a general property of uncertainty measures, yet is inherently necessary for the proof approach adopted by Cox. This axiom is the assumption that uncertainty can be measured by one real number. This is a strong structural assumption, implying that the uncertainty values are totally ordered. This prevents, for example, the applicability of Cox's theorem to calculi like Dempster-Shafer theory, which uses two real numbers for the representation of uncertainty.

The remaining question after the result of J. B. Paris is the following: are there extensions or modifications of the Cox axioms, which are justifiable as general properties of uncertainty measures and which imply a result essentially similar to Cox's theorem? One important step in this direction was taken by S. Arnborg and G. Sjödin. They replaced the axiom introduced by J.B. Paris by a more intuitive statement which they called "Refinability axiom". Furthermore, they dropped the requirement that uncertainty values are real numbers. By this step, they transformed the Cox approach to a genuine algebraic approach, constructing the structure of the domain of uncertainty values and not assuming it. But in order to get the result they want, they introduced a total of 16 axioms (when one counts every discernible requirement they formulate as a separate axiom, as we do for our core system), with different degrees of foundational justifiability. Additionally, at a crucial step in their proof they introduce a total order assumption for the domain of uncertainty values, thus restricting the range of their result in a fundamental way.

This was the situation when we entered the development, seeing that Arnborg and Sjödin made a crucial step in the amelioration of the original Cox's approach, but still leaving some major issues open, which have blocked the general applicability of their result. Accordingly, our goal was the following: to devise an axiom system as minimal as possible, with as weak and as general properties as possible, especially to drop the total order assumption, but still be able to derive a Cox-style result.

6   Relations to Existing Uncertainty Calculi

Today, there exist many approaches for dealing with uncertainty, for example lower probabilities, which have only partially ordered uncertainty values or non-monotonic logic, which can be interpreted as using infinitesimal probabilities. In the following, we try to analyse these calculi in the light of our results.

6.1   Lower Probabilities

The problem of dealing with "imprecise" probabilities has led to the development of calculi known under the common name "lower probabilities". The main distinction from the probability calculus is that the uncertainty of a proposition is judged by *two* numbers instead of one. Accordingly, there are two functions mapping the elements of a proposition algebra to $[0, 1]$, the *lower probability* P_* and the *upper probability* P^*. The most general notion of a lower probability is defined wrt. a set of probability distributions $\mathcal{P}$ (see, for example, [7]):

$$P^*(A) = \sup_{P \in \mathcal{P}} P(A) \quad \text{and} \quad P_*(A) = \inf_{P \in \mathcal{P}} P(A) .$$

One can show that lower and upper probabilities satisfy the following inequalities if A and B are disjoint:

$$P_*(A \cup B) \geq P_*(A) + P_*(B) \quad \text{and} \quad P^*(A \cup B) \leq P^*(A) + P^*(B) .$$

These properties are called super-additivity and sub-additivity, respectively. Furthermore, lower and upper probability are connected via the following relations:

$$P_*(A) \leq P^*(A) \quad \text{and} \quad P^*(A) = 1 - P_*(\bar{A}) .$$

The inequality says that lower and upper probabilities can be seen as defining an interval, thus making lower and upper probabilities an uncertainty calculus having a partially ordered domain of uncertainty values. The equation implies that from both uncertainty values, upper and lower probability, of a proposition one can derive the upper and lower probabilities of its negation. Hence lower and upper probabilities together satisfy axiom Not.

An application of our results to the analysis of lower probabilities is now the following: even if the domain of uncertainty values is only partially ordered, which is possible according to NC_{12}, there exists a function G which relates the uncertainty value of a disjunction of disjoint propositions and the uncertainty values of the single propositions by an equation, and not only by an inequality. If no such function G exists for an uncertainty calculus, it must violate at least one of the axioms Not, And_1, or And_2 (we assume that the infrastructure axioms are satisfied). Now, because lower probabilities satisfy axiom Not, they must violate And_1 or And_2. This implies that there cannot be any definition of conditioning for lower probabilities which satisfies And_1 and And_2. Seeing And_1 and And_2 as essential conditions for not loosing relevant information, this may explain why the definiton of conditioning for lower probabilities has turned out to be such a hard problem, which is still the topic of ongoing research.

This conclusion is also valid for Dempster-Shafer theory, which can be seen as lower and upper probabilities satisfying additional constraints. Accordingly, there are several proposals for conditioning in DS-theory, each having its own advantages and disadvantages. By the above analysis, this is not a transitory state until the "right" conditioning rule has been found, but a fundamental obstacle which cannot be resolved within the frame of DS-theory.

6.2 Non-monotonic Logic

A non-monotonic logic extends classical logic with a framework of "belief revision", i.e. conclusions derived at one point can be retracted at a later point. Non-monotonic logic can be seen as defining a hierarchy of "default assumptions", which are assumed valid until observed evidence directly contradicts them. If this happens, a revision process is executed, which incorporates the new evidence and eliminates contradictions while trying to preserve as much as possible from the old knowledge state. Now, as for example Lehman and Magidor have observed in [11], one can formalize default expressions of the type "if A then typically B" as "the probability of B given A is very high", where "very high" is equated to $1 - \epsilon$, for *infinitesimal* ϵ. This can be modeled by a generalized probability algebra using the $[0, 1]$-interval of *hyperreal* numbers as a domain of uncertainty values.

7 Conclusion

Despite many attempts, there is still no consensus on basic questions concerning uncertainty and the foundations of inductive logic. In [1], Arnborg and Sjödin note that reaching a consensus is not only a foundational issue but is also important outside the ivory tower: designers of complex systems struggle with difficult compatibility problems when they plan to integrate system components which happen to use different ways to describe uncertainty.

In this article, we have tried to contribute to the debate on uncertainty by discerning ontologically different types of uncertainty and introducing an axiomatic core system for uncertainty measures with the explicit aim not to prejudice structural properties of the domain of uncertainty values, but to derive them from basic assumptions.

References

1. Arnborg, S., Sjödin, G.: What is the plausibility of probability? Preprint, Nada, KTH (2001)
2. Cox, R.T.: Probability, frequency, and reasonable expectation. Am. Jour. Phys. 14, 1–13 (1946)
3. Dubois, D.: Possibility theory and statistical reasoning. Computational Statistics & Data Analysis 51(1), 47–69 (2006)
4. Gärdenfors, P. (ed.): Belief Revision. Cambridge University Press, Cambridge (1992)
5. Ginsberg, M. (ed.): Readings in Nonmonotonic Reasoning. Morgan Kaufmann, Los Altos (1987)
6. Halpern, J.: A counterexample to theorems of Cox and Fine. Journal of A.I. Research 10, 76–85 (1999)
7. Halpern, J.: Reasoning about Uncertainty. MIT Press, Cambridge (2003)
8. Hutter, M.: Universal Artificial Intelligence. Springer, Heidelberg (2005)
9. Jaynes, E.T.: Probability Theory: The Logic of Science. Cambridge University Press, Cambridge (2003)

10. Knight, F.: Risk, Uncertainty, and Profit. Houghton Mifflin (1921)
11. Lehman, D., Magidor, M.: What does a conditional knowledge base entail? Artificial Intelligence 55(1), 1–60 (1992)
12. MacLane, S., Birkhoff, G.: Algebra. The MacMillan Company, Basingstoke (1967)
13. Paris, J.B.: The Uncertain Reasoner's Companion. Cambridge University Press, Cambridge (1994)
14. Pearl, J.: Causality: Models, Reasoning, and Inference. Cambridge University Press, Cambridge (2000)
15. Schmidhuber, J.: Ultimate cognition à la Gödel. Cognitive Computation 1(2), 177–193 (2009)
16. Shafer, G.: Mathematical Theory of Evidence. Princeton University Press, Princeton (1976)
17. Solomonoff, R.: A formal theory of inductive inference, part I. Information and Control 7(1), 1–22 (1964)
18. Solomonoff, R.: A formal theory of inductive inference, part II. Information and Control 7(2), 224–254 (1964)
19. Spohn, W.: A survey of ranking theory. In: Huber, F., Schmidt-Petri, C. (eds.) Degrees of Belief. Springer, Heidelberg (2009)
20. Zimmermann, J.: A proof outline for the ring conjecture (2010), http://www.iai.uni-bonn.de/~jz/ring_conjecture.pdf

Author Index